Northampton: Patronage and Policy at the Court of James I

Northampton:
Patronage and Policy
at the Court of James I

LINDA LEVY PECK
Department of History, Purdue University

London
GEORGE ALLEN & UNWIN
Boston   Sydney

**George Allen & Unwin (Publishers) Ltd,
40 Museum Street, London WC1A 1LU, UK**

George Allen & Unwin (Publishers) Ltd,
Park Lane, Hemel Hempstead, Herts HP2 4TE, UK

Allen & Unwin, Inc.,
9 Winchester Terrace, Winchester, Mass. 01890, USA

George Allen & Unwin Australia Pty Ltd,
8 Napier Street, North Sydney, NSW 2060, Australia

First published in 1982

British Library Cataloguing in Publication Data

Peck, Linda Levy
    Northampton : patronage and policy at the court of James I.
1. Northampton, Henry Howard, *Earl of*
2. Great Britain – Nobility – Biography
I. Title
941.06'1'0924   DA391.1.N/
ISBN 0-04-942177-8

Library of Congress Cataloging in Publication Data

Peck, Linda Levy
    Northampton, patronage and policy at the court of James I.
Bibliography: p.
Includes index.
1. Northampton, Henry Howard, Earl of, 1540–1616.
2. Great Britain – Politics and government – 1558–1603.
3. Great Britain – Politics and government – 1603–1625.
4. Great Britain – Court and courtiers – Biography.
I. Title
DA391.1N67P42   1982   941.06'1'0924   82–8813
ISBN 0-04-942177-8   AACR2

Set in 10 on 11 point Plantin by Red Lion Setters, London WC1
and printed in Great Britain
by Billing and Sons Ltd, London and Worcester

To my parents

Contents

Preface

Writing a book is like a journey, at once solitary, yet filled with the sights and sounds of many places and, more importantly, of many people without whom it would be impossible to reach one's destination. It is, then, a great pleasure to acknowledge their assistance. First of all I want to thank Jack Hexter, who first encouraged my examination of the Jacobean court. He once expressed the hope that he had taught his students to ask interesting questions. He always does: with fine wit and penetrating insight he has questioned the historical verities for four decades. Joel Hurstfield, who did so much important work on Elizabethan and Jacobean government, encouraged my study of the Earl of Northampton. His death is a great loss to the profession and to those scholars, among them many Americans, to whom he became a friend.

Scholarship is communal; I have greatly benefited from the advice and criticism of colleagues. At an early stage of this project Duncan Foley listened to my findings and his probing questions always made our discussions worthwhile. Alan Kreider, Pat Patterson and Fritz Levy read early drafts of individual chapters and proffered helpful comments. Maija Cole has kindly loaned me a typescript of the newly discovered journal for the Parliament of 1614 which she is editing for publication.

I am especially grateful to Elizabeth Read Foster and Conrad Russell who read various drafts of this work. Elizabeth Foster has been most generous in sharing her unrivalled knowledge of early Stuart Parliaments. Conrad Russell, well known for his aid to fellow scholars, has been very helpful in providing wide-ranging references and commenting on several chapters. To Peter Clark, Derek Hirst, Ivan Roots and A. G. R. Smith go particular thanks for reading most or all of the book. Peter Clark's provocative comments have made me reconsider my interpretations at several points. Derek Hirst's own work on the relationship of court and country helped to shape my own treatment of the subject. Ivan Roots provided invaluable advice on the text, while Alan Smith suggested important parallels with Elizabethan administrative practice.

Coming closer to home, I owe a particular debt of gratitude to my colleagues at Purdue University. Donald J. Berthrong, head of the department, has always supported my research and I wish to thank him for that and for shaping an able and congenial department. Our faculty seminar has provided a useful testing ground for work in progress. Combining friendship with an unclouded eye are Darlene Clark Hine, Charles Ingrao, Lois Magner, Regina Wolkoff, Jon Teaford and John Contreni. In particular I want to thank two colleagues: Lester Cohen who brought to bear on some of these chapters the same keen sense of rhetoric that infuses his own work and Philip VanderMeer who, in the spirit of friendship, made me prove every point along the way. The department staff under the direction of Joyce Good, always the model of grace under pressure, produced the typescript with efficiency and skill. To my family and friends goes a special note of appreciation. They had little to do directly with this book but by their gifts of the heart helped me to bring it to fruition.

In addition I want to express my thanks to the American Council of Learned Societies, the Folger Shakespeare Library, Purdue University and the National Endowment for the Humanities for grants which helped me to complete the research for this study. In that endeavour I have had the invaluable aid of the librarians and staffs of the British Library, the Public Record Office, the Cambridge University Library, Trinity College, Cambridge, the Bodleian Library, Oxford, the Institute of Historical Research, the Library of Congress, the Folger Shakespeare Library, the Henry E. Huntington Library and the Yale Parliamentary Diaries Center. I should like to thank the Duke of Norfolk for allowing me to consult the manuscripts at Arundel Castle and Sir William Gordon Cumming for permission to cite family papers at the National Museum of Scotland. The *Historical Journal* has allowed me to draw on material in my articles 'Problems in Jacobean administration: Was Henry Howard, Earl of Northampton, a reformer?', vol. 19 (1976), pp. 831–58, and 'The Earl of Northampton, merchant grievances and the Addled Parliament of 1614', vol. 24 (1981), pp. 533–52. Throughout the text the spelling and punctuation of all quotations have been modernised.

In reaching the end of one journey, one longs to be off again. The questions of patronage and corruption that Northampton's career has thrown light on need to be more fully examined and I hope to do this in a future study. In the meantime, I alone of course am responsible for the errors that remain in this work.

West Lafayette
October 1981

Introduction

Reassessing the Jacobean Court

Commentators have long treated the Jacobean court as if it were synony-
mous with Jacobean drama: sinister, bloody, cynical and corrupt. On the
one hand, the traditional image of James I, pedantic and unwashed, fawning
on favourites and haunted by favour-seekers, has provided an irresistible
foil to the glory of Queen Elizabeth. On the other, following the patterns
established by Civil War propagandists, the moral failings of the early
Stuart court have been invoked to explain the 'Puritan Revolution'. Yet if
we lay aside the gory imaginings of Webster and the cynicism of Jonson, put
away the golden words and presence of Gloriana, and renounce predestina-
tion at least as it pertains to the outbreak of revolution, we are confronted
with the problem of understanding the Jacobean court on its own terms.
Henry Howard, Earl of Northampton, was one of James's most important
privy councillors; this study of his career provides a new look at the court
and some of the crucial administrative and political problems of the Stuarts
in the decades before the English Civil War.

The importance of this task has not gone unnoticed by historians. To
explain what he called the general crisis of the seventeenth century, Hugh
Trevor-Roper located the source of disequilibrium in the overblown
Renaissance state, whose bloated and corrupt bureaucracy pressed increasingly heavily on contemporary society. In England, he argued, the political
elite felt these pressures most intensely. There, significant segments of the
gentry and nobility identified themselves as the 'Country' and ultimately
took up arms against the 'Court'.[1] Although modified in part, this fundamental split between court and country in the reign of James I has become a
standard explanation of the English Civil War.[2]

Yet despite the prevailing paradigm of conflict between court and
country, there has been little study of the actual workings of the Jacobean
court. Instead, the attention of most seventeenth-century historians over the
past two decades has been on the country, either in the localities or in
Parliament. Focus on the county community has fostered careful studies of
social, economic and political structures within several shires. As a result, it
is now possible to understand in detail the issues and alliances which first
agitated individual counties in the early seventeenth century and later
shaped the local course of the Civil War. Not all local historians have
ignored politics at the centre. But several, in emphasising the insularity of
county communities, have argued that national concerns were of little

importance to any but a handful of courtiers.[3] Parliament has been the other focus of interest. The range of publications includes studies of individual Parliaments, as well as the debates and diaries of several sessions of the early Stuarts.[4] In the Whig view which many of these works reflect, the march toward parliamentary sovereignty began with the creation of a parliamentary opposition in the reign of James I.

Recently both these focal points have come under attack. Challenging the standard dichotomy of court and country, some historians have begun to stress the important underlying connections between the court, Parliament and the localities which, prevailing into the 1620s and perhaps beyond, overcame temporary differences of opinion.[5] Whatever the outcome of this historiographical debate, however, the reintegration of national and local politics will only occur when historians take another look at the court, for its activities were much more complex than usually portrayed. A reassessment of the court of James I is the necessary step to building a new model of national politics in the decades before the English Civil War.

Taking a fresh look requires in particular an examination of the critical issues of patronage, policy and administrative reform. These posed difficult problems which challenged the Crown and animated contemporary politics. Most discussions of patronage, the central link between monarch and subjects in the early modern state, have emphasised the striking differences between Elizabeth's husbanding of her bounty and James's profligacy. Sir John Neale argued that the Elizabethan patronage system faltered in the 1590s, broke down under James and 'the scandal and discontent caused by a putrifying political system helped to provoke the English Civil War'.[6] But little work has been done on Jacobean patronage networks or the process by which policy was formulated. Instead, patronage as well as domestic policy has usually been written off as the preserve of James's favourites, the Earls of Somerset and Buckingham, whose central concern was to provide as many payoffs to their faction as possible. Moreover, efforts at administrative reform within the court have either been dismissed as failures or compared unfavourably with contemporary French efforts under Richelieu.[7] Such analyses, however, tend to ignore the structural difficulties in early modern administration and the changing cluster of ideas which hedged office in the early modern state.

The practices of patronage and graft under attack both by contemporaries and later historians were rooted in a governmental structure in which a professional and salaried civil service with established norms of conduct pertaining to the public interest did not yet exist.[8] Stuart statesmen were forced to rely on the patronage system to recruit able officials, to reward the politically important and to restrain abuses within acceptable limits. Forced to formulate policy under increasingly stringent financial and political circumstances, the Privy Council was overworked and understaffed. It lacked administrative departments to provide advice on policy and to carry out decisions once made.[9] In their efforts to construct policy, reward the political elite, present the government's case in Parliament, oversee administration and reform corrupt practices, Jacobean officials resembled jugglers trying to keep too many objects in the air, any one of which might come quickly crashing to the ground. To ignore these aspects of the court is to misunderstand the nature of its problems, the reasons for its failures and the consequences for national politics even up to the outbreak of the Civil War.

One means of re-evaluating the court is to examine the activities of individual officials. Few have been studied, but the intensive work of Joel Hurstfield, Menna Prestwich and R. H. Tawney on the Lord Treasurers, Robert Cecil and Lionel Cranfield, provide models for understanding the contradictory concerns and pressures under which Jacobean policy was formed and patronage dispensed.[10] The career of an individual can provide a microcosm of the court itself.

If the Jacobean court has long been the target of moral strictures, Henry Howard, Earl of Northampton, has been condemned as perhaps the worst of all of James's officials. One eminent historian has characterised him as 'a nobleman left over from the high Renaissance days with the outlook – and morals – of one of the least pleasant Italian dukes'.[11] Certainly Northampton was the consummate Jacobean courtier, a clever analyst of the nuances of power. His combination of flattery and pedantry matched the tastes of his monarch, as did his predilection for young men. To James, who had written extensively on the divine right of kings, a courtier who was willing to expatiate at length on the royal virtues must have seemed a kindred spirit.

For decades, Howard had been poor, a client without a patron, cut off from royal favour. Under the Tudors, Howard's father, brother and nephew died attainted of treason and he himself was often imprisoned for his support of the causes of Catholicism and Mary, Queen of Scots. In the 1590s his fortune began to change when he was able to re-establish ties with the court. He became a follower of the Earl of Essex and was reconciled with Queen Elizabeth. Most important, Howard, along with Robert Cecil, became a close adviser to James VI of Scotland in the waning days of Elizabeth's reign. When James became King of England, he made Henry Howard Earl of Northampton and one of his most important ministers; as a privy councillor Northampton became an active proponent of administrative reform. Wielding the influence that his new offices and position afforded him, he fashioned his own patron–client connections to reinforce his position at court and in the countryside. At his death in 1614, Northampton had been in office only eleven years, but his faction controlled the distribution of much of the patronage at court, and he himself had amassed an estate worth £80,000. Northampton reflected qualities intrinsic to the Jacobean court, or so a contemporary thought, for he was 'of a subtle and fine wit, of a good proportion, excellent in outward courtship, famous for secret insinuation and fortuning flatteries, and by reason of these qualities, became a fit man for the conditions of these times'.[12]

During his lifetime, Northampton was condemned by some as an instrument of Spain and shelterer of Jesuits and lauded by others as the most learned noble in the land and patron of the scholarly. The Civil War provoked a different emphasis in appraisals of his character. When proponents of the Commonwealth and Protectorate sought to shore up their authority by attacking James and his ministers, Northampton proved a perfect target. He had been implicated posthumously in the biggest scandal of King James's reign, the imprisonment and murder of Sir Thomas Overbury, who had attempted to block the marriage of the earl's niece, Frances Howard, to the king's favourite, Robert Carr, Earl of Somerset. Commonwealth historians made much of the Overbury scandal, accusing Northampton of playing the pander in order to cement his family's alliance with the favourite. He was declared untrue to the sovereign he served with zeal and his attempts at government reform were put down to malice, to the 'venom of this monster ... who did flatter the king and dissemble with God'.[13]

Royalist writers counter-attacking found it necessary to rehabilitate Howard. One noted Howard's wisdom and learning and attributed his advancement to King James's great affection for men of letters: 'so [Howard] had the less occasion, to advance his fortune, by court-flattery or state-employment; nor indeed was he ever suitor for either.'[14] Neither side was accurate. But the warmth of the indictment continued to be repeated in the eighteenth and nineteenth centuries in the successive reprinting and rehashings of these histories.

S. R. Gardiner provided the first scholarly assessment of Northampton's career. Critical of James and his court, Gardiner's judgement was harsh: 'of all who gathered round the new king this man was, beyond all comparison, the most undeserving of the favours which he received.' He castigated Northampton for combining his Catholicism with an unmatched reverence for the royal prerogative, but grudgingly acknowledged his considerable abilities and noted that he 'took his share in the duties of government with credit'.[15] Little has changed since this Victorian verdict. The stigma of the Commonwealth writers continues to carry weight with modern historians. Faced with apparent dualities in Northampton's career, Menna Prestwich, in her study of Lionel Cranfield, Jacobean merchant and Lord Treasurer, observes that

> the irony of Cranfield's appearance at court lay in the facts that his patron was the corrupt Northampton, whose zeal for reform was merely a cloak for his ambition, and that Cranfield too saw no reason why the public interest and private profits could not coexist.[16]

Here then is the central difficulty, both in assessing the court and Jacobean officials: the imposition of nineteenth- and twentieth-century standards of public service on the early modern state. But as Joel Hurstfield persuasively argued, in a system where salaries were extremely low or did not exist, where service was to the king's person and not to the public, and where the Renaissance court prescribed grandeur of style for its servants, there was no necessary contradiction between private profits and public interest. Northampton's and Cranfield's attitudes were shared by most of their contemporaries. The measure of the early modern official was not whether he profited from his policies but what service he performed in return.[17] Were Northampton only the flattering, intriguing pedant, he might well be left to the clutches of his detractors. His historical reputation cannot, however, be reconciled with his activities at the Jacobean court. Northampton was both courtier and councillor: these were not separate roles, but functions inextricably linked by the nature of the early modern state. It is precisely because Northampton epitomises at the same time both the pursuit of personal profit and of governmental reform that he provides an interesting case study in Jacobean politics. His career casts light on the kind of expert opinion available to government and the way in which professional commitments shaped and limited the advice given. Northampton's work yields essential information about the making of a patronage network, the spectrum of clients connected to the court, and the structural difficulties which skewed the giving of favour. Furthermore, his pursuit of administrative reform underlines the means available to the Crown's officials, the political questions such means raised and the conflicting interests that reform engendered. Northampton illustrates the parameters within which Jacobean officials functioned and the complex structure of the Jacobean court.

Chapter 1

'A Man Obscured'

Renaissance culture emphasised the metaphors of theatre and of role playing. Henry Howard, Earl of Northampton, was a consummate actor. But if the roles he played changed, the script did not; despite continuing rebuffs that lasted over decades, he was drawn irresistibly to the court. Whether scholar, conspirator, or courtier, his goal remained the same: to gain the place and power to which his birth entitled him and in 1603, after a lifetime of poverty and danger, he laid claim to them. In a letter of gratitude to King James he spelled out the vicissitudes he had suffered in his search for favour, drawing his own political version of the Fall and Resurrection.

> To the place by birth my due, from which I was ejected rather by the wrongs of others than mine own deserts, your Majesty restored me. I was then esteemed a forlorn hope ... I am now admitted, though unworthy, by extraordinary grace to be your privy councillor. I was branded with the mark of reprobation; you have signed me with the character of trust. I was esteemed, and so termed, a man dangerous; you have trusted me with one of the strongest locks of your estate. To be well affected to the best prince in Europe was then my crime, it is now my credit. To have put myself in readiness against your golden day was then my danger; it is now my gaol delivery.[1]

To understand Northampton and his compulsive role playing, one must begin where he did, with the pre-eminence of his family. When he was born in 1540 to the Earl and Countess of Surrey, the Howard family had reached the height of its influence and power, by a combination over several centuries of judicious marriages and willing service to the ruling monarch both at court and on the battlefield. Henry Howard's grandfather, Thomas, third Duke of Norfolk, showed all the attributes which had elevated them. He had married well, in succession the daughters of Edward IV and the Duke of Buckingham, had served with skill both at sea and on the field at Flodden in 1513 and to these added a talent for court politics. As Lord Treasurer he led the conservative faction in the Privy Council opposing Cardinal Wolsey and later Thomas Cromwell. On the king's 'great matter', his divorce from Catherine of Aragon, he sided with the king and promoted Henry's marriage to his niece Anne Boleyn. By 1540, when Henry Howard was born, Norfolk was triumphant. He had engineered the downfall of Cromwell and survived the fall of Anne, by sitting on the tribunal which found her guilty of treason. Now he was grooming another niece, Catherine Howard, to be queen. The acquisition of monastic lands in the wake of the dissolution of the monasteries had made him one of England's richest landowners.

The court in 1540 swarmed with Howards: Norfolk and his family, the brothers of Catherine Howard, favoured by their relation to the new queen, and the offspring of the second duke, including Lord William Howard, diplomatic envoy for Henry VIII and later Lord Chamberlain to Elizabeth. Not least was Norfolk's eldest son, Henry Howard, Earl of Surrey, courtier and poet, who served valiantly in the army, won distinction in court tournaments, and introduced Italian Renaissance forms to English poetry. He married Frances Vere, daughter of the fifteenth Earl of Oxford, by whom he had two sons, Thomas and Henry, and three daughters, Jane, Catherine and Margaret.

The Howards' dominance did not last, however, beyond Henry Howard's childhood. Catherine Howard proved a fragile prop for the family's fortunes; she was executed in 1542. Moreover, as the aged Henry VIII worried about the succession in 1546, Surrey vigorously supported his father's claim to the protectorship of Prince Edward, and rashly quartered the arms of Edward the Confessor, supposedly limited only to the royal heir. To the king's suspicious mind, the Howards seemed bent on supplanting Edward.[2] Surrey and Norfolk were found guilty of treason; Surrey was beheaded in January 1547. His father dead, the family disgraced, Henry and the other children were taken from their mother and put in the guardianship of an aunt, the Countess of Richmond. Norfolk was saved from the block which had already claimed his son and nieces only because Henry VIII died the night before he was to be executed. For 6-year-old Henry Howard this sudden revolution of the wheel of fortune must have been traumatic; in later life he frequently emphasised the part destiny had played in his misfortunes as well as his successes.

Childhood experience marked his personality with insecurity and contradiction. Proud, pedantic and cynical, Howard combined outward flattery with inner resentment. Obsessed with his family heritage, he was frequently forced to abase himself before men of lesser lineage. Moreover, the reversal from luxury and position to poverty and dishonour fostered in him both a taste for conspiratorial politics and a strong will to survive. Throughout the rest of his life, Northampton was drawn to dazzling young courtiers such as the Earl of Essex and later Robert Carr, Earl of Somerset, who were much like his father, his hope perhaps to regain the golden days of his early childhood. Throughout Elizabeth's reign, he sought favour through the roles of scholar and conspirator. In the end, patronage, lifeblood of the Renaissance monarchy, was to bring him to power. It took thirty years.

I

An authorised biography written in the early years of James's reign commented on Howard's life under Elizabeth, 'this lord in his youth being very studious, and given to the knowledge of good letters, became for his great learning and eloquence in the Greek and Latin tongues the Rhetoric Reader in the University of Cambridge. Afterwards through his brother's misfortunes, and some other disasters happening in that noble house, he lived for the most part of Queen Elizabeth's days as a man obscured, or rather neglected.'[3] In an afterthought, however, 'neglected' was crossed out and 'voluntarily obscured' inserted. But this antiseptic version glossed over the drama.

Howard's education did not suffer from the family's disgrace. Among his tutors was Hadrianus Junius, a scholar of European reputation. Fluent in Greek and Latin by the age of sixteen, Howard read widely in philosophy, civil law, theology and history. After Elizabeth came to the throne, Howard was sent to King's College, Cambridge, at the queen's expense and there charted a career unusual for one of his birth and rank as scholar and teacher. Taking his degree in 1564, he went on to read civil law at Trinity Hall. To his classical and legal training, Howard joined a knowledge of modern languages including Spanish, French and Italian and a familiarity with contemporary European literature. In his first known work, a treatise on natural philosophy, dated from Trinity Hall, August 1569, and dedicated to his sister Catherine, Howard cited, along with the works of Aristotle, Plato, Seneca and Plutarch, 'that most excellent work of the Count of Castiglione called the Courtier', an important allusion in light of his continuing ambition for a position outside of the academy.[4]

While Reader in Rhetoric at Cambridge, Howard lectured as well on civil law. Certainly, he was the only nobleman of the Elizabethan era to teach at a university, apparently to augment his slender income. Later, under James, Howard was addressed by the universities as the most learned among the noble and the most noble among the learned.[5] Howard's education was reflected in his own writings, in his patronage of the scholarly, and perhaps even his politics. His training in rhetoric shaped his speeches and writings, characterised by Renaissance webs of metaphor contorted and spun in upon themselves by time spent in bitter hopelessness. His study of civil law, without corollary training in common law or experience of power, encouraged a viewpoint that strongly emphasised authority.[6]

At Cambridge, Howard made friends with Michael Hickes who, as one of Lord Burghley's secretaries, became a linch-pin of Elizabethan court patronage. Hickes proved helpful to Howard, for a time at least. He lent Howard money, advised him on fashion, lute-masters and the latest court gossip.[7] But Howard's problems also began at Cambridge. Trinity Hall was suspected of Catholic leanings and in 1568 Howard wrote the first of many letters to Lord Burghley to plead that he not be suspected of recusancy.[8]

Howard's religious beliefs pose some puzzles, for they reflected in part the changing contours of religious belief during his lifetime. John Fox, the

Protestant martyrologist, had been one of his childhood tutors. When his grandfather was restored as Duke of Norfolk by Queen Mary, he dismissed Fox and, following family tradition, sent Henry to serve as a page in the household of the Roman Catholic Bishop of Lincoln, John White.[9] It is probable that these years from age 13 to 18 spent in White's entourage were the primary influence in Howard's embrace of Catholicism. John Bossy has described him as 'the most permanent representative [of] . . . courtly Catholicism' whose central theme was that 'Catholicism was the natural religion for a courtly society'.[10] This assessment seems accurate. It is compatible with Howard's outward conformity, his emphasis on authority, order and degree, and his attacks on papal power while a privy councillor. There is no indication of Howard's association either with the Jesuits or with William Allen and Robert Parsons who emphasised the role of the priest rather than the layman in English Catholicism. Yet he differed from the loyal Catholic gentry of Elizabethan England by maintaining close if cautious contact with Mary, Queen of Scots and with the Spanish ambassador. At James's accession, he adopted the established religion, but at the end of his life was converted once more to Roman Catholicism, at the urging of Don Diego de Sarmiento, then Spanish ambassador. To Sarmiento's secretary, who was a priest, Howard made his general confession and 'with deep tears and devotion asked to be reconciled to the Catholic church'. On two other occasions in the spring of 1614 he made confession and, to provide encouragement to others, prepared a prayer for the king and began his will with the statement that he died a member of the same church into which he had been born.[11] In sum, Howard's religious outlook may not have differed greatly from the traditionalism of his grandfather, the third Duke of Norfolk.

In 1569 or 1570, Howard moved to claim his rightful place at court as brother to Thomas Howard, fourth Duke of Norfolk and premier duke of England, who had succeeded to the title on his grandfather's death in 1554. Thomas Howard had inherited his grandfather's pride of family but not his prudence; his talent for making advantageous marriages ultimately led to his undoing. He married three heiresses, Lady Mary Fitzalan, heiress of the Earl of Arundel, who died at sixteen; Margaret, daughter of Lord Audley, who died after bearing five children in five years, and Elizabeth Leyburne, the widow of Lord Dacre, who died in childbirth in 1567. Norfolk became guardian of the four Dacre children including three heiresses to whom Norfolk married his three sons. Each son received a different patrimony: the eldest, Philip, was seated at Arundel Castle as Earl of Arundel; Thomas, eldest son of the second marriage, became Lord Howard de Walden located at Audley End in Essex; and Lord William Howard succeeded to his wife's estates in the north, settling at Naworth Castle in Cumberland.

The financial difficulties of younger sons of the English aristocracy whose lands were often entailed on the eldest, were the cause of continuing complaint in sixteenth-century England. The duke's younger brother, Henry Howard, lived in Howard House as a poor relation. Because Norfolk now had nine children to look after, he was 'as yet unable to perform that which of a natural zeal he meant unto me'.[12] It was a dangerous moment for Henry Howard to claim his inheritance. His sister Jane had married the Earl of Westmorland who in 1569 was one of the leaders of the Rising in the North. In reaction to the Rising and the Pope's excommunication of Elizabeth in 1570, the government imposed stricter sanctions against Catholics. Moreover, when Norfolk became a widower for the third time, politics entered his consideration of a fourth wife. Although sworn into Elizabeth's Privy Council, he had been entrusted by the queen with neither office nor influence. To remedy his lack of political power Norfolk intended to make Mary, Queen of Scots, his next wife. Despite his knowledge that Elizabeth greatly disapproved, Norfolk became more and more deeply involved in conspiracy. Ultimately he agreed to put Mary on the English throne and support a national return to Catholicism. When the plot was discovered, Norfolk was arrested, tried and found guilty of treason. His lands were forfeited to the Crown and he died on the block in 1572. Norfolk's death was another important loss to Howard, though there is little evidence of closeness between the brothers. The duke did not even mention him in the moving letter he wrote to his children before he was executed, urging them to shun the court.[13]

In the year before his brother's execution Howard was unable to appear at court because of the queen's indignation at Norfolk. Indeed Howard worried that Burghley thought he should leave Howard House because of the 'small portion of living allotted unto me'.[14] After his brother's death, Howard was forced to live by his wits. For thirty years he dwelt in the houses of his nephews with whom he did form close ties and with other relations. He was mainly dependent on a small income given him by his favourite sister, Catherine, Lady Berkeley.[15] Now began the sycophantic letters, the pedantic tracts and the entrance into conspiracy; because of his Catholicism and blighted hopes, Howard became a supporter of Mary, Queen of Scots, despite his brother's execution.

The Elizabethan court was dominated in the 1570s by William Cecil, Lord Burghley, Secretary of State and Lord Treasurer, and Robert Dudley, Earl of Leicester, whose closeness to the queen made him a dominant figure on the Privy Council and the greatest patron of the period. Denied the presence of the queen, Howard lived on the fringes of the court. Between 1572 and 1586 he was part of a group of Catholic gentlemen including Charles Paget and his cousins, Charles Arundell and the Earl of Oxford, who strove to advance Mary's interests and improve the lot of English Catholics. From this group emanated *Leicester's Commonwealth* in 1584, a tract attacking the Puritan patron and what was seen as his monopolisation of Elizabeth's favour. Originally aligned with French interests, the group supported the wooing of the queen by the duc d'Alençon, brother to the French king. The discovery that the French would not support toleration for English Catholics brought disillusion and a decisive turn toward Spain.[16]

Howard established a close relationship with the Spanish ambassador and supplied him faithfully with court gossip, albeit second-hand, at a time when the ambassador was shunned by all other courtiers. Don Bernadino de Mendoza was not blind to the fact that Howard had become the leader of his family. Howard, he said, 'completely rules his nephews and constantly keeps before them the need for resenting the death of their father, and following the party of the Queen of Scots, by whose means alone can they hope for vengeance'.[17] Claiming that Howard was his most important contact at court, Mendoza persuaded Philip II to grant him a pension of one thousand crowns a year.

How important Howard's efforts on behalf of Mary were is not clear. She herself wrote to Mendoza that 'I will write you a word by Lord Harry to assure you that you may safely send by him any letters to me that you may think proper, but do not trust him with anything of importance'.[18] From a more comfortable time Howard recalled: 'I was ever reputed amongst many of the queen's allies, friends and servants [as] over cold in giving counsel for the furtherance and advancement of her Majesty's affairs ... I presented often-times by letters and discourses to herself the purpose of her enemies to take advantage of the first occasion that might give colour to that bloody course which they meant to take with her.'[19] As was the case later with the Earl of Essex, Howard always belonged to the faction around Mary urging caution.

Even if his work on Mary's behalf was not significant, Howard did not escape suspicion during this period. He was arrested and imprisoned five times, his papers searched and seized, and he was exiled to bleak country houses for months at a time. In the 1580s he was called one of the chief agents of the Queen of Scots.[20] His family was again and again tainted with treason and recusancy. Howard and his cousin Oxford accused each other of treasonable speeches.[21] Two of his nephews, Norfolk's sons, Philip, Earl of Arundel, and William, converted to Catholicism and were arrested several times in the 1580s and Philip was eventually condemned for treason and imprisoned in the Tower until his death in 1597.

Yet Henry Howard himself never suffered the more extreme penalties. He survived because he was cautious, hedging his bets in the 1570s and 1580s by seeking favour with Elizabeth and her ministers. In October 1572, shortly after Norfolk's death, Howard wrote to Burghley thanking him excessively for taking Norfolk's eldest son Philip into his own household, invoking Burghley's 'rare friendship ... toward the poor remain of our unhappy house' as well as the queen's 'unspeakable clemency'.[22] Howard wrote to her that he would 'gladly shorten and abridge my wretched days without offence to God, than live beneath the compass of my birth and ever pine in want as I have been constrained to do rather than I would estrange my self from the presence or the service of your Majesty'.[23] But his frequent banishment from court meant he was unable to compete with other court-iers by charm, wit or manner. Not trusted with official position, Howard fell back on his scholarship.

Even as he worked for Mary's cause, he composed works calculated to placate Elizabeth, Burghley and Sir Francis Walsingham. His writings during this period reflect current controversies: the discourses usually have 'Defence' or 'Answer' in the title, reflecting their intended role in Elizabethan propaganda. Thus his works included in 1574 a defence of the bishops against Thomas Cartwright the presbyterian and in 1580 an answer to John Stubbes's *Gaping Gulf*, which had attacked the projected match of the queen with the brother of the French king, the duc d'Alençon. He wrote two works celebrating Elizabeth: 'Regina Fortunata', composed about 1576 and 'A Dutiful Defense of the Lawful Regiment of Women'. Written somewhat belatedly in the 1580s at the suggestion of Lord Burghley, the latter attacked John Knox, whose untimely *First Blast of the Trumpet against the Monstrous Regiment of Women* had appeared just when Elizabeth acceded to the throne.[24] One of the few of his works to be printed was *A Defensative against the Poyson of Supposed Prophecies*, published in 1583. Dedicating the book to Walsingham, Howard upheld religious orthodoxy and attacked those who believed that by means of prophecy man rivalled God. This may have been a response to the circles around Gabriel and Richard Harvey and John Dee who dabbled in science.[25] Other works by Howard which circulated in court circles in manuscript included religious works, maxims and Charles V's instructions to his son, the King of Spain, Philip II, which he claimed to have translated in order to show how far Philip had fallen from his father's principles.[26] Each year he produced yet another learned discourse but none earned the hoped-for reward. He remained as distant from royal favour, he wrote, 'as others are distant from America'.[27]

Howard, the Catholic conspirator, was the upholder of orthodoxy, royal authority and tradition in his writings on politics and religion.[28] He collected materials for a work on passive disobedience, arguing against the right to take up arms against princes, even when they began 'to swerve from the right'. Howard justified his position 'by the scriptures, by the stories, by the laws, and by the wisest and best learned divines, either protestant or Catholics, that lived at this day in Europe'.[29] Attacking 'the importunate tattlings of these peevish Puritans', he argued that it was better with due severity to keep 'the unity of the spirit in the bond of peace . . . the unity of mind and opinion . . . and to cut off those that be troublesome: than with foolish levity to suffer pricking brambles to overflow the vineyard. Supreme authority is the only brake which restraineth such brain sick colts from their untoward affection.'[30] Howard's Renaissance education was reflected in such works by his reliance on classical authors, as well as the Bible and mediaeval legal precedents. As important as his use of classical and historical material was his method: a critical analysis and comparison of sources.

He framed most of his writings with historical questions in mind, and in his answer to the *Gaping Gulf* marshalled arguments based on both reason and 'the experience of past ages'. Striking an anti-Leicester stance he argued against the queen's marrying at home because among other reasons it would discontent the nobility. Howard urged instead the French match which might produce heirs as well as a useful alliance. Otherwise he feared a Bolingbroke might usurp the throne, while denying of course that the queen had the imperfections of Richard II.[31] It was a pregnant allusion which became dangerous in the 1590s: Sir John Hayward was imprisoned for comparing Essex with Bolingbroke in his *Henry IV*; Shakespeare had to remove the deposition scene from *Richard II* and, at the time of Essex's rebellion, the queen herself echoed the unhappy parallel.[32]

All Howard's works had in common three elements: all were decked in the apparatus of Renaissance scholarship, all upheld orthodoxy and all were intended to secure patronage from the great at court. All included dedications and letters of entreaty such as one to the queen in which he wrote of his difficult lot: 'All meditations are memories of favours past ... the small encouragement I find at any time is but a dim reflection of a wasted hope.'[33]

In 1594 Howard had his portrait painted,[34] which like many of the period is emblematic, revealing Howard's own view of his life. Tall, thin-faced, dark, sardonic, Howard stands holding a globe representing knowledge. In the background is a flower blasted by a cloud, as his hopes and his house (as he so frequently repeated) had been blasted. These feelings which Howard had lived with for years continued to burn within even as fortune's wheel took an upward turn.

The execution of Mary, Queen of Scots, in 1587 ended an alternative centre of power in England. For favour and restoration of fortune, Henry Howard could only look to the Elizabethan court. Time proved to be on his side for he outlived Leicester and Walsingham, who had been particular enemies. More importantly, in the 1590s a happy portent appeared. Howard's dazzling young cousin, Robert Devereux, Earl of Essex, became the queen's favourite.

II

It has frequently been observed that in the 1590s factions at the Elizabethan court resolved to two: the Cecils and Essex. Their rivalry coloured court life.[35] Each sought to control the queen's distribution of patronage and they carried the contest to the countryside, trying to influence local administration and elections. The 1590s proved to be the seedbed of Jacobean politics and Jacobean patronage networks. Howard's activities as part of Essex's faction shed light on their formation. But never one to choose sides irrevocably, Howard chose to maintain good relations with Cecil, and his career in the 1590s provides evidence that it was possible to remain on good terms with both pole-stars of the late Elizabethan court. The first indication that Howard's position had changed for the better dates from 1595. Anthony Bacon, Essex's closest friend, wrote to Howard to thank him for some books, adding, in a flattering way, that 'one of the greatest haps that can befall me [is] to be able by some acceptable service to acknowledge your Lordship's good opinion and favour, to deserve the increase'.[36] Howard served Essex in many ways. While Essex was at sea and in Ireland, Howard managed some of his correspondence, occasionally replacing Anthony Bacon as Essex's chief correspondent and transmitting letters to his followers. It was Howard who brought the first news to Bacon of Essex's victory at Cadiz. Howard told the earl of the intrigues which swirled through the court, tracked down rumours and provided information which Essex had requested.[37]

When in December 1597 Essex was made Earl Marshal, Howard applied his erudition to a description of the office. As Howard was later to employ scholars so was he now employed in outlining the powers and prerogatives of Essex's new position.

> Since my last being with you, I laboured above my strength, not only in rifling all corners of my dusty cabinet about notes belonging to an honour, that doth now concern yourself, but besides in sweeping down the cobwebs every other where, that I may rightly judge, and you may truly understand, what is due to your authority.[38]

Howard's labour was a lengthy treatise entitled 'A brief discourse on the right use of giving arms'. Of all the works he wrote during Elizabeth's reign, this most closely resembled the kind of work he would commission under James: an analysis of the abuses in an important office, in this case the office of heralds, with suggestions for reform.

Forced to live 'below the compass of my birth', Howard excoriated the fraudulent giving of arms to upstarts hungry for prestige by heralds hungry for money. His work is one of the most extreme statements against social mobility, made at a time when changes in fortune were occurring with unusual rapidity. Howard noted, for instance: 'I speak of merchants chiefly in this place because their spawn hath multiplied above all other fishes in the lake, their seeds increased faster . . . but my reason reacheth other occupations also of proportionable unworthiness.'[39]

His scholarship now found practical political outlet: Howard challenged the heralds' claim to exercise jurisdiction independent of the Earl Marshal. In addition to citing classical authors and biblical literature, he showed a sophisticated sense of historical analysis, drawing on mediaeval precedents, ancient account books, Exchequer records, the notes of early heralds and the ordinances drawn up when his brother was Earl Marshal in 1568. In 'sweeping down the cobwebs' he had questioned heralds and scholars, and examined evidence in government offices and private collections. Although the Earl Marshalship had been associated with the Dukedom of Norfolk, Henry Howard showed no resentment. Rather he declared that the life of the country and Essex were one, and vowed not to love any man that did not love the favourite.[40]

Patronage was the lifeblood of the alliance. Sir Robert Sidney spelled out the role of favour very clearly in commenting on the naming of two new members of the Privy Council in October 1596: 'Yet am I glad that our new councillors were brought in by the Earl. These which are lukewarm will trust more on him and such as be assured unto him will be glad to see he hath power to do his friends good.'[41] Howard sought the favourite's patronage for his family, writing to him to ensure his nephew Lord Thomas Howard a share of the booty from the Cadiz expedition. Essex's commendation of Howard's nephew to the queen and Cecil evoked thanks from Howard for promoting 'this happy branch...of a blasted stock', and a description of his own situation in these gloomy terms. 'My life is now...so far worn with care, as it is time for me to renounce the world, that affordeth me nothing in regard of any dessert but contempt, oblivion and secret nips.'[42]

Self-pity notwithstanding, Howard's position had certainly improved. He was now a familiar figure at court and, by 1597, had not only established himself as an intermediary between Essex and his followers but also had been readmitted to the presence of the queen.[43] Recalling that important occasion from the security of James's reign, Howard described how the queen decided

> some five years and more before her death at my Lord of Hertford's house in Cannon Row to receive me to her favour by the kissing of her hand with this further protestation that as those heavy crosses which I had so often borne had been too light upon proof of guiltiness in those things... suspected during the disgraces and disasters of my house and friends so now she must confess...too heavy for a man that had so cleared himself from imputation.

His misfortunes had grown from others 'so my satisfaction should grow from herself'.[44] She now granted him a £200 pension. No doubt Essex had promoted Howard's interests, as his letter to Sir Thomas Egerton makes clear: 'your favour is very worthily bestowed, for...my inward friendship with my Lord H. Howard doth make me know his many virtues.'[45]

Patronage depends on power. Without it any patron loses most of his following. The mood of the Essex faction changed from Sidney's gloating in 1596 to suspicion and despair in 1599 and 1600. A paranoid style developed, if in fact it had not always been there. Howard's own personality meshed with and perhaps exacerbated this view. He needed reassurance of Essex's love and support and grew apprehensive and defensive in its absence. Repeatedly the earl reassured him that only heaviness of business at court prevented his answering Howard's messages. Anthony Bacon described Howard on one occasion as 'greatly moved in countenance betwixt challenge and charging of your lordship and moaning of himself... saying he would not trouble your lordship again, to receive a third repulse'.[46] In one instance Essex replied sensibly but in a manner that suggested he shared Howard's world-view: 'take no alarms of me but from me . . . for the world is idle as it is false, and both these properties will vanquish us if we be not resolved before hand to let rumours pass in at one ear and out at another.'[47] When Essex went off to Ireland in March 1599 Howard expressed concern over the enterprise, and relayed his worries that the court in his absence had become of one party alone, presumably Cecil's.[48] Although this was necessary intelligence it could only feed Essex's own fear and hasten the return without the queen's permission which led to his downfall.

In 1599 when Essex returned from his expedition against the queen's express orders, she had him sequestered. Howard remained loyal to him, but others did not. Francis Bacon was one and rumours circulated that as one of the queen's counsels he had advised that Essex was guilty of high treason. Indignantly Bacon wrote to Henry Howard to denounce the rumour, and to solicit Howard's help in countering it. Admitting that he had been much bound to Essex, Bacon argued that he had devoted more time to the earl's well-being than to his own, and had a 'superior duty'. To this self-serving letter Howard wrote a seemingly sympathetic but ambiguous reply, masterful in its veiled attack on Bacon's short memory and self-justification. It deserves to be quoted at length since it describes Howard's notion of the *quid pro quo* of the patronage relationship.

> The travail of the worthy gentleman in your behalf, when you stood for a place of credit; the delight which he hath ever taken in your company; the grief that he should not seal up assurance of his love by fruits, effects and offices proportionable to his infinite desire; his study in my knowledge to engage your love by the best means he could devise, are forcible reasons and instances to make me judge that a gentleman so well born, a wise gentleman, so well learned, a gentleman so highly valued by a person of his virtue, worth and quality, will rather hunt after all occasions of expressing thankfulness (so far as duty doth permit) than either omit opportunity or increase indignation.[49]

During the time that Essex was forbidden access to the court Howard apparently advised him on how to write to the queen and her ministers and may even have helped him compose those letters. At Michaelmas, that is, on 25 September 1600, Essex's lease on the impositions on sweet wines fell in. Because the wine farm was the mainstay of his income, Essex anxiously pressed the queen to renew it. Howard counselled a different course. About 29 September, Edward Reynolds, Essex's secretary, wrote that Howard advised the earl not to write to the queen for four or five days but instead to send a few lines to Sir John Stanhope, Treasurer of the Chamber. Requesting the last letter that Stanhope had written to Essex, Howard composed a message to the Treasurer which he could then show to the queen to Essex's advantage. When he wrote to Elizabeth on 4 October, Essex referred to his letter to Stanhope. In its arguments, Howard's hand may perhaps be discerned: 'the other which I wrote since to Sir John Stanhope has, I hope, made you see that I let fall all suits which you are not pleased to grant, and enjoin myself never to speak in that style which you do not like to hear. If I may be but a mute in your presence, they that have most favours of fortune shall never be envied by me.' [50] Although Stanhope felt the letter had been successful, these soft sentiments failed to move Elizabeth's heart. Still in disfavour, his finances in disarray, his influence dissipated, Essex came to believe that his enemies were plotting against him and that he needed to seize the court in order to bring the queen to her senses.

Howard had devoted himself as wholeheartedly to Essex's interests as he had to Mary, Queen of Scots', but drew the line at overt rebellion and took no part in Essex's desperate revolt. He was apparently the leader of the faction of the earl's followers who opposed the action.[51] In 1601 two of Essex's followers, Sir John Davies and Sir William Constable, sought Howard's intervention to mitigate the effects of their participation in the uprising. Constable requested Lord Henry 'to assist him for the continuance of Cecil's favours'.[52] Whether or not Howard did intercede for them, both survived to prosper under James I.

There is something puzzling here. How was it that Howard was in a position in 1600 to advise Essex how to approach the queen, and in 1601 to influence Cecil? Did not his acceptance at court depend on Essex? Apparently not. Unlike Bacon, Howard did not dissociate himself from Essex after his disgrace in 1599, but he did protect himself by maintaining friendly relations with the other pole-star of the court, Sir Robert Cecil. Cecil knew where Howard's first loyalty lay, but showed him kindness anyway, probably out of friendship with his nephew, Lord Thomas Howard. In 1596, for example, Cecil had allayed Howard's anxiety about the battle of Cadiz and the fate of Essex with the first news that reached the court of Essex's triumph. Calling himself a 'bankrupt in fortune's exchange', Howard thanked Cecil profusely for informing him before many of Cecil's own friends.[53] By 1598 Howard had acquired a certain amount of influence with the Secretary. Of this there are several examples. Cecil expedited Howard's pension in 1598. The Earl of Shrewsbury told Cecil that Lord Thomas and Lord Henry Howard would favour the suit of his protegé Anthony Wingfield. William Tresham, a Catholic and old friend, applied to Howard in 1599 to further his suit to return from exile. Howard was able to use his contacts with Cecil to help mitigate the queen's displeasure towards Thomas Arundell, a kinsman of Howard's.[54]

Analysing court politics after Essex's return from Ireland points up Howard's success at the patronage game and his own already slippery reputation. Rowland Whyte wrote to Sir Robert Sidney, in September 1599, that Howard was among the members of Essex's faction, 'but he is held a neuter, and I pray you take heed of him, be not too bold to trust him if you have not already gone too far'.[55] But while issuing this warning, Whyte also took care to approach Howard about promoting Sidney's interests. There was talk at court that Howard was trying to mediate peace between Essex and Cecil and by the end of August 1600 Whyte wrote Sidney that 'my Lord Henry Howard hath infinitely travelled in his business, for surely, things were far out of square between him and Mr Secretary, which seems by his direction to be upon better terms'.[56] Yet at the same time, as we have seen, Howard continued to maintain his close relations with Essex. On 29 August 1600 Cecil wrote to Sir George Carew that Essex had received permission to go to his uncle's in the country, 'few resort to him but those who are of his blood, amongst which I imagine the Lord Henry Howard will not be long from him'.[57] Nevertheless, Howard's reconciliation with Cecil was to have the most profound effect on his future career.

Howard's travels through the thickets of late Elizabethan patronage suggest that the factional struggles of the 1590s need to be re-evaluated. It was not impossible to be on good terms with both Essex and Cecil. Moreover, it appears that such groupings were not ideological, formed neither exclusively around religious nor foreign policy issues. The efforts of a 'trimmer' such as Howard, motivated by personal gain, did have positive results. For Howard was mediating between Essex and Cecil on behalf of a most illustrious patron, James VI of Scotland. Howard's alliance with Cecil helped to lay the foundation for James's peaceful accession to the throne, and for the structure of Jacobean patronage.

III

The succession question which had agitated England throughout most of the sixteenth century remained unanswered in 1600. A variety of claimants including James VI of Scotland, the Spanish Infanta and several domestic aspirants, lobbied for precedence as the reign drew to a close. James was the most likely heir, but the queen refused to arrange for an orderly transfer of power. Anxious to gain the favour of a new monarch, several of her courtiers secretly contacted James to assure him of their support. Essex, in particular, established a warm friendship with James and in 1598 the French ambassador noted that the Scottish king entrusted all his negotiations at the English court to the favourite.[58] Essex's revolt in February 1601 ended that alliance and James quickly and cannily made new arrangements with Robert Cecil, whose supremacy at court he now recognised. At the end of May 1601 James and Cecil began a secret correspondence which ultimately led to James's peaceful accession to the English throne in 1603 and Cecil's political hegemony almost until his death in 1612.

This secret correspondence took place mainly through intermediaries, the Earl of Mar and Edward Bruce on the Scottish side and, surprisingly, Lord Henry Howard on the English. Whether Howard had taken part in

Essex's communications with James cannot be documented but seems likely, because the choice of Howard to act as go-between was made by the king himself. In his first letter to the Secretary James asked Cecil

> to accept of his long approved and trusty 3 [Lord Henry Howard]... to be a sure and secret interpreter betwixt 30 [K. James] and 10 [Sec. Cecil] in the opening up of every one of their minds to another; whom 10 hath the better cause to like of and trust, since long before this time 3 dealt very earnestly with 30 to take a good conceit of 10, offering himself to be a dealer betwixt them, whereupon 30 was contented 3 should deal betwixt Essex and 10... for the well [sic] of 30.[59]

To James's choice of Howard as intermediary Cecil agreed. Clearly the rumours in the summer of 1600 of a rapprochement between Howard and Cecil were correct. In a rather opaque letter of this period, Cecil wrote Howard that 'the Earl of Nottingham accuseth both you and me of morning jugglings'.[60] Howard's efforts to be on good terms with the Secretary as well as Essex now can be seen to have had as its goal the creation of a broadly based party on behalf of James.

The secret correspondence fulfilled the needs of both sides. In the absence of parliamentary legislation or a binding commitment from the queen, James required a party in England which could guarantee his accession to the throne. Cecil needed to ensure a peaceful succession and a friendly monarch to continue his hold on political power. These clandestine contacts were in line with Cecil's personality, for as Howard remarked, 'nothing makes him confident, but experience of secret trust, and security of intelligence'.[61] Howard also argued a more statesmanlike motive, that the prevention of dissension and misunderstanding with the Scottish king was in the queen's interest even though against her express wish. Certainly the confidence generated by the correspondence led James to a new harmony in his relations with Elizabeth, fostering consultation on foreign policy and putting an end to his importuning the queen about the succession. At the same time the correspondence spelled out future government policy: Howard wrote that 'the main foundations of the future buildings... is grounded upon peace with Spain and combination with the North'.[62]

But the essence of the secret correspondence was the establishment of a new patronage relationship between the future king and Cecil, and Howard, too, which was to characterise the new reign. Both Cecil and Howard sought to reinforce James's belief that Cecil provided the only means to the throne. All alternative sources of influence were to be denigrated or destroyed. Much of Howard's correspondence was taken up, in fact, with warning the king against other courtiers.[63] Henry Brooke, Lord Cobham, Warden of the Cinque Ports, and Sir Walter Raleigh, Captain of the Queen's Guard, became Howard's particular targets because they tried to make an independent approach to James through his favourite, the Duke

of Lennox. Since both had been enemies of Essex's, Howard had no difficulty employing his long-nurtured malice to their disadvantage. Furthermore, he felt that Raleigh had undertaken 'endless practice to disgrace
me'.[64] He suggested to Cecil various means of undermining their position
with the queen by accusing them of intriguing with James or the Spaniards.
Of Cobham he wrote,

> But as my Lord of Leicester dealt with my brother – finding his humour
> apt to deal with Scotland, when he thrust him into treaty about those
> affairs, assuring himself that either he should lose the queen for the
> present, or the other queen for the future – so must you embark this
> gallant Cobham by your wit and interest, in some course the Spanish
> way, as either may reveal his weakness or snare his ambition. . . . For my
> own part I account it impossible for him to escape the snares which wit
> may set, and weakness is apt to fall into. (The queen did never yet love
> man that failed in a project of importance put into his hand. . . .)

In Raleigh's case, Howard commented: 'by how much this man wanteth
better helps by nature, art, or industry, to countenance a pride above the
greatest Lucifer that hath lived in our age, by so much shall he sooner run
himself on ground in rage and make the queen more sensitive in scorning so
great sauciness in so great infirmity.'[65]

Howard convinced James and his officials that Cobham and Raleigh had
tried to poison the queen against Cecil. Bruce wrote to Howard that the two
were forlorn in the Scots' accounts, that no one could win ground to the
least disgrace of Cecil of whom they were greatly enamoured and that
Howard should tell those that he loved of Essex's friends that any ideas of
injuring Cecil would result in their own ruin.[66] As Elizabeth lay near death,
James's reliance on Cecil and Howard increased. Bruce wrote to Howard
that the king longed to hear from him, 'because of the multitude of advertisements we receive, you must be the more frequent in sending this time,
for we mean to sail by no other compass than your counsel and advice in all
things'.[67] As James made his triumphal entry into his new kingdom, both
Cobham and Raleigh rushed to greet him, the latter conducting many
suitors to the king. But Howard had done his work well. Raleigh was stayed
and Howard joined the king at Newcastle to counter Cobham and provide
Cecil with on-the-spot intelligence.[68]

In the case of Raleigh and Cobham, there is no way to defend Howard's
actions, and perhaps not much need. In those last hectic days of Elizabeth's
reign, as the queen herself failed to prepare for an orderly transition of
power, it was left to her courtiers. In the scramble for place under James, all
played for the highest stakes. Howard felt rightly or wrongly that his
brother and indeed his father had been vanquished in similar struggles; he
would not. Howard's attachment to Essex was emotional; he never forgot
those who had victimised Essex as he felt his father and brother had been.

Raleigh had plagued Essex and, it was said, had attended Essex's execution with glee. The venom of Howard's writings shocks, but how important were his convoluted insinuations to the fall of Raleigh and Cobham? It appears that, denied favour, they acted as he predicted. Confusedly conspiring to regain power in the early days of the new reign, they were entrapped in the Main Plot of 1603, tried and imprisoned. Responding to Lady Raleigh, who accused him of malice against her husband, Howard composed a lengthy letter of self-justification to be shown to the king perhaps as well as to her. Alluding to Raleigh's practices against himself, 'shooting me through and through so long as he had any powder left', and to his malice toward Essex, he went on:

> I could thank your Ladyship for putting me in mind of the griefs and sores of my own honourable family (because nothing more contenteth and pleaseth the dispositions of men than to look back to the rocks and billows of the sea after they are arrived in safe harbour) if I did not find this warning powdered with many grains of...bitterness...none of those was either committed thither nor convicted after they came thither upon so just grounds as we committed Sir Walter.[69]

Howard's personal triumph over adversity, over the enemies he saw around him, over *fortuna*, was complete.

In the secret correspondence, Howard served as hatchet man, but only along with Robert Cecil, Cobham's brother-in-law and Elizabeth's most important minister, whose interests he served as well as his own. The major results of the secret correspondence were positive and substantial: the peaceful accession of a new dynasty – and of a foreign monarch at that – for the first time in English history. After years of uncertainty, King James entered the promised land, grateful to Cecil and Howard for leading the way. As a result, Cecil continued to control patronage as he had in the last years of Elizabeth and in alliance with him, Howard took a leading role in Jacobean government. The late 1590s laid the foundation for Jacobean politics and patronage networks. What has not been sufficiently noticed is the extent to which these networks included Essex's followers.[70] Howard proved an important patron to old comrades. Cecil shaped a Privy Council which resembled that of the earlier days of Elizabeth; a group of officials each with his own following, who were able to foster widespread support for the regime and maintain its stability. It has frequently been asserted that Cecil and Howard were enemies from 1600 to 1608 or 1610;[71] in fact they were closely allied. This explains Northampton's access to power and the prominent part he played in English government from 1603 to 1614.

The future Earl of Northampton proved to be the consummate Jacobean courtier but in 1603 his political career was just beginning. After a lifetime of poverty and danger, he could now lay claim to his inheritance of power and influence. 'A cautious pilot', as he described himself, had 'brought his bark safe out of the broken seas' to a sunny port.[72] At the age of 63, Howard had finally achieved his life-long ambition of high court office.

Acknowledging his debt to Howard in the early days of his reign, James ordered the Privy Council to give him the precedence due to the son of a duke on the grounds that he would have held that status had not the fall of his ancestors prevented the descent of the title:

> Forasmuch as we have had long experience, of the honest affection of the Lord Henry Howard, to our person and well-doing; and are not ignorant how many crosses he hath sustained, in his own particular, in respect thereof. We being now desirous to witness our good opinion of his fidelity and zeal to our service ... for his better grace, both in respect of the house whereof he is descended and in regard of our desire, to notify the good opinion we have of his loyal and dutiful affection towards us ... both in the time of our late sister (to whom he ever reserved his honest duty) and since, to the uttermost of his power.[73]

But it was royal patronage, not ancestry, which proved to be his 'gaol delivery'.

Chapter 2

The Organisation of Influence

As King James moved southward to claim the English throne which was his by divine right, and for which he had waited on tenterhooks for decades, he was greeted by waves of well-wishers and favour-seekers. *En route* James came to stay at Burleigh, the seat of Robert Cecil's elder brother, Thomas, Lord Burghley. There, Henry Howard presented Lord Thomas and Lord William Howard: 'My Lord Henry Howard at their first coming ... brought them presently unto the king ... [who] turning unto my Lord Henry said "here be two of your nephews, both Howards, I love the whole house of them" ... the king said they should never repent his coming into the kingdom, and so drew my Lord Henry along the gallery with him.'[1] King James thus sealed in public the connection he had shaped in his secret correspondence. Henry Howard and members of the Howard family were assured of the king's favour. Granted the status of a duke's son, Howard was made a privy councillor, created Earl of Northampton and appointed Lord Warden of the Cinque Ports. Thomas Howard was also made a privy councillor, created Earl of Suffolk and named Lord Chamberlain. James granted both of them jointly most of the lands which had come to the Crown by the attainders which had marked their house. Northampton was to maintain close ties with the king until his death. In the early years of the reign this intimacy was symbolised by the joking letters the king sent his leading councillors, addressing Salisbury, Northampton and Suffolk as 'a trinity of knaves'. Never as powerful as Cecil, Northampton's influence fluctuated over the years, but it was to the ailing earl that the king turned for advice at the close of the Addled Parliament of 1614. While Northampton lived, the king's trust in him seems not to have wavered.[2]

But what might appear to be the happy ending to the story was, of course, just the beginning. Having once achieved royal favour, Northampton's task was to translate it into political power. This was not a simple equation. Northampton had established no organisation while he worked in secret on James's behalf. Now he had to construct a set of relationships which would perpetuate the promise of James's accession for the continuing benefit of himself and his family. To do so, he carved out a place for himself and his followers at court under Cecil's hegemony from 1603 to 1611. And as Cecil lost power and Robert Carr became the king's favourite, Northampton constructed an alliance with the favourite that gave him even greater access to court patronage. But power and status in Tudor–Stuart England required standing both at court and in the countryside. It was not enough for Northampton to have the king's ear himself, or even to gain favour for himself: he had to be able to promote the fortunes of his followers. This had been the Earl of Essex's difficulty, his inability to secure favour for his clients; it was also the great failure of Northampton's brother who, despite his status as the premier duke of England and his dominance of the county of Norfolk, was unable to gain favour with the queen at court.[3] Through his patronage Northampton sought to gain both ends. Despite the fact that he was literally 'created' by the king, he sought followers in the regions through his position as Lord Warden of the Cinque Ports and, through his landholdings in Norfolk and Suffolk, tried to fulfil his role of patron for traditional Howard followers. Moreover, at the Jacobean court it was necessary to be seen to exercise power. In a society which emphasised formal display, the successful patron required a swarm of followers whose pestering presence testified to his august standing. Northampton's transformation from humble petitioner to court patron provides an insider's view of Jacobean politics.

Examining how the Crown organised and dispensed patronage in the early years of James's reign helps to explain the political parameters and value system within which Northampton operated. While patronage was a traditional means of achieving stability in English society, instability, caused by the increasingly frantic scramble for reward by individual patrons and clients, was undermining the Crown's control in the late sixteenth and early seventeenth centuries. The king and his ministers sought in various ways to organise patronage for the Crown's benefit: James centralised patronage in one official's hands; Salisbury crafted a plan which laid out in detail how patronage was to be distributed; Northampton emphasised merit in government appointments and carefully constructed his own patronage network designed both to exploit the possibilities at court for influence and profit, and to provide servants for the king.

I

The patron–client relationship was the chief means by which the Crown won the loyalty of powerful subjects, integrated regional elites and local governments into the state and staffed its administration. Lacking coercive institutions such as a standing army or a paid local bureaucracy by which to impose their will, the Tudors had successfully made the court the centre of power, offering honour, privilege and office in exchange for service and obedience.[4] Robert Cecil characterised it clearly in 1610: 'For the king not to be bountiful were a fault, for that duty is best and surest tried where it is rewarded, which...makes men the willinger to do service.'[5] The monarch's resources were imposing. Honours such as knighthoods and patents of nobility were the traditional rewards the king bestowed on his supporters. Elizabeth's parsimony contributed to the demand for both at King James's accession by those who sought public confirmation of achieved or hoped-for status.[6] Grants of royal lands on favourable terms or the delegation of royal rights such as wardship[7] and concealed lands – those that should have been paying rent to the Crown – also attracted suitors. Furthermore, the privileges and offices in the Crown's gift had increased under Henry VIII as the Crown took over many of the social and economic functions of the mediaeval church and guilds. As a result, there were profits to be made from the enforcement of religious penalties and the exploitation of economic regulation including custom farms and monopolies. These grants became more and more lucrative as English trade grew in the sixteenth and seventeenth centuries. In addition, the court could dispose of perhaps 2,500 offices, 1,200 of which were 'worth a gentleman's having'.[8] Office conferred power, status and, most important of all, profit. In addition to age-old fees for the performance of official duties, there were gratuities which may have amounted to £250,000–£400,000, as much as 40 per cent of the yearly royal revenue.[9] Offices were treated as the private property of the holder and a flourishing market existed in which they were bought and sold.

The court patrons were the key to royal reward, serving as intermediaries between suitors and monarch.[10] A strong sense of the nuances of power animated suitors who sought out courtiers known to have access to the king. The relationship established between patron and client was a real one, sometimes labelled a contract, although it was not necessarily permanent or exclusive. Suitors changed allegiance with alacrity when their patron lost influence. The result was that even important officials needed to have the favour of those closest to the king. To the suitor, the patron offered access to royal favour. In return the suitor testified with both his presence – and his presents – to the power of the patron, thereby enhancing the patron's influence and prestige. Northampton received the thanks of Sir Thomas Edmondes, for whom he had secured a favour, by saying he held it a 'richness to my soul when I make a worthy friend rich in reputation by my labour'.[11] While cynicism might suggest richness to his pocketbook as well, the centrality of prestige in Stuart politics should not be underestimated. The suitors for this extensive royal bounty were primarily members of the landed aristocracy, those peers and country gentlemen who controlled power in localities. In addition, the educated, particularly lawyers who practised in royal courts[12] and wealthy London merchants, sought favour at court. These few thousand formed the political elite to whom the Crown gave favour.

Several developments in the late sixteenth and seventeenth centuries, however, worked to undermine the effective distribution of court patronage. First, in a period of marked population growth, as well as increased prosperity and access to education, the size of the political elite increased dramatically.[13] The growth in royal bounty during the same period failed to keep pace with the growth in population. Secondly, perhaps in response to this increased pressure on royal bounty and the active market for office, the king's control over office-holding diminished. The tendency toward life tenure for most middle-range offices in the central government was exacerbated during James's reign when many offices were granted for life which previously had been held at the monarch's pleasure. This meant that offices did not open up as frequently for patronage. In addition, the practice of attaching reversions to offices was characteristic of perhaps as many as half of the middle-rank offices.[14] Often granted for a succession of lives, offices became practically hereditary in certain families. Control over appointees was difficult because, in some cases, the rights of appointment were disputed between important ministers and, in others, importuning courtiers sought to supplant the patronage of heads of departments. Furthermore, once in office, officeholders frequently chose their own subordinates. Finally, the sale of offices created a group of officeholders who found it necessary to milk the public in order to recover their investment; to maintain their profits, they brought pressure on the king not to create new offices.[15]

These were difficult problems but so long as patronage was distributed by officials who were also in charge of government policy and administration, favour might still be distributed to muster support for the monarchy. The chief dispenser of patronage in the early years of James's reign was Robert Cecil, Earl of Salisbury. Through his offices, as Secretary of State, Master of the Court of Wards and later Lord Treasurer, and through his influence with the king, Salisbury dominated politics and administration.[16]

Northampton had built his fortune on his close relationship with Salisbury and, of course, with the king, in the 1590s and continued to do so now. Too much political significance has been attached to the supposed antipathy between Cecil and himself. Cecil himself referred to the 'obligation of our alliance' later in the reign. Howard said that those who had tried to destroy that connection had been disappointed because 'affection to our Master, regard of our own duty, love to the public . . . hath drawn both of us to that . . . fastness in affection and correspondent love which shuts up the gate to the Trojan horse'.[17] The Howard party, often described as dominating the court and the Privy Council from Salisbury's death in 1612 up to the emergence of the Duke of Buckingham as the king's favourite, in 1603 existed only in embryo. The basic reality of Jacobean political life was the pre-eminence of Cecil: it was as his allies that Henry Howard and his family became influential. Such factions have usually been described by historians in much too static a fashion.[18] While it is certainly possible to discern constellations at court and even continuing antipathies, in reality Jacobean politics were, as we shall see, quite fluid. Particularly at times of transition, such as Salisbury's death or Somerset's fall and Buckingham's rise, factions were in flux. For one thing, Suffolk had independent ties to Cecil created under Elizabeth. For another, not all Howards were included in this faction. Charles Howard, Earl of Nottingham and Lord Admiral, continued as a member of the Privy Council after James's accession, but did not participate in the Cecil–Howard alliance. Northampton was hostile to Nottingham and successfully excluded him from policy decisions on matters other than the navy. And by the end of his life Northampton was not on good terms with his nephew Suffolk, with whom he had enjoyed royal favour. Salisbury shared some of his own power. Most patronage and policy decisions were referred to an inner circle of the Privy Council of which Northampton was a constant member. Indeed it would appear that the central alliance of the early Jacobean period was that of Salisbury and Northampton. Perception of this powerful combine appears in petition after petition of earnest suitors, many of whom were important aristocrats in their own right. For instance, Sir John Harrington wanted the Earl of Shrewsbury to move Northampton and Salisbury on his behalf, while the Earl of Bath used Northampton's secretary John Griffith as an intermediary to Salisbury. To Salisbury and Northampton were referred the appointment of an allowance for the Countess of Oxford as well as the controversy between the Earl of Huntingdon and Lord Derby over the Isle of Man. Sir William Fitzwilliam obtained the remission of his father's debt after approaching Howard and Cecil. Sir Henry Danvers's Irish grant was signified by Howard to Cecil. In a controversy with Thomas Southwell over an annuity, Sir William Cornwallis was successful presumably through Howard's influence in staying proceedings until Salisbury and Northampton could consider it.[19]

Moreover, by frequently including the Earl of Suffolk as well as Edward Somerset, Earl of Worcester, who became closely identified with the Howard faction, the petitions reveal the beginnings of the Howard connection alongside Salisbury. Thus Lord Treasurer Buckhurst thought it expedient to consult with Northampton and Suffolk as well as Cecil when he wished to promote his son-in-law in 1603. George Bowes solicited their support for his project for gold prospecting while Henry Fanshawe asked them for the right to bestow the reversion of his office as Remembrancer of the Exchequer.[20] Sir Francis Hastings's wish to be restored to the king's good favour after presenting in Parliament what was considered a seditious petition of Northamptonshire gentlemen in behalf of deprived ministers had the support, he wrote to Salisbury, of Northampton and Worcester.[21] Evidently patronage at the Jacobean court was not limited by ideology; Hastings, often taken for a Puritan, had solicited and, more significantly, received the support of courtiers known to be crypto-Catholics. While Hastings may have shown political acumen, his successful approach to Northampton and Worcester suggests too that Jacobean patronage and factions were not polarised. Finally, the crucial importance of Cecil and Howard to the workings of the early Jacobean government was recognised by the Archbishop of Canterbury when he wrote to Cecil about the commission for ecclesiastical causes in 1605:

I sent the names for the commission ecclesiastical unto my Lord Chancellor, who will in no sort allow it that the Earl of Northampton's name and your Lordship's should be left out, because, as he says (and truly) that, these times considered, some occasion may fall out that the omission of them may be very inconvenient.[22]

Besides identifying the locus of power these petitions reflect something more about the organisation of court patronage. When Lord Harrington petitioned in 1607 that a new office be created to oversee the execution of the processes of outlawry from which he wanted half of all forfeitures, the request was referred to Salisbury, Northampton, Lord Ellesmere, who was Lord Chancellor, the Earl of Dorset, the Lord Treasurer and Sir Thomas Fleming, the Lord Chief Justice.[23] What becomes apparent is that these petitions reflect not only the realities of power and faction but also the effort by Salisbury to control patronage so as to ensure that the king received service in return for reward.

The need for such control was evident to James himself. In 1592 he had had the Scottish Parliament enact a statute establishing a procedure to insulate him from clients.[24] On his progress from Scotland to England the king had been besieged by favour-seekers and had with a glad hand bestowed knighthoods right and left, 906 in the early months of his reign, even 432 in one day.[25] In response to the outcry against such bounty, the English Privy Council apparently devised some sort of system as early as 1604 to provide for the orderly dispensation of patronage and to ensure that the Elizabethan practice of demanding service in return for reward continued. The grant to Sir Henry Lee of the keeping of Carlisle Castle is an example of this policy. Northampton stressed that while the terms in the grant should include keeping of the castle for life, there should be little or no fee attached. 'For since it behooveth his Majesty to cut off all waste charges of keepings by the best means and the most orderly that his council can devise, I would be loth, in the very extreme and first step to reformation, to lay down a rub, or advise that, out of partiality, which duty and affection doth countermand.'[26]

By 1608 Salisbury had drawn up a detailed set of instructions to manage patronage in the king's name. Their language provides evidence of the personal and reciprocal nature of the patronage system when it referred to the 'suits as shall be preferred unto us by any of our servants, or subjects who have cause to expect matter of rewards or recompense'. The instructions went on to describe both the difficulties of Jacobean patronage and its rationale: grants would only be made 'after so good and mature deliberation. As (for want thereof) the desire we have to use our liberality to men of dessert, may not (through overmuch haste) draw from us any grants that may afterwards be found inconvenient.' To slow down the process, to insulate both the king and the councillors who had more important matters to consider than the importunities of suitors, the instructions provided that such suits be referred to a subcommittee of officials including members of the learned counsel. The king's purpose was stated directly:

for as no Sovereign can be without service, nor service without some reward, so we confess that no prince is more desirous than we are to reward the merit of our servants, and other our subjects in things that might be fitting for us to give provided always that the same be not prejudicial either to the main part ... of any revenue which we are desirous to leave to our posterity for the better maintenance of the dignity of their estate, in no less honour and magnificence than our progenitors, kings of this realm, had held.[27]

In this personal relationship between the king and his servants those suits were ruled out by the instructions which were contrary to law or 'are fit to be wholly to our own use until our estate be repaired'.[28] These included grants of the benefits of penal laws, royal land, leases and rents, pensions and avoidance of customs duties. These prohibitions sought to prevent the giving away of royal revenues, as well as items that were oppressive to the subjects such as fines and inquiries into defective titles. Grants that could be asked for included offices, keeping of parks, forfeiture of lands and goods stemming from felonies, debts due to the Crown dating from before the thirtieth year of Elizabeth and projects or new inventions 'so they be not contrary to the law nor mischievous to the state by raising prices of commodities at home or hurt of trade'.[29] In this way Salisbury sought to safeguard the royal estate and to distribute rewards from among the minor favours in the king's gift and the obligations his subjects owed him. This Elizabethan policy of reward in return for service was one that Northampton attempted to continue after Salisbury's death.

But the making of policy was always contingent on continuing favour and connection, Northampton's to Salisbury, Salisbury's to the king. The alliance between Salisbury and Northampton survived despite occasional strains. Northampton wrote to Sir Charles Cornwallis, English ambassador in Spain, to deny a falling out between Salisbury and himself, suggesting that a difference of opinion at the council table had engendered the rumours. This assurance brought forth from Cornwallis the panegyric of the grateful client: by that 'perfect and faithful unity ... your prince shall be served ... your country secured, your own honours and strengths established, and my poor self shadow my head under that bay tree whereunto I wish perpetual greenness and plentiful blossom'.[30] Still strains there were. In 1607, and again in 1611, for instance, Northampton came close to overthrowing Cecil's arrangement for the Great Farm of the customs which had brought Cecil both profit and prestige. Northampton's patronage remained restricted while Salisbury explicitly denied Northampton and his clients access to the most profitable privileges the court had to offer. Salisbury kept close tabs on his ally including his correspondence. On one occasion Sir Roger Aston, Master of the Wardrobe, described in detail to Salisbury a packet of letters Northampton had sent to court. 'There was one letter to his Majesty which contained two sheets of paper written of all sides. After his

Majesty had read it he gave it to Lord Fenton; so far as I could perceive it contained such matters as had passed in Council since his Majesty's departing from you.'[31] Salisbury had been successful in almost all his government endeavours. The failure of his ambitious attempt to conclude the Great Contract in 1610, by which Parliament would grant the king a yearly revenue in exchange for his giving up feudal prerogatives such as wardship, led to a subtle lessening of his influence with the king. At the same time there was a new star on the horizon, the Scottish courtier, Robert Carr. Sir Thomas Howard, Suffolk's son, bitterly and wittily described Carr's new ascendance:

> Robert Carr is now most likely to win the Prince's affection and doth it wondrously in a little time. The Prince leaneth on his arm, pinches his cheek, smooths his ruffled garment.... We are almost worn out in our endeavours to keep pace with this fellow in his duty and labour to gain favour, but all in vain; where it endeth I cannot guess, but honours are talked of speedily for him.[32]

II

In the spring of 1611 Carr appeared to be part of a faction in opposition to the Howards and to Cecil. Sir Thomas Lake had accused him of fomenting trouble between Salisbury and Parliament and between Salisbury and the king. By October 1611 a sensitive observer noted that Carr, now Viscount Rochester, had more suitors following him than had the Lord Treasurer.[33] All signs pointed to a realignment of influence at court. Even before Salisbury's death in May 1612, Northampton had begun to ingratiate himself with the favourite, laying the foundation for a new alliance which would ensure his continuance in power. Among other things, he sang Carr's praises to the king, and lauded his handling of official duties. He only wished, he said, that Carr were a member of the Privy Council or that all who were members were possessed of his 'dainty parts', that is, nature, judgement and capacity.[34] With Salisbury's death Carr became the 'primum mobile of our court, by whose motion all the other spheres must move, or else stand still; the bright sun of our firmament, at whose splendour or glooming all our marigolds of the court open or shut. In his conjunction all the other stars are prosperous, and in his opposition malominous. There are in higher spheres as great as he, but none more glorious.'[35]

By allying himself with Carr, Northampton achieved access to a much more extensive patronage than he had enjoyed under Cecil. Cecil had derived his power from his control of the administration but Rochester derived his from his attendance on the king. By taking over many of Salisbury's administrative duties, Northampton shared in Rochester's supremacy. This becomes clear from the advice that Sir Walter Cope, who had served under Cecil, gave his kinsman Dudley Carleton. While Salisbury lived he had been the means of Carleton's advancement. Within a couple of weeks of Salisbury's death, Cope had reassessed the situation at court and advised Carleton to turn to Northampton and Rochester. Northampton took over the leadership of the Privy Council and was put on the treasury commission. It was thought that he would ultimately become Lord Treasurer. Thomas, Viscount Fenton, a Scottish courtier and a close friend of Northampton's, wrote to the Earl of Mar, Northampton's Scottish partner in the secret correspondence, of their friend's chances. 'He has not many friends but one strong one he has, or then both himself and I am deceived.'[36] Although there was little doubt that Northampton would be named Lord Treasurer, an alternative candidate was put forward by those who opposed him.

> So fearful are all such as followed the Treasurer, Suffolk and Worcester excepted, that there is not any exception that can be taken that is not proclaimed, both his religion, his love to his friends, and his hatred to his enemies. Yet I do not see but he shall carry the matter in the end. He has a great deal of his Majesty's own affection and besides he that is most powerful is a very great friend to him.[37]

By describing Suffolk and Worcester as Salisbury's clients, Fenton's letter illustrates the Cecilian hegemony within which the Howards and their allies had functioned. It also suggests that neither Northampton's religion nor his personality were of much weight in the race for favour compared to his connection with the king's favourite.

It has already been noted that in 1611 Rochester was associated with a faction in opposition to Salisbury. This was organised by Sir Thomas Overbury, a long-time friend of Carr's, and included the Earls of Pembroke and Southampton, Sir Henry Neville and other MPs. Much of the rivalry between Pembroke, Southampton and the Howards revolved around the quest for a new Secretary of State. After Salisbury's death the king decided to be his own secretary with Rochester's help. Sir Thomas Lake was chagrined to find that Carr had taken over the signet seals which had been in his custody. The many candidates included Neville, Pembroke's candidate, and Lake, the Howards' candidate. Northampton encouraged Lake's approach to Carr. 'I am very glad to hear of the good correspondence between you and noble Rochester and make no doubt but it will be fortunate to you in the end of the banquet.'[38] The secretaryship was important because it provided the holder with constant access to the king and made him privy to his every decision. Writing to Rochester, Northampton made clear Southampton's purpose (and his own) in pursuing the office: 'his end in making his dear Damon Secretary [was] that by him he might have understood which way to set his compass at all times.'[39] Northampton emphasised that the king was determined to make his own choice. In the end the secretaryship went to Sir Ralph Winwood, ambassador in the Netherlands, apparently on Somerset's nomination,[40] and Lake became a privy councillor. But Stuart government remained personal. The office of Secretary lost its importance with Salisbury's death, for the king did not allow its holder to exercise Salisbury's earlier dominance.

Alliances were fluid at the Jacobean court. Northampton proved once again a shrewd judge of the shifting sands of royal favour. He was able gracefully and effectively to move from Cecil's faction to Carr's as he had earlier moved from Essex's to Cecil's.[41] The influence which Northampton now enjoyed because of his connection with Rochester was extensive. Particularly striking are the privileges he was now able to secure for his merchant associates. He had developed and now extended contacts with Lionel Cranfield, Arthur Ingram and Sir John Swinnerton, who did business with the government, farming the customs and a variety of patents, selling Crown lands and providing loans. Each important court official had his own coterie among the London financial community. During the negotiations of the Great Farm of the customs in 1604 Dorset, the Lord Treasurer, sent Cecil the offer of 'my merchants' and suggested that he quickly send it to Northampton and the Lord of Barwick 'because it may be they deal with more merchants than you do'.[42] Northampton's financial and political relations with his merchant advisers will be discussed in later chapters. Here it is sufficient to note the rewards he was able to provide them. Lionel Cranfield was one of Howard's closest advisers, helping him buy land, farming his starch patent and at the same time providing him with expert advice on government problems. In return, Northampton helped Cranfield move from London merchant to government official, a move which ultimately led to his becoming Lord Treasurer. Much of this advancement occurred through Northampton's alliance with Rochester. In 1612 and 1613 Cranfield accumulated government pensions of £300. In 1613 he was granted arms and knighted. The news letter-writer John Chamberlain thought he might succeed Sir Thomas Waller as lieutenant of Dover Castle. 'I should hardly believe it, but that he is become lately in great favour with the Lord Privy Seal, and rides ordinarily in coach with him and by his means was knighted on Sunday last.'[43] Although Cranfield did not become lieutenant, Northampton did fight for his interests. In 1614 Cranfield obtained the right to purvey Gascon wines for the Household but only after Northampton had put down opposition. He wrote to Carr that 'it is given out in this place that Sir H. Neville hath been a mean to stay the passing of Sir Lionel Cranfield's bargain for the wines so greatly beneficial to the king . . . what his colours may be I know not but I am sure that if he have done it he did with a wisdom paramount to the king's servants in the Treasury'.[44] Northampton was also the patron of Sir John Swinnerton, the Lord Mayor of London, and through the favourite Northampton got him the farm of the sweet wines and the farm of the duties on silk. Arthur Ingram farmed Northampton's patent on starch duties and participated in a variety of government projects including the alum works. Handling Crown land sales in 1613 he arranged the purchase of some parsonages for Northampton. Ingram was knighted in 1613 and the earl got him and Cranfield the farm of the Irish customs the same year.[45] The year 1613 marked the pinnacle of Northampton's power and prestige founded on royal patronage and secured by his close association with the king's favourite.

III

As important as the structure and political configuration of Jacobean patronage was the way in which the patron viewed himself and the rationale of the system. Many of the Earl of Northampton's views are recorded in his extensive correspondence with Robert Carr. Northampton, now the most influential member of the Privy Council, received the king's instructions from the favourite and wrote frequent reports to Carr of the activities at Westminster while the favourite attended the king on progress. In the midst of one such report Northampton commended the king's reward of Lionel Cranfield. Underscoring the importance of reward in return for service much as Salisbury had in his memorandum of 1608, Northampton emphasised that the able official glorified his king and patron alike.[46]

In placing clients in office, Northampton made careful distinctions between offices which required special abilities and those which could be safely filled by the merely socially prominent. Merit was an important consideration in Northampton's promotion of John Daccombe, who had been one of Salisbury's secretaries.[47] Without a patron, after Salisbury's death he soon attracted Northampton's attention by his capable work for the treasury commission. Northampton asked Carr to

> vouchsafe to bestow upon him some livery of your love that he may be ever known to be your vassal. This contemplation had made me think of a Mastership of the Requests to which he is enabled by his wit, his experience and understanding in the law and as I think will very well discharge the place though with some envy which ever attends worth.[48]

As an example of Northampton's patronage, Daccombe's case is interesting. The naming of the Masters of Requests has been variously ascribed to the king himself[49] and to the Lord Privy Seal. In this case it was the king's favourite who actually controlled the nomination. Merit was an important element in Northampton's selection of a man for an administratively sensitive position, but status was important, too. Daccombe's undistinguished origins would make his rise envied, but promotion would increase his reputation and make him a more valuable servant. Shortly after Northampton wrote his letter, Daccombe became a Master of Requests. By June 1615 he had obtained the reversion to the chancellorship of the Duchy of Lancaster which, John Chamberlain sniffed, was a great step from what he was a few years before.[50] Daccombe had made the transition from personal to public servant so typical of early modern bureaucracy.

A contrary case was presented by Richard Preston, Lord Dingwall, one of the king's Scottish courtiers. Seeking a profitable office whose duties he could delegate to a deputy, Preston had focused on the receivership of alienation fines. The receiver's function was to collect those fines due when lands held of the king changed hands. At Rochester's request Northampton looked into the circumstances of the receivership and decided it was not for Dingwall. Although deputies were common in many offices of the central administration, Northampton felt that the receivership was administratively important enough to require the attendance of its holder. Yet because it was subordinate to the Treasurer and Chancellor of the Exchequer it would not be fitting for a man of Preston's prestige to attend in person. In addition the profits were limited because of the office's political sensitivity. The profits were scarcely anything but the salary of £120 a year because, Northampton noted, subjects clamoured against these exactions.[51]

But the distinctions which Northampton drew were not universally applied at court. When Rochester, who wanted to be Master of the Horse, ran up against the lifetime tenure of the Earl of Worcester, questions of merit went by the board. The Earl of Worcester was willing to give up the post only with proper compensation. He was offered the position of Lord High Steward but,

> finding that how transcendent soever the title were, yet the profits of the place were far inferior to that he already possesseth, would by no means budge, unless he might further receive in exchange a pension of £1000 a year for his own life and another whom he should nominate, which conditions being judged too advantageous, they have sought rather to content the former by an assurance which is given him of the first place that shall be void of these four, viz. admiralty, treasurership, chamberlainship, mastership of the horse, which offer, it seems, for want of better satisfaction he hath accepted.[52]

In this instance patronage, the scramble for reward, interfered with efforts to distinguish between the qualities needed for a Lord Treasurer and a Master of the Horse, or to enforce regulations for making such distinctions.

Northampton emphasised the importance of merit in promotion to office and strong administrative control of patronage. In particular, he wished to preserve the king's freedom of action, and to keep patronage in the gift of important officials rather than their subordinates. Northampton's arguments were sometimes used against political opponents such as the Earl of Pembroke, but they also made good administrative sense. Concerned to make the king's patchwork coat of revenues cover the bloated costs of royal reward, he insisted that promotion to sensitive offices was to be for service and competence.

When Charles Howard, Earl of Nottingham, the Lord Admiral, wished to make his eldest son Vice-Admiral in 1613 his only concern was whether to approach the king directly and claim the office as the last reward of an old servant or to solicit it through the Elector Palatine, who was arriving in England to marry the king's daughter Elizabeth. Northampton's concern was for the impact the appointment would have on the king's service. He argued against the office on several grounds: the admiral's direction of the navy had been derelict; the admiral's son was incompetent; the place, although it carried life tenure, was unnecessary and had been vacant for many years.

His Majesty, having found the state of that office as it is under him that hath some experience [Nottingham], if he had as much integrity and understanding, may conceive how it will stand under his son that wants all three . . . it will be a good answer to deny that the place, having stood so long vacant both in the queen's time and his own, needs any present supply when his wants do rather need abatement of expenses and pensions than multiplication. For though the wages be not great yet the impertinency in this time of peace and the example of filling other vacant places is considerable.[53]

Thus Northampton's concern went beyond the individual petitioner or the specific post to the important administrative issue: to fill this office would serve as a goad to the filling of other vacant places which the king could ill afford. When Robert Sidney, now Viscount Lisle and a member of the faction which opposed Northampton and the Howards at court, informed him that the king had authorised Lisle's son's reversion to an unnamed office he added that it had been invested in his father and himself for almost sixty years. Writing to Rochester, Northampton noted acerbically that this was indeed 'the term of their first coming into Kent which before never heard of them'. He then went on more seriously:

But God forbid that the favours which kings allow upon election should by an endless possession be made hereditary. I have done my duty in making a pause upon reversions 'til the king's gracious pleasure be understood. When I hear of that rather by my Lord of Rochester than himself I will observe what the king commandeth.[54]

The vesting of offices with life tenure in fathers and sons limited the number of places the king had to offer and freed officials from the king's control. To prevent this loss of authority, Northampton tried to maintain the connection between office and responsibility not only by challenging such appointments but also by upholding the patronage power of royal officials. Northampton had two cousins, Sir Francis Vere and Sir Horace Vere, both famous military leaders in the Low Countries. In 1604 Sir

Francis Vere composed a brief for Northampton on ways to expel the Spanish from the Low Countries and in the same year Northampton urged the Dutch ambassador to England and the English agent in the Netherlands to uphold Vere's authority. In 1612 when Sir Francis had returned to England he was expected to be made a baron and captain of Portsmouth because of 'the good correspondence he holdeth with the Earls of Northampton and Montgomery by the means of whom and of the rest of his friends in court, the king hath of late taken especial notice both of him and Sir Horace'.[55] In 1613 Northampton supported Sir Horace Vere's authority in a struggle between two of his own clients.

> My cousin Horace Vere is advertised that Sir William Constable means to procure his Majesty's letter for a place in the Brill under him which he hath promised long since to Sir H. Peyton a gentleman of great value and sufficiency in that charge, wherefore both he and I in his behalf are humble suitors to his Majesty to have the gift of those places which by patent appertain to his own election as it pleaseth him to deal.[56]

If the point of the patronage system was to secure the competent staffing of royal government and the political support of the king's most important subjects, this was most effectively achieved by connecting patronage with policy. This was the purpose of Salisbury's organisation of patronage in 1608 and as we shall see, the method suggested by Northampton in his efforts to reform the royal administration. When favour was distributed with the government's needs in mind, it was more likely to recognise merit and reward service than when it was distributed as a result of a free-for-all among competing courtiers or a favourite's hegemony. By emphasising ability and ministerial control, Northampton contributed to the effective functioning of the Jacobean patronage system. Yet at the same time many of his attitudes and actions in relation to patronage point up the problems of the system.

The influence of the important patron, particularly the king's favourite, suffused the court. When Northampton urged Rochester to act against the Howards' rivals, the Earls of Pembroke and Southampton and Viscount Lisle, he described the favourite's power:

> There is no better way to pare their nails . . . than by some withdrawing of your favourable countenance which I do assure you is a groundyard to their boldness and a discharge of many watchful ears and eyes that, setting your countenance aside, would attend them more narrowly.[57]

The influence of the favourite could even bring about the reversal of the king's promise. Northampton was the patron of William, Lord Cavendish. The long-standing family battles of Bess of Hardwick with her husband, the

Earl of Shrewsbury, and her son Henry Cavendish had extended into the second generation and in 1613 focused on a piece of property which Lord Cavendish held of the king, the manor of Hartington. As a member of the treasury commission responsible for increasing the royal revenues, Northampton had secured the king's promise that Cavendish might purchase Hartington. He feared, however, that Pembroke would seek to undo this engagement through the favourite. To counter that manoeuvre he wrote to Rochester:

> It is not unlikely that you will be pressed from my Lord of Pembroke to opine against the king's pleasure signified to Mr Chancellor of the Duchy and me that we should acquaint the Lords in commission with his gracious liking that my Lord Cavendish should [be] preferred being tenant in possession to Hartington if he offer well. For my lady of Shrewsbury, who graspeth all with her silver paws, I hear is almost mad with my Lord Cavendish's offering. Your Lordship may well be rid of importunity by casting all upon the king's word engaged and royal promise.[58]

The fact that James's word could be reversed under pressure exerted by the favourite tended to make the patronage system erratic.

Court life was a constant canvassing of advances and rebuffs not only for the throngs of suitors but also for the highest officials of the Crown. When Suffolk became Lord Treasurer, it was seen as a mixed blessing, for by removing from his place near the king as Lord Chamberlain, 'to a place of much distinction ... without leaving a friend in his room, he might peradventure take cold at his back'.[59] Northampton was always anxious about his own position at court, his relation to the king and the favourite and the judgement of his peers. He measured his status by his success in gaining favour for his clients. Whether or not a matter was important, he always laid his prestige on the line. Such was the case when Northampton was asked to secure a knighthood for John Steede, a wealthy Kentish gentleman related to the Culpeppers, who was about to marry Elizabeth Cromer, granddaughter of Sir Matthew Carew, Master in Chancery. Knighthood was one of the articles of the marriage contract. Northampton solicited Rochester's aid.

> Being infinitely pressed to procure the making of this gentleman a knight by my own dear friends ... it stand me somewhat upon my credit in respect of the quality of the interceders. Yet upon the hearing of a report that his Majesty hath made some dainty of this kind of suit of late, I somewhat staggered and had rather die than propound that to the king which he should not like of. . . . If it please your Lordship to procure this favour for me of the king, I shall be bound to you because the failing is more disgraceful than the prevailing is important.[60]

When Carr got Steede his knighthood, Northampton expressed his gratitude:

> I must account myself much bound to you for your favour to the gentle-
> man. I am not ignorant what strange conjects and fantasies have crept of
> late into vulgar conceits. . . . For though it be true that the scarcity and
> poverty of parts in me deserve not much, yet so much as amounteth to the
> making of a knight they would perhaps have expected from me.[61]

Jacobean patrons were often more acted upon than acting. Favour
mirrored the expectations of their peers as much as their own choices. In
one case Northampton asked Rochester to assert his influence even though
the office was minor and the candidates unknown to him, because 'the
world expected grace to one of them from you which is a kind of engagement'.[62] Moreover, Jacobean patronage was not only organised on the direct
relationship between patron and client; it also included the connections of
friends of friends and enemies of enemies. As head of a faction the patron
might find himself granting favour to those he hardly knew. Northampton
once wrote a letter of recommendation to Salisbury stating frankly that he
knew nothing at all about the favour-seeker. But the conclusion of his note
was significant: 'The rest I leave to your Lordship's good pleasure only
craving that since he hath made election of me to move in his behalf, your
Lordship will be pleased (the matter sorting in other circumstances agree-
ably to your good liking) to let him know that upon my request you do the
rather favour him.'[63] On another occasion, Northampton, privy councillor
and treasury commissioner, found himself serving as errand boy for the
favourite, trying to secure the place of a groom of the bedchamber for the
wrong client.[64] The stability of reward in return for service was undermined
by unusual structural pressures in the Jacobean period and Northampton's
actions sometimes reflected the instability thereby created.

IV

Over the Steede knighthood Northampton had described himself as 'in
some sort desperate'.[65] Such desperation was most clearly expressed in the
Essex divorce and Overbury murder scandals. Much debated by historians,
the evidence and results of each deserve to be reconsidered at length.[66] Here
I want to examine them only as the most extreme manifestation of Northampton's search for a patron. To assure that his family continued to be
connected to the sole conduit of favour after the death of Salisbury, Northampton undertook to separate Rochester from Sir Thomas Overbury and
his faction. By 1613, when Rochester became enamoured of Frances
Howard, Suffolk's daughter, Northampton had completed the process. The
nuptials did not begin the alliance as much as confirm Northampton's

successful campaign to secure his family's central position at the fount of power. Ironically, the means he adopted to conclude this match helped create a breach between the king and his subjects that in all his other work he sought to avoid.

To begin with, Northampton had to arrange a divorce for Frances. She had been married to the Earl of Essex for seven years; at 22 he might reasonably be expected to live several more decades. Northampton proposed an annulment on the grounds that the marriage had not been consummated, that Essex was impotent and Frances still a virgin. Northampton's loyalties to Essex's father gave way to his own family ties. The king, sympathetic to the new match, appointed a commission of bishops and legal officers to investigate the charges. While Archbishop Abbot marvelled that the king repeatedly cajoled the commissioners, Northampton noted with satisfaction that 'this last letter of our Master to those of the commission hath caused the lame to go, the dumb to speak and the sick to recover'.[67] Still the divorce was only granted after James named two more bishops to the commission. Always attuned to public presentation, Northampton urged Carr to ensure the presence of Lancelot Andrewes, the admired Bishop of Ely, when the verdict was announced to allay any aspersions that might be circulated.[68]

Secondly, in order to strengthen his ties with the favourite, Northampton played Pandarus. While the commission conferred, Northampton urged Somerset to reward Frances 'with a kiss from your own lips which shall pass for the broad seal till you come to the privy seal wherein if I make any stay let the king take my office'. In an elaborate conceit he combined his own love for the favourite with Frances's: 'think not that I can find pain in that which gives me greatest pleasure which proceeds out of your pen and flows from your mind ... though it were but that which a man takes in cracking a sweet nut to taste the kernel or but like the pain my Lady Frances shall feel when the sweet stream follows'. As Essex and Frances's brother prepared to duel over her honour, Northampton scathingly described Essex as 'my Lord the gelding'. 'If my Lord would draw his sword in defence of a good prick it were worth his pains but never to make such a poor pudding's apology'.[69]

Thirdly, Northampton had to deal with Overbury, who violently opposed the marriage and threatened Carr with exposure of unspecified secrets. To prevent his embarrassing the divorce proceedings both Carr and Northampton connived at his remand to the Tower, ostensibly for refusing an ambassadorship. In the summer of 1613 Northampton wrote daily reports to Carr of the progress of the annulment while urging the lieutenant, Sir Gervaise Helwys, whom he had placed in office, to force the prisoner to accept the marriage. There were, however, two plots on foot to remove Overbury, the one temporarily the other permanently. Northampton apparently did not know that Frances was engaged in a conspiracy to kill Overbury. In September 1613 he died, but of what – poison tarts or disease – is not known. In 1615, after Somerset lost his place as the king's favourite to George Villiers, Helwys admitted he had known about a plot to poison Overbury. Brought to trial, Frances pleaded guilty but Carr maintained his innocence. The role of Northampton, now dead, remained ambiguous. The most recent writer on the scandal has concluded that Northampton was not involved in the plot to murder Overbury.[70] There can be no doubt, however, about the impact of Northampton's letters when read in court. One observer noted that 'it would turn chaste blood into water to hear the unchaste and unclean phrases that were contained in them'.[71] From the beginning, the divorce, marriage and trial had been the subject of gossip both at court and in the countryside. Scatological rhymes and writings had circulated widely.[72] Northampton's efforts to put the best possible face on it had failed utterly.

The venomous character of Northampton's treatment of both Essex and Overbury recall his comments about Raleigh and Cobham in the secret correspondence. In that earlier struggle to secure James's favour, there had been no holds barred. As the centre of power shifted in 1612 and 1613, Northampton's rhetoric once again became tense and strained. But Northampton's letters which horrified court observers and contemporaries are not as damning in manuscript as in their published versions. Moreover, read in their entirety, not as selected by the prosecutors, the letters present a somewhat different picture of Northampton's activities in the summer of 1613, for they paint not only his juggling with Overbury, but detail the work of the Privy Council, the problem with the Irish Lords, Northampton's differences with Queen Anne over Greenwich Park and direct sharp digs at Coke and Neville over the secretaryship.[73] In short, they reflect the same mixture of patronage and policy matters characteristic of all his reports to Carr between 1612 and 1614. Finally, if we go behind the sensations of these scandals to examine the use that Northampton made of his patronage, we shall find that under difficult conditions Northampton created a patronage network which not only reinforced his own prestige but at the same time provided service to the king.

Chapter 3

A Jacobean Patronage Network

From the beginning of James I's reign, Northampton successfully translated royal favour into offices and reward for himself. Moreover, his close ties with Cecil and Carr allowed him to continue to enlarge his sphere of influence, to gain a set of followers and to provide them with favour. This patronage network was at once an exercise of power and its image, reflecting and confirming Northampton's new-found authority. Historians of the Tudor–Stuart period have paid a good deal of attention to court connections,[1] but not systematically analysed individual Jacobean patrons or who they rewarded. A closer look at the patron's resources, the methods by which patron–client ties were established, the variety of his clients, is in order to show how power was exercised and how local elites were connected to the central government.

The Elizabethan magnate, such as the Earl of Leicester, with close ties to the queen and to the royal bounty, had been able to dispense favour to a wide range of clients within the political elite. The eighteenth-century Whig patron with great influence in the countryside and prominence in Parliament thereby controlled a vast range of privileges with which to reward his followers. Both patrons enjoyed formidable standing in both the central government and the localities[2] and, as a result, generated ties between the central government and local political elites. Both tended to distribute favour across a broad ideological spectrum. Their successful wielding of patronage enabled the central government to rule its localities, even without a standing army and a paid local bureaucracy. What of the early Stuart patron? Unlike their Elizabethan counterparts, it is argued, Stuart patrons were unwilling or unable to maintain the ties that bind between the court and the politically important gentry. The domination of court patronage by royal favourites, particularly the Duke of Buckingham, is often cited as an important cause of the breakdown of the nobility and gentry into opposing political and ideological factions of 'Court and Country'.[3] It is possible to suggest, however, that the emphasis on royal favourites and the overriding concern to explain the outbreak of civil war has obscured the patronage dispensed by other Jacobean patrons and the extent to which Elizabethan patronage networks were in fact maintained at least into James's reign. Recent studies of the 1620s have suggested that court and country alliances did not become polarised but, in fact, continued. It is becoming evident that prominent gentry remained in contact with the court throughout James's reign.[4] Taking a closer look at the Earl of Northampton's patronage reveals how he used his offices to build a network of supporters in the countryside, who these clients were, and the purpose of these carefully tended connections. Finally, it suggests that Northampton tried hard to continue Elizabethan patronage practices linking court and country, and focuses attention on the structural difficulties which plagued stable patron–client ties, those traditional relationships which lent stability to the state.

I

The major sources of Northampton's patronage stemmed from his offices: Lord Warden of the Cinque Ports and Lord Privy Seal. He became Lord Warden in 1604 in the wake of the disgrace of Henry, Lord Cobham. It afforded him his own base of power in a region situated reasonably close to the court and a free hand in the distribution of its patronage. The Cinque Ports was a confederation of sea ports on England's southeastern coast which had been of major strategic value during the Middle Ages because of their control of the Channel. These seven, not five, towns – Sandwich, Dover, Hythe, New Romney, Rye, Winchelsea and Hastings – had been granted a corporate existence separate from the rest of the country. Although they were no longer of military importance, their distinct administration continued in the seventeenth century, headed by the Lord Warden. He oversaw an administration that repeated on a smaller scale that at Westminster. The Court of St James at Dover included a common-law court, a court of Chancery and Star Chamber. Dover Castle was the Lord Warden's seat and the centre as well of the executive administration headed by the lieutenant and the steward, the chief legal officer, who presided over the Court of St James. The Lord Warden acted as the Lord High Admiral of the Cinque Ports and also controlled the garrisons within the ports, their captains and soldiers.

Northampton has been considered an absentee Lord Warden, a courtier with few connections to the area he ruled, who paid little attention to matters in the Cinque Ports. This view requires some revision. Northampton moved immediately to exercise control over the administrative apparatus of the Cinque Ports; one of his first acts was to secure a copy of his predecessor's patent of office.[5] Furthermore, he enforced his control of patronage with an eye to the smallest detail. In 1612 the captain of Sandgate Castle removed his lieutenant, a minor event one would think in the busy life of one of the king's most important privy councillors. Yet Northampton angrily wrote to the lieutenant of Dover Castle, Sir Thomas Waller, to rescind the order. 'I will teach him to know the Lord Warden and himself to be captain...by my favour.' Invoking precedent, Northampton asserted that though the captain held his command by grant from the king, he was subject to the Lord Warden and could not remove the meanest soldier but upon due conviction under the ordinances governing the forts.[6]

An absentee Lord Warden insisting on his perquisites, relying on his honour and royal power would appear on the face of it to suggest just the sort of breakdown of court/country links which are thought characteristic of the early Stuart period. Instead a closer look presents quite a different picture: a reinforcement of court/country ties, an emphasis on the traditional rights of the Lord Warden and a refusal to allow middle-level officials to usurp these prerogatives. The purpose of that patronage is clear. On the one hand it provided Northampton, who had few supporters at James's accession, with a ready-made set of clients in the members of the local oligarchies and on the other with offices with which to reward his own servants.

Why was Northampton so concerned about the expulsion of a member of the Sandgate garrison? It is helpful to look at who they were. Most were town officials who were rewarded with appointments to the staff of the castles within his jurisdiction. Thus William Eldwood, an official of the Cinque Ports since the 1590s, jurat and later Mayor of Sandwich, was a gunner at Dover Castle at a fee of 8d per diem. John Hales, an official of Tenterden, was a gunner and soldier at Sandgate Castle at 6d a day.[7] Joseph Pelham and Francis Wiseman, officials of Hythe, were both soldiers at Sandgate Castle. So was Hythe's most important official: William Knight, Mayor of Hythe, was appointed gentleman porter of Sandgate Castle by Northampton. Richard Portriffe, bailiff and Mayor of Rye, described by Northampton as one of his servants, also held a gunner's position in Rye at 6d a day.[8]

It may appear rather strange that these prominent town officials were also manning the guns of the Cinque Ports. In fact, these positions were purely patronage jobs at the disposal of the Lord Warden and were much sought after. At 6d a day the gunner's position was worth £9 2s 6d and had a capital value of about £30.[9] Often they were considered the freehold property of their holders.

In addition to rewarding town officials by the judicious distribution of these places Northampton also used them to reward country gentry. Of the sixteen gunners at Dover Castle in 1613, for instance, only three actually performed any duties. Five of the sixteen were resident in Dover Castle itself, but three were gentlemen who did not take the watch. Their place was filled by others, servants of the lieutenant of the Castle. Two gunners lived in Dover, one nearby. The rest lived as far away as Canterbury and Gravesend. Eight were Dover residents, six country gentry. The remaining two lived in London because they were Northampton's own personal servants, Thomas Willowes and John Sotherwood.[10]

Other servants of Northampton's who enjoyed Cinque Ports sinecures were John Hicks, to whom Northampton left £50 in his will, and who held the position of gentleman porter at Dover Castle at 8d a day. John Jaggard, another of his servants to whom he bequeathed £100, was a gunner of

Arch-Cliff Fort in Dover.[11] Finally, John Heydon, son of Christopher Heydon, a Norfolk gentleman and follower of Essex, had been a servant of Northampton's. It was he who evoked Northampton's anger by dismissing an under-officer at Sandgate Castle where he was appointed captain. Significantly, Heydon apparently was not perceived locally as a carpetbagger installed by the central government. After Northampton's death, Heydon became the client of Edward, Lord Zouche, who emphasised local ties in his appointments, and later of the Duke of Buckingham.[12]

Treating these positions as patronage jobs, Northampton made no demand that these gunners be residents. After all he was a non-resident himself. But when Lord Zouche became Lord Warden in 1615 he reversed Northampton's policy, insisted that all these positions be filled by townsmen and turned out several of Northampton's appointees.[13] But Northampton had only continued traditional policy. Heightened sensitivity to non-residents reflected not only Zouche's own policy but changing political attitudes in the towns themselves in the 1620s. A controversy in 1627 between town and gunner makes this clear. When Rye complained to the Duke of Buckingham that Thomas Harrison, who then had the fee, was a non-resident, Harrison replied that the fee was not attached to the town but the cannon. The cannon had been given to Rye by Henry VIII during the war with France with the gunner's place to be disposed of by the Lord Warden. At the time of the Spanish Armada, the cannon had been removed to the Tower of London and since Harrison resided in London he claimed he was quite ready to do service when commanded. He pointed out that William Ratcliffe and Richard Portriffe, both local officials, had enjoyed the fee for thirty-six years after the cannon was removed. Harrison cleverly exposed the gunners' positions as sinecures. His argument was logical, but missed the point: Rye's plaint was that the positions were *their* sinecures. In a period of growing dissatisfaction with traditional patronage practices in the late 1620s, the towns began to refuse to accept nominees proposed by the Lord Warden.[14]

The most important patronage which Northampton dispensed as Lord Warden was the executive machinery of Dover Castle to which he named trusted associates, several of whom were Kentish gentry. Sir Thomas Waller became lieutenant and the real administrator of the Cinque Ports. He enjoyed further benefits in payment for his service. While lieutenant, Waller also became by Northampton's favour a member of the commission to oversee starch making, an important part of the machinery by which Northampton's starch patent was enforced. He was also granted prisage and butlerage of most wines as Chief Butler of England, with fees of £100. In addition, Waller enjoyed certain perquisites. When Northampton, his secretary, John Griffith and Waller expended their efforts to free the ports from the Privy Seal loan of 1612, the ports voted them gratuities, £110 to Northampton, £30 to Waller.[15] Matthew Hadd was a prominent Kentish lawyer who served as high steward of Dover Castle. As the chief legal officer he determined what constituted a wreck and what stray goods; the latter belonged to the Lord Warden. Hadd retained his office under Lord Zouche and eventually held most of the important legal offices in the county, serving as legal counsel to the cities of Canterbury, Hythe, Lydd and Sandwich.[16]

The tie between town government and the Cinque Ports administrative apparatus was a close one, reflecting the concerns of a councillor such as Northampton to oversee local government. William Ward, a gentleman of Dover, was the serjeant of the admiralty of the Cinque Ports and droit gatherer general for the Lord Warden. In 1613 Ward also became Mayor of Dover, a position he held for several years, while continuing to serve as collector of droits for Zouche. In 1618 he was appointed lieutenant of Dover Castle. The reward for such a useful client lay not in office alone. Like so many other of Northampton's officers, Ward was also a gunner at Dover Castle at 8d a day.[17]

While Northampton was Lord Warden, John Packenham, another Kentish gentleman, became clerk of Dover Castle which included the clerkship of the exchequer within Dover Castle and the registrarship of the courts of Chancery and Admiralty for the Cinque Ports. For this position he had a yearly fee of £3 6s 8d augmented by the more sizeable fees he collected from his legal duties. But always cautious, Northampton had Packenham enter into a £400 bond to keep the Lord Warden immune from law suits.[18] As with so many administrators in the Cinque Ports, Packenham kept his office when Zouche became Lord Warden. There is no indication that Northampton replaced such officials; many had served under Lord Cobham and continued to serve under Zouche.

While most of his appointees were Cinque Ports townsmen or Kentish gentry, Northampton did occasionally place courtiers in office. Sir Robert Brett provides an interesting example of the pecuniary aspects of Jacobean patronage. At the time of his appointment as lieutenant of Dover Castle, Brett sold a particularly choice piece of land at Charing Cross to Northampton for the enlargement of the earl's garden. Yet the appointment should not be seen as merely based on purchase. Brett was a close ally of Northampton's and a witness to his will. And even as he lay dying, the reciprocal nature of patronage remained on Northampton's mind. On his deathbed Northampton wrote to the Earl of Somerset, to ask that Brett be allowed to continue as lieutenant of Dover Castle. Brett did remain in the position about a year but was put out of office when Zouche became Lord Warden.[19]

The point has been made that the patronage system was centred upon the 'politically pre-eminent classes'.[20] An analysis of Northampton's clients who enjoyed positions in the Cinque Ports substantiates this view. In addition it provides concrete evidence of a Jacobean patronage network directed at maintaining court/country ties.

There were perhaps as many as fifty-two individuals who can be considered Northampton's clients in the Cinque Ports. As a group, they tended to be middle-aged gentlemen. It has been possible to determine the residence of forty-four clients. Many were pre-eminent in the affairs of the ports' towns. Of the twenty-two of Northampton's clients who lived in the Cinque Ports, eighteen served as mayors, jurats or bailiffs. In short, half of those sampled whose residence is known were town oligarchs. Ten others were substantial members of the landed gentry of Kent. Many of these served as members of the House of Commons for the ports on the Lord Warden's nomination. Northampton's parliamentary patronage will be discussed later. It is, however, important to note here that most of his parliamentary nominees enjoyed other forms of his patronage in the Cinque Ports as well. The remaining twelve were outsiders, eight of them Northampton's household servants who had been rewarded with offices or sinecures in the ports' administrative apparatus.[21]

What is particularly striking about Northampton's Cinque Ports patronage is that it is granted again and again to the same people. Clients, whether household servants or town officials, held positions simultaneously as officers, gunners, MPs or retainers. The rate of repetition was high: 71 per cent of the officers, 84 per cent of those identified as retainers, 77 per cent of the gunners and 60 per cent of the MPs enjoyed other instances of Northampton's favour in the Cinque Ports. Northampton's patronage in the Cinque Ports operated, then, in two directions. On the one hand, it brought into relation with the central government those men who held power in the towns. On the other, it provided offices and profit for the Lord Warden's servants and other of his courtier clients. Through patronage Northampton spun a web which had a larger purpose than his own self-aggrandisement.

The purpose of Northampton's patronage in the Cinque Ports went beyond his own need for followers, his prestige or his profit although as we have seen these were central to the creation of his patronage network. In the hierarchical view of society shared by the governors of early seventeenth-century England, the authority of the magistrate, whether that of the king or the local officeholder, was supreme within its sphere; the purpose of this far-reaching authority was the maintenance of public order. In dispatching a Privy Council order to Dover for the observance of Lent, Northampton added his own words concerning the role of the magistrate: 'it hath been observed that people are with nothing so much moved (as by the example of those that govern them).' Therefore the Privy Council required that 'the principal magistrates in themselves and their own families do make such demonstrations of conformity herein as may serve for examples unto inferior persons'.[22] In return for acting as such models as well as using their power and influence to maintain order, the local political elite were rewarded with royal patronage. Furthermore, in the absence of a paid local bureaucracy, the central government needed to reinforce its own authority. Here too patronage was the means to a larger end, to establish the central government's control over its local magistrates and through them all of its people.

An inquiry Northampton addressed to Robert Bowyer, as keeper of the records in the Tower, in November 1609 makes clear this overriding objective. It is described as 'Particulars desired by the right honourable, the Earl of Northampton, Lord Privy Seal and Lord Warden of the Cinque Ports out of records or other precedents on the authority of the Lord Warden in certain cases'. These cases did not concern Northampton's personal profit, although he paid enough attention to that, but, crucially, the imposition of royal authority in the person of the Lord Warden over local officials, local courts and local justice.

Bowyer was asked to search for precedents to support these assertions of royal power: that the mayor and other officers of the ports 'ought to assist the Lord Warden's ministers in the execution of his Majesty's processes' and 'execute the Lord Warden's mandate in causes that concern his Majesty's service'. Furthermore, Northampton asked the penalties for 'denying or neglecting such service', including freeing 'offenders committed by the Lord Warden's authority for refusing to serve his Majesty in juries', or committed for disobedience of the Lord Warden's authority or standing out against 'all process and commissions of rebellion issued out of any of the courts held by the Lord Warden or his deputies'.

Bowyer's response was not to point out that the Lord Warden was overstepping his authority but, on the contrary, to supply just the particulars he desired including a precedent from the reign of Edward III that provided 'in default of the mayors etc., the Warden to enter into the ports and to do justice'.[23] Relying on tradition and precedent to support his claims, Northampton kept a close eye on his own privileges and the king's rights in the Cinque Ports. This concern for the execution of royal justice in the ports, extended to his successor who sat in person in the court of the Admiralty in the Cinque Ports. This was a power Northampton delegated. But their goals were the same: the imposition of royal authority on local officials.

Northampton grasped the opportunities for patronage offered by the Cinque Ports in its offices and sinecures. He probed the limits of his power, insisting on his rights over the least member of a garrison and helped, as we shall see, to transform an assertion of parliamentary patronage into an immemorial right. But his power in the Cinque Ports was greater than in the Privy Seal office. A comparison of the two indicates both the extent and limitation of court patronage.

II

In 1608 Northampton became Lord Privy Seal, overseeing the Privy Seal office and, nominally, the Court of Requests and the Masters of Requests who sat as its judges. The Court of Requests, a civil court which dispensed equity law, was originally the court for poor people and Crown servants. Although its jurisdiction was challenged by the common lawyers, including

Sir Edward Coke, from the 1590s on, it survived until the Civil War. It was traditionally associated with the Lord Privy Seal although there is no evidence that between 1516 and 1630 any Lord Privy Seal sat with the judges.[24] As was the case with the other offices he assumed, Northampton received at his accession a tract discussing abuses in the court that needed to be reformed. It suggested that he attend the court occasionally and receive daily reports from the presiding judge.[25] But Northampton neither participated in the workings of the Court of Requests nor enjoyed much patronage in the filling of the offices of Master of Requests. These offices, usually divided between common lawyers and civil lawyers, were held for life, and fell vacant only infrequently. During Northampton's tenure between 1608 and 1614 only one vacancy occurred and, as we have seen, Northampton secured the post in 1613 for John Daccombe, former secretary to Salisbury, through the favourite.[26] As Lord Privy Seal Northampton did oversee the Privy Seal office, its four clerks and several deputies. Although at times he prevented the passage of certain grants, entrenched practices limited his patronage and control of the office's administration. The Privy Seal was the official seal of the Court of Requests and the seal used to administer forced loans. But the bulk of its work was as one of the three offices which authorised royal grants in a bureaucratic routine laid down in Acts of 1444 and 1536.[27] Even before 1536, suitors had tried to avoid paying fees to the Signet and Privy Seal clerks for their unnecessary work. But by the Act of that year, the clerks of those offices were allowed to receive fees even when a suitor got an immediate warrant, that is, a petition approved by the king and used as a warrant directly to the Great Seal. Although the Privy Seal had once had an important place as the king's personal instrument, by the seventeenth century it functioned primarily to provide sinecures for office-holders who received gratuities many times their authorised fees from those needing to have documents affixed with the Privy Seal.

Northampton was unable to establish control over the patronage of this office of the central government as he had in the Cinque Ports. The reasons for this appear very clearly in the extensive correspondence of one of the Privy Seal clerks, Edward Reynolds. Moreover, Reynolds's own career illustrates several aspects of Elizabethan and Jacobean officeholding: the search for a patron, the sales of offices, the importance of reversions and fees, and the limitations that Northampton or the king's other ministers faced in controlling offices in the central administration.

Reynolds was the Earl of Essex's secretary and it was through Essex that he first met Lord Henry Howard. Under Essex's aegis Reynolds scrambled for court office. Like most suitors he pounced eagerly on any rumour of illness or death. Writing to the queen to solicit the surveyorship of the ordnance he noted that the present holder was dangerously ill and that he had Essex's favour for the office.[28] While his eagerness for the surveyorship went unrewarded, Reynolds did obtain a grant in reversion of the clerkship of the Privy Seal. To his future wife Reynolds justified his lack of more immediate prospects on the grounds that Essex's absence from court for twelve weeks had allowed other competitors to get the advantage.[29]

The fall of Essex left Reynolds without a patron. He cultivated Howard's acquaintance and within a month of James's accession proposed to get a job in the Privy Seal office through the favour of 'my Lord Harry'.[30] He sought Howard's favour not only for himself but also for his brother Owen Reynolds. But favour was not enough. G. E. Aylmer has established that access to office was often dependent on patronage combined with purchase.[31] So it was with Reynolds. Reynolds spent years negotiating to buy the office of Thomas Kerry, clerk of the Privy Seal. He first offered £200 down and £200 to be paid in two years provided the office yielded £300 or £400 yearly. He had apparently overestimated the income from the clerkship because in 1605 he offered, in addition to ready money, £100 each year for two years if the proceeds of the Privy Seal office amounted to £250 a year.[32] But Reynolds did not wish to rely on his reversion, which was rather like an actuarial lottery, dependent on the life expectancy of those before him.

> Were it not for fear of the cunning and undermining tricks which are practised in this age, I would attend the full time until it should please God to give me my turn for this preferment, which in all probability cannot be long. But if I may prevent them by bestowing a part of my poor means, and be installed in the office which will quickly repay such a disbursement and remove all hazards, I do not see how I ought in discretion to let slip this opportunity but rather diligently to embrace it.[33]

But having embraced the opportunity, Reynolds had not removed all hazards. Shortly after his old friend Northampton took office as Lord Privy Seal in 1608 there began a controversy over fees. The Privy Seal clerks were entitled to certain fees from the public for writing and sealing documents as part of the process of royal authorisation. The Privy Seal clerks zealously guarded their position in the bureaucracy and complained of the loss of fees when grants were passed by immediate warrant to the Great Seal.[34] Upon his entry into office Northampton claimed that the clerks were withholding his share of the fees and demanded one-fifth of all the fees collected. Perhaps because of his ties with Northampton, Reynolds took the lead in trying to settle the argument. Fearing that the earl would order a sequestration of all fees until he had ascertained his rights, Reynolds drew up an apology to be signed by all the clerks. He begged the earl that the issue be settled without a public suit, saying that nothing had grieved him more since the fall of Essex than this controversy. But Northampton was not dissuaded. Reynolds and the other clerks asked Salisbury to intercede and Reynolds counselled that if Northampton pressed for a directory of the profits of office he should be put off until the controversy was decided.[35] Whatever Northampton's claims to supreme authority in the Cinque Ports, his authority over the

Privy Seal clerks was limited by politics and administrative practices such as deputies and reversions.

The clerks ultimately acceded to Northampton's demands but the question of fees continued as a *Leitmotif* in Reynold's correspondence. Northampton's death prompted the clerks to hope they could avoid payment of such large fees to the next Lord Privy Seal. Reynolds complained that he had suffered under 'the late testy Lord' by holding out against his claim to a fifth of their fees. Thus when the Earl of Worcester became Lord Privy Seal in 1616, Reynolds suggested that the clerks consult on how to oppose his demand for one-fifth of fees.[36] But Worcester proved more importunate than Northampton. He not only laid claim to his fifth share of the fees but also considered farming it for £200. Reynolds feared that such a farm would pose a threat to the clerks because it 'would subject the office to injurious siftings' – that is, the accounts would be audited. The farm did not materialise, but the clerks did agree to Worcester's demand for one-fifth of the fees. In addition Worcester demanded and got £20 per annum for two of his secretaries.[37] Where the town oligarchs in the Cinque Ports were dependent on the continuing goodwill of the Lord Warden, the Privy Seal clerks had greater leverage. Confronted with the lowering of their profits, the clerks actively tried to increase their fees in two directions, from the public and from the Crown. First they tried to tighten bureaucratic procedure by preventing the deputies, who did much of the work, from passing grants for free.[38] Secondly, they petitioned the Crown for diet. They asked Worcester for help but he suggested they petition the king. They tried giving the Secretary of State, Sir Robert Naunton, a gift but he returned it when he was unable to obtain their suit. Finally, Reynolds suggested they try Lord Villiers, the future Duke of Buckingham. This method proved successful. The Privy Seal clerks got what they wanted: not food, but £50 each in lieu of diet.[39]

The clerks did not concern themselves only with fees. They also spent a great deal of time competing for positions in the administration of Privy Seal loans and securing reversions of their offices for their relatives by means of constant pressure on their patron. In 1611 Reynolds suggested to Francis Mills that he serve as clerk for the Privy Seal loan. Reynolds wrote to Northampton to secure approval of Mills's appointment and to head off the competitive efforts of Thomas Packer, a reversioner and deputy in the Privy Seal office. Though Packer had the advantage of previous experience, Reynolds emphasised the matter of status. 'I do know your Lordship to be so truly honourable and so worthy a patron of our office, as I shall never see any man's deputy preferred before an ordinary officer.'[40] The earl acceded to the request and Reynolds crowed to Mills that they had outwitted Packer. He was quite chagrined to find that Mills did not want the job for fear it would damage his health. However, Mills did serve and petitioned Salisbury for £100 for expenses. Packer, not to be outdone, petitioned for expense money for working on the business of the loans three weeks before Mills came to town.[41]

Hereditary elements in the Privy Seal office were quite strong. Both Francis Mills and Sir Thomas Clerk, another of Reynolds's contemporaries, had their sons serving as their deputies. Reynolds wanted the reversion of the next available clerkship for his cousin John Castle but he had to contend with the efforts of John Packer who wanted the reversion for his own infant son. Packer's action may not have been unduly foresighted. When a reversion was granted in 1617 there were already five previous reversioners. After efforts to negotiate for the reversion with another clerk had fallen through, Reynolds was finally able to place his cousin as a clerk through the patronage of Worcester, now Lord Privy Seal.[42]

Reynolds's career provides ample evidence that in the Privy Seal office Northampton's patronage was circumscribed by elements familiar in Jacobean administration: deputies, long lists of reversioners, control of appointment in the hands of lower officials, practices which hampered officials who tried to exercise control over their offices. Unlike the Cinque Ports where his authority was more easily asserted and mostly unfettered, Northampton was stymied in the Privy Seal office. It is not coincidental that in his efforts to reform administration Northampton focused on the very elements that were present in the Privy Seal office and that prevented officials from gaining control of the bureaucracy.

III

The Lord Wardenship of the Cinque Ports and the Privy Seal office provided Northampton with the offices and the privileges with which to build a patronage network. In addition, these positions provided him with a group of followers drawn from the political elite, made up on the one hand of town oligarchs and country gentlemen and, on the other, officeholders. If we change the focus from the patron's resources to the variety of clients who were thus connected to the court, Northampton's network appears in greater detail. The pattern that emerges shows that Northampton systematically rewarded his own family connections, old followers of the Earl of Essex, and politically active gentry, particularly from Kent, his regional base as Lord Warden, and from Norfolk and Suffolk, centre of his Howard landholdings. The creation of the baronetage under James I provides the clearest and fullest picture of Northampton as patron. Inundated with requests for the new title, Northampton can be connected with as many as thirty-four of the recipients.

The dearth of honours distributed by Queen Elizabeth created a clamour for title from the nobility and the landed gentry when King James came to the throne. To meet that demand as well as the Crown's pressing need for money, the king created the new title of baronet in 1611 with a price-tag of £1095 and a rank which floated somewhere between knight and baron.[43] Floated appears the correct term because the exact privileges and status which came with the title were at first in dispute. Salisbury probably named most of the first baronets, but as his influence waned after the failure of the Great Contract, Northampton's increased. Both were approached by eager applicants who ranged from older gentlemen prominent in their counties to young men whose new titles seem to have been part of their marriage settlements with important families.[44] It is evident that both Salisbury and Northampton carefully selected the recipients with the same objective in mind: to cement court and country ties. Moreover, the distribution of the baronetage shows other characteristics of Jacobean patronage with which we have become familiar: the use of intermediaries, the invocation of family ties and local connections, and especially the pressure on the patron himself so that at times he was more acted upon than acting.

Lionel Tolemache, whose family was traditionally allied with the Howards, provides a case in point. Tolemache, a Suffolk gentleman, got his cousin William Strode of Kent to intercede with Northampton in person. Having secured Northampton's favour for Tolemache's baronetcy, Strode painted a picture of the pressure exerted on the patron by irrepressible suitors.

> I have been sithence your departure out of London three times with my Lord of Northampton.... I desired his Lordship that you might not be forgotten, but that his Lordship would place you as your self and the antiquity of your house deserveth.... He said to me that he would take all the care he might for your advancement, with many more protestations, and further said that if he could bring you with the first making he would do his best. But if it did not fall out so for the first, he would so place you that it should be to your content, and said I should not need to move him any more for it, for he could not nor would not forget you and your house.[45]

One can well imagine Northampton's mixed feelings and ultimate frustration at this process; such a testimony to his power brought with it both gratification and continuing harassment. While it is difficult to pin down just who named many of the baronets, among those connected to Northampton were George Shirley of Leicestershire who had married Northampton's niece, Frances, daughter of Henry, Lord Berkeley, and Catherine Howard, Northampton's sister, and Thomas Spencer, a cousin of Northampton's ward George Berkeley.[46] Philip Knyvett came from a Norfolk family which had traditionally served the Howards and were distantly related. Thomas Monson, Master of the Armoury, was a close associate of Northampton's; William Constable was an Essex follower who had appealed for Northampton's help after the earl's revolt; William Maynard of Essex was the son-in-law of William Cavendish for whom Northampton secured a seat in Parliament in 1610.

The importance of kinship in Jacobean society finds expression in the number of family connections in the new order. Miles Sandys, who was

Northampton's parliamentary choice at Cambridge in 1614, became a baronet as did two of his sons-in-law. Outnumbering the Sandys' group were those related to Sir Moyle Finch, a prominent Kentish gentleman, who had been a supporter of the Earl of Essex and became an important client of Northampton's.[47] Finch himself became a baronet and so did two of his sons-in-law: William Twysden who sat for Thetford in 1614 and got his Finch brothers-in-law seats in 1607 and 1614 through Northampton, and John Wentworth, Gentleman of the Bedchamber to Prince Henry. William Molyns, another Kentish gentleman, was also Twysden's brother-in-law. Another of the new baronets was Samuel Peyton of Kent, just twenty-one. He was the son-in-law of Roger Aston, Master of the Wardrobe and Northampton's choice for the Sandwich seat in the Parliament of 1614. Northampton thus appears to have connections with five of the eight Kentish baronets. Few courtiers who lacked local connections were made baronets. Indeed a significant number of country gentlemen who served as MPs appear to have received the new title.[48] The Crown deliberately distributed the new title to important local gentry.

Sir Robert Cotton, Northampton's aide and adviser, was himself among the first to receive the new title in return for his efforts in creating the baronetage.[49] Perhaps his more important reward was his close proximity to power, an unusual position for a scholar and country gentleman. Cotton's work for Northampton on questions of policy and reform will be discussed at length in a later chapter. It is enough to note here that, because of his close working relation with Howard, Cotton was besieged by suitors. He became thereby one of many intermediaries through which Jacobean ministers screened the endless requests for favour. His correspondence was coloured with suits from friends and strangers alike. In the midst of a letter about a book that Cotton was helping him get through the press, John Speed, the historian, prompted Cotton to remind the Lord Privy Seal of his suit. He refused the help of Mr Cole, one of Northampton's servants, and insisted on Cotton's own intercession. William Dethick, an antiquary and herald and old friend of Cotton, solicited his help in the restoration of his pension. Francis Tate, another antiquary, asked Cotton to recommend the bearer of his letter to Northampton, 'according to the powerfulness of that interest you have in that great lord'.[50] Cotton acted as an intermediary in the process of selecting the new baronets. Henry Montagu, Sergeant-at-Law, nominated Thomas Spencer; Richard Comack suggested Edward Seymour of Devonshire and when both were accepted, they wrote to Cotton to find out how to procure the patent and where to pay the price. Robert Bowyer, another old friend of Cotton, commended his cousin William Essex for inclusion on the list of baronets and asked that he might be first named in his county. 'This will much raise his reputation in that place, which by your kindness and the honourable favour through your means showed him, hath been both there and elsewhere supported when otherwise it had fallen.'[51] Bowyer's discreet reference was to Essex's financial difficulties. These had

been temporarily ameliorated in 1609 and 1610 when the Earl of Northampton and others had taken over the administration of some of his estates.
They became his feoffees authorised to sell some of his manors and hold the
courts in the hundred of Chipping Lambourn.[52] Cotton was apparently the
conduit for Northampton's favour to Essex. Essex's case reveals the extent
to which court patrons were successfully prevailed upon to support the aspirations and standing of country gentlemen. Moreover, the distribution of
the baronetage provides ample evidence that Salisbury and Northampton
consciously used the new title to reinforce existing court/country connections.

Among the members of the old, established gentry families whom the
Privy Council carefully selected as the first group of baronets, there were
several who were unusual. Of equally old and well-established gentry
families these men were either suspected Catholics or known recusants.
When James I acceded to the throne English Catholics had hoped for a new
spirit of toleration. The Gunpowder Plot designed to blow up king, Lords
and Commons in 1605 was engineered by a desperate group of recusants.
Its discovery ensured that the penalties assessed against Catholics would be
increased. It is therefore surprising to find at least fifteen Catholics among
the first ninety-two baronets.[53] It is not possible to discover who named
them all, but the evidence suggests an answer.

Many of the Catholic baronets were related to one another, reflecting the
same pattern of kinship ties found among non-Catholics. Lewis Tresham,
younger brother of Francis Tresham who had taken part in the Gunpowder
Plot, was a member of a family to which Northampton had been friendly.
His uncle, William Throckmorton, also became a baronet and so did his
brother-in-law Thomas Brudenell. Brudenell, cited for recusancy in 1609,
was a cousin of Robert Cotton and a friend of the Howards. A cousin of the
Throckmortons and the Treshams, Sir Francis Englefield, was the nephew
of one of Mary Tudor's privy councillors who went into exile during Elizabeth's reign. Englefield married Jane Browne, daughter of Anthony
Viscount Montagu, a well-known Catholic. The father of Thomas Gerard,
another new baronet, had suffered for the cause of Mary, Queen of Scots;
his brother was a Jesuit who was suspected of complicity in the Gunpowder
Plot, and his third wife was Mary Dormer, widow of Anthony Browne and
mother of Francis Englefield's wife. Another baronet, John Peshall, was
married to Englefield's cousin Anne Sheldon. William Sedley of Aylesford,
Kent was related to the Aylesford Culpeppers, one of whom was Northampton's ward.[54]

Salisbury and Northampton were careful to control the numbers and
quality of the first two hundred recipients. Yet despite the enthusiasm with
which gentlemen sought the title, the baronetage encountered some hostility from its inception. The open sale of the title was looked on unfavourably, at least in part, because it allowed the king to stave off a parliamentary
session. In addition, the distribution of the title generated grievances among

those omitted who felt themselves equal to the recipients. This hostility surfaced in 1614 when petitions were prepared in the Addled Parliament calling for the order's abolition. Although it is not clear how widespread the dissatisfaction was, it has been suggested that the large number of Catholics contributed to the opposition to the baronetage.[55] How did such a large number of Catholics come to be made baronets? It seems quite possible that Northampton's influence was crucial, for the earl was the major court patron of Roman Catholics in the early Jacobean period.

IV

Of Northampton's court clients, seventeen, or 25 per cent, can be identified as recusants or Catholic sympathisers. This is not surprising considering Northampton's own Catholicism. He had been an adherent of Rome until King James's accession. Then conscience had bowed to the realities of power. The Venetian ambassador noted the change. 'Old Howard, who has lately been appointed to the Council, and Southampton, who are both Catholics, declare that God has touched their hearts, and that the example of their king has more weight with them than the disputes of theologians. They have become Protestants, and go to church in the train of the king.'[56]

Northampton could not offer much advancement to practising Catholics and did not try. His own nephew Lord William Howard was barred from court office by the king himself. 'For notwithstanding the infinite trust I had in the faithfulness of his brother [the Earl of Suffolk] and uncle, yet I durst never bestow any preferment upon him in my days only because of his religion and devotion to the Jesuits.'[57] But the kind of patronage Northampton could offer Catholics was extensive. Among other things he could mitigate the punishment of an old man who had petitioned for the removal of laws against Catholics, ameliorate the confinement of Lord Vaux and his mother who had refused the oath of allegiance, and occasionally prevent the exploitation of recusancy. Hardret, jeweller to the queen, said the earl dashed his hopes for the profit of three recusants.[58]

Northampton established close relationships with many Catholics. He was the executor of the will of Henry, Lord Windsor, and became the guardian of his eldest son Thomas. Northampton also took up the wardship of William, son of Sir Thomas Culpepper, of Aylesford, Kent, a member of a widespread and well-known recusant family which could claim kinship to the earl through the Culpepper mother of Queen Catherine Howard. Another Culpepper served in Northampton's household.[59] When Sir Henry Carey, a kinsman of Northampton's and suspected Catholic, returned from the Low Countries, 'so Spanish in attire as if he were in love with the nation', the earl sought to extricate him from the difficulties in which he had become embroiled while abroad.[60] Sir Robert Bassett, an English Catholic living in Rome, wishing to return to England to attend to pressing financial problems, made his request to Northampton. Despite the fact that legal charges were outstanding against him, Northampton arranged a conditional licence for him to come to England for six months.[61]

Robert Dudley, son of the Earl of Leicester by Douglas Howard, the sister of Charles Howard, Earl of Nottingham, lived, a convert to Catholicism, in exile in Italy. Although Leicester had been Northampton's enemy, Dudley's religion and his connection to the Howards recommended him to Northampton. Dudley found favour with the Medici Duke of Tuscany who wrote on his behalf to Northampton:

> The Earl of Warwick . . . has come to my dominions in order to be able to live quietly in the religion which he has so far observed. I have received him the more willingly for his relationship to you, and extended him the affection I have for you. . . . And as he regards you as his father, I would ask you to treat him as your son and keep him in the good graces of the king.[62]

While Northampton was unable to do that he did undertake to administer Dudley's English estate. The lands were escheated to the Crown but Northampton arranged to have the sums due to the king paid to Lady Dudley and to Dudley's creditors. Thomas Chaloner informed Dudley, his one-time pupil, that 'you have received through my Lord of Northampton's especial care (as I may justly term it) the life of your estate, which through your debts and other intricacies was ready to perish'.[63] After Northampton's death Dudley turned to the earl's ally, Robert Carr, the Earl of Somerset, as his patron.

It is important to stress that Northampton's patronage was directed at Catholic gentry, not Catholic ideologues. When Thomas Morgan, a long-time agent of Mary, Queen of Scots, arrived in England in 1608, he expected a warm welcome from her son. From Dover he wrote a long letter to James detailing his service to Mary.[64] Instead of being succoured he was sequestered for refusing to take the oath of allegiance. To Northampton, Morgan's associate in intrigue, fell the duty of explaining why he should leave. He reminded Morgan that though they had worked for the same cause, circumstances had prevented their friendship. Howard emphasised that of all Mary's advisers he himself had urged her to caution. 'For I did ever advise her to win time, to abate the sails of her royal spirits in so great a gust, to discourage practice with patience', while others out of ambition acted 'to cut off the reward of hope by anticipation of opportunity'.[65] Northampton, conspirator turned courtier, now stressed the importance of obedience to the established state. The king, no sentimentalist, would settle for nothing less. Morgan returned to the continent.

Northampton's ability to employ Catholics even within his own service was subject to limitation by the king. On one occasion the king asked if he had any and Northampton replied that he only knew of one named Penny.

The king replied jokingly, 'well, you have had so much from me that you can surely spare me a Penny'. Northampton took the hint and discharged George Penny and three or four others.[66] But despite these limitations Northampton could and did use his patronage to help old allies and forge links between Catholics and the new king.

V

If Northampton appears consciously to have favoured Catholic gentry, it is significant that he did *not* use his power at court to influence ecclesiastical appointments or his own extensive lay patronage to shape the direction of the English church. Northampton was a sincere Catholic who at times valued status above religion and was patron to moderate Puritans as well as papists. He made no effort to impose his religious views on or through his clients. Between 1603 and 1610 Cecil and Archbishop Bancroft chose most of the bishops; between 1611 and 1619 the king himself.[67] And if Northampton enjoyed little influence over important church offices, he showed little interest in the church livings which were included in the extensive lands granted him in Norfolk by King James. Some of these lands were put in the hands of trustees who thereby became the patrons of these benefices. In other instances he allowed clients of his to make the nominations.[68] Of the clerics he did nominate himself several already held benefices. Although he promoted well-educated clerics,[69] Northampton gave scant personal attention to this area of patronage. Such an analysis, however, may be excessively negative. For the result was to increase local ecclesiastical patronage in the hands of the leading gentlemen of Norfolk, who thus became recipients once more of Northampton's favour.

Yet suitors for high church office, ever hopeful, still sought his favour with an eagerness apt for more secular callings. Thomas Dove, Bishop of Peterborough, wanted to be Bishop of Lincoln. William Cotton, Bishop of Exeter and Robert Cotton's cousin, longed to be transferred. He lamented to Cotton that 'there have been two and twenty bishops created and translated and I sit still as one nailed to this stool and unless my never failing and most honourable good Lord (the Lord Privy Seal) do become my godfather, I shall never have other name of place whilst I live'.[70]

Another suitor was William Tooker, Dean of Lichfield, whose promotions seemed to fall through at the last moment. Tooker claimed in 1604 that Northampton and Suffolk had recommended him for the bishopric of Gloucester. In 1610 the Gloucester see seemed within his grasp only to fall to another.[71] The year before he angled through Sir Robert Cotton for Northampton's help in becoming Bishop of Lichfield. 'His Lordship is so noble that looketh for no remuneration to be fastened upon him: by so much the more I may engage myself to his follower.'[72] Tooker's letter suggests that Jacobean patrons frequently demanded payment for favours given;

Northampton was unusual in asking for no remuneration. But Tooker knew what might interest the earl: he drew up for him a discourse on the difficulty of collecting parliamentary assessments with suggestions for improvement. Nevertheless the politically minded Tooker remained Dean of Lichfield.[73] In only one instance did Northampton contribute to the making of a bishop and that was not in England. On the recommendation of Sir Arthur Chichester, Lord Deputy of Ireland, who was himself one of Northampton's clients, the earl nominated Mr Main, Dean of St Patrick's, for the Bishopric of Kilmore.[74]

VI

If we move away from individual cases of favour to the aggregate, we can see quite plainly who Northampton's clients were.[75] Most were middle-aged and well-educated, many of them gentlemen and esquires but more often knights. It is useful to compare Northampton's clients with those surveyed by G. E. Aylmer in *The King's Servants, The Civil Service of Charles I*.[76] They share many similarities; differences are few. In age they tend to be somewhat older than Aylmer's sample, perhaps reflecting Northampton's own advanced years. In status both groups are dominated by knights although Aylmer's contains more peers and esquires than Northampton's. (It should be noted that this refers to the status achieved by Aylmer's civil servants.) Many were the offspring of those classed below gentlemen. In education a great many of Northampton's clients had attended university and 44 per cent of these had had some legal training. This is a much higher percentage than the 13 per cent of university men whom Lawrence Stone has cited as attending the Inns of Court and may indicate that the earl, sometime reader in civil law at Cambridge, particularly favoured the educated.[77] In general, Northampton's court clients came from the highest level of the wealthy gentry. Aylmer's cover a broader spectrum. Geographically, Northampton's clients reflected his family's traditional ties with Norfolk and his own ties with Kent, site of his country seat at Greenwich and much of his Cinque Ports administration. It does not reflect the large number of officeholders that Aylmer found living in London.[78] Politically, many of Northampton's people had been allied with Essex, fewer with Cecil.

Comparing Northampton's court clients, those who secured court offices or honours, with those of the Cinque Ports, yields certain contrasts. His clients at court were better educated, of higher status and younger than those on the coast. At the court, 32 per cent were under 40, in the Cinque Ports, 12 per cent. This may have reflected the higher status of Northampton's court clients, 40 per cent of whom were knights, 19 per cent gentlemen. At court, rank was important; in the Ports, local officeholding was more significant. Because of their higher status it is not surprising that more court clients had gone to university: 58 per cent as opposed to 27 per cent.

And 44 per cent of these had then gone on to the Inns of Court while 21 per cent of the Cinque Ports clients had had legal training. Despite their differences, however, it is important to note that both sets of clients were drawn from a homogeneous group, the well-born and politically active. This same social group is represented in Northampton's household servants.

VII

Northampton's household might represent in microcosm the web of patronage he had spun continuing the traditional Tudor practice of using favour to link court and country.[79] Despite the enormous pressure on the patron, what emerges from Northampton's letters and activities is the loyalty he felt for his followers.

Of the forty-five men identified as Northampton's servants, seventeen were gentlemen or esquires while only one's status was below that of a gentleman. Since it has only been possible to identify the status of about one-third of Northampton's servants, it is probable that many of those who have remained unidentified were of non-gentle origins. Seventeen of the forty-one, or 38 per cent, had attended Oxford or Cambridge. Of these 35 per cent had had legal training. What is most striking about Northampton's servants is their age. Of the sixteen whose ages can be identified, eight were in their twenties, or 18 per cent of the total. This should be compared with the other two groups of Northampton's clients. Of Northampton's court clients 13 per cent were under thirty; of the Cinque Ports group only 6 per cent. The youthfulness of Northampton's servants can be traced to the tradition of placing the sons of leading gentlemen in the households of important nobles. When the court became the fountain of favour, this tradition brought these young gentlemen into the service of leading courtiers. As Sir John Neale pointed out, 'the gentlemanly profession of "serving men" was a common career of younger sons of the gentry and the vast households of court magnates offered attractive prospects. The pressure to enter some great man's service, or place a protégé, was constant.' [80]

Northampton evidently had many such ambitious young men in his retinue and he remembered some of them generously in his will. Hugh Cholmondeley was the third son of a well-known family of Cheshire. His elder brother, Robert, became a baronet in 1611 and shared a grant of £1,200 out of old debts due to the Crown. High Sheriff of the county in 1631, he was made a viscount in 1638 and Earl of Leinster in 1646. Aged twenty-two when Northampton died, Hugh was the recipient of a £100 legacy.[81] Robert Poyntz was the younger son of Sir Nicholas, a leading member of the Gloucester gentry. Descended from Sir Nicholas Poyntz, the Tudor courtier, he was related to the Finches and Twysdens of Kent, Northampton's clients. He was also a cousin of George Berkeley, Northampton's ward and great-nephew.[82] It seems quite possible that the Henry

Mildmay who was Northampton's servant was the well-known monopolist and parliamentarian. The latter was brought up at court, knighted in 1617 and made Master of the Jewel-House in 1618, although some considered him too young and too mean in estate. In 1614 Northampton bequeathed him £50.[83] There is an interesting connection between Northampton's servants and the first baronets. Thomas Mildmay was a cousin of Henry Mildmay, and Roger Appleton, another Essex baronet, was Thomas Mildmay's son-in-law. Two other of Northampton's gentlemen retainers may have been related to new baronets: Giles Savage to John Savage, grandson of the Earl of Rutland and High Sheriff of Cheshire in 1607 and John Wynn to John Wynn of Gwŷdir in Caernarvon, an active courtier under Elizabeth and James whose family enjoyed the patronage of the Howards. John Wynn inherited £50 at Northampton's death.[84]

Aiming to make their mark at court were other well-born members of Northampton's retinue. Thomas Rant came from the Norfolk gentry as did Francis Windham to whom Northampton left £100. John Heydon of Norfolk, whose father and uncle had been followers of Essex, was left £100; Ferdinand O'Kelly was a follower of the Earl of Clanricard and probably related to John O'Kelly, Lord of the Manor of Screen, in Galway. To him Northampton left £20.[85]

Northampton did not fail to reward his gentlemen followers. In addition to legacies, he placed thirteen in office. He procured patents for William Bland and for Thomas Jermy, a Suffolk gentleman whose debt of £100 he forgave. John Griffith, his secretary, enjoyed fishing rights, a patent for the measurement of sea coal, and a couple of wardships in addition to the office of assistant to the Lord Warden of the Cinque Ports for which he had a fee of £36 6s a year and gratuities.[86] Owen Shepherd, Northampton's receiver-general in Norfolk, 'much advanced his fortunes; by that office'.[87] In his household as elsewhere Northampton endeavoured to engage the support of the gentlemen who held power in England's localities by holding out the promise of royal favour.

The dynamic interrelationship established by the dispensation of court patronage to local governors is best illustrated in two cases where Northampton took into his household young scions of Cinque Ports oligarchs and later appointed them to positions in the region. William Bing, younger brother of George Bing, who was active in Dover politics, matriculated at Trinity College in 1602, entered Northampton's service and in 1608 was named captain of Deal Castle which had a yearly fee of £20. In the 1610–11 session of Parliament he sat for New Romney and in 1614 for Winchelsea. Northampton left him 500 marks in his will and named him as one of its executors.[88] Thomas Godfrey was the son of a Thomas Godfrey who had been jurat of Lydd for over twenty years and Elizabeth Pix whose father was jurat of Folkstone and Hythe. Born in 1585, he attended Cambridge and the Middle Temple. The way in which he entered Northampton's service points up the earl's close relations with the ports' power structure. Godfrey was recommended to Howard by his father, and attended the earl as one of his gentlemen in ordinary for two years. He returned to the ports when he married the daughter of William Lambarde, the historian of Kent.[89] Though he left Northampton's household he did not leave his service.

For Northampton oversaw the ports' politics as carefully as their patronage. He gave Godfrey orders to take back to Winchelsea: 'according to these orders I was sworn a jurat . . . [these] orders . . . commanded that . . . though Mr Farmer and Mr Cooper had been long on the bench yet Mr Greene and myself were to take the place of them and to be mayors in succession before them.'[90] Patronage inevitably meant that some were left out and one may wonder how Mr Farmer and Mr Cooper felt at losing their seniority. Yet the oligarchy of the Cinque Ports towns were supported by and to some extent dependent on the authority of the Lord Warden and the central government. The town government was glad to make use of Godfrey; in 1609 he was employed by the corporation to carry a petition to the Lord Warden concerning their disobedience in the election of a mayor. Godfrey sat for Winchelsea along with Bing in the Parliament of 1614.[91]

Northampton struggled to continue the traditional pattern of giving favour in return for service in the changed and increasingly stressful structure of Jacobean politics caused by increased pressure on shrinking royal resources. Drawing on his regional office and his influence with Salisbury and Carr, Northampton created a tissue of relationships which provided him with a set of followers and the means with which to reward them. Patronage was an increasingly fragile tie in the early seventeenth century, yet Northampton's support for his clients was constant, his willingness to work for their interests when they coincided with his own unflagging. While his ability to shape the Privy Seal office was limited by administrative practices, Northampton managed to build an extensive patronage network in eleven years. Despite his own fierce reputation as a deadly enemy, his patronage tended to be inclusive and non-ideological, focused on the traditional leaders of the counties and the town oligarchs. He made no consistent effort to plant courtiers in local offices. Rather, his overriding concern was to ensure the Crown's control of its principal subjects, by providing them with royal reward. It is possible to view his patronage of Catholic gentry as inadvertently undermining the stability of the Jacobean court because of the hostility it engendered. Conversely, it may be viewed as a carefully selective process by which loyal Catholics found new connection to the court, after the persecution of the late Elizabethan period. Northampton, then, was quite traditional in his use of patronage as he himself had stated in challenging his own captain's action at Sandgate Castle.

Northampton emphasised that he followed the prescription of his predecessors. Urged by Prince Henry to recommend Dr Lionel Sharpe for the provostship of King's College, Cambridge, in 1612, Northampton praised the prince's tutor 'for learning, good conversation and integrity', but spelled out his reservations to Sir Charles Cornwallis who had become the prince's treasurer:

> According to the prince's request . . . I have commended Dr Sharpe to the king . . . this is all I can do and somewhat more for the prince's sake than I should do. For though the Dr for his qualities may take his turn with other competitors, yet I know that the king must break a statute before he thrust him in. . . . I . . . fearing now in the twilight of my age an eternal judgement for a temporary trick dare go no further. . . . To the last point which he requires, that I should press the king to put him in against the voices of the college, beside the bond of conscience, I dare not for fear of damnation.[92]

The importunities of suitors and Northampton's reluctant acquiescence to Dr Sharpe and Prince Henry himself appears vividly. Even more apparent is Northampton's continuing concern for those who might well be called his constituents, for he was chancellor of the University of Cambridge. Northampton claimed that in a similar election at St John's College he had prevailed with the king 'against the violence of many importuning suitors', to leave the election at liberty. Northampton emphasised that were he to argue against free elections by the college's fellows, 'in recompense of all their love and favour I should return ingratitude and make myself among them the most hateful man ever was brought up in that body'.[93]

A man with few clients or standing in the countryside when he came to power, Northampton developed a powerful loyalty to his followers, particularly in the Cinque Ports. Northampton even tried to control the patronage of the Cinque Ports from beyond the grave. John Chamberlain noted that the day of his death Northampton wrote to the Earl of Somerset requesting that 'the Earl of Pembroke and the Lord Lisle should not have any of his offices, because accounting them his enemies he would not they should triumph over him when he was gone. These and such other passages made the world speak hardly of him, and to say *ut vixit sic morixit*.'[94] Chamberlain's account was in part accurate. Northampton did ask Somerset to prevent Pembroke or Lisle from becoming Lord Warden of the Cinque Ports. But the reason Northampton gave differed significantly from Chamberlain's report. He wrote, 'I humbly beseech your Lord to stay with all the power you can the conferring the office of the Cinque Ports either upon Pembroke or Lisle, for as they hated me, so *they will plague my people and those whom I loved*.'[95] Patronage was to Northampton a tightly woven fabric in which all threads were closely bound up. To snap one would be to unravel all. Somerset yielded to Northampton's last request and the office remained empty until granted to Lord Zouche the following year. Northampton attached at least as much importance to the region he ruled as to Greenwich, his home, or Norfolk where his ancestors lay buried. At the time of Northampton's death, one courtier observed the importance the earl had attached to the Lord Wardenship: '[he] did either esteem it, or thought himself to receive so much estimation from it, as he hath willed his body to be laid in the Castle of Dover.' [96]

Chapter 4

Profit from Office

In his last public appearance, the Earl of Northampton travelled in state from Greenwich to London, his coach accompanied by a procession of sixty gentlemen on horseback. *Sic transit gloria mundi* was the comment of one onlooker.[1] On 15 June he died in his newly built palace in the Strand, amid the tapestries, paintings and furniture which he had bought with an extravagant hand. He left a large estate to his heirs, including land worth £3,000 or £4,000 a year, his house in the Strand and his country seat in Greenwich as well as jewels, furniture and plate worth over £6,500. In addition, he provided generously for the setting up of three almshouses.[2] At his death he may have been worth as much as £80,000.[3]

It is not surprising that a man of Northampton's political importance and family connections should live lavishly or die possessed of a sizeable fortune equal to that of others of his rank. By virtue of the extent of their landed estates the Howard family had enjoyed a power base independent of the Crown for over a century while at the same time they served successive Tudor monarchs as influential court officials. But in view of his previous career nothing could have seemed less likely than Henry Howard's worldly success, for 'he had proved much variety and vicissitude of fortune in the course of his life'.[4] Although Howard had spent the decades of Elizabeth's reign in poverty, he was able to amass a fortune at the Jacobean court within the short space of eleven years. The rewards of the patronage system which characterised the government of the early Stuarts included not only the promotion of followers but access as well to the fountain of official profits. Thus as one of James's chief ministers, Northampton enjoyed the fruits of his labour in the form of a large income and an imposing establishment. Although he was notoriously proud of his family's traditional aristocratic status, Northampton was as much the creature of the court as the newest of new men. His freshly made fortune illustrates the ways in which the Jacobean courtier might enrich himself from office.

I

Northampton moved to consolidate his official powers and exploit all possible profit in the same vigorous way that he had organised his patronage. As we have seen, when he was named Lord Warden of the Cinque Ports on 6 January 1604, his first act was to secure a copy of his predecessor's patent of office. Then at Northampton's request Francis Thynne,

Lancaster Herald, drew up a list of the Lord Warden's prerogatives. Citing a precedent of the reign of Henry VIII, Thynne noted among these the yearly salary of £160 due to the Constable of Dover Castle.[5] Northampton was granted this £160 in September 1604, along with the salary of £102 which he collected as Lord Warden. The Lord Wardenship also provided other profits. As Admiral of the Cinque Ports, the Lord Warden was entitled to shares of pirates' goods and wrecks amounting to one-third to one-half their value. Much of the business of the Admiralty court in the Cinque Ports concerned the collection of these profits.[6] In each port the Lord Warden had a personal droit-collector as well as a collector-general. Throughout his tenure, Northampton asserted this right of shipwreck as well as coroner's jurisdiction and within a month of his assuming office served notice on the officials of New Romney that his fishmonger was to be provided with the best at the most reasonable price.[7] He launched several projects from which he expected a sizeable cut, but all failed. These included the farm of the tenth fish, by which foreign fishermen would pay the king a tax equal to one-tenth the value of their catch, and a project to exploit a new invention to recover lost anchors, which would yield Northampton one-third of the amount for which the anchors were sold. Even without these imaginative devices, the Lord Wardenship apparently yielded £700 a year in the 1620s.[8]

Northampton administered the Cinque Ports from a distance, but nevertheless maintained a close interest both in its patronage and the possible profits the position afforded. Northampton's efforts to impose the Lord Warden's authority politically and financially did not go unopposed. In 1608 his claim to coroner's jurisdiction in Dover harbour was challenged by the General Brotherhood meeting held at New Romney. Underlining their own historical rights they directed that 'all town clerks are to search their records for precedents regarding the jurisdiction'.[9] Although the towns questioned Northampton's power they also made use of it. Through his influence at court they were freed from a forced loan in 1611 and in gratitude voted the earl a gratuity of £110.[10]

Northampton was also Lord Privy Seal from 25 April 1608. Shortly after taking office he accused the clerks of concealing the true amount of the fees that came into the office and withholding his share.[11] Although the Lord Privy Seal and the clerks divided fees according to a fixed schedule, Northampton's income from this source remains unclear. None the less, G. E. Aylmer's estimate that the Lordship of the Privy Seal was of little value appears incorrect. In fact, Northampton claimed his income from the office was £960, of which £627 6s 10½d was granted to him in lieu of the Lord Privy Seal's ancient allowance of sixteen dishes of meat in the king's house.[12] Certainly, Howard tried to maximise the profits which the Cinque Ports and the Privy Seal brought him, both in salary and perquisites, but these did not account for most of his revenue. That flowed from the favour he enjoyed from the king and the influence he wielded as a privy councillor.

II

Although the legitimate heir to the fourth Duke of Norfolk's estates, Thomas, Earl of Arundel, was alive and well in 1603, Henry Howard and his nephew, the Earl of Suffolk, were granted much of the Norfolk property in reward for their political support for the king. In 1604 they reached a settlement dividing their grants between them.[13] Over the next years, as they continued to enjoy the king's favour, additional parts of the Norfolk holdings were given to them. Northampton also received other family lands in Dorset which previously had been in possession of a cadet branch, the Howards of Bindon.[14] Moreover, Northampton added to his lands through purchase. To assess with any exactness Northampton's landed income or profits from the management of his estates is impossible. There is little relevant evidence extant and his extensive correspondence does not shed any light on how he handled his property. What can be said with some certainty is this: while Northampton's holdings were centred in Norfolk and Suffolk, traditional Howard country, with scattered manors in other counties, his relation to his lands seems to have been purely titular. There is no indication that he took part in their administration at all.[15] Unlike his predecessors the earl did not establish a country seat in Norfolk, nor spend much time there. Instead he located himself close by the court in the royal park at Greenwich. Yet as in the Cinque Ports, he was willing to use his influence at court when his tenants in Bishop's Castle, Salop, appealed to him as lord of the manor to prevent the erection of a market in nearby Stratton, a rival town. Their plea successful, they presented him with £10. But in the main he appears to have been content, as an absentee landowner, to collect his rental income.

Northampton's income from land appears to have been quite low at the beginning of the reign; the first year's receipts from his Norfolk and Suffolk manors amounted to about £700.[16] This is deceptive, however, because it does not include the income from all of his holdings, such as the manor of Clun in Shropshire, and Bishop's Castle which probably yielded another £325.[17] Furthermore, it does not include aspects of landed wealth which did not bring an immediate return, but which contributed to the total value of Northampton's landed estate. The manor of Earsham in Norfolk provides an example. Part of its lands were rented out for £16 a year on a lease which was to run another forty-seven years. Owen Shepherd, Northampton's receiver-general, estimated, however, that the rent could be increased to £200 once the lease ran out. In addition, he reported, 'there belonged to the manor a leet and the Lord hath the royalties of fishing, fowling, hawking and hunting. There belongeth also to the manor the advowson of Earsham worth by year £40. The timber in the park is valued to be worth £600.' In another manor, Acle, in Norfolk, the current rent was £13 but might be improved to £50, after the sixty-seven-year lease was up.[18] In general, Northampton's yearly income from his valuable properties seems low because of the long leases on which many were let. Their potential value was much greater. Northampton also added to his holdings by purchase. At a time when some peers were selling land, Northampton was buying. In 1606 he bought the manor of Reydon in Norfolk for £1,150 and added the hundred of Frebridge for £596 in 1613.[19] In the same year, to round off his property in London, Northampton purchased one parcel for £760, and another, from Sir Robert Brett in St Martin-in-the-Fields, for £2,240. He then leased the latter back to Brett for a rent of £150. He had also acquired by his death the manor of Sedgely, which was estimated in 1616 to have a capital value of £2,500.[20]

Lawrence Stone has estimated that in 1602 peers enjoyed an average yearly rental income of £2,340 and the mean of all their yearly landed profits amounted to £3,020.[21] Northampton's yearly income from land did not rank with Salisbury's which was £6,080, or that of his nephew Suffolk, estimated at £5,800.[22] Still, by 1614 it was generally estimated that his yearly landed income, acquired through the king's grant and by his own purchase, totalled more than £3,000 and may have amounted to as much as £4,000. At Northampton's death Sir Henry Wotton commented to Sir Edmund Bacon, 'to the Earl of Arundel he left all his land (which will amount to some £3,000 of yearly revenue), besides three or four hundred [a year] to Mr Henry Howard'. To Arundel, a friend hastily penned that although 'to write your lordship particulars of my Lord of Northampton's last testament, may argue some zeal... he had given your lord £3,000 a year, furnished Mr Henry Howard £1,000 a year'.[23] If the letter-writers are correct, Northampton had made a large fortune quite rapidly and was investing the proceeds of royal favour in land, the usual repository for gains from office or trade throughout much of English history.

An important form of that royal favour was the patent of monopoly, conferring the exclusive right to manufacture, import or control items of trade with the right to enjoy the profits of licences or customs duties. Granted by the Crown to increase employment and trade, such patents reflected the diversification of the English economy and the growth of new domestic industries in the sixteenth and seventeenth centuries. Monopolies were also means by which the monarch could reward his servants at little cost to himself. In the long run, however, the inconveniences and elevation of prices these monopolies were thought to cause rendered them noxious to the king's subjects.

In 1607 the domestic starch industry came under attack in Parliament for wasting wheat, causing food shortages and fostering higher prices. In fact this grievance was planted in the House of Commons by merchants interested in organising the industry both foreign and domestic for their own profit. Although Parliament refused to act on the Bill to regulate the industry, these merchants succeeded in getting a royal commission established in September 1607. It was empowered to oversee the proper making of starch in authorised places, to issue licences and collect dues and fines.[24]

Then, on 14 March 1608, Northampton was granted for the period of twelve years new duties of ten shillings per hundredweight on imported starch and five shillings per hundredweight on starch made in England, in return for paying the king one-quarter of the revenue.[25] He sublet the customs to Lionel Cranfield, Arthur Ingram and other merchants. Cranfield had been active in the starch business from the beginning and it provided him an early opportunity to be of service to the Earl of Northampton. Between the royal commission set up for the socially useful purpose of overseeing starch production and the profitable customs duties farm, there were strong ties. Six of the seven farmers to whom Northampton sublet the customs duties were also on the commission. The starch patent was part of a twenty-year programme begun by Lord Burghley to balance the requirements of an adequate food supply with the benefits of new industry.[26] Now it was taken over by Northampton and a group of city merchants in the name of proper regulation and increased royal revenue.

Concern for the king's revenue was not, however, evident in Northampton's negotiations for the starch patent. To Salisbury, whom he called 'the sole solicitor of my suit since it first began', he wrote:

> my end is with your favour to convert the king's third to the next degree which is a fourth, and will prove unto me a benefit at the beginning of the farm while certain values are *sub horizonte* and to the king either a very weak or no great hindrance when beams of bright splendour breaking out he may after my time make his best commodity.[27]

Northampton's rent was set at a fourth of the revenue, and some months later, in November 1608, the rent was reduced further to the certain sum of £333 6s 8d.[28] Since Northampton sublet the farm for £3,000, he enjoyed a large profit, and the value of the farm, far from being *sub horizonte*, was apparent from the very beginning. The starch duties were revoked in 1610 because of parliamentary disapproval but by that time Howard had already made £4,500.[29] To compensate him for the loss of this lucrative income, the king granted him £4,000 a year for twelve years. Two years later, however, he had not yet received one penny of his pension, so he offered the king the following bargain: he would abate £2,000 of the arrears and accept a pension of £3,000 instead of the £4,000. The king accepted Northampton's proposals, and at Michaelmas 1612, authorised the payment of £6,000 to the earl out of the customs of England, as well as an annuity for life of £3,000. This last pension was to be paid out of the customs of Ireland organised for the Crown in 1613 by Cranfield, Ingram and other merchants.[30] From 1608 to 1614 Northampton may have received as much as £15,750 from his starch patents and those pensions which took its place, that is, £4,500 from the starch duties, £6,000 paid in 1612 and £5,250 due on his pension between Michaelmas 1612 and his death in June 1614. Patents of monopoly were important rewards for royal servants; under attack in Parliament they were often converted into pensions, further straining royal resources.

The Norfolk lands and the starch patent were the principal props of Northampton's new fortune. He enjoyed one other important form of royal favour, the grant of profitable wardships. When a minor succeeded to land held of the king by knight's service, he was considered incapable of supplying the requisite military support and the king was allowed to make the minor his ward and lease the lands to another until the heir came of age. In the early seventeenth century, although feudalism had been long dead, wardship was not. Administered through the Court of Wards and Liveries, wardships were sold by the government to courtiers who could resell them either to the ward's family or to strangers at a handsome profit.[31] Northampton was granted those of Lord Windsor and of Lord Berkeley. Northampton paid £570 for Lord Windsor's wardship which was worth at least £940 by Howard's own calculation.[32] In the case of George Lord Berkeley, profit came together with family feeling, for George Berkeley was his great-nephew. The Berkeley family hoped that Northampton would allow the ward's mother to educate him and arrange his marriage and in this they were not disappointed. They had other hopes too. For twenty-six years Catherine Howard, Lady Berkeley, had provided her brother with £50 a year from her household allowance during his decades of poverty. Perhaps because of his sister's support in darker days, he would remember George in his will. This was not an idle wish. To the child's mother Northampton had written:

> your care, your counsel and desires shall be regarded as mine own, in anything that concerns him in any way, and when I die, my will shall testify both what I think of your virtue, and in this case what I owe to your affection. During mine own time, I confess the height of my ambition is to express by care of this child in what account I held the grandmother, that for her virtues and rare parts besides her love to myself deserves to be recorded in a grateful memory.[33]

The publication of Northampton's will in the summer of 1614 must have been a shock to the Berkeley family. Not only did Northampton leave nothing to George, he listed the wardship as part of his estate, to be sold to the family for £1,500. When the disgruntled mother refused to pay, the executors took her to court and forced her to agree to remit the entire sum.[34] In this case the promptings of gratitude competed unsuccessfully with extravagant building schemes, charitable endowments and personal display. Royal grants of wards, land and patents were the direct means by which Northampton turned place into profit; indirect means such as the peddling of influence could be no less profitable.

III

Influence was the courtier's stock-in-trade, and it provided him with an income from the high hopes of those anxious to do business with the Crown. At times influence was translated into cash through the specific soliciting of the courtier's intercession by a suitor prepared to pay for the service. At other times payments were more of an insurance policy, a precautionary measure to maintain the goodwill of the courtier who as much by sins of omission as of commission could control the financial futures of those dependent on the court. Transactions of these kinds are often hard to pin down, but some of the Earl of Northampton's wealth stemmed from this source. His income from the Spanish government, for example, was a lucrative type of influence-peddling. Howard had been paid a pension by the Spanish ambassador in the 1580s, both to secure the allegiance of the Howard family and to pay for some diplomatic information. In 1582 Mendoza, the Spanish ambassador, had suggested the pension because:

> Lord Harry continues to serve with his usual care and intelligence. I understand that we cannot give him less than 1,000 crowns or 1,200 crowns a year . . . whereas if your Majesty makes him a present, you could not give him less than three times that sum. If he gets the 1,200 crowns in two half-yearly payments from me, it will have double the effect in encouraging him, and will pledge his house; and if he slackens or things change, the payments can be stopped.

In reply King Philip authorised the gift of 500 crowns to Howard as well as a pension of 1,000 crowns.[35] This arrangement was short-lived, however, because Mendoza was expelled from England in January 1584. As Mendoza's letter indicates, presents and pensions were on a continuum, the line between them thin or non-existent.

When Howard became a privy councillor his relationship with the Spaniards changed from that of a dutiful servant to a distinguished sympathiser. The Constable of Castile arrived in England to sign the peace treaty in August 1604, bringing with him letters of credit for 300,000 crowns allocated for those involved in the negotiations. Northampton shared in this largesse as one of the five English commissioners and Cecil's principal assistant in the negotiations. The ambassador of the Spanish Netherlands also brought gifts for the English negotiators and presented them publicly. The Venetian ambassador commented, 'this leads everyone to conjecture that what is done in secret is far greater'.[36] In secret dealings, Dr Robert Taylor, another envoy of the Spanish archduke, sought freedom of religion for Catholics and an offensive and defensive league with the English. He claimed that the Countess of Suffolk had offered to promote these goals in exchange for £20,000 for herself and £10,000 each for her husband and the

Earl of Northampton.[37] There is no evidence that such sums were ever paid the Howards, but Northampton did begin to receive a yearly pension of £1,000 as well as occasional gifts of jewels soon after the establishment of peace with Spain. Such payments were common at European courts. But the publication of tracts in 1620 attacking Spanish pensioners caused a political uproar in England.[38]

Northampton could not count on the prompt payment of his Spanish pension. It was often in arrears. The Venetian ambassador noted in 1611 that 'as yet not a penny of the pensions which he [the Spanish envoy] was to distribute to various courtiers has been paid so far'.[39] In October 1613 Don Diego de Sarmiento informed King Philip III that he was behind in paying his 'confidants', and in February 1614 noted in his accounts that he had paid Northampton, code-named *El Cid*, two years of his pension.[40] Curiously, if Northampton's rewards were in arrears, he did not concern himself with them nor did he press Sarmiento for payment. Indeed, he wished to pass these profits on to another. Compiling his accounts for 1615, Sarmiento added this note. 'The Cid's pension is not mentioned here, for 4,000 ducats that I had sent him were returned to me begging me to keep them until he sent me a message and sign saying who they were to be given to.'[41] In this case, perhaps patronage preceded profits in importance. Northampton may have preferred to put someone else in his debt than to collect his own pension.

Spanish payments to the earl are recorded in the ambassador's accounts and dispatches. The profits that Howard may have made from promoting the interests of merchant associates cannot be documented as easily. It is possible, even probable, that he profited from his association with John Swinnerton in the negotiations for the Great Farm of the customs and the farm of the sweet and Rhenish wines and from his association with Lionel Cranfield and Arthur Ingram in the negotiations for the Irish customs farm. Certainly Swinnerton and Cranfield both paid off Northampton's ally, Robert Carr, Viscount Rochester, in the negotiations for wine farms and in fact, Northampton forced Cranfield to increase his kickback to Rochester from 1,000 marks to 2,000.[42] But there is no concrete evidence that Northampton himself made a profit from influence-peddling.

The difficulty in pinpointing these kinds of profits can be illustrated by the Cockayne project. Alderman Cockayne proposed to develop the dyeing and dressing of cloth within England instead of shipping it to the Netherlands to be finished as was the custom. He claimed this would increase business profits, employ more workers, augment the king's revenues and, not incidentally, do away with the monopoly of the Merchant Adventurers which was a long-time grievance of those merchants outside the company. In the actual case, the project helped precipitate a major crisis in the English cloth trade because the Merchant Adventurers refused to participate in the new scheme, not enough capital was invested in the new industry and the Dutch refused to buy the dressed cloth which undermined their own home industry. The year before the Cockayne project was adopted, 1614, proved to be the highpoint of the English cloth trade; the project was followed by the depression of 1616 during which cloth fell in price, unemployment was widespread, and the king's cloth customs declined by 25 per cent.[43] In the aftermath of this disaster came recriminations. Several historians, including Menna Prestwich in her major study of the career of Lionel Cranfield, have cited and accepted as very plausible the allegation of a contemporary pamphlet that Northampton, his nephew Suffolk and Robert Carr were bribed to promote the Cockayne project. The pamphlet, 'Truth Brought to Light', makes the following statement: 'My Lord of Rochester, my Lord of Northampton, and my Lord (blank) then Treasurer, were great agents in this business, and were thought to have been promised great sums of money to accomplish it.'[44] This statement, both speculative and indefinite, is all the evidence there is that Northampton profited from the Cockayne project. In fact, it is not even certain that he promoted it.

In much the same way as Burghley approached projects, Northampton solicited expert opinion. Furthermore, Northampton convened the Privy Council to hear discussion of the issue for over four hours, 'everyone receiving great contentment by the full liberty which was admitted of effectual and pithy discourse to every man that was either prepared or disposed to argue'.[45] To provide the king with the best advice all parties had been ordered to commit their arguments to writing, which would then be submitted to their opponents for analysis and rebuttal. That this process did not produce the wisest decision is clear from hindsight. None the less, Northampton's careful presentation of the case made by both sides does not bear out the charge that he was a 'great agent in the business' of the Cockayne project. If he had been promised great sums to advance the project, his papers provide no evidence that he promoted it.

New Year gifts were a source, albeit a minor one, of official profits. The fifth Earl of Rutland, for instance, paid his fealty to Northampton every first of January with sizeable presents. The Catholic Roger Manners, fifth Earl of Rutland, had been as a young man a follower of Robert, Earl of Essex, as had Henry Howard. Howard retained a sentimental fondness for other followers of that lost cause as well as connections with his co-religionists. When Howard came to prominence under James I, Manners cemented the connection with his yearly tribute. Silver and gilt basins and ewers shaped variously like a snail, a mermaid, and Bacchus and Ceres were among the gifts he sent which ranged in price from £28 to £47.[46] In every year between 1608 and 1614 Northampton was the recipient of Rutland's largest gifts, receiving more than several Chief Justices, Lord Chancellor Ellesmere or King James himself.

The period between 1609 and 1615 saw the greatest investment by landed groups in trading and colonial enterprises. Along with other leading officials Northampton participated in the Irish plantation, undertaking by way of nominees the settlement of 12,500 acres. The Lord Deputy, Sir Arthur Chichester, congratulated the earl on his choice of undertakers for the plantation project, but added pessimistically that the work promised to be great and difficult.[47] He feared that the neglect of the Irish would provoke rebellion and, of course, he was right. Furthermore, the plantation was a financial failure, losing £40,000.[48] During this period Northampton joined several other ventures which held out the hope of great discoveries but not immediate profit, such as the Hudson Venturers of 1610 and the Northwest Passage Company of 1612.[49] In 1610 he and Sir Francis Bacon and forty-six others, thirty-six of them merchants, were granted a plantation in Newfoundland.[50] The goal of the company was the establishment of a colony and a monopoly of the carrying trade in fish to the Mediterranean. Northampton evidently maintained a continuing interest in the project for in 1612 Sir Percival Willoughby, one of the leaders of the company, suggested that the earl be asked to support a scheme for governmental protection of the fishing fleet at Newfoundland. The colony in its first years was successful but later ate up the profits beginning to be made in the fishing trade. Although Northampton apparently realised no return on his investment, he continued to be one of the 'practical and persistent supporters of the expansion of English trade'.[51]

IV

These were some of the ways in which a courtier tried to make his fortune. Just as important as the getting was the spending. The role of the courtier demanded a display equal in lavishness to his importance. Lawrence Stone has estimated that an earl in the early seventeenth century could not maintain his household in appropriate style on less than £5,000 a year divided among wages, clothes, kitchen, stables, tradesmen and repairs.[52] Without a family to maintain, Northampton's expenses were rather less, but the abrupt change in his political fortunes impelled him to construct an elaborate establishment in a short space of time.

A house in London and a country seat were the usual domiciles considered appropriate to the dignity of an earl. Henry Howard lacked both in 1603 but by 1605 he had purchased property in St Martin-in-the-Fields parish, pulled down the existing tenements and erected a turreted and towered palace which stretched to the river, its 162-foot length fronting on the Strand.[53] After its construction he continued to buy up property in the neighbourhood. In 1610 he bought stables and coachhouses and in 1613 added land to extend his gardens. This mansion, called Northampton House, was considered one of the finest residences in Europe.[54]

At the same time he acquired land in Greenwich. Having spent both his childhood and some of his adult years there, in his old age he came to see Greenwich as a refuge from the daily pressures of the Council. He picked up some of the property through Lionel Cranfield. Sir Nicholas Stoddard, for instance, offered to sell his Greenwich real estate to Northampton through Cranfield's means, 'holding myself almost assured of your desire to gratify my Lord of Northampton with manifesting of your love towards him, and I having an especial desire that his lordship may have good satisfaction in his desire towards the enlarging of his house at Greenwich'.[55] Another Greenwich landowner was not so sanguine. Simon Basill, an officeholder, complained to his patron Salisbury that at Northampton's wish he had taken down part of the upper garret and second story of his house, which had resulted in the loss of two good rooms. Not satisfied with that, Northampton now insisted that he take down the whole side of that wing.[56] Whether or not Basill was successful in getting Salisbury to intercede, Northampton continued to increase his holdings in the royal borough. He bought the lease of the meadow and parsonage for £1,500, the keeping of Greenwich Park for £200 and spent about £2,000 on it.[57] In 1613 he became embroiled with Queen Anne over the stewardship of the park which she desired to claim for herself. Enlisting the favourite, Robert Carr, in his cause, Northampton indignantly denied that he made any money from the office. 'With the park there goes no other benefit than the fee of three pence a day and those four kine. . . . My charge is treble to the gain and to enjoy the lodge without the care of the park would make me ridiculous.'[58] On 20 December 1613 Howard triumphed and was confirmed in his office of keeper of Greenwich Park.[59] By locating his country home in a royal park, he had given himself a head start on the establishment of his estate.

Such transactions reveal the value system of the Jacobean courtier: power and prestige were invoked even in seemingly minor matters. In the first case, Northampton felt free to force another to dismantle his house, presumably because it spoiled the earl's view; in the second, he begged the king's intervention so that he might not appear ridiculous at court. Status at the Jacobean court was not inherent in birth or office but in the eye of the court observer, and that caused anxiety. Northampton's anxious rhetoric was more appropriate to his poverty in earlier days than his power under James. The king, he said, was 'much more sensitive of his poor servant's humble patience and blasted credit than others that emblemish it'.[60] Northampton was not poor, humble or patient; neither in 1613 at the height of his power was his credit blasted.

During his few years of affluence Northampton amassed moveables worth over £6,700; his household goods accounted for almost half that sum.[61] Both his city palace and country house were richly fitted up with tapestries; some of the Brussels work had belonged to Cardinal Wolsey. Leather hangings in gold and azure, Persian and Turkish carpets, inlaid cabinets, velvet chairs and pillows filled the rooms. As many as 105 paintings hung on the walls of his galleries, one of the largest art collections of the period. Northampton's own history and sympathies could be read in his collection. Most were portraits of the Howard family and their kin and various members of the royal family. Five of the portraits were of Mary, Queen of Scots.[62] He also amassed a large library, collected gold and jewels, diamonds, rubies and sapphires and plate, both gilt and silver, worth over £3,500.[63]

Combined with the conspicuous display typical of the period, Northampton manifested an atypical concern for good works. Lawrence Stone has estimated that a prototypical Jacobean earl, who spent about £5,000 a year, would allocate about £100 a year in gifts and alms.[64] Northampton proved quite a contrary case. He established the largest almshouse in Kent founded in the period between 1480 and 1660, another that was one of the largest in Norfolk and a third one of good size in Shropshire. These foundations constituted one man's effort to revive aspects of the monastic system. Howard founded first in May 1607 the Hospital of the Holy and Undivided Trinity at Clun in Shropshire, a traditional Howard seat. He authorised the admission of twelve poor men and a warden and endowed it with lands yielding about £200 a year (that is, with a capital value of about £4,000).[65] In 1608, the year of his lucrative starch patent, he set up an almshouse at Castle Rising, Norfolk. He spent £451 14s 2d for the building which consisted of twelve apartments for twelve poor women, the governess's room, a spacious hall, kitchen and chapel, and endowed the almshouse with £100 a year from some of his Norfolk holdings. The twelve poor women at Castle Rising each received eight shillings a month, the governess twelve shillings, with additional sums on feast days. One gown was provided every year and in the seventh year a gown and hat of blue broadcloth with Northampton's badge embroidered on the breast. In regulations which recall the nunnery, chapel was required twice a day, and prayers were to be said three times a day. Admission was open to single women over 56, who were literate, of good character and possessed of goods worth under £50.[66] His greatest foundation was Trinity Hospital at Greenwich. He endowed it with much of the land he had purchased there, with a capital value of £3,833. Trinity Hospital was to care for twenty poor men, twelve from East Greenwich, eight from Howard's birthplace in Shotesham, Norfolk. For the support of each almsman £9 17s 8d was provided plus £1 a year for clothing and £2 a year as a stipend. A cook, laundress and barber were also included to care for the almsmen. The Mercers' Company was named to administer Trinity Hospital, perhaps because Northampton's associate Lionel Cranfield was a member. In all the Earl of Northampton expended 'upwards of £9,000 for buildings and endowments'.[67] In his will he provided that all his goods and lands were to be leased for ten years to his executors to pay his debts and legacies, and particularly to finish the building and endowment of his hospitals. Any excess at the end of those ten years was to be divided among the treasuries of the three foundations.[68] Although much of the endowed charity of the period has been attributed to Protestant gentry and merchants, the Roman Catholic Northampton spent a good part of his income on good works.

Despite the fact that he was an invalid in the last months of his life, Northampton maintained his interest in building up his estate. Through the efforts of Arthur Ingram, who along with Cranfield had managed his starch business, he struck a good bargain for several rectories. Buying them at the low rate of sixteen years' purchase, he spent £1,639 for these properties and used them to endow his hospital at Clun.[69] He continued to buy jewels and plate although not always for himself. To mark the marriage of Robert Carr and his niece, Frances Howard, he presented the couple with £1,500 in plate. For the groom he had made an elaborate sword which cost £566.[70] A watch in the form of St George and the dragon, which he had ordered for himself, remained at the goldsmiths at the time of his death and another George to be set with diamonds was on order.[71] When he died his heirs were faced with debts of £6,000.[72]

Favour had made Howard's fortune. To the Earl of Suffolk, who was also the recipient of Northampton House, he bequeathed the symbol of that favour, 'my jewel of the three stones which his excellent Majesty sent me out of Scotland as his first token, which jewel I cannot better repose with any than with him that is so faithful and trusty as my said nephew is'. Acknowledging that he had benefited from the king's gift of the Duke of Norfolk's lands which might have belonged to his brother's children, he left most of his land to the Earl of Arundel and £2,000 to Lord William Howard to replace the manor of Clun intended by his father for him and now in Northampton's hands. But to poor George Berkeley he left only 'the suit of new dressed hangings which were my Lord Berkeley's'.[73] Northampton rewarded his servants with generous bequests ranging from £200 down to forty shillings for Will the kitchen boy. For his funeral each gentleman was provided with twenty nobles, each yeoman five marks, to buy black clothing for mourning. In an elaborate procession his body was carried through Kent to Dover, his men standing watch by the candlelit coffin at inns along the route. Nicholas Stone, master mason to James I, was commissioned to make a monumental effigy and tomb for the earl to be set in Dover Castle. At £500 it was one of Stone's most lucrative assignments.[74] In death as in life, Northampton proclaimed his importance.

Northampton owed his title and fortune to James I. Although he received half of the Howard lands held by the Crown in 1603, much of his fortune came from court office and influence. Northampton's substantial fortune was made quickly. Like his contemporaries Salisbury and Suffolk, he spent the proceeds in an extravagant building programme, on Northampton House and his three hospitals, and he claimed to be eaten up with debts because of it. Why, then, did he leave such little debt compared with these other master builders? His nephew Suffolk owed as much as £40,000 at his death.[75] Biology provides a reasonable answer. A lifelong bachelor because of poverty and sexual preference, Northampton had no daughters to provide with marriage portions, no sons to support in expensive living at court. Structural factors influenced Northampton's income in another way.

It may be that the long leases which tied up some of his Norfolk holdings forced him to lean more heavily on court reward.

There was a complex relationship between profits and policy at the Jacobean court. It would be a mistake to see projects, patents of monopoly and pensions as contrary to the king's interest. They were in fact the king's primary means of rewarding his servants. Moreover projects and monopolies often had socially beneficial ends. But increasing pressure on the royal bounty in the early seventeenth century meant that suitors had to search harder for plausible and implausible projects to solicit from the king. These were more likely to be burdensome to the subject. Moreover, it is not at all clear that because a courtier accepted gratuities he then represented or spoke for the interests that had paid him off. The case of the Spanish pensions provides clear evidence of this. Northampton would have been a supporter of a pro-Spanish foreign policy even without an annuity. Similarly it is not clear that influence-peddling affected policy as directly as is usually supposed. Faced with the Cockayne project, Northampton followed his usual practice in organising debate in the Privy Council with a hardheaded examination of the issues and presentation at length of both sides of the argument. It may well be that the gratuities or bribes ensured a contract already secured, or the continuation of favour already granted. Bribes were thus often brokerage fees. Finally, profits and policy were linked in another way. Often the Crown had to ensure private profits if it wanted public policy carried out. Elizabeth had run her navy in a mixture of public and private enterprise; the plantation of Ulster was undertaken in the same manner. Northampton made a fortune from his influence at court. As a policy-maker, we shall see that he aimed to harness the processes of patronage and profit for the king's own service.

Chapter 5

The Jacobean Privy Councillor

The Earl of Northampton was both courtier and councillor: concern for his own power, patronage and profit intermingled with energetic efforts to shape a rational royal policy and to reform royal administration. The combination of personal and public interest characterised early modern government. From the image of the king as *pater familias* as well as monarch, of the magistrate as god and father, personal relationships between king and subjects, between patron and client permeated English society. Royal officials, known as the king's servants (not the public's), had to make their own private arrangements as to appointment, remuneration and tenure in office. In looking at Northampton's work as a privy councillor it is well to remember the importance of personal ties even to members of that body.

The English Privy Council held an importance in royal government higher than that of councils in other European countries such as France or Spain.[1] Unlike bodies in those countries, where responsibilities were divided, the Privy Council was omnicompetent: it not only provided advice to the king on all issues of policy both foreign and domestic, but it also sat as the Court of Star Chamber dispensing justice on a wide range of matters both public and private. Over the six decades prior to James's accession to the throne, the Privy Council's functions, routine and membership had become stabilised. The *Acts of the Privy Council* provide a formal record of its deliberations. Unfortunately, those records for the first half of James's reign were destroyed in the Whitehall fire of 1619. But we possess an informal account of the actual workings of the Privy Council in a series of letters written between 1612–14 from the Earl of Northampton to the king's favourite Robert Carr, Earl of Somerset, detailing not only the decisions taken by the Council, but the difficulties it confronted and sometimes only partly overcame. The peculiar mix of the personal and the public is sharply drawn in this correspondence.

While Northampton served on the Council, it conducted certain aspects of foreign policy, looked for new ways to raise money and to reform government spending and administration, as well as hearing petitions, conducting musters, providing licences to travel. But if the Privy Council was omnicompetent, it did not have the technical capacity to supervise government departments, to oversee the carrying out of its orders. Balanced delicately between an ideology which stressed the awfulness and absolute power of the

monarch and his ministers and a political system which depended on voluntary local government, privy councillors had to make their way carefully, to
use every means both coercive and persuasive to implement royal policy. It
has been convincingly argued that the strain of war in the 1620s overwhelmed this delicate balance.[2] The following chapters focus on how an
early modern minister made policy, and the structural and personal difficulties which hampered his efforts.

From 1603 to 1612, the Earl of Salisbury dominated Jacobean government as Secretary of State and the central figure on the Privy Council. All
official (and much unofficial) correspondence passed through his hands.[3]
He was able to organise and regulate the business that came before the
Council. During these years Northampton acted as Salisbury's aide, on the
one hand by serving as a major spokesman on public occasions and, on the
other, by concentrating on administrative detail. Northampton perceived
himself and was perceived by others as a notable public speaker and on
important occasions his rhetorical skills were tapped. In 1604 he took a
leading role at the Spanish peace treaty negotiations challenging Spanish
pretensions to control trade to the East Indies. In 1606 he elaborated much
of the case against Henry Garnet and the Gunpowder plotters. In a similar
way, as we shall see, Northampton used his rhetorical skills to present the
Crown's case in Parliament on such issues as union with Scotland and the
Great Contract. In April 1607 Northampton wrote to Sir Charles Cornwallis, the English ambassador to Spain, that he had been delayed in
answering his letters first because of illness, afterwards his discourse on
Garnet and most recently his work on behalf of the union.[4]

That was his public role. Northampton also carried out the efforts of
Salisbury and the Council to improve the royal finances. In 1605 Northampton noted, 'this day's labour wholly spent about the reformation of his
[James's] house the flaws and excesses of which are infinite'.[5] When Salisbury became Lord Treasurer he tried to develop a long-term plan to organise court patronage which was embodied in the Book of Bounty, published
in 1610 but drafted in 1608, and to put the Crown's resources on a new
footing via the Great Contract formulated in the years leading up to 1610.
Northampton contributed to this effort by establishing investigative commissions to reform the navy in 1608 as well as the Earl Marshalship and
other royal offices. These efforts at administrative reform, which will be
treated below, have often been characterised by historians as Northampton's
way of undercutting or challenging Salisbury's hegemony. It would not be
possible to suggest that the alliance between Northampton and Salisbury
was based on warm personal feelings. But that it was a working partnership
is suggested by Northampton's letter to Sir Thomas Edmondes at the time
that the naval commission was established. 'We are all now set upon the
point of thrift but my Lord Treasurer above all who . . . bends his whole
endeavour both to clear the loans that hang upon us heavily and to equal the
king's receipts with his expense out of those fragments that are left rather by

chance than providence of a rich fortune.' Northampton described himself as one of Salisbury's assistants 'of which I am both the weakest and worst'.[6]

Northampton's work and correspondence provide the flavour of the functioning of the Privy Council. This chapter will suggest the process by which that body made policy and the variety of issues it faced. The advice Northampton sought in order to solve these problems, his work as an administrative reformer and his major role in the presentation of the council's programme in Parliament will be considered thereafter.

I. Star Chamber

It is useful to begin an examination of Northampton as privy councillor with a brief look at his work in the Court of Star Chamber. This is not in fact a detour. While the Court of Star Chamber had developed as a separate court by the seventeenth century with its own procedures and records, the overlap of its membership with that of the Privy Council meant that the division between the two bodies was one of administration, not one of personnel or policy.[7] Sitting as the Court of Star Chamber, the privy councillors heard cases on a wide range of issues, most of which concerned the preservation of order. Cases ranged from rioting, disputes of title and libel to punishment of government officials for corrupt practices. Northampton's activities as a member of the court suggest attitudes which characterised his work on the Privy Council and in Parliament as well.

To begin with, he usually supported Salisbury's position in the court's decisions. On more than one occasion he said that 'he was in everything of the same opinion'.[8] He often attended Star Chamber when Salisbury did not, acting perhaps as his proxy. This was repeatedly the case, as we shall see, in parliamentary sessions.[9] Furthermore, he was one of the major government spokesmen at meetings of Star Chamber. While Lord Chancellor Ellesmere dominated the proceedings, Northampton spoke often and elaborately, particularly on issues pertaining to title and honour. The earl asserted that 'he would wrestle with any man in skill, and endanger any man by arguments'. His speeches were studded with references to the Bible, classical history and Roman writers, including Cicero and Scipio. There is little evidence of rigid factions in Star Chamber decisions; Northampton and Ellesmere, sometimes described as the leader of the strongly Protestant faction on the Council, often agreed. Moreover, in the case of a libeller of the late Archbishop of Canterbury, Northampton, like Salisbury who spoke before him, specifically argued against dissension, for 'amongst us there are no essential impediments in doctrine'.[10]

Northampton presented the case for reconciliation among the king's subjects particularly on matters of religion, while always upholding royal authority. Long a Catholic, Northampton's willingness to go to the established church and serve the king boded well for Catholic support of the new regime and in return a moderation of their treatment. Northampton was frequently called on to present the Crown's case against Catholic conspirators and defend the king's commitment to the established religion, as his speeches in Star Chamber graphically illustrate.

Early in the reign, in answer to a petition expressing concern that the king was considering toleration for Roman Catholics, the privy councillors sitting in Star Chamber took care to reassure their Protestant subjects that he was not. Northampton was on thorny ground here since there is some evidence that he himself had asked the king for toleration of Catholics.[11] None the less, in the united front that the Privy Council tried to present on such overriding matters of policy, Northampton dutifully pointed out that the king had sent him to foreign ambassadors to forbid them to press the issue. Northampton protested, however, 'that there were many Catholics which otherwise, but for their consciences, were men well qualified, and good subjects, and loyally disposed to the state'. This statement preceded the Gunpowder Plot. In an elaborate speech delivered in Star Chamber after that event, Northampton explained the king's stand on religion. Now there was no emphasis on the good qualities of Catholics but an emphatic denial that the king had ever promised toleration. Stressing the importance of his own role in James's accession, Northampton noted that during Elizabeth's reign he had warned the king that such rumours were damaging his claim to the English throne. He did acknowledge that at the accession he had solicited the king for juster treatment of Catholics but emphatically denied that the king had ever promised toleration. Indeed the king had sent him to Watson, the priest found guilty in the Bye Plot, to get him to deny such a rumour. As a result Watson avowed prior to his execution that the king never had promised toleration.[12] Northampton's speech suggests that he served as patron and contact to loyal Catholics during James's reign. Yet he always upheld royal authority even if it meant speaking on behalf of the established religion and scotching rumours of the toleration he wished for.

Even so, Northampton was not believed. In 1612 he discovered a widespread report that accused him of writing to an important Roman Catholic polemicist, Cardinal Bellarmine, to take no notice of his denunciation of Father Garnet and the Gunpowder plotters. To Robert Carr Northampton wrote to 'bemoan' the wrong.

> But to call a man of my birth, my rank and interest in my royal master's favour in question for packing in a more execrable villainy this day or at the least with covering the crimes of those that were engaged in that horror is almost above belief. . . .
>
> His Majesty belike made a very ill choice of his affectionate and humble 3 to be an examiner in this cause of Garnet and his complices if he carry in his heart an inclination to favour any man that smelt of that smoke and Northampton was a brave hypocrite in hunting Garnet and all the rest from the bar to the gallows. . . .

> To be accused often for my resolute affections to the most worthy queen and king that ever lived in the world was meritorious and glorious and these persecutions I confess out of the joy of conscience have made me somewhat proud, but for a coverer or concealer of any of the blackguard of Lemathen I was never brought upon the stage before and therefore your Lord shall perceive that in this white age like an ill comediant I will not so much as trip *in extremo actu quia finis coromat opus*.[13]

Northampton notified Carr that he intended to bring the matter before the Lords, and to proceed by ordinary form usual upon like affronts. He did so by bringing suit in Star Chamber.

In examinations taken before the Lords, the defendants confessed to having circulated the rumours that since Northampton had become Lord Warden of the Cinque Ports more priests had come into the country than previously and that he had excused his book against Garnet to Bellarmine as composed only to placate the king. Significantly, the gossips described George Abbot, Archbishop of Canterbury, as having 'informed his Majesty such matters against my Lord of Northampton which if he could prove he should never be treasurer'.[14] The circulation of this rumour in the months after Salisbury's death suggests that it may have been fostered by court politics and intended to have just that effect: to deny Northampton the Lord Treasurership. The identity of the defendants reinforces this possibility, too, for they were a collection of court officers and gentry: Sir Richard Cox, son of a bishop of Ely, Thomas Lake, possibly the son of the Second Secretary, Henry Vernon, a member of the minor gentry, Serjeant Mynours, clerk of the carriages, Thomas Goodrick, a student at Gray's Inn, and James Ingraham, a merchant.

In November 1612 six publishers of the libel were given heavy fines and imprisoned. John Chamberlain commented on the strangeness of North-ampton's pursuing gossip with such vengeance.[15] But Northampton believed that rumours which virtually accused him of treason would sound the deathknell to his ability to function as a privy councillor. Indeed such steps as he took were common. For instance, in Fourde's case, an unsuccessful plaintiff complained in a petition to the king about the judicial conduct of Lord Chancellor Ellesmere. For sowing sedition between the king and his peers, Fourde was sentenced 'to have perpetual imprisonment, to lose his ears upon the pillory, having papers on his head, to ride with his face to the horse tail and to be fined £1,000'. The sentence was in the end rescinded, but the councillors used the occasion to reinforce their authority. 'All the court being a great presence condemned him bitterly and commended the Lord Chancellor excellently.... Let all men hereby take heed how they complain in words against any magistrate, for they are gods; and he must have very good matter that will go about to convince them, for fear he overthrow not himself.' In another case, Lord Chief Justice Popham called libel a breach of the peace and a poison to the commonwealth. Salisbury emphasised that such libels had one goal: 'their end is faction, their zeal blind fury'. Northampton agreed, arguing that 'the seed of schism and sedition springs every day'.[16] Yet it is important to note that at his request five of Northampton's six libellers were released from incarceration within a month of the sentence and their fines remitted. Furthermore, the case does not seem to have affected their subsequent careers at court: Lake became Clerk of the Council; Mynours, Master of the Otter-hounds. Only Ingraham, the unlucky merchant who had begun the rumour and probably lacked the court connections of the others, languished in the Fleet for close to six months.[17] In short, there was a gap between the rhetoric of divine magistracy, the punishments proclaimed in Star Chamber and the extent to which these were carried out.

For the councillors had to maintain that delicate balance between their own extraordinary majesty and practical politics. The result was that Northampton often argued for moderation in the fines and punishments of those who came before the Court of Star Chamber. One case concerned a potential riot in Wales caused by a local justice of the peace who brought 140 men along with him to quarter sessions to challenge an antagonist. The two chief justices, Lord Zouche, the two bishops and Northampton judged it a small fault. Recognising the importance of the gentry in local government, they sought to mediate between the parties, calling the defendant 'a gentleman that had done good service in the country' and the plaintiff 'a recusant, but otherwise a man of honest and civil conversation'. For the sake of example they fined the defendant £40. Northampton's majority opinion noted the defendant's residence 'within Wales, which as they thought was punishment enough'.[18]

Northampton often spoke to issues pertaining to title and honour. Such decisions were difficult: 'He was like, he said, to a man upon a narrow bridge, either swerving, slipping, or must go leasurably; and that he that hath a weak eye, and reads a small print with spectacles, had not need to go upon this bridge.'[19] He found against his client Dudley in his quest for recognition as Earl of Leicester and his cousins, the Fanes, in their claim to the Barony of Abergavenny. He had no trouble in again upholding the dignity of the nobility, a favourite theme of his, in the case of the Countess of Rutland against the claims of a merchant to whom she owed money. All the judges agreed that peers' wives could not be arrested except for contempt. Yet Northampton's view of women, with the exception of Mary, Queen of Scots, tended to be rather jaundiced. Reflecting an attitude characteristic of the *ancien regime*, he noted that by the civil law women were favoured in cases of treason, *'propter unbecillitatem sexus'*. By way of an astronomical metaphor he argued that wives' dignity reflected that of their husbands: 'it is with them as it is with the eclipse of the sun by the interposition of the terrestrial body, for if she marry ignobly, or live dishonourably her glory is altogether eclipsed and vanished and she loseth her privilege.'[20]

In a case concerning the custody of the castle and manor of Dunnington,

Elizabeth, Lady Russell, had the temerity to argue with the judges. Well educated and a spirited defender of her own case, she attacked the Earl of Nottingham, the other claimant, and volunteered that if her husband, Lord John Russell, had lived longer he would have excelled Nottingham, hero of England's victory over the Spanish Armada. The Lord Chancellor chastised her and Northampton followed, saying 'out of the place I hold, as one to whom the office of Earl Marshal is committed, that by the law of arms you are no Lady Dowager', pointing out that her husband had died during his own father's lifetime. In this unusually lively session of the court, Lady Russell responded by grasping Northampton by the cloak, and told him that the law was otherwise before he was born.[21] This battle of the septuagenarians provides an amusing counterpoint to the councillors' stern pronouncements of the god-like magistrate.

The purpose of Star Chamber was to maintain order. The judges did that by several different methods, upholding hierarchy and patriarchy, directing and inspiring the local governing elite, putting down riots, providing exemplary sentences which were at times revoked, and punishing corrupt government officials.[22] The statements of the judges of Star Chamber repeatedly emphasised the ideal of order and exalted the authority of the Privy Council. There was, however, an essential contradiction between ideology and practice, as becomes clear when we turn from public pronouncements to council procedure.

II. The Workings of the Privy Council

From 1612–14 Northampton dominated the Privy Council, replacing Salisbury. No love had been lost between the two but Northampton had worked rather harmoniously with Cecil, certainly through to 1610 or 1611. With Salisbury's death, Northampton had now to organise and orchestrate the Council's business, an assignment different from carrying out the commands of the king and Mr Secretary.

During Northampton's dominance of the Council there was no Secretary of State. Instead of all information flowing to and from a central figure such as Salisbury who also served as the king's chief adviser, power was dispersed. Northampton conducted Privy Council meetings, reported results to Carr and the king and in return received royal decisions and new issues to be placed on the Council's agenda. Unlike Queen Elizabeth's Council, which tended to follow her on progress, met wherever she was in residence, and was thus ready to proffer advice on the spot, the Privy Council during Northampton's pre-eminence remained rooted in Whitehall. At James's side, however, were Robert Carr, Sir Thomas Lake and other councillors. Divided by personalities as well as issues, the Council now laboured under this further burden: in a fundamental way, the Council was functionally as well as physically divided. D. E. Hoak has suggested that in the 1550s the co-ordination of work between the Council that remained in Westminster and that attendant on the king 'placed an undeniable burden on both councillors and clerks'.[23] This remained true in 1613 when in administrative terms at least the king was so often on progress.

The only Acts of the Privy Council that have survived for this period begin in May 1613. Between May 1613 and June 1614, the month of Northampton's death, the attendance records provide an interesting picture of the process by which the Privy Council functioned. Almost all meetings of that period, seventy-five out of eighty-eight, were held at Whitehall, nine at Greenwich, two at Hampton Court. One convened at Northampton House, during Northampton's last illness, in February 1614. The rhythm of the meetings depended on the time of the year, more taking place in June and July, October and November and during Parliament time in March, April and May of 1614. Presumably the fact that James's Council remained at Westminster reflected the need to oversee the machinery of government. It also dictated who the central nucleus of its members were. Over these thirteen months, the attendance at meetings averaged close to ten (9.7) of the twenty-three members sworn to the Privy Council. Large numbers of members, as many as fifteen and sixteen, attended in Parliament time, in spring 1614. More often, however, the numbers who attended ranged from eight to twelve. Frequently meetings were held with fewer, often with only six or seven councillors present. Only twice did as few as five meet. This perhaps reflects Tudor policy, the rule established in 1553 that four councillors constituted a quorum, but six at least were necessary for 'a perfect conclusion and end of things'.[24]

Who, then, attended these meetings? The seven councillors who attended two-thirds of the recorded eighty-six meetings were the Archbishop of Canterbury, George Abbot, Lord Chancellor Ellesmere, Northampton, who was Lord Privy Seal, his nephew Lord Chamberlain Suffolk, Sir Julius Caesar, the Chancellor of the Exchequer, and the Household officials, William Knollys, the Treasurer of the Household, and Edward Wotton, the Comptroller. Another four councillors who attended more than half the meetings were Sir John Stanhope, Vice-Chamberlain and Treasurer of the Chamber, Edward Somerset, Earl of Worcester and Master of the Horse, William Herbert, Earl of Pembroke, and Edward, Lord Zouche. This composition is not unlike that of the Tudor Council under Edward VI and Elizabeth.[25]

The prominence of Northampton's position after Salisbury's demise is borne out not only by his attendance at Privy Council meetings, his extensive correspondence with Carr, Secretary Lake and the king himself, but also by the comments of observers. The Venetian ambassador, for instance, noted in 1612 that Northampton had become 'Lord Treasurer in petto and does almost all business in James's absence'.[26] His work on the treasury commission, which will be examined later in this chapter, overlapped with his work on the Council. Northampton frequently detailed conclusions from meetings of both bodies; often the treasury commission sat in the morning, the Council in the afternoon. Northampton's letters to Rochester provide an insider's view of the Privy Council, its processes as well as certain issues of policy and finances with which it wrestled.

In the early days of his convening the Privy Council, Northampton described his role rather mechanically, as 'only now a London pipe to convey the liquor which the Lords infuse (as I was before) which I hope will plead for me'. Northampton suffered from some difficulties in those early days, the lack of a quorum, of data and of a method to provide the king with the advice he wanted as rapidly as possible. The lack of councillors shows up repeatedly. In August 1612 Northampton asked the favourite to acquaint the king with their endeavours, 'though we now are present but three'. In the same month, when attendance was in fact normally low, he commented that the three chancellors and the Privy Seal made up all the company.[27] Returning from Greenwich to London to discuss some treaties as well as a new instruction of the king's to investigate the illegal transport of wool, Northampton could not find a single councillor at hand. He expressed hope that the Lord Chancellor and Caesar would join him. A few days later, business was being dispatched by 'those of the Council that are in town'. Yet the paucity of councillors appeared not only in the summer but in October as well. On an issue relating to the Savoy marriage proposals, Northampton wrote that 'the greater part of our fellows are out of town', and put off the matter until the king designated specific members to deal with it.[28]

Regarding the payment of English troops serving in France, the Council was unable to find the crucial document authorising continuance with pay. 'We find nothing on our side but tradition . . . a letter of the French king's to require a longer stay was once among the papers but surely by the tossing and transposing of the papers by the little Lord who made his own cabinet the treasury of the state's whole evidence and intelligencer (which no man ever either durst before his time attempt nor in his time reprove) is not now to be found by all the search that hath been made hitherto.' The result was that the Council reluctantly accepted the French interpretation of the treaty. 'We find no just cause to detain the shadow when the substance is fled,'[29] Northampton noted.

English government was still personal despite the bureaucratic innovations of the 1530s.[30] The difficulties imposed by the king's absence are apparent in Northampton's unhappy letters of August 1612 when it was clear that the king was not satisfied with the advice proffered by the Council on a trade dispute with the Spanish Netherlands. Northampton wrote to the favourite that he was much grieved, had expected approbation rather than censure and had done everything he could to gain intelligence on the question from English merchants. Northampton therefore needed intelligence of another sort, too, to understand the workings of the king's mind and the permutations of the court while it was away on progress. Thus he thanked Sir Thomas Lake, Second Secretary, for 'your last letter which was full of good advice and traced out a path which is fit for me to bear'.[31] Policy-makers then and now depend on information not only on issues but on personalities. It was not only in the Star Chamber that Northampton felt he was treading a slippery path.

The king proved impatient with the Council's advice in the early months after Salisbury's death. Northampton was abject. 'Could any man do more as the case stood with us that were not to create light but to convey that light which their experience should cast in so dark a business?' Casting about for a way to excuse this failure, Northampton fastened on the supposed failings of the Earl of Salisbury. The difficulties faced by the councillors without Salisbury were spelled out in letter after letter both overtly and subconsciously. Confused without him, Northampton blamed Salisbury for the inefficiency and deficiency of the Council, because he had usurped its functions. In a matter concerning Ireland, Northampton blamed Salisbury because he had not kept them informed. 'The little Lord was the cause of all this stir by some direction without the Council.'[32] But as Northampton got a greater grasp of the rhythm of issues, meetings, reports and discussion, he brought decision-making more under control and his criticism of Salisbury lessened.

The search for consensus was a very strong motif. Difficulties were thrashed out and if major disagreements continued members were selected to bring in the positive and negative sides of the argument. On this later hearing the board would make its decision and send it for confirmation to the king. Such was the process which extended over several meetings in deciding to call Parliament in 1614. A subcommittee was established to examine the matter and to report back. On issues of great importance, Northampton adopted the legalistic procedure of formal position papers listing the pros and cons of the project which then required answer from their opponents. At the end of this lengthy process which often lasted several sessions, the Council proffered its advice.

The Privy Council dealt with foreign ambassadors often in the same legalistic way, by argumentation and presentation of formal documentation. In a letter to Carr, Northampton described how 'Sir Noel Caron held us all the afternoon yesterday in points which included Greenland and the 3d surcharge' recently imposed on imports. Although many Dutch merchants accompanied Caron, Northampton boasted that 'we proved the possession to have been so properly our own . . . as he gave it over confessing plainly that he had been deceived'. Another matter of dispute 'was referred to certain on both sides . . . and the conclusion will then follow certainly'.

On the same day the Spanish ambassador came before the Lords of the Council to beg the release of a well-to-do Spanish woman arrested as an abbess along with five young women suspected of being probationers or nuns. After emphasising the importance of enforcing English law the Lords turned to the king for his pleasure. Northampton advised the king to grant the release speedily, but strictly as a matter of his own grace. In addition the councillors sent a proclamation to the printer and reported that the *Pearl*, a ship freighted with Indian goods, had been seized in Ireland. Northampton ended his despatch by saying that though it was long, it was 'yet indeed but a brief abstract of so many weighty businesses as are couched in a narrow room'.[33]

If outsiders sometimes attended meetings to petition the Lords, so too did the Lords call before them those who might provide useful advice. The difficulties faced by early modern administrators can be seen in the case of the ratio of gold to silver which proved a continuing problem affecting the outflow of bullion. Northampton asserted to Rochester that 'the Lords, the officers of the mint and others have laboured their wits and imparted their readiest stock of invention and observation . . . to stave the silver from transport and the state from penury'. Though the discussion had borne little fruit, Northampton asked Carr to assure the king that at his return 'we shall be able to deliver to his Majesty the uttermost of our conceits upon a subject so shrewdly snarled and entangled'. Northampton complained of the hard labour that left him bleary-eyed and his handwriting shaky.[34]

Frequently the issues presented to the councillors were minor. An altercation between the Venetian ambassador and a coachmaker whom he had neglected to pay came before Northampton. The Venetian secretary argued that the coachmaker should be tortured. Northampton committed the coachmaker briefly but said 'that must be the end of punishing' and he urged the coachmaker's wife to 'move her complaint humbly to the Council board who will take that order that shall be most agreeable to honour with equity'.[35]

The functions of the Privy Council were many and included foreign and domestic policy, matters of high estate and low comedy. Yet its institutional base was inadequate. Long-range planning gave way to short-term response. While coping with the king's finances in a major effort to get the City to extend credit, the Council was forced to put aside its work and see the French ambassador. Northampton wrote to the favourite in frustration: 'this day the French ambassador comes before the Lords and hinders our proceeding to the consideration of other causes recommended by the king. For we never receive any direction by rule that is not crossed by some springing occasion before unlooked for that must likewise be considered.'[36] Northampton's efforts, as we shall see, depended not so much as Salisbury's had on fundamental restructuring of the state's finances as the use of suasion, administrative reform, and pitting one interest group against another to bring about a sought-for conclusion.

To deal with important issues, Northampton had developed a legalistic procedure both to decide questions and perhaps to insulate himself from the king's demands for action and advice. He described such a procedure to Sir Thomas Lake in 1613: 'we have appointed a day wherein the proffers of the Spanish ambassador, which in show seem very fair, having been examined by conference before hand and after in his presence or his ministers with our merchants we shall be able to advertise his Majesty both what is solid and what is hollow.'[37] A closer scrutiny of Northampton's work on issues before the Privy Council reveals close attention to available facts, consultation with experts and those affected by the policy he formulated.

III. Ireland

James I reserved the making of foreign policy for himself and Salisbury. The Privy Council as a body appears to have had small part in its formulation. To be sure, Northampton was well informed, receiving reports from both the English ambassadors in Spain and in France. Drawing on these, he frequently invoked foreign policy considerations to influence decisions taken in Parliament, noting that foreign observers carefully monitored English politics. During his pre-eminence on the Council he dealt with routine matters concerning foreign ambassadors such as the Spanish envoy's smuggling in mass books for English Catholics. The most important Spanish sympathiser at the court, it is not clear what impact he actually had on policy-making; although Sir Charles Cornwallis wrote him frequently from Spain, his letters were often taken up as much with discussion of domestic issues as with diplomacy.[38] While he encouraged negotiations for the marriages of the king's children with Spain and with Savoy, Northampton was no doubt aware that the king preferred to handle these negotiations himself. In the latter instance he reported that 'I find the appetite of Savoy to be very sharp; if his purse be suitable the match may be prosperous. But his Majesty, who ever holdeth in his hand the balance of advised consideration, will choose by God's direction which I both pray and look for.'[39] Clearly, in matters like these Northampton and the other Lords of the Council awaited the king's direction.

In Ireland, King James replaced Elizabeth's policy of military conquest with peaceful colonisation. Northampton administered a policy that was at once pragmatic and moderate. In fact Northampton's work on Ireland presents in microcosm several aspects of his work on the Privy Council: the necessity as well as the difficulty of keeping hold of several threads of policy at once, the crucial importance of patronage in maintaining the links between minister and official, and the need for oversight of royal policy, once promulgated, which proved particularly difficult in Ireland. The plantation of Ulster and the Irish Parliament of 1613 provide excellent examples.

The Lord Deputy of Ireland was Sir Arthur Chichester, an extremely able official who came into office in 1605. Chichester presided over the establishment of the plantation of Ulster with words of warning to his superiors in London, repeatedly describing those actual conditions in Ireland which were to modify fond dreams of projectors and privy councillors. While it has been suggested that the king with Salisbury managed all foreign affairs, especially in Ireland,[40] Northampton became involved in

Irish affairs even before Salisbury's death. The editor of the *Calendar of State Papers Ireland* notes that many were addressed to Northampton, others passed through his hands. 'He was one of the Lords constantly in correspondence with the Deputy and the Council.'[41]

A striking aspect of Northampton's work as a privy councillor was his recruitment and support of able officials. It is therefore interesting to trace the establishment of a patronage relationship with Chichester which formed the basis of their mutual trust. Northampton developed close ties with the Lord Deputy about 1608 and promoted his career. He wanted to recommend him for the Presidency of Munster, but Chichester declined. Northampton favoured the Deputy's choice for the Bishop of Kilmore and Chichester placed friends of Northampton's in positions in Ireland. In 1609 Chichester wrote to Northampton that 'I was never so much beholding and bound for favour received to any lord or other great personages'. Northampton not only received messages from Chichester's servants but 'do sometimes call upon them to remember you in whatsoever concerns me and therein to give your gracious furtherance far beyond my expectation or dessert'.[42]

Chichester noted that 'a common wealth is nothing more than a commercement or continual suppeditation of benefits mutually received and done between men'.[43] This might suggest that little more was involved here than the private stroking of courtiers. This is too limited a view. Indeed the necessary nexus of early modern administration was created by appropriate rewards for those in the king's service. Chichester spelled out this version of the political contract in asking for favour for Sir Edward Brabazon, 'an ancient councillor of this state, for the space of thirty years or thereabouts, in all which time he hath yet received neither entertainment nor reward (notwithstanding his attendance and service in most of the consultations and expeditions from the beginning)'. In return for the transformation of his lands into free and common socage, 'in recompense of all his former services', Chichester promised that Brabazon would rest more contented and 'the more encouraged to continue in the same during the rest of his life'.[44] Throughout his official correspondence Chichester combined his relation of governmental problems with continuing concern for his own standing with the Council and with Somerset. Thus, as much as the privy councillor, the successful official needed continually to jockey for position.

Having established a strong tie with Chichester, Northampton looked to him not only for the administration of royal policy but also for advice on its formulation. The issues they dealt with ranged from the continuing problem of piracy, the recruitment of soldiers for continental warfare, Irish rebels and royal proclamations. In one case Chichester sent back a proclamation with his reasons and those of his Council for staying it; an official such as Chichester had the leeway to advise change or reject policy of the privy councillors who were a long way off in London.[45] Nowhere was this clearer than in the matter of the plantation of Ulster. Chichester, with extraordinary clarity fostered by his presence in Ireland, predicted the problems and suggested some solutions for that major undertaking. Both he and Northampton consistently stressed the need for administrative oversight to ensure that the undertakers carried out the policies drawn up by the Council.

The plantation of Ulster was a counterpart to the plantation of Virginia. Both plantations promised unrealistic reward; both were undertaken by ill-prepared settlers; both had to cope with native people who were perceived as essentially alien. In the case of Ireland the large indigenous population and critical religious differences between the settlers and the Irish posed as many problems as in the New World. The Privy Council attempted to provide guidance but the limitations of early modern administration made it frustrating and difficult.[46]

Northampton himself had begun a consideration of such a plantation during Elizabeth's reign. Discussing 'rules to reduce the state of Ireland to obedience', he suggested the establishment of a colony which would provide benefits to Irish and English alike. It would 'draw all the wild Irish that dwell now dispersed in woods... or wander up and down without any certain dwelling, to dwell in towns ensconced, to suffer themselves to be united to the English by law and mutual commerce and trade and to set them to husbandry'. This optimistic vision promised a variety of benefits to the English, too. First of all it was a way of disburdening England of many poor families. It thus provided an answer to the chronic problem of over-population and underemployment. Secondly, Northampton argued that the distribution of lands would make younger brothers and men of courage not only adventure willingly but fight bravely. Finally, such a colony would renew decayed trade with English merchants and bring prosperity to corporate towns. To those who argued against it because it would breed great changes in Ireland, Northampton answered that the plan would take only the lands that were in the hands of rebels.[47]

Once in office Northampton continued this interest. His usual procedure was to tap the views of those with expert knowledge and his papers from the period 1607–9 contain 'certain notes... touching... colonies' which argued that the use of English husbandry in Ireland, that is, a stable form of agriculture, would permit easier control by the central government, much the same point as he himself had made some years earlier. This writer contemplated that the English could take over two-thirds of Ulster. Northampton collected other briefs on trade, and 'the present state of Ireland' in 1612.[48]

While Chichester's main contact in the early years of the reign was Salisbury, he was in close touch too with Northampton and spelled out to both the difficulties with the policy adopted for Ulster which treated Ireland as a 'white sheet of paper'. Chichester had come to believe after several years in office in the importance of safeguarding the property rights of the Irish. In a letter of 1608, he called for the interspersion of numerous small Irish free-holders among the British and pointed out that the cost of creating such a settlement would be one-tenth of what it had cost to pacify Ireland during Tyrone's rebellion from 1598 to 1603. Chichester lost this policy campaign, as important as any on the battlefield. In September 1610, when the Council adopted the plan to remove the Irish from parts of Ulster, Chichester wrote a strongly worded letter to Salisbury and a month later a similar one to Northampton. Complimenting him on his choice of 'undertakers' for the plantation, Chichester went on to iterate his own deepseated concern: first that those who had come in person were not the men to perform the difficult business, for 'to displant the natives who are a warlike people, out of the greatest part of six whole counties, is not the work for private men who seek present profit'.[49] Chichester put his finger on what was at once both the motor and the brake of early modern government: the integral connection of policy and profit, a theme Northampton developed independently in his own investigations. Secondly, Chichester argued that in the distribution of land 'the natives and servitors were greatly neglected'. He had thought that at least half of each county should be left to the Irish, but in fact they had been often left with much less. The result, the Lord Deputy thought all too accurately, was to cause great discontent and provoke rebellion.[50] Chichester's views then coincided with Northampton's under Elizabeth I.

But the policy pursued had been established before Northampton's dominance of the Privy Council. After Salisbury's death one of the myriad problems that faced Northampton was to implement the effort to colonise, settle and develop Ulster. Here the Privy Council indeed ran into problems similar to the settlement of Virginia: the failure of colonists to cultivate the land adequately, to construct fortified buildings and to establish friendly relations with the inhabitants.[51] Chichester argued that the undertakers should be required to come to Ireland in person. Furthermore, he asked that a commission of oversight be sent out to survey the work of the plantation. It would encourage those that had carried out the work and let the king know whom to punish for contempt of his directions. Problems with the undertakers continued to mark the plantation. In the 1620s, the Council was still trying to exercise oversight from afar with only middling success, undermined by war with Spain in the later 1620s.[52] In the 1630s the Earl of Strafford's attempt to implement some of Chichester's recommendations provoked widespread discontent.

The Privy Council also had to reckon with the Irish Parliament of 1613. The session broke up in disorder over accusations of court packing because the king had created forty new boroughs to give the Protestant undertakers control of the lower House. The recusant representatives refused to accept the speaker prearranged by the Lord Deputy and staged a walkout on the proceedings so that Parliament could not be organised.[53] When the Lords followed suit the Privy Council under Northampton's direction asked that a delegation explain themselves. While Chichester worried that force would be required to secure an orderly Parliament, Northampton took a different tack, listening patiently to the wide range of official abuses they complained of. He shaped a small workman-like committee of four to investigate with one of its members, Sir Charles Cornwallis, reporting directly to himself.[54]

Despite the rhetoric of the god-like magistrate so often heard, particularly in Star Chamber, the privy councillors did not crack down ferociously on the recalcitrant Irish Lords and burgesses. These were, after all, the people with whom they had to work. While supporting Chichester's authority Northampton took seriously the possibility that Chichester's officials might have abused their power. One of the secret instructions to the commission, therefore, was to investigate such abuses:

> in case his name or countenance have been abused by others put in trust, upon notice taken he may give redress; and beside, in the secret instructions to be put into the hands of the commissioners that shall go, one chief point shall be to examine the true state of that perplexed business that the Lords upon their information may give satisfaction to any grief that in the mean time shall not be cured.[55]

Northampton understood that the redress of grievances was crucial to the defence of authority.

Chichester laid out his defence in a lengthy letter to the commissioners in November 1613, claiming credit for 'the reformation of manners and barbarous customs . . . and [making] the king's writs and laws to run current throughout the land'. Furthermore, he argued that imposing the oath of supremacy, reforming religion and preparing for Parliament had engendered the opposition reflected in the petitions, as he had forewarned Salisbury when the policy was developed. He emphasised also the necessity of supporting the magistrates. 'Our lives are . . . to be subjected unto a multitude that will regard nothing but their own wills if magistrates shall be deprived of their honour and due respects'.[56] The King and Council, in almost all respects backed up the Lord Deputy, chastised the recusants but, significantly, also declared invalid some of the new corporations, which had been at the centre of the controversy. As a result the Parliament was recalled and settled down to work without the resort to force that Chichester had feared would be necessary. Northampton deserves some of the credit for the peaceful and fruitful resolution of this crisis. Of constitutional significance, James's concessions shrewdly protected his right to make new boroughs and the legality of virtual representation which had been challenged by the Irish delegation.[57]

But the fundamental problems in Ireland remained. Chichester wrote that 'there hath no treasure arrived here in specie since February last'. He labelled it 'a great error of state indeed' in letters to Northampton and to Sir Julius Caesar, Chancellor of the Exchequer. With little or no money, the populace had been reduced to a barter economy in corn and cattle. Without pay, the soldiers had been preying on the population.[58]

In short, the issue of money or rather its lack proved to be critical in

Ireland as in Jacobean policy generally. While Northampton dominated the Council it was the key question to which he addressed himself, the central issue to which all the strands of policy were inextricably tied. If the Privy Council had to deal with a peripatetic king who demanded policy decisions, the presentation of an ideology which exalted the role of magistrates and the omnicompetence of the Council without workable bureaucratic mechanisms to back up its authority, the central problem was that of financing government. In the period of Northampton's dominance, the Council sought out projects to fill the king's coffers. As the work of Star Chamber overlapped with that of the Council, so the work of the treasury, put into commission by James after Salisbury's death, overlapped with the Council. Northampton was at the centre of both.

IV.   Finances

The great financial straits in which James's government found itself appear vividly in Northampton's description of the Council's negotiation with City lenders to finance the royal debt. Without a national bank, the Crown was forced to resort to short-term loans primarily from prominent merchants at high interest which constantly had to be rolled over. The relationship was symbiotic. The awesomeness of Stuart government so apparent in Privy Council pronouncements does not appear in these negotiations. Describing his 'Herculean labour' Northampton stressed how difficult it was to change the date due on the loan repayment, particularly because the previous time repayment had been delayed, the king promised it would be the last. 'The little wit and oratory gift that some of us had in struggling against humble but yet peremptory negatives was hardly able to keep out the force by which they wrought upon our former engagements.' The councillors managed to rearrange payment by having the customs farmers cover the debt, but only after much persuasion, urging on them the chaos they would bring upon both king and state. Northampton asserted that James had contrived 'some secret courses' rather than fail to perform his promise. His point was not to suggest the king's resort to arbitrary taxation. Rather, the king would put himself 'into a greater strait than any man conceives rather than his word should faint in case their repugnancy had been invincible'.

The lesson that Northampton drew from his meeting was the necessity for 'his Majesty beholding into how great strait these heavy debts do lead may hereafter crush the seeds and bruise the motives that induce these degrees of perplexities'. And he added that 'without some better care than hath been taken to stop these endless leaks that make the ship less able to live in a broken sea and to maintain herself against those necessary storms which kingdoms must accept as accidents inevitable it is not possible for the king's estate to be either secure or happy'.[59]

This encounter points up two major issues that the Council had to deal with: on the one hand ways to increase the royal revenue and on the other to cut unnecessary expenditure. Throughout the reign Northampton took an important part in dealing with both, by the development of new means of revenue and, as a treasury commissioner and administrative reformer, carefully examining and seeking to change the spending patterns of Jacobean government. Since these activities were at the centre of his work as a privy councillor, they will be dealt with at length in succeeding chapters, but his approach is considered in general here.

How could the Jacobean privy councillor raise the necessary money to supply the deficit that inflation, a large family and an unfettered royal hand had produced? For the king could not, as was traditionally hoped, 'live of his own'.[60] Several means which immediately suggested themselves proved inadequate. The first, parliamentary subsidy, had proven unequal to needs even when Parliament voted it. In a system in which assessment was made by neighbours, subsidies tended to fall short of expectations and that little was made even less by inflation.[61] The sale of royal lands always brought in money but as it cut down on future revenues from rent, was essentially self-defeating. Yet the Privy Council wavered between tying up royal lands in entail so that they could not be touched and breaking into that legal piggy bank to meet current expenses. Northampton noted that 'we that have forborne thus long to sell anything at all will be cautious in reserving whatsoever present necessity doth not extort'.[62] Even he, however, was forced to sell royal lands.

Northampton was concerned with finances both as a councillor and as a treasury commissioner. Chamberlain noted his appointment in June 1612, and added, 'he is willing the state of the revenue ... should be thoroughly looked into, before he meddle withal, and then he to be accountable only for the time forward that he enters upon it'.[63] While Northampton was Lord Treasurer in all but name the Council raised money through an aid on the occasion of Princess Elizabeth's marriage, collected money due on the knighting of Prince Henry despite the fact that he was dead, and even tried to make money from goods seized from private ships such as the *Pearl* and *Peppercorn* freighted with riches from the East Indies.[64] No stone was left unturned.

But most promising were the projects. It is a mistake to assume that projects, proposals, both imaginative and venal, to raise royal revenues, were an alternative to the Great Contract. Projects were typical of the Tudor–Stuart state;[65] in investigating projects between 1612 and 1614, Northampton was in fact continuing a policy of Salisbury's. Historians have often treated projects as if they were merely created for the financial benefit of highly placed courtiers. Many did provide a cover for extortion, such as the alehouse patent. Others proved irritants to the landed gentry, such as those for concealed lands which should have been paying the king rent but were not. The use of informers to enforce the law, the sharing of profits from judicial proceedings, in short the intimate connection of private profit and public policy were, of course, characteristic of the period.[66] It is necessary to remember, however, the strain under which the Council laboured to provide some new revenues to cover the king's expenses. Projects promised and sometimes achieved the diversification and expansion of home industries.

Northampton's own painstaking attentions to such suggestions are found in his annotation of the collection of projects in Cotton manuscript Titus B V, ranging from John Keymer's well-known projects for encouraging home manufactures and fishing to others urging the cultivation of diverse thistles for cloth manufactures, the offer of French undertakers to transmute iron into steel and even a project involving coneyskins.[67] Northampton annotated these and others including those on starch and the farms of the customs on sweet wines with which he was connected. It is not extraordinary to see Northampton's blocky handwriting on projects of even marginal significance. Without a formal administrative structure he was forced to evaluate, enforce and oversee policy all at the same time. Making a virtue out of necessity, early modern officials made use of the projector's self-interest to raise money for the Crown and even to streamline government operations. At least this was the fond hope. But Northampton emphasised the importance of checking the feasibility and political implications of the varied projects that came before him. In the case of one concerning furnaces, Northampton encapsulated in a letter to Salisbury the difficulties of early modern administration. A patent had recently been granted to a group of projectors which Northampton had previously promised to

a poor man . . . upon approvement of his travail by such persons as were of experience in the faculty. . . . My Lord Knyvet having the diligent examination of the matter referred to him by the king gave good allowance to this invention more than six months past whereupon no doubt the patent had found passage often times but that my meaning was to call the brewers and the dyers for a proof, before I put it to a point if I had not been diverted by the perplexities of a parliament.[68]

This example suggests that the king tried to ensure some review of patents, that Northampton made it a practice to consult those with knowledge about the problems before him and that the pressure of business on the privy councillors without adequate administrative departments ensured that some matters were put aside without decision.

In making major policy decisions Northampton always consulted those whose interests were affected. His procedure can be traced not only in position papers in the state papers but in private letters, particularly on those projects that he concerned himself with, such as Cockayne's project, farthing tokens and alum.

The great question of dressing and dyeing cloth within the land came to be heard at great length and with strong instance on both sides before the Lords; every one receiving great contentment by the full liberty which was admitted of effectual and pithy discourse to every man that was either prepared or disposed to argue.

Those in favour of the project forecast an increase in customs and promised a contribution of £20,000. The other side argued that its adoption would stay much of the trade and thereby destroy the livings of many families; they doubted the skill and industry of those that dyed and dressed cloth within England and asked that provincial clothiers be heard before the clothworkers and dyers that advocated the plan be credited. The last point suggested a division along regional lines that resembled that between the outports and London on matters of trade. Those who favoured the project replied lauding the skill of English workers and concluded 'that the benefit would be as great and much greater to the subject by transporting cloth to the very points (dyed and dressed at home) which now bought them of the Merchant Adventurers'.[69]

In fact, Cockayne and his people proved unable to sell their cloth in former markets. Northampton had not accepted the blithe assurances of the projectors but insisted on hearing all sides. A subcommittee was set up to confer with the interested parties.[70]

The purpose here is not to detail the negotiations over the Cockayne project for which Northampton was not primarily responsible but rather to suggest the sort of issues with which the Council wrestled and how Northampton attempted to solve them. If it be asked why the Council focused on such schemes one cogent answer is given by a tract advocating several different projects to increase the royal revenue. 'Whatsoever you abate or approve at home comes out of your subjects' purse and if it be never so just is hardly drawn from them without clamour or murmur but what you catch or win out of the seas or work and fetch out of the earth magnifies the glory and wisdom of the state and infinitely enriches your kingdom and people who will then be as ready to requite this your gracious care with full hands.'[71]

With the consideration of farthing tokens to replace small silver coins or tradesmen's tokens, the Council culled historical precedents, compared contemporary usage in other countries including Spain, France, Italy and the Low Countries, and collected tracts that emphasised the need to prevent the export of silver. Gerard de Malynes, an assay master and one of the major participants in the well-known debate of 1622–3 on the causes of the trade depression, blamed the outflow of bullion on erroneous valuations by merchants who influenced the mint and urged recoinage. He was an active proponent of the farthing project and, in fact, became one of the farmers of Lord Harrington's project for farthing tokens. Malynes's activities as writer, adviser and projector are characteristic of the Jacobean court, illustrating that project literature needs to be read not merely as a bundle of get-rich-quick schemes but also as efforts to improve the English economy. The ill-fate of many suggests the limits of economic expertise and the problems of economic structure in the period as much as corrupt motives. Northampton, to whom Malynes dedicated one of his tracts, responded cautiously. When the patent for farthing tokens was about to be awarded to Lord Harrington to cover his debts, Northampton insisted that their use be voluntary and the king reserve some of the profit for himself.[72]

The alum works was a project that provoked continual interest among privy councillors ever hopeful of profit, but those hopes were invariably dashed as farmers and merchants came and went, each group claiming it would enrich the king. Northampton's approach was as reasoned and cautious as usual. Although Sir Arthur Ingram was his client Northampton insisted that he and the other projectors 'give sufficient assurance for the whole works and for the whole time, that the king be not cast in an arrear upon a trick . . . and withal, that skilful surveyors that do thoroughly understand the craft be selected to attend their operation with a continual and watchful care that there be no lavish or hurtful waste made of the materials and that the full quantity be performed that is promised'.[73] As the leading commissioner for the treasury, Northampton sifted many such proposals. His analysis of these projects always emphasised careful oversight and measured political implications. Often he called for commissioners to certify the value of the project. Moreover, Northampton repeatedly added up the figures of the royal revenue and the royal expenditures, no doubt hoping each time they would tell a different tale.[74] They did not.

The second prong of Northampton's attack on the problem of finance was to investigate and oversee government spending. These problems were recognised early in the reign. Archbishop Matthew Hutton wrote to Northampton about the slow payment of the first subsidy of James's reign, arguing that it was caused 'by reason of the excessive wasting of the treasure of this kingdom, which if it should continue, England is like to be the poorest kingdom in Europe and the chief blame will be laid upon you great councillors . . . now it hath pleased God to make you a great councillor of state and the best learned of any especially'.[75] Financial difficulties had, of course, plagued Elizabeth, especially in her last decade when the cost of war on the Continent and in Ireland had far outrun her revenues. James and his ministers had to deal with those debts as well as a larger Household and continuing inflation.

Northampton agreed with Hutton. For his part he launched investigations of government offices and insisted that oversight be exercised in the dispensing of royal patronage and projects. As a treasury commissioner he continued to press such investigations, reviving the naval commission in 1613. Moreover, he requested a survey of the king's revenue and disbursement as well as a list of officeholders and rewards. Most strikingly, the free gifts to the Scots were extraordinarily large, as much as £11,000 to Rochester.[76] The king continued to dispense favour with an open hand, to the despair of his administrators.

While a treasury commissioner, Northampton drew up an extensive memorandum analysing how expenditures could be reduced and revenues improved. He kept a careful eye on the Household. He noted that 'the sum of £4,000 which the Lords presumed would abate in pensions . . . is very likely to be made good . . . so as his Majesty be pleased to abstain from granting reversions, from exchanging old lives for young, and from giving any new, till the gross which is now too heavy for the state, be drawn down to that moderation which the state itself can bear without any such waste as is now found in the treasure'. This £4,000 of course was little compared to what the king was giving away. Furthermore, the Lords suggested that £5,000 would have been saved 'by the care and diligence of the king's officers in Household . . . if a new charge of £1,200 had not been raised in the stable'.[77]

Such savings depended on the king's willingness not to dispense favour lightly. Thus the Lords urged once again that 'new grants not grounded upon just causes nor reasons justifiable by the law shall be reviewed by his Majesty's learned counsel who out of their judgement will observe what may be spared for the king's benefit'. And they asked the king to have a special look at the Wardrobe and to compare expenditures with those under Elizabeth. This was a veiled attack on the administration of James, Lord Hay, later Earl of Carlisle, one of the most extravagant of James's Scottish favourites. Furthermore, Northampton, in noting the difficulty of controlling pensions, called for the establishment of a subcommittee to examine the book of fees and pensions in the Exchequer, Duchy of Lancaster and various government departments. He emphasised the particular difficulty of controlling government spending without sound accounting practices when 'pensions paid privately . . . are not recorded in the receipt but taken from the receivers or farmers whereupon it happens that the receipt is never certain but falls short of the sum expected'.[78]

In his survey Northampton held out conditional hope of 'improvements not in being but depending'. On the keeping of old castles and their grounds, the treasury commissioners urged the king to abstain from granting such reversions since so many had already been distributed. Northampton's views had obviously changed with experience in office since he had urged the king in 1604 to grant the keeping of Carlisle castle to Sir Henry Lee. By 1613, the Lords in Commission were counting on every bit they could get their hands on. There were other possibilities but they were always tempered by legal obligations and political expediency.

Northampton was acutely attuned to the political significance of modes of raising money. Increased profits might be made from Crown lands, for instance, but only if carried out with political acumen. Enclosure, he thought, should come at the suit of the tenants and was careful to argue that the casual profits (from Crown lands) might be rented out only so long as subjects were not oppressed.[79] He did think that copyholders would be willing to give 'between thirty and fifty years' profit of the ancient rent according to the nature of the soil so that they might have fines certain'. In return they would receive both the king's assent and confirmation by Parliament. Northampton wrote, too, that 'wards sold to best advantage may improve £50,000 more than before: a higher strain will cause great clamour'. Far from arguing for arbitrary taxation, Northampton quite literally urged royal officials 'to feel the pulse of the subject'.[80]

Time, distance and institutional inadequacy posed great difficulties to the Privy Council. Northampton was often frustrated, particularly between 1612 and 1614, in handling the issues that the king in his absence pressed his councillors to answer. This chapter has examined aspects of the issues that confronted the Council. How then were they decided? How were solutions to the king's pressing problems generated? The king himself suggested one of the difficulties later when he told the Parliament of 1621 of projects that 'each had as fair a face'. One way was through an informal structure which grew up to fulfil necessary functions which still had no administrative basis in the early seventeenth-century state. Much as patronage provided for the needs of social and political bonding and recruitment for government office, so too an individual councillor like Northampton established his own 'brains trust', first, to advise him on policy matters the king had laid before the Council, secondly, to generate solutions particularly to the massive financial problems that the Crown faced and thirdly, to administer these solutions, either through the establishment of reform commissions or by bringing gifted individuals into government. The next several chapters show how Northampton, with the help of experts, struggled with the lethargy of early modern bureaucracy and the vested interests that challenged him. Finally, we shall see the structure of thinking that shaped and at times limited the advice such experts gave.

Chapter 6

Advisers on Policy: Scholars and Officeholders

How governments make policy is a question that excites the interest not only of historians and political scientists, but of ordinary citizens who must bear the consequences. To answer it requires going beyond formal acts and proclamations to look at the process by which decisions are made. This is difficult to discover in the early modern period, but Northampton's career provides a particularly useful lens through which to examine policy-making. The Jacobean Privy Council with its omnicompetent jurisdiction had to construct policy on a variety of issues without the advice of govern-ment departments or permanent under-secretaries. To bridge this institu-tional gap, Northampton created an informal group of advisers, a 'brains trust', made up of scholars, merchants and officeholders, to advise him on issues that came before the Council and arose in the several offices he held. By analysing the sorts of questions Northampton asked and the answers he received, it is possible to discover the range of advice available to a seven-teenth-century government as well as the attitudes that shaped that advice and at times limited its usefulness.

Northampton's selection of merchants and officeholders as advisers does not surprise; their knowledge about areas of the administration and the economy is obvious. But his choice of the antiquary as expert requires explanation.[1] The new status accorded to antiquaries was the result of the emergence of history as a discipline in the late sixteenth and early seven-teenth centuries. The study of history had become fashionable and import-ant in England for a variety of reasons: the new political rhetoric of policy shaped by Cromwell under Henry VIII, the exaltation of the common law, the reception of Italian and French historical writings, the appearance of an educated public eager for the fruits of antiquarian research, and even the grasping for social prestige. Historical activity was further spurred on by the development of Anglo-Saxon studies. In the 1560s royal officials, in particular William Cecil and Archbishop Matthew Parker, began collecting the manuscripts loosed by the dissolution of the monasteries. The circles around Cecil and Parker developed the tools to read and understand the documents and began to investigate Anglo-Saxon history. Parker used these studies to underpin the Elizabethan church settlement by arguing that it represented a return to the original English Church.[2] Social developments also intensified interest in historical study. Genealogy and heraldry became popular in the second half of the century, providing means to respectability.

The independent power the landed interest enjoyed before the Tudors was in the process of becoming transmuted into coats of arms, crests and family history.

But despite two generations of historical work, of Leland and Bale and Nowell, it was only with the establishment of the Society of Antiquaries in the 1580s that this diffuse field of inquiry became a discipline. Formed by a group of lawyers, record keepers, heralds and country gentlemen in the wake of the publication of William Camden's *Britannia*, the Society was the first 'learned society' in England.[3] Camden's *Britannia*, a history of Britain informed by the critical method of the Renaissance humanists and legal historians, and based on original documents, provided the paradigm, the 'concrete artefact' in Kuhnian terms, which established the Society's tradition, the questions to be asked and the methods by which to probe the answers to the origins of England's institutions. From the late 1580s to the early years of James's reign, the Society met during term-time and considered questions and presented papers on the history of English institutions, following the direction pointed by *Britannia*. The antiquaries' central quest was for origins and the method they adopted was a critical one. They used original sources, whether documents or relics, weighed conflicting evidence and fell back on conjecture only when their sources gave out.

This organisation of antiquaries shaped a new role for the historian which was to outlast the Society itself. Its professional nature found reflection in a petition for incorporation as a library and research body at the end of Elizabeth's reign.[4] The suggestion, predating the establishment of the British Museum by over a hundred years, points to a new relationship between the government and the antiquary, not merely the administrator or the propagandist but the 'expert'. For this scholarly community represented a pool of easily accessible information about traditional solutions to public problems. Several scholars eagerly drew up papers on royal institutions, provided precedents on questions before the Privy Council and suggested solutions to fiscal mismanagement. From the standpoint of history the scholars sought answers to contemporary financial questions in the annals of mediaeval kings. In this way they were not far different from contemporaries who sat in the House of Commons; often indeed they were themselves MPs. The attitudes and procedures of the Society of Antiquaries are particularly relevant to this study since several of its members provided advice to Northampton, among them his most important aide, Sir Robert Cotton.

Northampton had an understandable affinity with the scholars of his day. As we have seen, he had lectured for several years at Cambridge on rhetoric and civil law, composed discourses on a variety of historical, philosophical and religious topics and published a work against astrology. During James's reign he became High Steward of Oxford and Lord Chancellor of Cambridge. Often called the most learned noble in the land, Northampton was known for his patronage of scholars. It is little wonder then that he sought information and advice from his friends in the Society of Antiquaries. That

Northampton was a member seems unlikely; that he drew upon the skills and libraries of its members there can be no doubt.

I

Sir Robert Cotton, a founding member of the Society of Antiquaries, was the earl's closest adviser. Born in 1571 into an old gentry family of Huntingdon, Cotton attended Westminster School where he began a lifelong friendship with William Camden. Graduating from Jesus College, Cambridge, in 1585, Cotton divided his time between his country estate in Connington, Huntingdonshire, and his London house close to Westminster. He went on expeditions with Camden to collect artefacts of Roman Britain; helped edit the fifth edition of *Britannia*; revised John Speed's *History of England*, supplying the volume with notes on Henry VIII's reign; maintained a wide correspondence with the leading scholars of his day; and built his library into a national resource, providing information both to the Privy Council and Parliament.

While the Cotton collection was very strong in Anglo-Saxon works, its great strength lay in the extraordinary number of Tudor state documents it contained.[5] The government recognised the importance of Cotton's library. George Calvert, Secretary of State, wrote to Cotton in 1620 that the Privy Council, in looking for past treaties between Denmark and England, had found some missing and wondered if Cotton had them. Calvert added that Cotton had to be at the Council chamber with 'precedents of present use or we are all undone'.[6] How the antiquary had got his hands on such important documents is not completely clear, but record keeping in the first half of the sixteenth century was quite slipshod, decentralised among many departments, the records left to the mercy of damp and vermin. Under Elizabeth the records were centralised and record keepers installed to maintain the collections, draw up catalogues and write histories of departments.[7] Many were close friends of Cotton's, and manuscripts were freely loaned back and forth between government office and Cotton's library. Sir Edward Coke, the eminent jurist, for one, requested Cotton to 'send unto me certain of those records which you have found in the Tower that I may compare them with mine, we having all one end to find out truth'.[8] When Arthur Agarde, Deputy Chamberlain in the Exchequer, died, leaving his private collection of manuscripts to Cotton, representations were made to keep Cotton from influencing the selection of a new keeper of records because of the documents Cotton had already got hold of.[9] However he had amassed his collection, Cotton was generous in making his library available to others, including some leading officials.

Cotton's loan lists are a roll call of the political and intellectual elite of early seventeenth-century England. While the Earl of Salisbury borrowed manuscripts concerning foreign affairs,[10] the manuscripts that Northampton borrowed reflected the whole range of questions that came before him both in his offices and as a privy councillor. Thus several concerned the Earl Marshal's office and the heralds, what Cotton described as 'my book of all taxations, loans, and subsidies since the Conquest to Henry VIII drawn out of old stories and records', a packet of projects and means to increase the revenue in the time of King Philip and Queen Mary, and 'my red book of parliaments'. Others included documents concerning the University of Cambridge, leases in Ireland, as well as Lambarde's Saxon Laws, Knighton's ecclesiastical histories, Taverner's *The Tree of the Commonwealth*, a book on Spain from 1568–78 and one on the navy written in 1585.[11] Cotton himself used his library as the basis of his work for Northampton. In one case, it will be seen, he supplemented a proposal with hundreds of original documents.

In the years between 1603 and 1614 when Cotton served as Northampton's adviser, he used his antiquarian skills both to support government policy and to reform government practice. In fact, their connection had been formed earlier. Cotton was probably one of those Northampton called on for aid in preparing his tract for Essex on the office of Earl Marshal in 1597. In his memorandum on the office, prepared in 1602 when Howard was named to the subcommittee to investigate the office, Cotton noted: 'thus much I have hastily gathered, not knowing by your paper which way you labour to fortify. Receive this as part of more debt, if you give me longer day I will pay you.'[12] Cotton fortified many of the government positions that it fell to Northampton to present. But Cotton's role went beyond that of propagandist. His usefulness to the government was summed up in Northampton's letter when Cotton lay ill. 'I will not cease to call upon God by endless prayer for your perfect recovery which shall not only make me happy in a worthy friend but my master . . . in an industrious servant and the whole state in an active and sufficient minister.'[13] The extent of Northampton's ties with Cotton is enormous and many areas such as patronage and parliamentary connections find their place in other chapters. Here I want to focus on the kind of questions that Northampton posed to Cotton and other antiquaries, the sorts of advice they proffered, and the framework within which these were constructed.

II

'The Somerset House Conference', the group portrait of the commissioners for the Treaty of London ending the Anglo-Spanish war, is the first of its kind in English portraiture.[14] For Northampton, it was one of the first public occasions in the reign in which he took a prominent role. Cotton served as his adviser on the negotiations from the beginning of the reign. When James I came to the throne he was committed to peace with Spain. The war begun in 1587 had lasted for the rest of Elizabeth's reign and had become a long-drawn-out one of attrition in support of the Dutch who had rebelled against their Spanish overlords. It constituted a major drain on the Crown's resources. While politically popular and profitable to some in the City and at court, it seriously strained the slender royal financial resources. Of several issues that had to be decided at peace negotiations, the most important and most intractable was the right to trade to the East and West Indies. In particular the English very much desired to augment the profits begun in their privateering raids on the West Indies; the Spanish were no less eager to prevent it.[15] In 1604 representatives of Spain and the Archduke of the Spanish Netherlands met with delegates from the English Privy Council: Thomas, Lord Buckhurst, the Lord Treasurer, Charles Howard, Earl of Nottingham, the Lord Admiral, Charles Blount, Earl of Devonshire, Robert Cecil, Viscount Cranbourne, and Henry Howard, Earl of Northampton. The commissioners settled down to months of bargaining. In a pattern that was to become familiar in the Council and in Parliament, Cecil and Howard led the negotiations.

Cotton's work for Northampton during the Spanish peace treaty negotiations serves as an exemplar of their frequent contacts. Northampton asked for advice: in response Cotton drew up analyses and provided the materials for Northampton's speeches; in other cases he was even to work on their publication. He created the structure for Northampton's public performance. But Northampton was not content merely to read Cotton's words. Where he went beyond his brief is of some interest as well.

On the question of making peace, Robert Cecil might well have been of two minds; it has been suggested that he was patron to several of those involved in privateering expeditions in the West Indies and may even have had a financial stake in such raids.[16] Making peace, then, would mean that such ventures would no longer have the protection of the Crown. Yet Cecil supported James's desire for peace, and by accepting a Spanish pension after the conference mitigated any such losses. Northampton had long been a Spanish sympathiser; in the wake of the negotiations he, too, became a Spanish pensioner. Juan de Tassis, one of the Spanish envoys, claimed that he had been of great help.[17] What this meant in concrete terms is not clear, but Northampton's prejudices would come as no surprise either to the king or Cecil, the shapers of English foreign policy.

Northampton's prominent part in the negotiations must be sought in the role he played in the new government. Pro-Spanish and pro-Catholic in sympathy, Northampton was completely loyal to James, who had restored his family to power and given the aging aristocrat office and estate long denied him. In return, his value to the Protestant king lay in part in his visibility as a Catholic, willing to serve any government cause even when papal authority or English Catholics were on trial. Moreover, Northampton's patronage of Catholics helped keep them loyal to the state. By appointing Northampton to the commission, the government gained a twofold advantage: it gave the appearance of being willing to conciliate Spain, while at the

same time availing itself of a civilian able to counter Spanish legal and theological arguments.

Well known for his learning and oratorical skills, Northampton took a
prominent role at the Somerset House Conference in spelling out Crown
policy in language steeped in classics and mediaeval precedent. Indeed it
was Northampton, no doubt appointed by Cecil, who provided the lengthy
exploration of English claims to trade with the Indies over which negotiations almost broke down. But he had already explored the prospects for
peace earlier in the reign.

Northampton was in favour of peace. In a letter to Sir Charles Cornwallis he
emphasised that the Spanish were on the edge of exhaustion: 'though it be
true, that by war we are as poor as they, that the realm would give no more, the
revenue could afford no more, and that the queen sold her land by lumps, yet
all are now persuaded, that without a peace the King of Spain would have
resigned up into the king's hands his whole dominions.'[18] Northampton
solicited the views of others on the issue in 1603, among them Robert Cotton.
The first piece, dated June 1603, three months after the new government was
in office, argued the historical justness of the Netherlanders' war. 'Those that
are versed in reading of histories' knew that the Netherlands had in ancient
times been ruled by no monarchy but by an aristocratic government. Indeed
Philip II was contracted to govern them 'after their good old customs, charters
and privileges'. When the king tried to rule them absolutely and to impose the
Spanish Inquisition, contrary to those customs and privileges, there was
disorder to which the Spanish had responded by executing both rich and poor
and driving thousands into exile. All the United Provinces were asking for
was peace with liberty and 'some exercise of reformed religion'.[19] In another
brief the same year, Cotton argued in similar fashion that Spain intended to
conquer England and would use Catholics to stir up factions. In terms of
analysis similar to early twentieth-century fears of German hegemony, he
argued that once at peace with England, Spain would be able to turn its
attention to the Netherlands. Having made herself indomitable in Europe,
Spain would threaten England again and exterminate reformed religion. He
ended by calling for the continuation of Elizabethan policy to maintain the
Netherlands in their defensible war 'and the king's Majesty laudably be
entitled the protector and defender of the Belgians' liberty'.[20]

The treaty between England and the United Provinces in 1603, in which
England agreed to continue supporting their cause, defused that problem so
that the central issue in the Treaty of London in 1604 was the English claim
to trade to the East and West Indies.[21] Now Cotton changed his focus, and
wrote 'Reasons for the trade into the East and West Indies by the merchants
of England gathered for the treaty between his Majesty's commissioners
and those of the King of Spain and the Archduke July 1604'.[22] In
preparation for the conference Northampton had himself drawn up an
analysis of reasons for and against permission to trade to the Indies. On the
Spanish side he argued that since the time of King Ferdinand, traffic

to the Indies had neither been spoken of in a treaty nor been allowed to any other prince in Europe, not even such relatives as his cousin the emperor or his brother the archduke. Finally, the negotiators were without authority to agree to the demand. On England's behalf, Northampton pointed out that the Spanish themselves had asked for a universal league and so this exception had to be cancelled.

> The long impostumation of quarrels and heart burnings between England and Spain cannot be easily reconciled without some such sweet condition as may make them to be more confident in amity. But none can work more in this case than the traffic to the Indies.

Without it English mariners, dependent for work on foreign trade, might join the Dutch to Spain's disadvantage. Finally, he argued that because commodities that came out of England and Ireland were of far greater value and use than those of Spain, they required 'this vent to the Indies to piece out the want of the other'.[23]

Of the two sides in Northampton's disputation England had the better of the argument. On grounds both diplomatic and economic he argued for the right to trade to the Indies. When Northampton addressed the conference on this central issue, he relied not only on his own cogent analysis of current circumstances, but on an historical and legal brief prepared at his request by Sir Robert Cotton.[24]

The Spanish and Portuguese hegemony in the Orient dated back to the fifteenth century. Confirmed by papal edict, their spheres of influence were joined in 1580 when the two countries were united. English monarchs and merchants had claimed the right to trade to the Indies throughout the sixteenth century. In 1601 the English East India Company was formed to participate in that trade. There is a great similarity between Cotton's tract and Northampton's speech urging England's right to trade to the Indies. Both cited treaties negotiated by Henry VII and Henry VIII with the Emperor Maximilian and Charles V as precedents for freedom of trade.[25] They enumerated civil-law definitions providing freedom of the seas, and disputed the authority of the Pope to assign the trades of the Indies to any prince. To the Spanish claim of dominion of the Indies by right of first discovery, Cotton and Northampton interposed the historically dubious relationship of Henry VII with Columbus, both citing as evidence the biography of Columbus written by his son Ferdinand.[26] Cotton wrote of the mirage of Spanish control in the Indies:

> And for the Spanish Territories . . . wherever you shall view not the 20th part of them possessed, and interruptions sometimes of a 1000 and 1500 leagues between the ports or places of any their just interests, and how basely they are enforced to attend the devotion of barbarian lords, making their safety by continual purchase.

Northampton made the same point:

> Besides, that if anybody may bar us from trading into those ports, the
> right of that exclusion belonged properly to those Indian princes them-
> selves . . . for that the Portuguese did not possess the 20th part of that
> which is open, 1000 leagues lying sometimes between one port possessed
> by them and another and they paying to those Indians pier custom and
> tributes for their freight, etc.[27]

The many similarities of Cotton's tract to Northampton's speech lead to
one conclusion: Cotton wrote his memorandum at Northampton's request.
Northampton used it as the basis of his speech on free trade to the Indies.

It is significant that Cotton's arguments for free trade were legalistic and
historical as befitted a brief prepared for a diplomatic conference. Summing
up his arguments, Cotton asked Northampton to 'note out of this hasty
gathering how far it is estranged from the Laws of Nature, and nations, the
rule of contract, our former practising with them, and other princes, and to
their own dealing even with barbarians thus to list and bound us'.[28] Cotton
omitted, however, the most important reason to maintain the navigation of
English merchants into the East and West Indies: that it was extremely
profitable.

Cotton never mentioned the East India Company and indicated only
briefly at the end of his tract that there were other reasons to encourage free
trade, 'other politic considerations . . . as the high venting of our own commodities, the cheap lading to us their necessaries, the assured and greatest
maintenance of our navigation, and the readiest instructing of our
mariners'. Instead he urged that history provide concrete solutions to
current problems. Thus he insisted that King James respond to Spanish
demands in the same way that Elizabeth did, and offer the same arguments
to them that Charles V did to the Portuguese in 1522. But Cotton was a
conscientious historian. After citing the examples of Elizabeth and Charles
V combating monopolistic claims, he did note that in some cases they had
agreed to the restraint of their trade.[29] Northampton made use of almost all
of Cotton's arguments in his speech, but he deliberately omitted any
mention of such precedents which told against English claims to free trade.

The strong stand taken by Northampton in favour of England's right to
trade to the Indies and the resistance of the Spanish threatened to put an
abrupt end to the negotiations. To avert that danger it was finally agreed to
insert a general article on trade in the treaty, similar to the one recently
drawn between Spain and France. Its application to the Indies was left
deliberately ambiguous, referring its interpretation to previous treaties and
ancient usage.[30]

At one point in his discussion of trade to the Indies Northampton went
beyond Cotton's brief. This concerned the papal right to share out the globe
between Spain and Portugal, an authority the Pope had exercised in 1493

by the Bull of Demarcation. By that Bull all new discoveries to the west of an imaginary line drawn through the Azores were to belong to Spain, those to the east to Portugal. Cotton had merely noted that under the doctrine of the freedom of the seas the Pope had no such authority.[31] Northampton argued the same point at length on theological grounds, attacking the temporal power of the Pope. Although no prince could limit traffic which had been left at liberty by nature, he said the Pope was uniquely unfit because he drew his pre-eminence from Christ whose kingdom was of another world. At most, papal authority extended only to those that recognised it, 'as Saint Paul refused plainly to judge those that are without the church, so likewise, it might be thought hard by some princes which were not within the fold, to hearten (*sic*) to the voice of a strange shepherd'.[32] In this exposition, Northampton was performing his assigned role to counter Spanish postulates with legal and theological arguments of his own.

To the Jacobean government it was important not only to negotiate peace with Spain, but have its policy, which was not politically popular, presented in as positive a manner as possible. As we shall see in examining Northampton's other public performances, their purpose was not only to persuade diplomats or juries, but public opinion as well. In the aftermath of the successful conclusion of the negotiations, Sir Thomas Edmondes, English ambassador to France, put together a full report of the negotiations intended perhaps for publication although it was not printed until the eighteenth century. Northampton's important role as spokesman and propagandist finds verification in a series of letters he wrote to Edmondes.

'Worthy knight, with much ado in tossing my papers I have found out the place that so much importeth the question and perplexed others which I beseech you both for my credit and for the credit of the cause to insert in the proper place . . . as I now deliver it and then expressed it . . . after that which I gave you yesterday.' What Northampton wished inserted was one of Cotton's most telling points, the citation of an important Spanish jurist who had emphatically disputed any nation's right to deny the liberty of the seas. Northampton had built up to this by saying

> but to omit that heap of testimonies and arguments which the great Senate of the learned writers offers in this cause I will only vouch one, for his understanding to be reverenced and so his integrity to be preferred in this cause before any, in respect he was of counsel to the King of Spain, whose interest is chiefly pinched in the conclusion, Ferdinand Vasquiez who, glancing at the Venetians and Genoese for assuming to themselves an interest in their several gulfs, in the end concludeth . . . the common law of nations . . . which do absolutely prohibit all prescriptions of those things which God and Nature have left in community and liberty.

Northampton's letter recalls his own great moment: 'You may remember Sir Thomas Edmondes how deeply this text pinched them, how narrowly they scanned both the print and the time of printing and yet later . . . how slight their answer was that this being the judgement of one and though subject to the King of Spain yet they were not bound to it.' He closed by saying, 'I beseech you let me have one of your copies fully set out as soon as you can and by this bearer send back my oration for I have no more but that sole copy.'[33] That sole copy had of course been drawn from Cotton's 'Reasons'.

If Northampton was one of the major negotiators of the peace and oversaw the construction of the official report, he also handled the ceremonial aspects of treaty-making. To him fell the task of welcoming the Constable of Castile who came to London to sign the treaty in August 1604. Cecil was perhaps too busy, the Earl of Nottingham, although outranking Northampton, had played such an important role in the war against Spain that he was inappropriate. But who better than the minister most interested in making peace? His excitement is apparent in his letters. Awaiting the Constable's arrival Northampton reported to the king that he did not know how he meant to arrive. 'I live in suspense whether I shall prove to be a land fowl or a water fowl or like some of those birds that live upon the river Nilus mixed between both but so long as I furnish myself with boats and boots . . . I need the less to regard how the compass vary.'[34]

In a long and enthusiastic letter to James, Northampton described the Constable's arrival in words meant to cement Anglo-Spanish amity. The Thames was filled with boats and there were 'many good wishes of blessing and God saving breaking out of the mouths of many'. The Constable proved a good tourist. Viewing the Tower, he declared it famous in foreign parts, asked many questions about its history, and looked forward to visiting Hampton Court and Windsor. Admiring the king's learning, sweetness of disposition and princely dealings, the Constable went on to say that 'England had made a happy change by the late alteration and that herein God had witnessed that his wrath was assuaged towards Christendom'. If the Constable paid compliments to the king he did not neglect his emissary. Attuned to the nuances of rank, Northampton waxed lyrical that the Constable had met him at the head of the stairs in his inn in Gravesend and at the end of their conversation accompanied him even to the foot of the stairs. Northampton ended by saying, 'he took notice of my manifold afflictions in former times whereof he had often heard for the queen martyr as he called her that was your queen mother adding that at one time or other they that endeavoured for a good cause and a worthy person should be rewarded either temporally or eternally'.[35]

With Cotton's aid, Northampton carried off his leading role in the Spanish peace treaty negotiations, and in the happiest of moods looked forward to the reconciliation between England and Spain, Catholic and Protestant. That hope was shattered by the discovery of the Gunpowder Plot.

III

The Gunpowder Plot, the apocalyptic scheme of a band of disillusioned Roman Catholic gentry to blow up Parliament – Commons, Lords, king and all – when it met on 5 November 1605, was meant as the reprisal to the king's refusal to grant toleration.

The Gunpowder conspirators were tried and executed in January 1606. Two months later, on 28 March, Henry Garnet, head of the Jesuits in England, was brought before a jury to face the charge of being privy to the plot. Here the government faced a public relations problem. The horrendousness of the plot itself was apparent, but Garnet claimed to know nothing of it but what he had heard in the secrecy of confession, which he could not violate.[36] Although the government did not recognise this defence, they did recognise it as a nice point. Rumours were being spread that the evidence implicating Garnet had been retracted by its author, and 'that king-killing and queen-killing was not indeed a doctrine of theirs [the Jesuits], but only a faction and policy of our state, thereby to make the papish religion to be despised and in disgrace'.[37] Robert Cecil, now the Earl of Salisbury, stated the government's answer to those rumours at the trial. 'But this day shall witness to the world, that all is false and your self condemned not by any but by yourself, your own confessions and actions. Alas M. Garnet, why should we be troubled all this day with you, poor man, were it not to make the cause appear as it deserveth.'[38] To make the cause appear as the government desired, to allay any doubts, the government published *A True and Perfect Relation of the whole proceedings against the late most barbarous Traitors, Garnet, a Jesuite, and his Confederats*. . . . The bulk of that volume was taken up by a long dissertation on the papal usurpation of temporal power and a history of jesuitical conspiracies. Northampton was its author.

Robert Cotton was again Northampton's aide, this time editing his writings and preparing the manuscript for the publisher. The antiquary had to cope with Northampton's continuous rewriting and emendations. Sending him the first sheet of the manuscript, Northampton noted that 'you see how I have scribbled presuming as well upon your pains as your love . . . I have written so much as you crossed over again'.[39] But Northampton relied on Cotton for more than editorial duty; he looked to him for support and encouragement. He wrote to the antiquary of his latest composition that

I think you will like it well enough as it is and therefore I dispatch it out of sight, for though I should read it a hundred times I should every time upon a review alter it. I will proceed to the rest with all the speed I can, observing your counsel not to push too fast or stint myself to my own wrong.[40]

When the manuscript was completed Northampton asked that a copy of the book be sent off in haste to the king.[41] While the actual date of publication is not known, the Venetian ambassador announced the appearance of the book to the doge in December 1606.

> The Earl of Northampton, one of the great Lords of this kingdom, a man of letters, member of the Privy Council, has . . . complete[d] a book on the late plot; starting from answers by the Jesuit who was condemned he has compiled a treatise, hostile to the pretended superiority of popes over princes in matters temporal. The work is highly commended by all, by the king in particular, he has ordered it to be translated into French, Latin and Italian. The fact that the author has been and still is reckoned a Catholic is expected to lend the work a greater authority.[42]

How important was Cotton's help in the composition of *The True and Perfect Relation*? Certainly he was its editor. In fact he did more. He supplied the historical framework on which Northampton built his case. First of all, he provided the primary sources for the work. Northampton requested Cotton to send him any collections of Saxon laws he might have in his library[43] and cited in his essay Saxon histories, the 'laws' of Canute, Edward the Confessor and William the Conqueror. Northampton also mentioned several other mediaeval documents which Cotton may have brought to his attention. More important, Cotton may have influenced the central argument of Northampton's tract, that the church had to justify its authority by its history: 'the charter which the Church of Christ receiveth by her Spouse is limited and tied to the validity of the evidence and the strength of witnesses, with the prescription of antiquity.' Northampton marshalled his evidence to prove that the papal claim to temporal power, to the right to dissolve the bond of loyalty that bound subject to monarch, was without precedent before the reign of Gregory VII.

> None of the patriarchs before the law, none of the priests and prophets under the law, not Christ or his apostles at the last expiring of the old law, nor any of the godly bishops that governed the Church of God for the space of 1000 years by the new law, did ever exercise . . . that kind of jurisdiction . . . that is deprivation of right, suspension from rule, or sequestration from royalty. For this I take to be that ball of wildfire, which hath caused so great loss of lives and states by combustion in monarchies.[44]

Northampton proposed therefore that the church return to the purely spiritual jurisdiction it had exercised at the beginning and cut off all temporal encroachments.

This story has a postscript. Northampton must have found it ironic when, seven years later, rumours were spread in London that he had written to Cardinal Bellarmine asking that no response be made to his book, written solely, it was said, to placate the king. To combat the rumours, the earl brought suit, as we have seen, against several well-placed gentlemen, and the case was heard in November 1612. Judgement was found for Northampton under a statute of Richard II which made finable the slander of the nobility. No evidence was ever produced to support the allegations, but its currency reveals that the strategy of using Northampton in a prominent position may actually have served to bring his entire endeavour into question.[45]

IV

Northampton brought Cotton into the very machinery of Jacobean government. Speechwriter and adviser, Cotton did not make policy and there is no convincing evidence that he, or Northampton on his behalf, sought high government office. Rather, Cotton was the seventeenth century's version of a technocrat; his role to organise royal commissions, to compile data – in this case historical precedents – for use in backing government decisions and to offer policy options from which Northampton could choose. Northampton's reliance on Cotton's precedents for his public speeches was not mere convention. On the contrary, Northampton sought Cotton's advice precisely because history was central to contemporary policy-making. Cotton was particularly sensitive to the method by which Crown objectives were carried out and it was a sensitivity that Northampton valued and indeed relied on.

Among the many position papers that Cotton drew up for Northampton between 1603 and 1614,[46] the most extensive was a long analysis of the king's finances with proposals for reform and ways to increase revenue. Lack of money was the most pressing problem of James's reign. Repeated attempts were made by Salisbury and Northampton to increase revenues and abate expenses, particularly after 1608. The failure of the Great Contract turned Jacobean officials back to traditional methods and to projects to raise funds. Northampton commissioned Cotton's 'Means to Repair the King's Estate', which he carefully perused, underlining and annotating about half of it.[47] In this paper Cotton had two aims in mind: to give an historical account of all the ways kings had raised money and to cite the 'prescription of antiquity' in suggesting how to increase revenue at the present time. Cotton made clear that he was offering Northampton a variety of options drawn from the past. 'I only can my Lord observe unto your honour such fragments of records as I have collected, wherein perchance somewhat your Lordship may observe whereof your judgement can make far better application than any bold direction of mine'.[48] Far from undue modesty, these lines sum up the role Cotton played in the formulation of policy.

If history was the crucial determinant in making policy, Cotton did not use it uncritically. A sophisticated historian, he looked to the nation's archives for answers to contemporary problems. The bulk of Cotton's historical account of royal finance consisted in fact of a collection of documents of all 'subsidies, desmes, fifteenths, reliefs, contributions, taxes, gifts, grants, benevolences and payments . . . as have been exacted . . . of the subjects of this realm of England since the Conquest'. One, for instance, described the proceeding in 'the benevolence collected out of such papers as I have left with your honour of the proceedings in the time of King Henry VIII'.[49] Although these 400 folios of mostly original documents might appear to be mere appendages to the tract itself, they were its heart. From this crude ore, policy might be mined. Northampton emphasised their importance when he requested Cotton to 'bring the book with you that you showed me yesterday touching all the grants from the subjects to the king because I desire very much upon that point to confer with you at some leisure'.[50]

Cotton's tract which prefaced the documents took a sharp look at why the Crown was in debt and how it might be relieved, both by cutting down on expenses and finding new sources of revenues. Reforming the household, for one, had a venerable history. Cardinal Wolsey had drawn up a book of ordinances for its regulation which were still supposed to be in force. But despite these ordinances, the household had become corrupted, to the king's great loss. 'For there is never a back door in court that costs not the king nearly £2000 yearly, and few mean houses in Westminster that are not maintained with food and firing by the stealth of their court-instruments.'[51] In addition to suggesting that leaks in the household be plugged by enforcing old regulations, Cotton focused on a more important breach in the dyke: the king's openhandedness. All suggestions for repairing the revenues were founded on, and ultimately foundered on, the assumption that James was seriously willing to curtail his spending and cut off new grants. Cotton drew Northampton's attention to a pertinent precedent. 'Hence was it the wisdom of former times forseeing the mischief that the open hand of the sovereign may bring, the state made a law 21 Richard II that whatsoever cometh to the king by judgement, escheat, forfeiture, wardship or any other ways, shall not be given away, and that the procurer of any gift shall be punished.'[52]

Cotton evaluated ways of increasing the king's revenue from the standpoint of history, emphasising the importance of making the means palatable to the subject. Kings had traditionally raised money by forced loans, but Cotton pointed out that a statute of Richard II allowed the subject his reasonable excuse.[53] When he proposed that the king might profit from farming out wastes, he put forward a way of going about it without arousing antagonism. Because 'there are many that have right of common *sans nombre*' he urged the use of neighbours as assessors, 'and the first demise to the inhabitants and under an easy value'.[54] Cotton's strategy of local initiative obviously impressed Northampton. When the earl drew up his own 'Considerations for Repair of the King's Estate', he insisted that 'to make the best of wastes and commons, skilful surveyors must be chosen to bring on some by example of others and working the motion to come by the joint suit of tenants and homeless'. He added this caution that 'the subject of enclosing wastes, commons, . . . further than the tenants themselves shall make suit, upon consideration . . . is not holden fit for improvement . . . before the next parliament'.[55] Cotton summed up the political difficulty that the Crown faced; forced to 'live of his own', especially on the revenues of Crown lands, the king was inhibited from systematically exploiting those lands by surveying and farming because of the political repercussions, particularly from the landed gentry.

Cotton was sensitive to the possible conflict of the king's right and local custom, but his proposals in the main were not new. He endorsed the farming of the customs, which had proved quite lucrative since it was begun in 1604. He suggested that the king sell Crown land, a device the Privy Council resorted to periodically but with reluctance. Re-establishing the ancient bullion exchange, tripling the fee-farm rent, coining base money, exacting first fruits and tenths from lands previously belonging to the church – none of these proposals recommended itself to the treasury commission. In fact, Northampton himself labelled fee-farming of the king's land and 'black money' as 'doubtful, dangerous, offered but not advised by us'.[56]

Similar financial problems plagued Charles I too. William Noy, his attorney-general, was said to have prepared a tract in 1634 entitled 'A Treatise of the Rights of the Crown, Declaring How the King of England May Support and Increase his Annual Revenue, Collected out of the Records in the Tower, the Parliament Rolls and Close Petitions'. In fact, 'A Treatise of the Rights of the Crown' is Cotton's tract mistakenly attributed to Noy when it was published in 1715.[57] Unchanging problems and solutions linked the Crown's financial policies of the 1610s and the 1630s in an important way, as this misattribution suggests. But by 1629 Cotton's library had been confiscated by the Crown, one of the signals of the sea-change in perception and communication between the king and Parliament.

One of Cotton's suggestions, however, as we have seen, did meet with success: the creation and sale of the new title of baronet. Believing that the gentry would be willing to pay for prestige, Cotton proposed 'for his Majesty now to make a degree of honour hereditary as baronets, next under barons, and grant them in tail, taking of everyone £1000 in fine, it would raise with ease £100,000 and by a judicious election be a means to content those worthy persons in the Commonwealth'.[58] The baronetage, created in the spring of 1611, proved to be a good moneymaker, although not quite so lucrative as Cotton had forecast. Calculated on what it would cost to maintain thirty foot soldiers for three years at 8d per diem for the defence of Ireland and the plantation of Ulster, the title was offered at £1,095. Subjects who had an income of at least £1,000 a year were eligible, and the king's ministers selected those to whom the baronetcy was to be offered. In three years the device had brought in £90,885.[59]

Cotton acted as an intermediary between those seeking the honour and Northampton, a role which put him in an embarrassing position with old friends who like himself had been made baronets in the first batch. The problem was the definition of the privileges of the rank. One version had suggested that they would include the right to sit in the House of Commons and freedom from arrest for debt.[60] The established rank included neither.

Moreover, the question remained of the baronets' precedence. They were to rank directly under barons and before all knights except knights banneret made on the battlefield in the presence of the king or the Prince of Wales. The new baronets, however, were not worried about the bannerets but wondered did they take precedence over the sons of barons? Over this question, Cotton and Northampton split, albeit temporarily.

In December 1611 Cotton joined with other newly-created baronets, Sir Moyle Finch and Sir William Twysden, to bring the issue of precedence before the Privy Council. Twysden had enjoyed Northampton's patronage in the past. But Northampton and other members ruled against them, insisting on the precedence of barons' sons. Not content with this decision, the baronets, this time significantly without Cotton, unsuccessfully pressed their claim in the new year. In a temper the Finches, the father and his son, Heneage Finch, both baronets, demanded their money back.[61] The king then agreed to hear the case and make the final decision on 29 April 1612. It was important to the baronets' cause that Cotton should use his antiquarian abilities on their behalf. Finch and others with some asperity asked him to attend the hearing, uneasy that he might stay away.[62] They were right. Twysden then charged Northampton with keeping Cotton away because he had records which would prove their right to precedence.[63] The baronets lost their case for a final time, but as a sop received minor additions to their patents, urged by Cotton for the better marketability of the title. He suggested that 'three or four of the ringleaders would easily devise what would best please themselves'.[64] Despite their differences over the baronets' privileges, Northampton was again patron of the Finch connection in the Parliament of 1614.

Cotton had now become Northampton's unofficial assistant, his counsel valued because he provided information which might be relevant to governmental policy-making on subjects which ranged from diplomacy and law to fiscal reform. Once asking Cotton about the pros and cons of coining base money, Northampton emphasised that 'though I have in my own experience observed many weighty reasons in the point, yet I value much that which the experience of former times adds to speculation'.[65] It is not surprising that a traditional society whose institutions were based on custom and immemorial usage should look at the process of governing from a traditional point of view. The development of a critical historical method in the sixteenth century sharpened this viewpoint by the use of original records, defined and interpreted in the light of the latest historical knowledge. Cotton could lend credibility to government positions by supplying precedents but, equally important, his suggestions on policy carried the weight of an authority derived from a long, searching study of England's past. This historical approach characterised the thinking of most of the king's ministers. Many of the questions that Northampton put to Cotton and other antiquaries, whether of the Earl Marshal's prerogatives, escuage, or the coining of base money, were couched in historical terms.

V

When Northampton became a commissioner for the Earl Marshalship, he vigorously applied himself to reforming abuses in it. Proposals to deal with such problems as the rights of heralds and the improper grant of arms had been drawn up in 1597 but were only fully implemented during Northampton's tenure. In the interest of reform, Northampton sought the expert opinion of two other members of the Society of Antiquaries besides Cotton. John Dodderidge, the solicitor-general, and Francis Thynne, the Lancaster Herald, composed memoranda on heraldry which together with his own researches into the operation of the office, laid the basis for his later reforms.

Dodderidge was an eminent common lawyer and student of history who had become James's solicitor-general. He wrote 'A consideration of the office and duty of an herald in England drawn out of sundry observations . . . at the instance of Henry Earl of Northampton in August 1605'.[66] The central thrust of Dodderidge's argument concerning the origins of the heralds' functions and the jurisdiction of the Earl Marshal went to the heart of Northampton's efforts to reform the office and to control the giving of arms. Dodderidge argued that heralds had traditionally fulfilled four functions in England: they served as messengers between leaders of opposing armies, as ministers of ceremonies, as administrators of the right to bear arms and as registrars of the proceedings in the Court of Earl Marshal. But the heralds had no right to claim a jurisdiction independent of the Earl Marshal. No new arms could be granted to anyone without his consent except by the three Kings of Arms, Garter, Clarencieux or Norroy, jointly or separately. And each year they were to deliver to the Earl Marshal a book containing all the patents and new grants of arms they made.

These provisions were rationalisations of the traditional institution, drawn up in 1568 by Thomas Howard, Duke of Norfolk, Northampton's brother, and Dodderidge's scholarship supported them. Indeed he pointed out that the duke had established a useful precedent by issuing ordinances aimed at rooting out abuses.[67] Finally, in perhaps his most significant point, Dodderidge squarely supported a jurisdiction for the Earl Marshal in the matter of arms, which though limited was separate from the common law. Dodderidge noted that the authority of the Earl Marshal's court in the matters of battle and arms was acknowledged by the common law judges as 'the law of the land concerning those causes and affairs'.[68] This statement was significant because the jurisdiction of the Earl Marshal would come under attack from heralds and common lawyers continuously over the next four decades and was abolished by the Long Parliament. Yet Dodderidge, writing in 1605, saw no difficulty in supporting the powers of the Earl Marshal.

Thynne's approach was less legalistic. Though equally grounded in history Thynne, as Lancaster Herald, also sprinkled his paper with the insights of an insider. His hope that 'your Lordships will repair this ruined state of ours' emphasised the purpose of his memorandum, to establish the basis for reform of the office; the reference to 'your honourable brother the Duke of Norfolk' points conclusively to Northampton as Thynne's patron. Thynne had provided Northampton with information on other questions including the Lord Wardenship of the Cinque Ports and it was for Northampton as one of the commissioners for the Earl Marshalship that Thynne wrote 'A Discourse of the Duty and Office of an Herald of Arms' in March 1605.[69]

Thynne traced the history of the heralds, pointed out their special education and condemned the publication of books on arms which made each man his own herald. Northampton was sensitive to this point and in his efforts at reform he always emphasised the necessity of safeguarding the prerogatives of the heralds. He understood the need for the support of officials in the departments in which he sought to bring about change.

Noting the number of heralds and of their fees in the fourteenth and fifteenth centuries, Thynne wistfully remarked on the handsome New Year gifts then bestowed on the heralds by all the noblemen and knights of the court. Heralds had been entitled to whatever accessories fell from a jouster while competing in a tournament. 'But now will not they which newly being to tourney pay their fees, but further bring with them so many pages and servants into the tilts, that they take the heralds' fee of whatsoever falleth from their masters, with opprobrious speech to the heralds, against all reason, order and custom.' Thynne's argument was not solely self-serving. He spoke out forcefully, too, on the abuses of the heralds themselves. 'By the lewd behaviour of some, the name of herald is become odious, and will fall to the ground if your Lordship, whose honourable mind and painful endeavour do tie all the heralds to acknowledge them your new framed, or at least revived creatures, do not put to your helping hand, and continue the credit of the office, and of such officers as shall deserve well.'[70] Thynne's suggestions included special training for the heralds, orderly behaviour, restoring traditional fees and barring painters from dealing with arms. In criticising the present state of the College of Arms, Thynne compared it unfavourably with the glorified position it had enjoyed during the Middle Ages. In fact, heraldry, in terms of popular interest, was at its apogee at the time Thynne wrote; the impulse to reform the heralds' office had arisen out of that interest.

Thynne went on to stress the precedents which put teeth into the Earl Marshal's jurisdiction. Faced with mediaeval precedents that emphasised the power of the Constable (an office lapsed since Henry VIII) whose deputy the Earl Marshal was, Thynne, in accordance with sixteenth-century legal opinion, conflated the powers of the two offices, giving the Marshal judicial powers where once he had only executory. Like Dodderidge, he pointed out that the law of the Constable and Marshal was independent of the common law. In addition he argued for the right of the Earl Marshal or commissioners for that office to imprison offenders without bail or *habeas corpus* until judgement in the Marshal's court.[71] These opinions, which strongly supported the jurisdiction to which Northampton laid claim in order to reform the office of heralds, did not go unchallenged.

VI

Northampton continued to solicit advice about the office of arms. In 1610 he encouraged Edmund Bolton, the antiquary, to publish a book on heraldry entitled *Elements of Armories*.[72] Born around 1575, Bolton was educated at Trinity College, Cambridge, and the Inner Temple. He was a student of English history all his life and the friend of the leading scholars of his day. But his career was hampered by his Roman Catholicism. Asked to contribute to John Speed's *History of England*, his life of Henry II was rejected as too favourable to Thomas Becket. Bolton acknowledged his handicap in a letter to Sir Robert Cotton, writing that 'this honourable cause... makes me publicly incapable of employment'.[73] But his Catholicism was no bar to Northampton's patronage.

Bolton provided Northampton with programmes and precedents on a variety of subjects. His counsel was always founded on historical example but was at times impractical because of its narrow antiquarianism. He diagnosed England's central difficulties as lack of treasure for the king and idle multitudes 'for which this realm useth the vent of Virginia among others'. Bolton proposed two solutions: first, the stringent enforcement of sumptuary legislation, not through the law courts, 'but directly and immediately, after the stern and juridical manner of the Romans in the person of a potent censor (one of the most necessary magistrates which ever they enjoyed)'.[74] To the objection that the royal customs actually benefited from the importation of expensive clothing and other 'means of riot', Bolton answered that it would find favour with God and through his intervention somehow bring in three times as many commodities as the hated apparel. Bolton's proposal overlooked the fact that in 1604 Parliament had repealed all Acts of apparel. Indeed, none was ever passed again. Sumptuary regulation, mediaeval in spirit, had ended in England just when Bolton urged it to be enforced most severely.

Bolton proposed secondly the settling of England's 'idle multitudes' on royal lands. 'For the king hath infinite forests, chases, wastes, and spare parks, and depopulators have perilously engrossed the livings of multitudes by monopolies of destroyed farms, contrary to express penal laws, which do command that tenements should be built and apportioned with grounds.'[75] According to Bolton's plan, not only would the realm profit from the re-establishment of thousands of honest families, but also from rents paid by the new royal tenants and the fees paid by depopulators. The enclosing of common fields for the purpose of grazing sheep had occurred for over a hundred years. Neither commissioners empowered to investigate nor stat-utes with stiff penalties had been able to reverse the new pattern of land-holding. None the less, Bolton's suggestion may have been a thoughtful response to the 1607 Midland revolt over enclosure. The resettling of a displaced rural population on royal estates might have provided the Crown with greater social control and revenue. There is no evidence, however, that Northampton acted on this suggestion. Instead, the Council was forced to sell Crown land throughout the reign for ready money.

Bolton's historical-mindedness characterised not only his counsel to Northampton but also his ideas about government. Attacking the notion that scholars were not fit for governing, Bolton called it 'senseless, and alto-gether as barbarous, as senseless opinion (as your Lordship can excellently witness) hath no manner of countenance in books of credit'. Scholars were uniquely prepared for office, Bolton thought, by 'the wise and diligent perusal of practick theology, ethics, history, and Caesarian or imperial laws, exactly compared with the present states of opinions'. Bolton believed in the aristocracy of the intelligent and vehemently wrote to Northampton, 'the proud and ignorant would be thrust down into those ranks to which God, nature and justice doth decree, that is to be subservient and subordi-nated to the learned'.[76] Under a monarchy, however, the only realm that scholars could rule was that of scholarship. For that purpose, Bolton suggested in 1617 the Academy Royal. Its function would be to write the official chronicle of English history, supervise the translation of foreign works, and authorise all books other than theological.[77] If the learned could not rule England, they could at least rule England's culture.

Barred from office himself, Bolton inflated the theoretical role of scholars. He did not perceive that they could influence government policy in subtler ways. He had only to look to his friend Sir Robert Cotton. Cotton derived much of his influence from his close relationship with Northamp-ton who often had him serve as his middle-man with clients. Thus when Bolton wished to contact Northampton, he wrote to Cotton and when Northampton wanted Bolton to do something for him, Cotton was again the agent. Did Northampton who, Bolton declared, 'breathes nothing but noblesse', reward Bolton's efforts, flawed as they were? Perhaps he did. As his patron, Northampton had written letters to the Lord Deputy of Ireland and others concerning Bolton's affairs there. But Bolton's Roman Catho-licism, although appealing to Northampton, made patronage difficult. In order that 'for want of a fit subject, his Lordship's noble inclinations toward myself may not be frustrate or barren', Bolton suggested to Cotton that a cousin be rewarded in his place.

Despite Bolton's many references to Northampton's favour and interest, he later claimed to have received nothing from him. 'You [Cotton] understand how sincere and full goodwill I always bore and bear to the house of Howard, particularly to that our late and noble Lord and friend, yet am I, in nothing richer, or the stronger for my relations to that family'.[78] Perhaps in Bolton's case Northampton had decided that scholarship was its own reward.

Northampton's questions to his advisers were often couched in the language of history and precedent. He sought answers from many scholars, whose advice ranged from Cotton's clever project of the baronetage to Bolton's Christian theories of commonwealth. If some of this advice was of limited value it was a result of Northampton's narrow focus as much as his advisers'. The problems facing the government of James I did not always yield to historical solutions. On fiscal policy in particular Northampton found it useful to turn elsewhere.

Chapter 7

Advisers on Policy: The Merchants

In 1624 Lionel Cranfield, Earl of Middlesex and Lord Treasurer of England, was impeached by Parliament, ostensibly for bribery and extortion, but in reality for offending the Duke of Buckingham and Prince Charles. During the impeachment proceedings, King James recalled in a speech to the House of Lords his first meeting with Cranfield when he was still a merchant. 'For the person of the man, the first acquaintance I had with him was by the Lord of Northampton, who often brought him unto me a private man, before he was so much as my servant. He then made many projects for my profit.'[1] Perhaps this was the greatest achievement of Northampton's patronage of experts: to discover and recruit for the royal administration the man who was to fight most vigorously, though in the end fruitlessly, for its reformation.

But the Earl of Northampton was probably not the only Jacobean minister to surround himself with a 'brains trust' of sorts. Certainly other royal officials, such as Salisbury and Lord Chancellor Ellesmere, for instance, had advisers who offered their opinions on government problems. Little note, however, has been taken of the role played in government affairs by private men and the influence they wielded. Northampton's patronage of experts is especially valuable because it reveals how one royal official sought advice, the attitudes that informed it and the way in which it was translated into practice.

The earl's counsellors were mainly scholars, officeholders and merchants. It was the argument of the previous chapter that those scholars who advised Northampton, and in particular Robert Cotton, viewed contemporary problems from the perspective of the past, that they couched their ideas in historical terms and that at times this historical attitude limited the usefulness of their advice. In this chapter the proposition will be advanced that those merchants whom Northampton consulted, of whom the foremost was Lionel Cranfield, based their opinions on their own experience in business, and were often pragmatic in solving political problems. But this distinction between scholars and merchants is not a dogmatic one. It neither supposes that historical and practical modes of thought are antithetical, nor does it mean that these seventeenth-century men can be placed in exclusive categories. It does not mean the historians were never pragmatic or that merchants did not read history. This distinction does suggest, however, that when confronted with an issue, antiquarians usually asked how it had been decided in the past. In contrast, some merchants asked about the current economic relationships involved.

Early seventeenth-century writers and policy-makers alike emphasised the importance of positive bullion flows without much regard to the changing realities of the balance of trade and have often been labelled mercantilists. In analysing the crucial impact of foreign trade on England's domestic economy in this period, Barry Supple has convincingly argued that what has been called mercantilism was not a highly articulated ideology but short-term responses to problems in trade, particularly in cloth, and to the unfavourable flow of gold and silver.[2] Much of the policy that Northampton helped to shape in this period was indeed generated in response to current crises. From his advisers he sought precise information on economic and financial matters which could be applied to the immediate government problems of foreign trade, monetary policy, customs duties and royal revenue. In addition, Northampton was coming to understand the need to liberate the economy from its dependence on the cloth trade. Northampton's patronage of economic advisers and the elaboration of project literature, much of which passed through his hands in this period, provide evidence of a new direction in the English economy.

Economic historians have pointed out the lack of economic expertise among privy councillors in the early Stuart period, despite their dutiful calling in of representatives of the important merchant communities on specific issues.[3] Northampton's 'brains trust' allows us to look at the spectrum of information available to the government and how a Jacobean privy councillor threaded his way through conflicting advice to develop policy. Northampton's informants ranged from City merchants like Lionel Cranfield, the Lord Mayor and customs farmer, Sir John Swinnerton, and Francis Needham, a member of the French and Spanish Companies, to Thomas Milles, the customer of Sandwich, whose views reflected the interests of the declining outports, and Tobias Gentleman, a shipbuilder, who urged the expansion of the English fishing industry.

Francis Needham's 'A discourse of the first beginning of clothing in England',[4] provides an excellent start to an analysis of Northampton's attention to the economy and his merchant advisers. It bears Northampton's careful annotations in which he summarised Needham's main points. By examining the text closely we can see both the advice given by the author and how the councillor read and understood it. Needham described the history of the cloth industry, emphasising the excellence and abundance of wool which had established England's important economic relation to the rest of Western Europe; the customs on wool had paid for the conquest of France in the fourteenth century. Noting the attributes of English cloth as 'warmth, cheapness, lasting', Northampton focused on the many commodities brought to England in exchange. In addition he underlined the custom duties paid in the reign of Edward III and the interconnections of trade with Flanders, Italy and France. Northampton followed Needham's lesson carefully, underlining the development of the Merchant Adventurers and jotting down 'why the Moscovy trade is to be maintained'. Describing trade to Turkey, Needham argued that the benefit England received 'by these infidel loving people is the increase of our navigation and that, by these long voyages, many tall ships are built and good mariners built up'; Northampton translated this tersely as 'good for the navy'. Needham summed up the importance of the cloth trade in these terms: 'our English cloth is of that consequence to the realm...the great woolbearers of the country... encouraged to breed sheep, the clothier, spinner, weaver, and infinite other poor people set on work, and made able to live by draping the wool into cloth, the merchant by traffic thereof enrich the revenues of the Crown by customs, the...shipping and mariners, by which our king is made master of the seas.' As his marginalia indicated, Northampton heeded the message Needham was anxious for him to hear as to the importance of the English cloth industry to the health of the English economy and in return he forwarded Needham's attempts to secure an auditorship.[5] When confronted with a boycott of English cloth by one of its chief foreign customers in 1612, Northampton dutifully consulted the merchants who engaged in it. But he found their advice on policy not particularly useful until he called in Lionel Cranfield.

I

Cranfield was born in 1575, the second son of a London merchant. He attended St Paul's School but at 15 was apprenticed to a cloth merchant to begin his real education. An apt pupil, by the age of 23 Cranfield had travelled abroad to purchase silk, become a member of the Mercers' Company, and amassed £1,000 more than his father who was worth £1,725 at his death. Although the turn of the century brought a trade depression, the peace between England and Spain in 1604 ushered in an expansion of the European market for those northern kersies in which Cranfield specialised. But to avoid being at the mercy of those expansions and contractions which continually plagued the cloth market, he diversified his commercial interests to include business dealings with the court. The royal government and many of its officials suffered from a chronic lack of ready money. By farming out the administration of its revenue to London merchants, the court and its officials could count on steady rents, and more important, a ready source of loans. Cranfield invested in several farms, including the Great Farm of the customs and the silk, tobacco and currant farms. His first contact with the Howard family occurred when he invested in the monopoly granted by the king to Charles Howard, the Lord Admiral, and his son, to license the keeping of taverns and the sale of wines at retail. Needing cash, the Howards sold off portions of their anticipated rent to their merchant associates. Within four years, the Howards had capitalised two-thirds of the yearly rent of £3,000, in the form of £100 and £200 annuities, which Cranfield and others sold at a profit.[6] Cranfield also enriched himself by participating in the syndicates organised to sell Crown lands on those frequent occasions when the court needed money. In fact, it was through the sale of Crown lands that Cranfield was first able in 1608 to perform a favour for his future patron. When Northampton indicated an interest in some parcels of land in Greenwich where he had his country home, 'Mr Cranfield did not only procure this, but persuaded the rest of the contractors to bestow it freely upon his Lordship, being of so small a value'.[7] A small gesture perhaps, it had rich reward. As we have seen, in the same year, Cranfield and Arthur Ingram, a prominent London merchant with whom he was associated throughout his commercial career, helped Northampton to establish his profitable monopoly of the duties paid on starch.

Up until 1612 Cranfield was content to build his fortune in the City and to cultivate his contacts at court. In 1612 and 1613 Cranfield made the transition, under Northampton's tutelage, from City merchant to court adviser, by solving a trade dispute, creating a new royal revenue, and critically analysing the farms of the customs. He was rewarded for his service with pensions and wages amounting to £500 a year, the office of surveyor-general of customs and a knighthood. That Cranfield's star enjoyed a rather meteoric rise emerges from John Chamberlain's inaccurate assignment to him of the newly vacant office of lieutenant of Dover Castle, which was in Northampton's gift as Lord Warden of the Cinque Ports. He added, 'I should hardly believe it, but that he has become lately in great favour with the Lord Privy Seal, and rides ordinarily in coach with him, and by his means was knighted on Sunday last.'[8] Indeed, Cranfield had supervised the purchase and outfitting of that carriage.

By January of 1613 Cranfield calculated his worth at £24,000 and his yearly income was perhaps £3,000. He had not given up his commercial interests when he became a court official and, with Northampton as intermediary and Ingram as partner, organised the farm of the Irish customs. He also obtained the right to purvey Gascon wines to the king's Household.[9] Cranfield's last service for Northampton was to sit in the Parliament of 1614 as a representative of Hythe, a Cinque Port. After Northampton's death in June 1614 Cranfield continued his attachment to the Howards until the rise of Buckingham who became his most important patron. Cranfield became successively Master of Requests, Master of the Court of Wards, and Lord Treasurer. He showed great initiative in undertaking administrative reforms,[10] cutting his teeth on those economic questions presented to him by his first patron, the Earl of Northampton. In the summer of 1612 Cranfield was able to demonstrate the usefulness of his pragmatic approach to policy by slicing through the welter of tradition which encumbered the Crown's ability to make decisions.

II

Albert, Archduke of the Spanish Netherlands, had precipitated a trade crisis when he banned English cloth from his domains. Although an ancient Flemish law prohibited the importation of English cloth, its enforcement had been modified by treaties and licences which proved lucrative additions to the archduke's treasury. In the autumn of 1611, however, four of his provinces petitioned to enforce the Act against English cloth in order to provide employment for their own people. The archduke acceded to their request, announcing on 12 April 1612 that after completion of the current licence no more would be granted. In July, with the expiration of the licence, the archduke ordered parcels of English cloth returned because the quantity permitted to be imported had already been exceeded.[11] The English ambassador in the Spanish Netherlands wrote home urgently for instructions and the king ordered the Privy Council into session.

With Salisbury's death in May 1612, the task of laying business before the Council and reporting its deliberations to the king had fallen to Northampton. He began his report on the crisis by criticising the late Secretary's handling of relations with the archduke. 'We did all wonder that my Lord deceased would engross unto himself the notice of such a growing fraction, considering how ready we should all have been and at all angles both oblique and straight upon this overture if he had acquainted us.'[12] In this way, Northampton scored off the memory of Robert Cecil and absolved himself and his fellow privy councillors of any responsibility for the crisis. Unwittingly, he also drew a picture of an administration not in control since the reins had slipped from Salisbury's hands. Northampton presented Rochester with a long report of the discussions the Privy Council had undertaken with the leading cloth merchants. To his bitter surprise, he found the king was not impressed. Northampton insisted to Rochester that he had questioned the merchants 'upon those heads that were proposed by his Majesty ... God is my judge that I cannot for my life conceive what should displease the king in all this nor in what one point he should rest unsatisfied'.[13] The king's dissatisfaction lay in the delay of the Privy Council in devising a coherent response to the archduke's action, stemming from the Council's reliance on the merchants to advise on policy. Northampton noted sourly that 'the merchants are not yet so ready with their answers as in half the time they would have been for a good bargain'.[14]

Policy is always dependent on information, and the soundness of any policy is directly related to the accuracy, completeness and relevance of the information on which it is based. In the case of the cloth-trade crisis, the merchants were willing, although slow, to supply the Council with answers. Unfortunately, the questions asked were the wrong ones or were much too narrowly focused. They were entirely historical and legal, for example, by what authority did the archduke undertake and justify the banning of English cloth, and how could England counter that authority?

Although the archduke relied on the traditional law which prohibited English cloth from the Netherlands, Northampton noted that the law had often been relaxed. He took the tack, therefore, that the archduke's authority could be undermined by an appeal to history, specifically as embodied in treaties between the two countries entered into since the reign of Edward IV.[15] The most recent treaty was that of 1604 which ended the war with Spain. At the time, the negotiators, one of whom was Northampton, had dealt with the problem of trade by drawing up a vague article which reinstated the state of commerce as it had existed prior to the war. In 1612, however, this ambiguity had become a problem and to settle the question, the Council directed two officials to examine the treaties and note all the variations in the enforcement of the ancient Flemish law. The merchants were charged to make a report of the state of trade as it existed before the war began. Their usefulness lay, Northampton said, in 'their experience and readiness in the treaties ... the poles of their trade'. This experience was drawn not from contemporary trade, but the recorded evidence of the forms of commerce almost fifty years before.

As the king waited impatiently for the Privy Council to devise a policy, Northampton bewailed the slowness of the cloth traders: 'though I have often called on the merchants yet they could not put themselves in point to answer in a matter that stood upon many treaties and variations.'[16] Still perceiving the trade crisis in historical terms, he continued to hope that the perusal of the treaties would yield the legal sanctions to challenge the archduke's decree.

Northampton's assessment of the crisis changed, however, when he called in Lionel Cranfield. Cranfield pointed out the economic realities of the trade crisis which (if Northampton's letters are an accurate guide) had not been presented before. The novelty of his approach was such that Northampton insisted that he travel north to Newark to present his views personally to the king, then on progress. Northampton wrote to Rochester in triumph, enthusing over Cranfield's usefulness and comparing the slowness of the merchants with his quick-witted appraisal. Though he still had hope that the study of the treaties might yield some advantage, Northampton, with Cranfield's assistance, now focused on the contemporary nature of the problem. 'For howsoever the Archduke bear himself in show upon ancient grounds yet I do certainly believe that new spurs have incited him.'[17]

The impact which Cranfield's advice had on Northampton must be attributed to its concreteness and immediacy, breaking through to the basic economic issues. In the memoranda he wrote at the time, Cranfield addressed himself to the question of what the recent trade figures revealed about England's cloth trade with the Spanish Netherlands. Not that Cranfield eschewed history altogether. He rehearsed the historical background to the dispute, the enactment of the law banishing English cloth, its frequent modification by treaty and the recent petition of the four provinces for its strict enforcement, the expiration of the last licence and the arch-duke's refusal to issue another. But history for Cranfield was the icing on his argument, not the argument itself.

Two facts appeared to Cranfield noteworthy: the archduke profited by eighteen shillings for every long cloth and nine shillings for every short cloth when he licensed English cloth for import and the trade figures for the period from Christmas 1610 to Christmas 1611 showed that the English had exported 6,967 cloths to the Spanish Netherlands. The archduke had made £5,076 18s in licences alone. Cranfield structured his analysis 'to show that the banishment of English cloth out of the Archduke's dominions will be much more prejudicial to the Archduke and his people than it will be to the King of England his subjects, and therefore by all likelihood will not long continue'.[18] Several reasons seemed to him to argue persuasively against the archduke's action. He would lose £7,000 in licences and cus-toms; his subjects who made their living from the cloth trade would go begging; his principal cities of Antwerp and Lille which had opposed the petition of the four provinces would be discontented. He broke down the trade figures further, to point an interesting conclusion. Of the 6,967 cloths shipped to the Spanish Netherlands 3,440 were coloured, 3,527 white. He contended that at least as many white cloths would be sold anyway to that country because the citizens of Antwerp, many of them in the cloth trade, maintained the right to import them by way of Middleburg. English mer-chants would save up to 24 shillings per long cloth which they had previously paid for licence and transportation. 'The greatest prejudice then that the execution of this law can do to the state of England is but the hazard of not venting of 3500 coloured cloths yearly in the archduke's dominions . . . that number being but a handful in comparison of the quantities made in England.' Cranfield thought that English merchants could easily sell those cloths in other lands and that the complaints of the archduke's own subjects would force him to rescind his ban. In a protest he drafted against the archduke's ban, Cranfield pointedly argued that it was not only

against the direct words of the treaty made in *anno* 1604, but against common sense, for now, in a time of peace and amity . . . he hath revived a law long since made for the banishing of our English cloths, which in the time of war and hostility were permitted to come in upon licence without any contradiction.[19]

Common sense dictated that in addition to an optimistic economic assess-ment Cranfield provide some concrete proposals to deal with the dilemma. Therefore he suggested that the king banish all the manufactures of the Spanish Netherlands from England. Since England bought from the arch-duke's domains twice as much as any other state and three times as much as the archduke's lands bought from England, this would be an effective blow against that state's economy. It might keep the archduke from collecting the

£300,000 that he had demanded of his provinces, 'by reason of the discontent induced in almost every one of his towns and villages by the stay of the sale of those goods whereby they live'. Cranfield noted that some of the archduke's subjects had foreseen and feared England's retaliation, and protested against the archduke's action back in April of 1612. Cannily, Cranfield scotched the idea that the archduke might declare war if England resorted to this measure. His land was too poor. He had owed his soldiers 3,000,000 crowns since the truce with Holland in 1609. The Hollanders would seize the opportunity to break that truce should conflict develop between the archduke and England. And lest it be thought that the King of Spain might come to his rescue, Cranfield pointed out that Philip III, too, was in extreme need. He had only been able to pay the Genoese one-seventh of what he had owed them since 1607. Cranfield ended his analysis by emphasising that 'we ought without any longer delay to fall to banishing of the said Archduke's manufactures as a present means to bring forth the reimportation of the cloths of this land into his country again there to be vented'.[20]

That Cranfield's approach was an unusual one finds substantiation in the archduke's answer to England's remonstrance. The archduke argued the legality of his edict on the grounds that English cloth had always been banished from Flanders, that the treaty of 1506 did not contravene this usage and that the English king had failed to observe the conditions of the peace concluded with the archduke in 1604.[21] In short, the archduke, like the Privy Council, appealed to history for justification. At this point it may be objected that if both the Privy Council and the archduke viewed the matter in historical terms, then that, in fact, was its real nature and it was Cranfield's economic analysis that was unmindful of the central issues of law and sovereignty. On the other hand it might be said that though the Privy Council and the archduke framed their arguments in historical terms, it was for form's sake only. Both knew the heart of the conflict lay in a commercial rivalry and its outcome would depend on who would hold the upper hand in a trade war. In that case Cranfield's analysis merely stated the obvious. The truth is more complex. Cranfield's ability to analyse with exactness the economic implications of the ban provided a new weapon in England's arsenal, one the Council steeped in precedent was hesitant to adopt. For though the argument was about trade, the archduke grounded his action on Flemish law and international agreements. And when the Privy Council met to devise an answer, they instinctively turned to tradition and treaties to guide their deliberations. Even when the cloth merchants were called on for advice, the Council directed their attention to the state of trade as it had existed in the early years of Elizabeth's reign. Cranfield's analysis, therefore, was of unique value and, more importantly, drew from that situation the principles to guide English policy. Cranfield's vision of the conduct of foreign affairs and foreign trade meant a painful if potent readjustment of the Council's views.

His vision ultimately prevailed although it took almost another year. In January 1613 the Archbishop of Canterbury noted that 'this last summer the matter was in hand but their honours thought the Archduke would not dare proceed therein'.[22] Sporadic attempts were made between August 1612 and June 1613 to resolve the crisis. In each case the Privy Council began again by setting up a committee to investigate the relevant treaties.[23] Each time it was without result. Only when the Council decided in the spring of 1613 to move against Flemish manufactures as Cranfield had suggested the previous August did the archduke reconsider his position. 'Finding the errors of the informations whereupon he restrained the sale of English cloths in Brabant, and the great loss his people are like to sustain in their traffic if your Majesty should prohibit the utterance of his manufactures in England',[24] he sent an emissary to settle all his differences with England. Under this threat, the archduke acted as Cranfield predicted. Cranfield's economic analysis had proven accurate enough to ensure Northampton's enthusiastic and continued patronage. On financial questions, Cranfield became an invaluable adviser, combining a keen sense of the possible with a statistical precision upon which his money-making depended. He was soon put to work making sense out of the king's finances.

III

The problem of making the royal revenue stretch to cover the royal expenses proved the most intractable of James's reign. In 1612 and 1613 Northampton examined dozens of projects to find those designed to increase revenue as well as to line the pockets of court projectors.[25] Most of these recapitulated or expanded on long-familiar devices. Newer proposals did not often confront the political problems inherent in tapping new sources of revenue. Northampton's central concern was to oversee the royal administration and, as we have seen, to establish only projects that would do the king the greatest good and the subject the least harm. Drawing on his analysis of trade with the Spanish Netherlands, Lionel Cranfield was able to develop a revenue measure which proved both lucrative and politically viable.

Cranfield had already pointed out that England imported three times as much from the archduke's domains as she exported. To combat England's unfavourable balance of trade, increased by the activities of 'strangers', and to raise funds, Cranfield proposed an additional imposition of threepence in the pound to be levied on goods imported and exported by alien merchants only. When Salisbury had imposed new duties above the regular customs in 1608, he had levied them across the board, making no distinction between native and foreign traders. These impositions, Cranfield said, upset the traditional customs arrangements whereby aliens had always paid threepence more than English merchants.[26] Salisbury's impositions had raised an

outcry from Parliament, but Cranfield's would have the advantage of carrying no political liability since it was levied upon an unrepresented minority.
To make sure of its acceptance, however, the Council sent up a trial
balloon, calling together at the end of September 1612 'the merchants in
generality as well strangers as English . . . about the threepence asked of the
foreigners'. When it had successfully faced this first challenge, Northampton, as Cranfield's patron, was delighted to present the plan to the king.
Informing James of the feeble objections put forward by some of the
English merchants who traded with France and feared retaliatory duties,
Northampton wrote, 'if the merchants can allege no better reasons . . . for
the disproof of this proposition, his Majesty shall know his humble 3
[Northampton] hath found out another 3d to serve him the more suitably'.[27]

But while the threepence aroused little domestic opposition, it was objected to, naturally enough, by its intended victims. On several occasions the
Privy Council obligingly heard the arguments of foreign merchants, and of
Ambassador Caron of the United Provinces representing Dutch mercantile
interests. Cranfield's role in the formulation of policy now changed from
that of private adviser to public servant. Instead of merely occupying a position in the wings, Cranfield was brought forward by Northampton to
defend his brainchild. At a meeting of the Privy Council in the spring of
1613 attended by Ambassador Caron and several foreign merchants, Cranfield justified the imposition by historical precedent, referring to the *Carta
Mercatoria*, a charter of liberties granted by Edward I in 1303 to foreign
merchants in return for their paying what was then called the 'new custom'.
This 'new custom' included threepence per pound on general merchandise.
Cranfield argued by analogy that the king was entitled to receive an extra
threepence from aliens any time new duties were imposed.[28] When the
foreign merchants said they did not dispute the king's right, but insisted
that it had never been levied to the extent proposed, the reply was that the
merchants should rather 'hold themselves bound to the king to forbear the
just arrearage of sums unpaid than to take exception to lawful demand by
charter which no time could abolish'. The strength of the government's
case overwhelmed Caron and the merchants, Northampton reported
happily to Rochester. And he praised 'Cranfield [who had] carried himself
with great pregnancy and sufficiency in this business'. The new imposition
was levied from 28 September 1613; Cranfield was its receiver with a fee of
£150 a year and the right to keep any monies he collected above the £3,000
which was allotted to the king.[29]

IV

The threepence proposal was merely the start. At Northampton's request,
Cranfield proceeded to take on the revision of the Great Farm of the customs
and the farm of the French and Rhenish wine customs. By a careful statistical

analysis of the customs receipts, the king's rent and the farmer's profits, Cranfield enabled the king to increase his revenues.

From the fourteenth to the sixteenth centuries the English customs were administered in each port by a customer who farmed the duties, guaranteeing the Crown an annual rent and reserving to himself revenues above that rent. Under Elizabeth attempts were made to consolidate the customs by category, by variously farming the customs on woollen cloth and wines at all ports, and by farming the customs of all the outports. In 1590 the Crown again took over the administration of the customs, but farming continued to promise greater profit.[30] In 1604, with peace with Spain and the prospect of expanded trade, the Privy Council revised the Book of Rates on which the customs were based, and decided to farm almost all the customs as a unit. Lord Treasurer Dorset, Salisbury and Northampton entered into negotiations with several groups of merchants with whom each was associated: Dorset's group headed by William Garway of the Levant Company, Cecil's by Francis Jones, an official of the customs house, Northampton's by Sir John Swinnerton, wine farmer and later Lord Mayor of London.[31] Although it had been hoped that the merchants would set as the base value of the farm the average of the receipts of the past ten years, Dorset settled for a medium of seven years.[32] But when the submitted bids were unsatisfactory, he demanded £28,600 above the medium and got it from Cecil's group who, joining with Dorset's, froze out Swinnerton.[33] The Great Farm covered customs on all imports and exports with the exception of petty farms covering items such as silk, gold thread, currants and French and Rhenish wines. Paying an annual rent of £112,400 and administering the customs offices, the farmers provided the king with both a regular revenue and a national organisation which facilitated collection and the raising of new duties. Of greatest importance, the organisation of the Great Farm provided the government with a pool of London merchants willing to advance to the Crown its own revenues at 10 per cent interest. Robert Ashton has effectively argued that 'the chief utility of the system of customs farming was . . . to be found in the regularity and efficiency with which the farmers were able to meet the royal demands for loans'.[34]

Both as Swinnerton's disappointed patron and in the name of reform, Northampton fought for several years to overturn the farmers' patent, or at the least, to increase the king's income. In 1607 Swinnerton accused the Great Farmers of fraud, claimed that the medium was inaccurate and made a new offer for the farm. The imminent success of this offer was related in a letter of John Chamberlain's:

the Earl of Northampton [is] further in grace than ever or than any man, whereby it is thought he hath overthrown the Earl of Salisbury's patentees of the customs and a new patent is making for Sir John Swinnerton and his associates, who they say offers an hundred thousand pounds for a fine, and £4,000 more yearly rent than is now paid.[35]

Through Salisbury's support the farmers did maintain their patent but were forced to raise the king's rent to £120,000. When the farm fell in again in December 1611, Swinnerton made a new bid, offering a fine of £100,000 in addition to a yearly rent of £120,000. According to Northampton, Salisbury sent for Swinnerton and told him in a fury that he would never enjoy the farm despite the efforts of his 'best friends' at court.[36]

The renewal of the farm was almost complete in 1612 when Northampton wrote to the king of a fraud perpetrated by Dorset when he negotiated the Great Farm in 1604 and continued by Salisbury when he became Lord Treasurer. The earl's informant was John Suckling, Dorset's secretary until his death in 1608 and brother-in-law to Lionel Cranfield. Suckling told Northampton that Dorset had distributed £1,700 in royal pensions to participants in the customs farm who were now holding offices in the customs administration. Each pension had carried with it the price tag of three or four years' purchase which Dorset pocketed.[37] Salisbury had been moved to revoke the patents but refused even though it would be to the king's benefit. His reasons were two, Northampton wrote to the king. 'First because some of the purchasers were his chiefest instruments in probing for money when his vast demands did urge, and affording bribes as vast out of the customs which they farmed by a false trick of *leger-de-main* at their first election . . . the second was to make the things more vendable when they should fall in by vacancy.'[38]

Northampton's attack on Salisbury, whatever its accuracy, was obviously not disinterested. His malicious description of the late Lord Treasurer's actions allowed him to blacken his dead rival's name, present his own efforts as treasury commissioner in a good light and enhance the position of his client Swinnerton. On Dorset and Salisbury's side it could be argued that by placing the farmers in important customs offices with commensurate rewards, a certain amount of reformation had been achieved. It has been suggested, for instance, that the farmers stopped the extortion practised on merchants by the traditional officers.[39] The intimate link between high officials and their merchant clients exercised an ambiguous influence on policy. On the one hand payoffs to privy councillors, such as Salisbury's £6,000 profit in 1604, often prevented adequate assessment of competing offers. On the other, losers in the race for profits could be tapped by disconsolate officials for information with which to undermine their rivals. The king stood to profit from such controversy. A distinction must be made, however, between the accusations of fraud initiated by Swinnerton which were aimed at getting the Great Farm for himself or making the other merchants pay dearly, and the statistical analysis of the English customs undertaken by Cranfield which provided the basic information essential to formulating policy.

On 14 August 1612 Northampton sent Rochester Swinnerton's most recent offer for the farm, urging that it be shown to the king and considered with speed because the farmers' new patent was about to pass.[40] Northampton's plea was successful; the patent was stayed while Cranfield investigated

Northampton: line cors Disc 79 (dk) file cors

the farm. He compiled statistics on the customs receipts for each of the previous seven years, analysing them according to port, specific duty and imports and exports. Using these figures Cranfield challenged the farmers who claimed that they had been driven to a hard bargain. 'These statements are false, for the contractors have made many thousand pounds and diverse of them, who before were but mean officers in that place, have raised themselves to great estates.' Cranfield calculated that the farmers had grossed £1,081,359 in the seven years they had held the patent. After paying the king rent amounting to £824,800 and management charges of about £8,000 a year, he reckoned they had cleared over £200,000. The farmers had made a large profit, but the king had suffered almost as large a loss. Cranfield specified five defects in the patent. First of all, the seven poorest years had been deliberately chosen from the previous ten to make up the medium, by which the farmers benefited and the king lost over £16,000. Secondly, the port of Carlisle had been omitted from the medium which had meant a loss of over £7,000. The Great Farm was to pay the king £28,600 above the poor seven years' medium of £85,272, which amounted to £113,872, but the rent had been set at £112,400. This third defect brought a loss of £10,304. Fourthly, by omitting the improvement in the Book of Rates the king had lost £98,000. Finally, the customs on stuffs newly in use since the time of Queen Elizabeth had not been allowed for in the rent, and the king, Cranfield estimated, had lost thereby £28,000. The sum total of these losses he set at £157,697.[41]

The farmers drew up a brief in which they justified their administration, claiming that any defects in the patent were not of their making, that they had increased the king's rent several times, furnished him with a loan of £120,000 and administered the impositions instituted in 1608, even though it cut down on their customs income. Cranfield answered this point by point. He insisted that the farmers had indeed introduced the defects in the patent because many were customs officers and had an intimate knowledge of 'which were the best years upon a medium for themselves to ground an offer and how as well by omissions as by improvements ... most benefit might be raised'. Contrary to their assertion, they had only increased the king's share under the pressure of Swinnerton's counter offers. They advanced £120,000 to the king not to do him service but to earn their 10 per cent.[42] To the farmers' claim that they had sustained a loss by the levying of impositions, Cranfield countered that they had been paid an additional £1,160 to collect them. As with all the customs revenues, the farmers had the use of the revenues until they came due, a not insubstantial asset. Cranfield concluded that

nothing at all doth thereby appear to have been brought in by their industry, but many thousand pounds do appear to have been withdrawn unto themselves which otherwise might have been brought into his Majesty's coffers with the said fines of £110,000 and £105,000 twice offered by others.[43]

On 8 October 1612 Northampton composed a letter to the king based on Cranfield's analysis, informing him of the errors in the Great Farm. Northampton focused on the defects in the medium, but he transformed Cranfield's statistical analysis into a political attack on the king's highest ministers, specifically charging them with corruption. Although the government had wanted a medium of ten years, Dorset had settled for seven. Moreover Dorset and Salisbury had purposely omitted items from the medium and based the king's revenue on the old Book of Rates while allowing the farmers to collect the customs according to the new. Even when an attempt was made in 1607 to right these defects, Dorset and Salisbury conspired to leave out other merchandise from the medium in order that the farmers might profit. The Lord Treasurer had, he concluded,

> made the benefit of the farm to swell to that proportion which came to be sharked and shared after by the free-booters, that, casting lots upon the robe imperial and shredding the same into shares, made it so short as with much ado it could be stretched out by tricks . . . to cover indignity.[44]

Northampton translated Cranfield's statistical analysis into the baroque prose with which he was most at home. To maintain their patent, the farmers were forced to pay the Crown a fine of £20,000, lend the king £18,000 for seven years and, in 1614, increase their rent to £140,000.[45]

V

In addition to the Great Farm, the Garway and Jones syndicate also held the farm of the duties on French and Rhenish wines. This combination appeared to increase their bargaining power for they could threaten, as they did in 1612, to give up the Great Farm unless they got the terms they wanted on the wines.[46] Such leverage, however, proved illusory because of the repeated attacks and counter offers made by their rival Sir John Swinnerton. He had farmed the wine duties from 1595 to 1607 at which date the Earl of Devonshire through nominees was awarded the farm and immediately compounded with Garway. Northampton as Swinnerton's patron had already accused Devonshire of fraud when he held the farm. In 1612, in addition to criticising the conditions on which the Great Farm was let, Northampton expressed the hope that the wine farm could be revoked.[47] On 11 October he and Ellesmere formally notified the king of his legal counsels' opinion that the wine farm had been obtained by fraud, and that he was entitled to have the profits sequestered and the lease recalled.[48] Under the contract of 1607 the farmers paid the king an annual rent of £14,000 with a fine of £6,000 and a loan of £12,000.[49] In January 1613 Swinnerton offered a rent of £22,000 and a £6,000 fine. Cranfield, fresh from his successful work on the Great Farm, undertook to weigh the two offers, applying his expert knowledge to the accounts of the French and Rhenish wines.

If the Great Farm was a lucrative investment, the wine farm was a gold mine. Specifying the wine customs collected at London and the outports and the price of wine per tun, Cranfield put the receipts of the French and Rhenish wine duties at an average of £35,444 over the previous five years. Deducting the king's rent of £14,000 and other expenses, he reckoned the farmers had made a profit of about £15,228 a year.[50] The wine farmers were keeping almost 43 per cent of their gross receipts. In addition, he noted that the money the farmers could make by investing the receipts until the rent came due more than covered the costs of managing the farm. These farmers had few management costs at all, since they administered it jointly with the Great Farm.[51] In June 1613 Cranfield drew up a brief weighing the farmers' offer for the renewal of the French and Rhenish wine farm. He pointed out that at first the farmers meant to offer only a fine of £12,000, with no increase in rent, counting on the king's lack of ready money to meet pressing needs. At the time of this proposal Northampton had written urgently to Rochester that 'a worse bargain cannot be made for the king himself whatsoever licking of fingers may be found out otherwise in close cookery'.[52] But the sequestration of the farmers' profits had had an unlooked for advantage; it had brought into the king's coffers an unexpectedly large amount of money. Cranfield stressed that the profit for the year ending on 29 September 1613 would be at least £18,000 and by 25 March 1614 the king would take in £20,000 over and above the rent of £14,000 that the farmers were now paying. On these figures, he rejected both the farmers' original offer and their new one of a rent of £20,000 with a fine of another £20,000. Even this would mean, Cranfield claimed, a loss to the king of £18,000 in money and £9,000 in rent.[53]

Since there was nothing to be gained by accepting the Garway syndicate's offer, it might be assumed that it was not accepted. But in fact it was. Reform had its limits. In the making of policy, two or three options may be offered: a fourth is taken. The cogency of Cranfield's argument could not be denied, but it did not take into account the patronage relationships which determined the distribution of rewards at court. In January 1613, when Sir John Swinnerton made his offer for the wine farm, he also promised to pay Rochester £6,000 for his favour in obtaining the farm. Rochester was, however, already engaged to the present farmers. As powerful and persistent as he was, Northampton could not compete with the king's favourite, to whom he admitted defeat.

> I pass over willingly where they showed themselves under the grace of Sweet Rochester, but otherwise they should have had their hands full of a business so well advanced by my industry and so safely carried, before they had been freed upon those conditions that now do fall to them.[54]

The farmers still paid dearly. Cranfield was authorised to draft a letter in the king's name addressed to the Lord Chancellor and Lord Privy Seal commending their efforts in increasing the customs revenue beyond expectation and directing them to accept Garway's latest offer because it contained a larger amount of ready money than Swinnerton's,[55] a not inconsiderable selling point to a king with an empty treasury. The final agreement with the farmers called for them to pay a fine of £16,000 and an annual rent of £20,000 to which was added £6,705 in lieu of providing the king's household with 200 tuns of wine and the nobility and gentry with 1,050 tuns of wine duty free.[56] Cranfield's successful revision of the terms under which the customs were rented out led him to suggest, and Northampton to promote, the creation of the office of surveyor-general of the customs to provide 'exact information on the terms of trade'.[57] The new office, which Cranfield intended to occupy himself, would institutionalise the role that he had just recently played in the customs negotiations. Emphasising his service to the Crown, Cranfield asserted that he had increased the king's revenue by £21,150; £10,000 from the new Great Farm patent, £6,000 from the wine farm, £4,000 as initiator and collector of the threepence imposition and £1,150 as the collector of the impositions. Northampton agreed on the efficacy of the office and urged Rochester to forward it on the following grounds: 'first the fruit which the king shall receive by his service; 2 the curb of cousinage and 3 the reward of industry.'[58] Reform and reward could go together. Cranfield was named to the surveyor's office with an annual salary of £200. Combined with his pension for his work on the Great Farm and the threepence imposition, Cranfield was now earning £500 a year as the government's expert adviser on economic policy. And his rewards were not only financial. In March 1613 he was knighted.

Under the patronage of the Earl of Northampton, Cranfield had made the transition from City merchant to court adviser. The contraction of his business investments in kersies, logwood and ordnance 'coincided with the crisis in Crown finance which cried out for the skill of a businessman'.[59] Cranfield's familiarity with the customs administration and his own participation as an investor in several of the customs farms enabled him to uncover the monies the king was losing by the defective and dishonest patents by which the Great Farm and the wine farm had been let. The method by which these farms were let, the marriage of convenience between court officials and City merchants, did not work to ensure an adequate revenue to the king, but it could be made to turn a profit for the king if syndicates were played off against one another. This Northampton accomplished in 1612 and 1613 with Cranfield's help. Unlike the other merchants of whom Northampton was patron, Swinnerton and, to a lesser extent, Ingram, and the group called in during the cloth trade crisis, Cranfield combined his experience and analytical ability with a concern for governmental reform. Northampton rightfully took pride in bringing him into the king's service, describing him as 'a merchant, a special friend of mine own, more witty and of better judgement than any'.[60]

The letting of the king's customs, it has been pointed out, offered advantages to several different interest groups. To the farmers who undertook to collect customs, it meant a tidy profit; to the merchants engaged in international trade, freedom from extortion practised by local customs officials; to the king, a steady income, a source of loans and, after Cranfield's work, an increased revenue. But the Great Farm had its opponents, chiefly those very customs officials who had been displaced or whose fees and functions had been downgraded by the new administration. Of these the most vocal was Thomas Milles, who presented his economic views in several books dedicated to the Earl of Northampton.

VI

Northampton spread his net wide. He was in touch with those outside the privileged circle of City merchants. Northampton's connection with Milles seems likely to have come about in one of two ways. Milles was chief customs official of Sandwich, one of the Cinque Ports, and in that position came under the jurisdiction and perhaps the notice of Northampton as Lord Warden. In addition, Robert Cotton was a friend of Milles, and may have served as intermediary. To Cotton Milles wrote quite forcefully of his disapproval of the customs farm, enclosing a memorandum on the subject, 'the reading or showing whereof I refer to your best discretion'.[61] Milles's works had circulated among royal officials in the 1590s and he had occasionally found himself in trouble with the authorities. He was admonished by the Privy Council on one occasion; on another, one of his books was stayed from publication. To ensure the acceptance of his writings, Milles needed a patron who would guarantee, as was the custom, the licensing of his works and protect him against his critics.[62] It would appear by Milles's laudatory dedications that in Northampton he had found one.[63] The argument of this chapter has been that those men involved in commercial affairs based their advice on policy on their own experience in trade. Milles's ideas reflected his experience as customer of Sandwich which, like the rest of England's provincial ports, had lost much of its foreign trade over the previous two centuries to London.

Milles was born in Kent in 1550, had a grammar-school education, and entered government service, serving for sixteen years in France, Flanders and Scotland. In 1585 he assumed the position of customer of Sandwich which he retained for thirty-eight years. He became secretary to Lord Cobham, Lord Warden of the Cinque Ports, in 1598. His experience on the continent and his knowledge of England's import and export trade ensured his ideas a hearing. When the Dutch concluded a peace treaty with Spain in 1609, Milles wrote to Cotton that his opinion had indeed been solicited by

Northampton. 'I busy myself in setting down certain acroamata spelled out of mine late *Alphabet* by my Lord of Northampton's direction, with whom I had discourse of late at Greenwich about bullion and traffic now upon the Truce of Holland.'[64] The 'Alphabet' to which Milles referred was his book, *The Customer's Alphabet and Primer*, which he published in 1608 and dedicated to Northampton.

Foreign trade had an important impact on the local economy of England in the seventeenth century. The interconnection of the balance of trade and bullion flow was only slowly being recognised by the government which attempted to deal with scarcity of capital signified by outflows of gold and silver by the enhancing of one metal or the other. Northampton's concern for the impact on English trade of the United Provinces' peace with Spain was a prescient one, since the two countries were at once partners and competitors. The Dutch finished English woollen products and provided the shipping for much of European commerce. Unfortunately Milles, a bullionist, did not provide useful insights into the complex relationship of trade and the movement of bullion. Still, he did provide Northampton with the views of the outports' merchants.

Milles asserted that traffic was being strangled by private monopolies such as the Merchant Adventurers who concentrated trade in their own hands and in London, at the expense of the outports. He advocated, like other representatives of the outports, the freeing of commerce from company regulation. The peace treaty with Spain in 1604, with its expected effect of expanded trade, had lent impetus to their demands. In Parliament that same year free trade was vigorously debated and in 1606 an Act was passed ensuring unregulated trade to France, Spain and Portugal.[65] But unlike most of the other outport 'free traders', Milles proposed to replace the regulated trading company with another and older structure, the home staple, market towns which handled specific commodities, controlled the quality of these commodities and the conditions under which they were traded. Milles complained that 'merchants by societies monopolising our staple commodities and royal wares have found the way to staple them beyond seas, and so confounding both our customs and diverting all our bullion'.[66] Milles urged the king to bring the staples home to increase his customs and his treasure.

Furthermore, Milles argued that under the new system of farming, customers such as himself, who served 'at the altar of trade', were deprived of those fees and rewards which their function deserved. 'We dip but our dishes in our neighbour's cisterns to quench our thirst, and at noon in his garden, crop a few of his leeks with his own consent, to keep us from starving.'[67] Milles's description differed from that of merchants who had complained of extortion and bribery practised by the customers. Under the Great Farm the customers were subordinated to a hierarchy of controllers, supervisors, farmers, searchers and waiters, about which Milles complained bitterly.[68]

Miles had little understanding of why bullion moved from one country to another – that it reflected the balance of trade, harvest fluctuations, and currency manipulations throughout Europe.[69] He blamed it on evil and usurious merchants. Despite his vigorous and prolific presentation of his views and his government contacts, Milles's ideas had little effect. It was suggested in the previous chapter that Edmund Bolton's historically minded advice on policy was not useful because it was too narrowly focused. The same was true of Milles. His experience of the real loss of trade by the provincial ports to London which controlled two-thirds to three-fourths of England's imports and exports led Milles to several erroneous conclusions. For instance, he claimed that monopolies were strangling English trade. In fact, England had a surplus of exports in both 1613 and 1614, as Lionel Cranfield pointed out. Moreover, Sandwich and its member ports, which exported mainly cloth and beer, yielded in one year of Milles's tenure £3,125 in customs: the second highest of the outports.[70] Milles also claimed that customs duties were too high, 'the utmost is thought too little'.[71] Actually, except for the export duty on wool and the import duty on wine, duties were very low. And duties became lower and lower as the Book of Rates, which established the wholesale value of the commodities on which duties were assessed, reflected less and less real values. There was no change in the Book of Rates between 1558 and 1604, and the 1604 revision only increased duties overall by 13.17 per cent.[72] Characterised by hyperbole, religious imagery and incorrect information, Milles's books may nevertheless have influenced parliamentary debate on the outports. Northampton provided him a forum, but did not adopt his advice.

VII

Milles hoped to promote the prosperity of the provincial ports by the re-establishment of the ancient institution of the home staple. Tobias Gentleman proposed another solution which aimed at the expansion of industry. A fisherman and shipbuilder who had served in the navy and the merchant marine, Gentleman advocated the creation of a state-supported fishing industry in his book, *England's Way to Win Wealth and to Employ Ships and Mariners*, which he dedicated to Northampton when it was published in 1614.[73]

Northampton's attitude toward the encouragement of the English fishing trade, like that of the king and Council as a whole, had tended to focus on restrictive measures against commercial rivals. As Lord Warden of the Cinque Ports, Northampton's power extended to the regulation of fishing within that domain. When Cinque Ports fishermen complained against the incursions of the Dutch fishing fleet, Northampton's authority to issue licences to foreign fishermen was extended and made the model for the nation. King James issued a proclamation in 1609 that no foreign fishermen were to fish off the British coast without a licence.[74]

In 1608 and 1609 the Council, acting on a petition of merchants, proposed another restriction, that of the tax on the tenth fish, called the assize herring. As well as laying claim to sovereignty over coastal waters, the king stood to gain a sizeable rent from a farm of the tax on foreign fishermen of one-tenth of their catch off British coasts. The petition had been referred to Northampton, and he went so far as to undertake negotiations with a London syndicate, perhaps to lease the farm if he himself secured its grant. Urging the merchants thoroughly to acquaint Salisbury with the matter, he suggested they 'rely upon his favour . . . I would be glad that his hand and mine might concur in this as they do in many other prosperous effects and have the same success both of honour and utility'.[75] The words are silky and ambiguous but the intimate connection of patronage, policy and profit is clear. Richard Rainsford, Northampton's client, did contact Salisbury; the king was, however, forced to delay the licensing of fishing after strong protests by the Dutch and French.[76]

Policy was uppermost in Northampton's mind in 1612 and 1613 when he dominated the Privy Council. As we have seen he examined an enormous range of proposals whose end was not only to increase royal revenues but also to improve the English economy. Among these were projects to build fishing vessels. It is often difficult to link such tracts to their dedicatees; often there existed no relationship other than the writer's desire to ensure publication or flatter the great. This case is different. Gentleman's work was written specifically for Northampton's information and provides an example of the links forged between adviser and policy-maker. More importantly, it marked a change from the restrictive policies of the past to a new emphasis on economic expansion. This change of views was one in which Northampton participated: he was, for instance, an eager promoter of the Newfoundland fishing expedition.

William Monson, Master of Armoury, Admiral of the Narrow Seas, and a client of Northampton's, advised him on the issue and commissioned Gentleman's work. Years after Northampton's death Monson wrote:

I confess this fishing is a business I have long taken into consideration. My Lord of Northampton, if he were now living, were able to witness how much it was solicited and desired by me, and no less wished and desired by his Lordship. I caused one Tobias Gentleman, a mariner by profession, but indeed a man of better parts than ordinary seamen, and much practised in the northern fishing, to dedicate a book to his Lordship which gave particular notice of the Hollanders' proceedings in their pinks and busses and what we shall do in the imitation of them. But by the death of my Lord it rested unthought by me till the late Duke of Richmond revived it and importuned me once more to it. His death in the like manner made it die, till his Majesty of late . . . took more than an ordinary care how to effect it.[77]

Monson's comments point up the personal nature of policy-making when proposals were dependent on the support of individual privy councillors. In his dedication Gentleman recognised this by emphasising both Northampton's eminence and the corresponding importance of the fishing project.[78] Based on his experience in 'fisher affairs' Gentleman presented a detailed description of the Dutch fishing trade with advice as to how England could establish her own profitable enterprise by the building of ships and repairing of her sea towns.

The energetic pursuit of deep-sea herring fishing by the Dutch had aroused the envy of Englishmen since the 1570s but the Dutch had actually been fishing off the coasts of Great Britain for centuries. English fishing had been in decline since the Reformation. Neither a political Lent, prescribing certain days of the week as fish days, nor barring the import of fish caught by foreigners – both Tudor expedients – had revived it.[79]

Signalling a changed approach to commerce, seventeenth-century pamphleteers urged more expansive methods, such as the building of fishing boats and changing the work habits of British fishermen to get them to ply longer hours during a longer season.[80] Commenting on the popular preference for leisure rather than profit, John Keymer complained that as soon as their boats were filled, the anglers went off to the alehouse even if it were only nine in the morning. In the course of his investigation of the fishing trade Keymer consulted Gentleman, whose collection of notes he wished to lay before the Privy Council. When nothing came of Keymer's plan, Gentleman decided to cast his notes and proposals in book form as *England's Way to Win Wealth....*[81] His was the first work to give an accurate account of the Dutch trade, a specific description of England's sea towns of Norfolk and Suffolk, the ways in which they had to be revitalised, and a breakdown of the actual costs of building herring boats.

The Dutch, Gentleman said, sent out 1,000 ships, 600 of them busses of as much as 120 tons carrying 20,000 men, to fish in the North Sea from 14 June to 24 August, and filled each boat two or three times over with herring. 'Herring-Yagers', merchant ships which sailed out to the North Sea to pick up the herring, played perhaps the most important part in the Dutch routine. Not only did they allow each buss to triple its capacity, they brought provisions and supplies to the fleet and carried away the herring to be sold in other countries. By this sophisticated system of fishing the Dutch took in £1,000,000 a year.[82] England, he argued, had the natural resources to emulate the Dutch: the fish off its own shores and the supplies of cordage, barrel-boards and tar which the Dutch themselves had to import. The benefits from the exploitation of herring fishing were typical of seventeenth-century project literature: it would provide employment, generate capital and strengthen the country's defences. Thousands of poor people 'which now know not how to live',[83] would be put to work. The outflow of bullion would be stayed. Gold and silver were scarce, Gentleman thought, because Englishmen were paying out their own specie for fish from their own streams. He pointed out that between Christmas 1613 and 18 February 1614, £12,000 had already been paid in London for barrelled fish. And England's ships and mariners would be increased, strengthening the kingdom against foreign invasion. The decayed state of English seamen was such that 'this last year there was a general press along the coast of England from Hull in Yorkshire into St Michael's Mount in Cornwall, only for sailors to furnish but seven ships for the wafting over of the Count Palatine and his most noble Princess but 28 leagues'.[84]

For England to develop a profitable herring industry, two conditions were requisite: her sea towns had to be rebuilt and a fleet of fishing boats had to be constructed. Gentleman offered a minute description of the sea towns of Norfolk and Suffolk, the number of their boats and fishermen, the condition of their piers as well as their place in the English economy. Sowld, for instance, was often so stopped up with stones that it was impossible to get in or out of the harbour. Ipswich, on the other hand, he thought the perfect place to build and sail busses, with plenty of timber and excellent workmen. Though the city had no fishermen, it could draw on those of surrounding towns. In addition, Ipswich cloth merchants had factors all over Europe who would be able to sell herring. Yarmouth, of course, was the centre of the English fishing trade, frequented by the fishermen of the Cinque Ports, the west and north counties, as well as the Dutch and the French. Given busses and barrelled fish, the port could excel all of England and Holland, for it was the best handler of fish and fishermen of the North Sea. Yarmouth's potential was at present wasted, however, because its harbour was in disrepair and its merchants lacked incentive to build or back busses because they made their profit by buying herring from the Dutch and selling it to the French.[85]

For building busses, Gentleman offered his own services as shipwright and provided exact figures on how much the ships would cost and how much they would bring in. With furnishings, sails, cables, anchors, the vessels would only cost £500 each to build. Provisions, wages, barrels and salt would come to £335. The season's haul, which he estimated at a hundred last of barrels at £10, would bring in £1,000. With £100 set aside for repairs, that left a clear profit of £555 per vessel from a summer's sailing.

The creation of a new industry required capital which Gentleman thought should be provided by the state and the well-to-do. 'Let all noble, worshipful and wealthy subjects put to their adventuring hands for the speedy launching and floating forward of this great commonwealth business ... for that these that be now the fishermen themselves be not able to begin.'[86] Like Cranfield's, Gentleman's survey and his conclusions were based on his personal experience in the fishing industry and the statistics of his trade. The recommendations he offered were equally pragmatic. If the fishermen themselves could not develop a viable herring industry, then it was up to the state to supply the money, the protection and the impetus. If

Monson was right, Northampton was moving in the direction of state support for new industry. In this sense efforts to build fishing vessels paralleled Alderman Cockayne's project, undertaken as Supple has suggested, to improve and diversify the English economy.

In his immediate object Gentleman was disappointed. The Earl of Northampton was gravely ill and attended his last Privy Council meeting in late February, four days after Gentleman's book appeared. In June he died. Gentleman's advice was not taken. Its accuracy and acuity, however, recommended it to later writers such as Malynes and Mun who cited it with approval in the 1620s debate on the economy.[87] Attempts to establish a state-supported fishing industry were made under Charles I in the 1630s, but they were not successful. Not until 1661 was the Royal Fishery established.

In any government the connection between patronage and policy is often a close one. In early Stuart England, with its unwieldy administration and ministers whose functions were undifferentiated, that connection was particularly crucial. A privy councillor such as the Earl of Northampton, who was diligent in his office, had to advise the king on a wide range of issues, including foreign policy, finance and commerce. The method that Northampton adopted to fulfil this responsibility was to seek out and rely on the advice of experts.

Northampton's patronage of merchants representative of different companies, different industries and different outlooks did not guarantee the making of good economic policy. None the less there is plenty of evidence that he was diligent in seeking such advice. More important, he recognised good advice when he heard it. Cranfield's handling of the trade dispute with the archduke, the threepence duty and the customs farms was masterly. In addition, Northampton showed indications of breaking with the restrictive measures generally favoured by the Council in his attitudes toward the fishing industry, the Cockayne and starch projects. The last usually seen as simply a profit-making venture, also bore the hope of the creation of a domestic starch industry, part of the diversification of the economy that occurred in the first half of the seventeenth century. Finally, by encouraging the works of Thomas Milles, Northampton ensured the outports were not without their spokesmen at court. Northampton's 'brains trust', his network of advisers, served at once to provide advice, and to build links between various interest groups and the court, thereby strengthening ties between the king and his subjects.

With Cotton and Cranfield, Northampton's patronage went beyond the gathering of information. Both were brought into the operation of the government itself; Cotton through his preparation of government propaganda in the aftermath of the Gunpowder Plot, his participation in the naval commission and the setting up of the baronetage, and Cranfield through his drafting of official government documents in the dispute with the archduke, the reassessment of the customs farms, and his new office as surveyor-general. Perhaps the highpoint of Northampton's work was his attempt to reform several government departments towards which he concentrated his patronage. By soliciting and publishing the views of his scholar and merchant clients, Northampton may also have been seeking the tacit consent to government policy of those groups of which they were a part. Reform was the goal of Northampton's policy, for which patronage and the creation of his 'brains trust' were the means.

Chapter 8

Administrative Reform and the Problems of Corruption

The overriding problems of the Jacobean court were financial and administrative. We have examined the variety of such issues that confronted Northampton as an official, the way in which he sought advice and the sorts of advice he received. How then did he act on that advice? A useful answer is provided by the indignant letter he wrote to James. Attacked by other courtiers who labelled his investigations of the navy and customs farms as 'spleen', Northampton argued:

> It was a spleen that descried the false trick in the ... ordnance, that sought to stop the leaks of the ships, that advised your Majesty to look to the gleanings and purloinings of the old Treasurer, that stops unworthy, dangerous and unjust demands at the Privy Seal, that seeks to reform the corruptions of the office of arms with a check to the purchasers of arms and gentility ... I am charged privily with spleen for moving my master in his wants rather to make use of springing profits to himself than to cram those that, in my knowledge, are full to the throat, and beg rather out of wantonness than necessity.[1]

By following the path laid down in Northampton's letter, it is possible to unravel not only his efforts to reform and remodel Jacobean administration but discover as well the reasons for his failure.

The characteristics of early modern bureaucracy are well known.[2] In Weberian terms it combined both patrimonial and rational elements. Appointment to office and promotion were made through patronage connections; officeholders were paid by those requiring their services; private servants were often brought informally into office and, if they stayed long enough, became royal officials. An informal market grew up for the buying and selling of offices and their reversions, with the profits going to the officeholders, not the Crown.

English administration had greatly expanded in the sixteenth century as the state took over the functions previously performed by church and guild and involved itself minutely in the country's social and economic life. Historians have generally characterised this bureaucracy as increasingly burdensome, by the seventeenth century, to the king and country it served.[3] Equally, however, it provided the government with new offices and privileges to parcel out to the political elite, centralising reward and obedience at court instead of in the hands of the landed magnates. The recipients of these royal favours were principally the nobility and gentry who oversaw local government and a lesser number of lawyers, both common and civil, and merchants whose services the Crown could not do without. One essential problem for the early Stuart monarchy was to make sure that its administration did not operate simply in the interests of its many officeholders. Yet to do so required the co-operation of some, at least, of those very officeholders. Failure effectively to monitor the distribution of office and privilege meant not only an unworkable administration, but more vitally, the alienation of the elite on whom the government relied. For without supervision, early modern government was prone to bribery, extortion and outright thievery, with a hand in the pocket not only of the king but his subjects. In short, while court patronage was the key to control of administration, it was also the cause of corrupt practices. Therein lay the Jacobean dilemma.[4]

Although there is a difficulty in characterising as corrupt those practices which may not have been considered so in the early seventeenth century, the term 'corruption' was defined with increasing stringency in this period. For the purpose of analysis, it is useful to apply the modern Western definition of corruption to delineate such practices.[5]

Northampton fought for administrative reform as the means to the Crown's financial and political stability. His work included investigations of household expenditures, purveyance, ecclesiastical courts, the ordnance office, the navy (the corruption of which he described as 'damnable and infinite') and the Earl Marshal's office.[6] Such reform was necessary because 'no age ever granted leave to disburse at will, to ask at will, proportion at will, to pay their own conditions with the king's money and seek out the very heart blood of the regal majesty without accompt, and the kingdom thrives accordingly'. It was no marvel, he thought, that the king was 'pressed more than his progenitors to borrow of kind subjects when his unkind servants have more abused and deceived him than any of his antecessors that had been less bountiful'.[7] In Northampton's mind the problems of financial solvency, administrative reform and loyal subjects were thus intimately connected. To solve them Northampton as always sought expert advice from scholars and merchants, but as often he turned to officeholders. Their opinions were not disinterested. Indeed they often had vested interests in the continuation of their jobs and the procedures of their offices. They were familiar, however, with the workings of the bureaucracy, and Northampton usually began his systematic attack on government abuses by asking the opinion of members of the office under study. In his search for solutions he frequently annotated the memoranda prepared for him and they provide us not only with his own reading of these briefs, but often with a vivid picture of Jacobean government and society.

Two examples provide a sense of the tangle of issues touched on by administrative reform, the goals pursued and the difficulties in the way of change. The first assessed the abuses of the purveyors, the second Irish finances. Northampton's concern was generated by parliamentary discontent as well as bureaucratic disorder; his goal was not only to repair the office but also to cement the good feelings between the king and his subjects.

I

Purveyance was the king's prerogative to take supplies and carts for the royal Household at a price he set himself, below the market price. The activities of the king's purveyors, such as taking carts at harvest time or threatening to take foodstuffs unless they were bribed not to, constituted a chronic source of abuse and complaint. Attempts at reform dated back to Magna Carta. Stringent legislation had been passed by Parliament relating to the purveyors' office, amounting to some forty statutes up to the time of Elizabeth's accession.[8] The question of purveyance and demands for further statutory limitations were raised in almost every one of her Parliaments, and continued into James's reign. Periodic efforts were made in both reigns to substitute a tax on the counties to replace the ancient right. The king shared his subjects' indignation at the abuse of the purveyors. Concentrating on this connection between purveyance and politics, he urged Cecil in 1604 to 'be earnest in trying and severe in punishing the thievish purveyors and take all pains ye can to inform and tune well the parliament men'.[9] In October 1605, when Northampton was engaged with Cecil in reforming the Household, he asked the chief cart-taker, Robert Fletcher, to prepare a brief on the purveyors' office not only to aid in reform, but also to forewarn the earl of objections that might arise in the session of Parliament already planned for the next January. Noting that 'these grievous afflictions laid upon the poor subjects by puling purveyors and unconscionable cart-takers were a just cause of clamours', Fletcher presented 'a view of certain evils grievously complained upon which in the next Parliament may be remembered and reformed'.[10]

   In colourful language Fletcher detailed the bribery, extortion and administrative laxity of his department, staffed by incompetents and 'bowling alley mates'. During the king's first progress, while the court was at Winchester, the cart-takers covered all Hampshire and 'bribed and abused ... as that grievous was it to hear the general complaints. But all was smoothed up and passed over, a second bribe in court answering for sundry ones inflicted upon the country.' The London cart-takers daily commandeered carts whether there was cause or not in order to extort £4 or £5 from each poor carter. Lord North, Treasurer of Queen Elizabeth's Household, took away the commissions of the cart-takers of London but later preferred a servant of his 'into that office which himself before had condemned for no office'. In fact the proliferation of offices characteristic of the central administration also occurred among the cart-takers, caused by court patronage.

Fletcher was not afraid to name names: Edward Cousins was 'a cunning briber' who had managed to be named clerk of the cart-takers with a fee of £100 even though the office was unnecessary.[11]

Fletcher's attack points up some of the complexities of Jacobean administration. Was Cousins's office a sinecure as Fletcher maintained or was it created in fact to provide the very oversight the office lacked, as Cousins's oath of office suggested?[12] Whether or not new offices were reforms would only be decided on in practice. What, then, did the Crown do about purveyance? It was, after all, worth between £25,000 and £50,000 a year. Salisbury and Northampton followed different paths. In the Parliament session of 1606 the king responded to Bills against purveyance by saying that he wished 'both the corruption and name of them to be utterly taken away and abolished'.[13] In an initiative that served as a preview for the negotiations over the Great Contract, Salisbury offered to abolish purveyance entirely in return for a lump sum to be used for the king's Household expenses. The Commons argued that to compound for purveyance would be to acknowledge the legitimacy of corrupt practices, while Bacon on behalf of the Crown told them that they would be buying the easing of inconvenience. One MP noted pessimistically, 'if we compound for the avoiding of purveyance and purveyors, we shall bind our posterity, and when our grievance shall notwithstanding continue . . . we shall be urged to new composition'.[14] The hostile reaction of the Commons forced the Crown to backtrack on purveyance. Salisbury wrote after the debate that 'we are now only seeking to temper that particular grievance by making a law to punish the abuse, but in no case to put down the use'.[15] King and Commons were one in condemning the corruption endemic in the process of purveyance. Where they differed was in what to do about it. Lord Protector Somerset had proposed in 1548 a similar *quid pro quo* which was briefly adopted during his rule. In the reign of Charles II, the Crown finally gave up the prerogative of purveyance in return for a parliamentary grant for life.[16] In between, the Parliament of 1606, in a foreshadowing of the fate of the Great Contract, refused such an exchange, cast their refusal at least in part in ethical terms and made corruption a political issue.

While Salisbury's proposal was the bolder, its failure made Northampton settle for Fletcher's advice: to reduce the number of cart-takers. They reached their lowest number during Northampton's dominance of the Council between 1612 and 1614.[17] The number rose again, however, after his death. For if patronage and policy were personal in early seventeenth-century England, so too was the impulse towards reform.

While Fletcher's description of purveyance tied administrative abuses quite accurately to public discontent, Sir Robert Jacob's made the potent connection between corruption and loss of revenues. Jacob was solicitor-general of Ireland. After Salisbury's death, he became a client of Northampton's and at his request composed two briefs on the government of Ireland.[18] In the first he called for the maintenance of a standing army in

Ireland to be paid for by an imposition on the Irish kingdom, levied either in Parliament or out, whichever was more convenient. (This notion, and the Crown's management of the Irish Parliament in 1613, suggest that practices which might give pause in England were acceptable, perhaps even tried out, in Ireland. Northampton argued the converse: that the Irish Parliament carefully watched the activities of the English and duplicated their actions.[19] Either way there was a close connection.) The second of Jacob's tracts focused on how to reduce official expenses in Ireland and increase royal revenue. Because Northampton had asked for such memoranda, Jacob was willing to try his hand at it although he thought it did not fall 'properly within my element, which is to study by all means to increase his Majesty's revenue, and not to project courses for the diminishing of his expense'.[20] If Jacob's specialised job description is accurate, it provides some insight into the Crown's failure to control its bureaucracy.

Since Jacob's lengthy tract on how to improve the king's revenue bears Northampton's annotations and underlinings, it is possible to see not only the advice proffered but what Northampton thought important enough to highlight; it is those sections which are discussed here. Jacob described several means used by Irish officials to augment the king's revenue; Northampton not only underlined but numbered them. They included increasing revenues from concealed lands, reviving large numbers of tenures *in capite*, taking stricter account of composition rent than formerly, settling Irish counties and reducing them to be held of the king by English tenures while reserving good rents, letting fishing rights, drawing the profit of the Great Seal into charge, setting fines on original writs and laying fines upon all those pardoned for treason or felony. The result was to increase total revenues from £14,000 to £24,000.

Jacob wrote that he had provided suggestions for further increases to Salisbury who, along with the Lord Deputy, referred it to the Irish attorney-general, Sir John Davies. But Northampton, sensitive to the use of Crown patronage, put a sign next to Jacob's contention that 'some of them that concern the private commodity of some great men, have been neglected . . . and so are alike to be still until we shall be awaked with a new summons out of England'.

In addition to possible gains not realised within the past two years, £1,500 in annual revenues had been given away 'by direction out of England'. Those who had picked up those revenues included Lord Hay, never one of Northampton's favourites, who had an impost on wines; herring merchants who had made off with the imposts on herrings; the well placed who received the first fruits of Irish bishoprics which were under-assessed anyway; and Sir James Harrington who had been given £200 sterling a year out of the land of an abbey in lieu of his fishing rights. Such compensation was required because the king had given the fishing rights away for nothing. Jacob argued cogently that it would have been better to grant Harrington some other recompense in concealed land for which he would render rent to the king 'and not to have given away £200 of his Majesty's annual revenues that must maintain the Crown'. Northampton underlined Jacob's words: 'that so much hath been given away after we had gotten it.' [21]

Discussing customs, Jacob noted that they had been raised of late, but might be further improved. Among the several varieties of customs Lady Rich had a profitable licence for the transport of 1,200 packs of linen yarn worth about £2,500 a year. It had only two years more to run but then was granted to John West for twenty-one years. Jacob suggested that the Crown resume this profitable customs duty and West redeem the licence with some other suit which would not diminish the king's yearly revenue. Were West to refuse, the king might license others and so make his grant of less value, or have the statute prohibiting the transportation of these commodities repealed so that West's licence would be void. Northampton was clearly interested in this approach and noted in the margin: 'West's licence way to defeat it.' [22] West's licence had been questioned at its original granting, but Salisbury had failed to act on that advice. [23]

Finally, Jacob emphasised that the king's revenue should not be raised without regard to the subject. Reproduced below are Jacob's comments and Northampton's underlinings:

> my intention is not to show how the king's revenue here might be racked to the highest by all manner of ways, good and bad: but to make an over-ture of the means how it might be improved in a good and moderate fashion, without oppression or grievance to the subject, and without drawing any more from them than they pay at this hour: whereof part is subtracted and purloined by sheriffs, undersheriffs, collectors, clerks and other officers; and part is given away in rewards to the deputy's follow-ers. [24]

The Crown needed money badly, yet it was difficult to increase revenues without significantly alienating the subject. Furthermore, patronage and corrupt practices had a significant impact on raising revenue. In seeking reform Northampton wanted to increase royal income, cut down costs and maintain administrative accountability in the interest of both king and country. Such efforts at reform engendered conflicting interests, prompting political questions as to the means adopted. Was it spleen or administrative reform?

II

The Privy Seal office had become an almost entirely formal part of the royal government by the mid-sixteenth century, bearing all the hallmarks of early modern administration. [25] Sale of offices and reversions, use of deputies and extractions of sizeable fees from those needing their services made the clerks somewhat independent of the Lord Privy Seal. Northampton tried to bring the office under his control. One week after he became Lord Privy Seal in 1608, Edward Reynolds presented him with a report of the defects in the office with suggestions for reform which were adopted.[26] The dispute with Reynolds and other clerks that arose over fees revealed that Northampton was not able to restore complete administrative control but he did use the office to repair some of the damage caused by a patronage system which he thought did not serve the king's best interests.

Northampton refused to seal grants of which he did not approve. In this he was not unique: Ellesmere too refused to seal a few in Chancery.[27] Northampton was, however, unusually persistent. In the year before he took office only one grant was stayed; in the year after his death, again only one was stayed.[28] But during his six years in the office forty-six grants were refused the Privy Seal. When in 1612 Northampton became the king's principal minister, he tried to increase his control of the administrative process and in the last thirteen months of his life stayed twenty-six grants. His work on the Council and the treasury commission to reform the patronage system and prevent the squandering of royal revenues was reflected in his actions in the Privy Seal office. Four falconers, a musician, the assistant to the assay-master at the Tower of London, the chief joiner of the realm, the keeper of the hare warren at Windsor and the king's cockmaster lost their fees and rooms. All fell victim to Northampton's battle against the proliferation of offices and perquisites within the royal Household. Northampton even stayed a grant which purported to reform abuses in the weighing of hay and straw in London and its environs, because it would have been a windfall to its projector who, in return for providing weights and seals for a true weight, would be entitled to demand from both buyer and seller threepence for a load of straw and sixpence for a load of hay.[29]

Most significantly, grants were stopped which authorised payments to those naval officials whom Northampton found derelict – an annual £40 to naval architect Phineas Pett, or several hundred pounds to Sir John Trevor for pipes and conduits at Windsor Castle. Another grant would have established the new office of Surveyor of all Ships.[30] These were blocked as a result of Northampton's year-long investigation of the navy.

III

Northampton's investigations of the navy in 1608 and 1613 have long been left in the shadow of the 1618 commission, which was hailed as one of the most important investigations of the period, with a wide-ranging set of recommendations for reform.[31] Northampton's commission has been written off as merely his desire to curry favour with the king and score off his aging cousin, the Lord Admiral, the Earl of Nottingham. Northampton's inquiry was more important than that. It suggests an early example of efforts to rationalise the bureaucracy ultimately successful only in later centuries when resources were available to implement its findings. The 1608 commission illustrates Northampton's systematic approach to administrative reform, his sophisticated understanding of the structural causes of corrupt practices and the means to remedy them.

The difficulties of the navy were not created by King James: he inherited them. The royal navy had begun to deteriorate in the 1590s. As early as 1602 an investigation was launched, but its leadership was entrusted to the leading naval officers. In 1603 Captain Thomas Norris complained to Sir John Coke that the 'whole body is so corrupted as there is no sound part . . . the great men feed on the less and enforce them to steal both for themselves and for their commanders'.[32] Both Norris and Coke served on the 1618 commission; Norris was one of Northampton's chief informants in 1608.

The letters patent which established the commission spoke of the 'intolerable abuses, deceits, frauds, corruptions, negligences, misdemeanours . . . perpetrated . . . against the continual admonitions of you our high Admiral by other the officers of and concerning our navy royal'. Its powers were broad: it could interrogate all who had been naval officers since 1598, their deputies and all suppliers of provisions to the navy, and indeed anyone else the commissioners thought fit. Access was provided to all the records of the office and the king's auditors enlisted to check the accuracy of the accounts. The fifteen members, mainly privy councillors and legal officers, were led by Northampton and Sir Robert Cotton, who acted as special counsel, assembling both witnesses and data with the aid of three naval officers, Norris, John Clyfton, a purser, and Hugh Meritt, one of the master attendants.[33]

During the year of the commission's existence, Northampton conferred repeatedly with his advisers, personally inspected naval yards, and wrote extensive reports and recommendations for reform. His aim was to uncover those who had 'kept Robin Hood's audit'.[34] As he had made use of John Swinnerton, loser in the battle for the customs farms, so Northampton made use of disaffected naval officers to provide first-hand information of abuses. The commission examined over 160 witnesses ranging from merchants who supplied the navy, to officers who served at sea and underclerks at the naval shipyards. Three examples of venality provide striking examples of the impact of inflation and the interconnection which proved impossible to break between the personal and the public in early modern government.

First of all, supplies were often stolen: lumber, for instance, was used to build private houses while the king's ships were constructed with green wood. Traditionally suppliers provided gratuities to officials to ensure prompt payment. Now, suppliers of wood planks were required to pay Sir John Trevor 2s 6d for every hundred four-inch planks they sold the navy, whether they were paid immediately or not.

Secondly, lower naval officials, captains, pursers, and victuallers conspired to keep crews short and shared out the allowances amongst themselves. Of 100 crew men only 70 would be employed; the victuals money was divided in three: the captain received 7s 6d, as did the victualler, and the purser ten shillings. But that ten did not remain in his pocket long: six had to be passed on to the captain. This practice too dated back to the Elizabethan period, but had been extended after 1603 under Sir Robert Mansell's aegis. Although Mansell tried to explain away testimony linking him to corrupt practices he proved the bane of all those who sought to reform the navy. Northampton failed to dislodge him, as did the commission of 1618.[35] Despite evidence of malfeasance he was protected by his close relationship with the king and Buckingham. The third example involves Mansell too.

The *Resistance*, owned by Sir Robert Mansell, Sir John Trevor and Phineas Pett, the shipwright, was ostensibly one of the transport ships in the Earl of Nottingham's embassy to Spain in 1605. She took on munitions, victuals and sailors at the king's expense, but her real destination was the south of Spain to deliver a cargo of lead. The king paid for a private venture, Norris testified. He had learned as much when he was clerk to Sir Richard Leveson, Admiral of the Fleet. Originally Leveson had told Norris not to draw up instructions for the commander of the *Resistance* because the ship was not part of the embassy fleet. But Leveson was asked by the senior officers to include it in the fleet or they would lose their cargo. Evidently he complied.[36] The mixture of personal and public interest characteristic of the Elizabethan navy whereby the queen might own or disown Sir Francis Drake at will now worked to the disadvantage of the king.

When their work was completed, Northampton and Cotton drew up an extensive report, detailing corrupt practices, naming names, dates and places and corroborative evidence. Northampton's optimism about their results was apparent in his letter to Cotton on the eve of the presentation of its findings.

> The work of reformation hath begun at Hampton Court . . . with the most gracious acceptance of the king and the applause of all my fellows. . . . The Admiral himself . . . was willing at the last to look on rather with an approving eye . . . which is more than half a miracle . . . you have been a faithful and industrious and happy assistant in the main course of our whole proceedings hitherto . . . I would not miss you in this conflict for a thousand pound. . . . It is the best ever was undertaken for the country's good, the most evenly and uprightly carried for the workmen's reputation.[37]

But reformation ran aground on the reef of patronage relationships. During the naval investigation the king had undercut its effectiveness by granting the Lord Admiral a pension of £1,700 and allowing the navy to build the *Prince Royal*, the largest ship constructed during the reign. Royal reward did not await results. When deponents before the commission questioned the honesty of the shipwright Phineas Pett, the king himself, acting as judge and jury, inspected the *Prince Royal* at Woolwich and declared it fit. Furthermore, when the commission presented the king with chapter and verse of abuses in the navy, the king's response was to urge the errant naval officers to beg for pardon and promise to perform their duties justly in the future. The Venetian ambassador, commenting on the 'endless' abuses Northampton had uncovered, noted pessimistically that the trials of those indicted were either suppressed or put in the hands of the Lord Admiral's underlings.

Northampton had come to understand the king's inability to deal with the conflicting claims of his courtiers. In his report he suggested the offenders be tried in Star Chamber, his purpose no doubt to ensure their punishment.[38] As we shall see in his work on the office of arms, Northampton learned that reform required the restraint of the king as well as of his officials.

James did commission Northampton to draw up a book of ordinances for the navy. Despite the charge of 'spleen' which contemporary critics and later historians have attached to his investigation, Northampton's analysis was systematic, relying both on a comparison with earlier procedures in the Elizabethan navy, and a close analysis of the structural difficulties which produced corrupt practices. He located the difficulties in the patronage system and the workings of early modern administration. The 'bitter root' of corrupt practices lay in the sale of offices and preferment. This was his diagnosis in the navy, the office of arms and the ecclesiastical courts. 'Without recovery of some part of those means by filching, which they laid out for the purchases at large, they should famish both themselves and their families.'[39] Northampton, who had built his career at court by carefully cultivating his own patronage, was not calling for an end to favour, but rather for its use in government to recognise and promote ability. Differentiating between departments of institutional importance and those whose work was routine, Northampton insisted that in the navy there must be no sales of offices, no reversions, no life tenure and no deputies. Appointments should be by merit and promotion gradual. Indeed officers were to be bound in recognisance, money they would have to forfeit should they neglect their duties. In sum, Northampton sought to rationalise the administration so that it might more efficiently serve the king and his subjects. It must have been tempting to the Council to contemplate the French innovation of the *paulette*, a levy on officeholders by which the sale of office was managed on behalf of and for the profit of the Crown, but Northampton considered it doubtful and dangerous.[40]

Northampton struck out, too, against conflict of interest by which officials acted also as suppliers to their own departments. He argued strongly against the grant of the monopoly of making hand-guns and daggers to Thomas Lavorock in reversion after his father. In addition to damaging the living of those already engaged in the trade, creating middle-men by which 'one man ... makes benefit of the poverty of other poor workmen' and driving able workmen such as those on Tower wharf out of work, Northampton argued it would also damage the king's service.

> When the subject at large serves the king and the king's officers put the pieces to the proof that be naught they may be cast off, but when Lavorock shall serve in the store himself, good and bad shall be all one so that he have the money and so provisions shall be weakened and the king confound. Beside here is the same inconvenience whereof we complain in the navy for Lavorock makes the provision and rates the pieces.[41]

Northampton's recommendations for reform only began to be realised in the Restoration period and during the reign of William and Mary.

IV

In the sixteenth century, the appetite of increasing numbers of gentry for arms, crests, pedigrees and monuments which would testify to their status grew, picking up speed at a rate that alarmed the authorities. Reflecting the importance of their duties, the officers of arms, heralds and pursuivants moved to new offices in Derby House and were incorporated in 1555. During Elizabeth's reign the number of grants of arms continued to increase and the heralds, paid by the grantees, claimed to exercise their jurisdiction without supervision. In 1568 Thomas Howard, fourth Duke of Norfolk, drew up a scheme to regulate the office of arms and bring it firmly under the control of the Earl Marshal. His execution cut short these efforts and by the 1590s there were continuous pleas from disgruntled gentlemen and even the heralds themselves to correct abuses.[42]

Northampton's efforts to reform the Earl Marshal's office dated back to his lengthy tract of 1597 for the Earl of Essex which drew on both his brother's reorganisation of the office and the information of his expert advisers. The tract had a twofold thrust: to reform the workings of the office of the heralds, and to control social mobility. These efforts continued when he became the leading commissioner for the office under James and led to efforts to control both the giving of arms and duelling.

In his tract, Howard upheld the authority of the Earl Marshal to oversee the heralds, challenged their pretensions to give arms without supervision, and launched a violent attack on the inflation of honours. Invoking historical examples of arms granted for valour, Northampton challenged the upstarts of his day:

> proves this that a merchant or his factor coming with a fair wind out of Spain on a ship freighted with oranges may at this first arrival receive arms at Billingsgate? ... shall Garter ... make a gentleman for carrying

his tankard with a comely grace from the Condit in Cheap to Bucklersbury? If he can but one be chosen warden of his company or before if he pay well? . . . shall a greasy grasier be timbered and helmed for his diligence in taking care that the kine cast not their calves to the weakening of his commodity? Because King Ferdinand and Queen Isabella granted arms to Christofero Columbo and the queen our sovereign in like manner to Sir Francis Drake for surrounding all the world by sea, shall merchants live in the hope of the like privilege for frequenting traffic by sea only out of avarice without the least regard for any ground that may give honour?[43]

To ensure 'the right giving of arms' Howard called for the implementation of the orders drawn up by his brother for reform of the office. These decrees emphasised the accurate keeping of records, the maintenance of a general library for the use of all the officers of arms, the establishment of the form of serving in office, the precedence of the senior officers and the division of fees.[44]

It has usually been thought that Northampton held no office prior to James's accession. This is incorrect. Despite his attack on the behaviour of the heralds, a deputation of officers of arms asked in 1601 that he be made a commissioner to investigate long-standing abuses associated with Sir William Dethick, Garter King of Arms.[45] After a commission of peers had failed to secure redress, the heralds suggested Lord Henry Howard should join Lord Zouche, Sir Robert Sidney and Sir Edward Dyer, 'being men both learned, and of great experience in these causes'; Henry Howard, Sidney and Dyer were duly named.[46] This subcommittee 'by due and deliberate examination found the complaints to be just and lamentable' and drew up a report on how 'these abuses and oppressions may be redressed and amended'. But 'their commission became void by the death of our late Sovereign'. At James's accession, the officers suggested that Dethick had escaped investigation because of his court connections and asked James to command Howard, Sidney and Dyer to deliver a true report of the cause to him so that he might order redress.[47] This episode provides another example of unhappy officeholders aiding the cause of reform.

Recognised now as an authority on the workings of the Earl Marshalship and the office of arms, Northampton was named a Lord Commissioner and came to dominate the commission. Northampton focused on reform of the office, the proper giving of arms and the control of social behaviour through the Earl Marshal's court. In 1601 Lord Hunsdon, one of Howard's cousins, had written to his brother-in-law, the Earl of Nottingham, a commissioner for the Earl Marshalship, to complain about Dethick. Among the complaints catalogued by the officers, Hunsdon noted that Dethick had struck another herald publicly at a funeral, detained fees and, contrary to the custom of the office, sought to make one of his sons Windsor Herald. Hunsdon urged Nottingham to ensure that one of the pursuivants should be promoted instead and suggested in particular William Smith, rouge-dragon pursuivant of arms, 'a man both for learning and language every way suffic- ient'.[48]

Smith did not get the promotion and in 1606 he wrote a piece for North- ampton, 'considering your honourable inclination', entitled 'a brief dis- course of the causes of discord among the officers of arms and of the great abuses committed by painters'.[49] Smith argued that the causes of the difficul- ties in the office were 'the want of due preferment and the unequal parting of droits'. Speaking from the point of view of the lowest ranking, Smith urged the steady promotion of lower officers skilled in their profession, attacking appointment based more on favour than skill. Smith's argument was much like that of Northampton and Cotton in the naval investigation; he detailed how strange it was that a man 'travaille many years in strange countries for obtaining skill and languages; shall sue long for the place, before he get it; shall serve long in the place before he have fees and profits thereof: and yet shall be over leaped by his inferiors in skill . . . which peradventure have not sued a month nor yet served a day of it'. Naming previous officers who could not read or write Latin, French or, indeed, English, Smith urged that none be named a pursuivant unless he had sufficient abilities to be a king of arms, the highest rank in the office of arms.

The second cause of discord was the unequal distribution of fees by the heralds who allowed the pursuivants but crumbs from their overladen table. Smith's discourse casts an important sidelight on the implications of the large number of knights created by James I that has not hitherto been noticed: the fees that the newly dubbed had to pay ever-present officials. Traditionally, the payment for becoming a knight was 20 shillings of which the pursuivant got 8d. Since the king's coming, 'through his gracious bountifulness' some heralds now received £5 after the manner of Scotland, and 'diverse other officers also have fees of new-made knights, which in times past had nothing'. But the heralds did not give half of the £5 to the pursuivants as in the manner of Scotland. (In his tract Smith did not mention how the new knights felt about this increase in fees.) As for earls, the heralds received £20 for each creation while the pursuivants received nothing. But if the heralds were to be made to give up graft, their interests had to be protected as well. Smith pointed out that painters, willing to do coats of arms and funerals on the cheap, were capturing the heralds' business. As a result Northampton ordered that no one was to meddle in any matters belonging to the office of heralds. 'Notwithstanding their . . . excuse of being brought up in the painting of arms . . . [they] have unjustly intruded themselves into matters belonging to our said officers of arms contrary to the privileges and corporation of our said officers.'[50] But Northampton's efforts to reform the office went beyond reinforcement of the traditional rights of the heralds or his brother's regularisation of procedure. There was, in fact, great similarity in his approach to reform in the navy and in the Earl Marshalship. In both he drew on expert advice, invoked Elizabethan practice and, most importantly, emphasised the necessity for structural changes to prevent the continuation of corruption.

Northampton's writings on the Earl Marshalship were both scholarly and practical. These attributes were not opposite but the very basis on which a traditional court functioned; to know the past was to know the purpose of the institution. And if the past was not sufficient to supply current policy, it served at least as the guidepost. Northampton compiled several treatises on the office of Earl Marshal, its antiquity and jurisdiction; probably begun under Elizabeth, one includes a list of Earl Marshals down to Essex.[51] He also drew up 'Certain rules to be prescribed and ever preserved for the reformation of all abuses and corruptions that have crept into the office of arms and for the prevention of all means which may bring in the like hereafter'.[52] While Northampton provided specific cases, including the ubiquitous William Dethick about whom other heralds had complained for years, his primary focus was systematic and structural as in his report on the navy. To begin with he reinforced the oversight of the Earl Marshal. No arms were to be given without his consent, all orders were to be recorded, fees were to be regularised. To the regulations of 1568 Northampton made some important additions. All officers of arms were to sue only in the Earl Marshal's court; preferment in office was to be orderly, officials serving by turn not at the pleasure of others, and appointments were to be made to gentlemen, not upstarts. As Cotton had written in the naval report, 'the charge is great requiring skill and cannot be discharged by persons ignorant, by formality or bravery', referring slightingly to 'threadbare fortunes utterly unable to maintain their part without spoil of the king's treasure'.[53] Naming men of property to office would prevent peculation. And given the circumstances of early modern administration this Whiggish formula might seem plausible. Northampton adopted Smith and Cotton's argument: ignorant and unskilled deputies were prohibited.

If the remedies were similar in both the navy and the office of arms, it was because the causes of corrupt practices were the same. Like the pursers and victuallers whose plight Northampton evoked in 1608–9, officers of arms, unable to maintain their families by ordinary wages, had been 'provoked by the spur of want to pursue the track of corruption'.[54] Proper payment, judicious recruitment, steady promotion in office and constant supervision were Northampton's remedies for the bureaucracy whether in the navy or office of arms.

One of Northampton's 'rules' was the calling in of all arms given since the tenth year of Elizabeth's reign when his brother had ordered that none be granted without the Earl Marshal's consent. Northampton had first urged this in 1597. He continued to be concerned that 'corrupt affections . . . bred confusion in this state as the world begins to set light the quality of a gentleman'.[55]

Given these attitudes and findings, how can Northampton's endorsement and support of the creation of the baronetage be explained? Northampton underwent a shift in view once in office. Necessity proved truly the mother of invention. Northampton discovered that some administrative and financial problems might be solved at a single stroke. Control over the office of arms could be instituted, the orderly dispensation of arms might be established and even be made to yield much-needed revenue. Indeed it was only by maintaining such 'quality control' that the Crown could ensure a continuing market for its titles. Thus Northampton supported the baronetage over which he and Salisbury exercised oversight. Moreover, Northampton's suggestion for the calling in of all patents of arms since 1568 was meant not to end their issuance but to control the recipients. And this too might be a moneymaker. In 1615, after Northampton's death, Sir Robert Cotton drew up a minute to force those recipients of arms since the tenth year of Elizabeth's reign who were unable to provide sufficient justification not to give them up, but to pay for them. There was thus a close link between administrative reform, bureaucratic control and financial stratagems in the 1610s which may suggest a model for the 1630s. How close a connection was there, for instance, between these Jacobean expedients and distraint of knighthood fines under Charles I?

V

I have suggested that Northampton's efforts as a commissioner for the Earl Marshalship moved in two directions simultaneously: the reform of abuse in the office and the reform of behaviour in society. His extended discourse written for Essex in 1597 emphasised that the evils of the office undermined hierarchy and authority in society at large by the granting of arms to the unworthy, the merchants, the players, the shopkeepers who now claimed gentility. Once in office, Northampton took a somewhat different tack, continuing his investigation of abuses but now presiding over the dispensation of honour for money, so long as the applicants were gentlemen.

In his last work, 'a publication of his majesty's edict and severe censure against private combats and combatants', Northampton returned to the issue of controlling social behaviour. The tract was written to accompany the king's proclamation against duelling in February 1614. Few proclamations were drawn up during Northampton's dominance of the Council between 1612 and 1614. There were thirteen in all; three concerned violence and duelling.[56] Northampton's interest in the subject was of long standing. He had compiled material on every aspect of the code of duelling, collecting information from Sir John Finet, Sir Francis Cottington and Sir Henry Wotton on laws regulating duelling abroad, and discourses by Sir Robert Cotton, Sir Edward Coke and members of the Society of Antiquaries on practices in England. He had apparently already written a piece himself entitled 'Duello Foil'd'.[57]

Northampton shared King James's antipathy to duelling and the code of honour which, imported from Italy and France, had become characteristic of Elizabethan and Jacobean England, reflected in contemporary drama and played out in earnest by courtiers and country gentlemen. More immediately, several duels involving courtiers preceded the king's proclamations. The most recent between Lord Henry Howard, Northampton's namesake and grand-nephew, and the Earl of Essex stemmed from controversy over the honour of Lady Frances Howard who was in process of divorcing Essex. Northampton was not the only privy councillor whose relatives engaged in duelling. Ellesmere's cousin was slain in a duel shortly after writing to Ellesmere that he feared for his life. From 1613 on the Crown led a campaign against duelling enforced in Star Chamber and the court of Earl Marshal. Northampton was its author and most active propagandist until his death.[58]

Several important themes inform Northampton's 'severe censure' that give this last tract a significance beyond the immediate circumstances that shaped its writing in late 1613.[59] Writing in the king's name, Northampton asserted the power and authority of the monarch to rationalise social behaviour. He called for methods of social and political control that were challenged in following decades.

Northampton argued that much as equity preserved subjects' goods in a civil court, so the king desired to preserve his subjects' lives and, most significantly for the argument, could not want lawful means to do so. He looked to Parliament to increase penalties against duelling but worried that many might be cut off 'before the parliament have time and opportunity to amend these errors.... The skill of government doth more consist in preventing harms ... than in taxing them.' Throughout Northampton emphasised the role of the judges, urging them to impress on defendants the horror of God's judgements, perhaps in the manner of Ellesmere's orations in Star Chamber. Indeed Northampton believed they might increase the penalties assigned by juries. The role of the clergy was not neglected either. The ecclesiastical hierarchy were to consider excommunication of offenders. Again Northampton's metaphor was reformative: 'more diseases are cured by good diet than by letting blood.' Such phrases suggest a different view of government than that shaped by the common lawyers, one in which precedent and parliamentary statute, while important, always gave way to present necessity.

Adopting a mode that James had made familiar in speeches to Parliament, Northampton asserted that 'the majesty and prerogative of kings ... acknowledge no superior but God only ... the subjects are presumed to have put the sovereigns in trust at their first election, and their successors, with the care of stopping any present mischief that is likely to break out, before the three states of the kingdom can be formally assembled'. Thus the king could command an end to duelling but, 'for a better earnest ... of our ... intent', pleased to set down chastisements for these quarrels with reason not passion for guide.[60]

This passage does not explicitly recognise the rights of the subject either in Parliament or out. But it does recognise the king's need to explain what he was undertaking. In short, it might be argued that, for Northampton, rhetoric had replaced political rights. Moreover, in Northampton's usage, 'birthright' and 'liberty', so common to seventeenth-century political debate, have a different meaning than might be expected. Reputation and the carrying of swords and daggers are the 'birthrights' with which Northampton was concerned.

Attacking those who 'dance in the net of novelty' Northampton painted a vivid picture of Jacobean London and those who feared to be pointed out in the streets as cowards. He traced the origin of giving the lie and, in the manner of sixteenth-century antiquaries, argued that it originally meant merely a negation. But by error and time it had become a 'conceit of horror' so that the king now ranked it with the highest of verbal wrongs.[61]

Unlike the usual argument from English precedent which characterised much of the political writings of the period, Northampton cited continental practice. To break an agreement made by the Court of Chivalry in France was considered sacrilege. He confidently proposed a similar method for England, 'because honour in all parts of Europe will be ever like itself'.[62] While specifically denying the uniqueness of the English experience, he did acknowledge that England could not adopt the severe punishments of foreign states.

Northampton stressed the need for an alternative means of providing satisfaction for damaged reputations to avoid resort to the sword. 'Without satisfaction upon the proffer of offence . . . it will be found almost impossible to stay the current of quarrelling.' The king had forborne to prohibit such quarrels without providing an adequate remedy. The method now devised was twofold: one, for the commissioners for the Earl Marshalship to give satisfaction for all kinds of offences; two, to provide a set of sharp punishments for those who disobeyed.

Northampton recognised that as members of the Council the Lords in Commission could hardly strike agreements between all those gentlemen in the kingdom on the brink of duelling. He limited their province to the court, the City of London and a distance of twenty miles around, as well as cases involving peers and nobles. All other areas were committed to the care of the Lord Lieutenants and their deputies. Procedures were left to the Lords' consideration, 'using the same moderation which they do commonly'. Whosoever stood convicted before the commissioners, the Lord Lieutenants, or their deputies, by sufficient proof, was to be committed to prison, until he acknowledged 'both an error in his judgement, and a breach in duty, in upbraiding any man with that uncivil term which our tender caution hath very sharply prohibited'.[63] Penalties applied not only to the principals but to all involved. Publications that invited a continuation of the quarrel had been prohibited by an earlier proclamation now reiterated. Their authors were threatened with proceedings in Star Chamber and banishment from court. Asking the keepers of gaming houses and their servants – it is clear that Northampton saw such places as provoking quarrels – as well as 'our own groom porter', keepers of tennis courts and bowling alleys to report quarrels on the pain of imprisonment, Northampton urged those in difficulty to repair to the Earl Marshal's court, 'for the cleansing of all green wounds, as for the healing of old ulcers'.[64] Worse than giving the lie, offence given by blows threatened the state with disorder. Northampton focused on the hazard should persons 'powerful in their own countries, strong in party and alliance', be involved. Such issues, as we have seen, he had already dealt with in Star Chamber. His remedy was to conduct offenders before the Lords or the Lieutenants and 'either by the strength of witnesses or by their own confession, of striking hastily for any other cause, than their own defence upon assault, shall instantly and before the Lords take any course for reconcilement of them, be committed to prison'.

The eradication of duelling required tough measures: a change in ideology which made honour a public not a private affair; a penalty which gentlemen would take seriously: removal from the governing body of the country; prison; refusal to bury the slain in church ground; banishment from court and office, and condemnation of intermediaries as much as the principals. 'The false colours and pretences of erring custom, have been counter pleaded and corrected by reforming severity.'[65] Much as John Keymer had advised the rationalisation of fishermen's habits in the interest of the economy, Northampton's end was to rationalise behaviour in the interest of the state.

Having established a method to punish those engaging in quarrels or duels, Northampton moved to plug the loopholes. In so doing he attacked practices similar to those that obstructed reform in the navy and the office of arms. Were a dueller to slay his enemy, Northampton argued there were only two ways for a gentleman to escape death, ways legitimated not by law but by court practice; by royal favour and 'by the practice of his own friends and allies in corrupting the pure fountains of justice itself . . . by their sly tricks and intermeddling'. As to the first, Northampton in the king's name acknowledged 'many have adventured too far upon secret confidence in the credit of some persons deeply interested in our gracious conceit, making therein our clemency, to be rather a receptacle for malefactors, than a scourge of inhumanity'. Royal patronage had got the gentlemen off. Now, Northampton wrote, the king would leave all delinquents to the law, and charged all members of his Privy Council, nobility, Household, all officers and other subjects, whatever their rank, to refrain from pressing him for pardons. Much as he had tried to do in his articles for the navy, Northampton sought to stay the king's generous hand. If both combatants emerged alive from the field of battle, they were to be banished from court for seven years, stripped of those offices and grants that depended only on the king's pleasure. The purpose of the banishment was to create greater care in the onlookers. Treating the offenders as 'fruitless branches cut off from the vine', royal patronage might prove a more potent weapon even than the law. 'Upon this resolution, we have hereby engaged our word, which is the word of a king, constant both to his honour and his promise.'[66] The tract thus contains this paradox: Northampton sought to bind the king, not by law, by which the king could not be bound, but by rhetoric. If the king would stay his hand so too must kinsmen and allies of the slayer. He would not tolerate intimidating juries, coroner's inquests or grand assizes by proud looks, heavy threats or bringing in precedents of pardons by 'those who bore themselves above their equals with the bladder of ambition'. 'Friends, allies, tenants and all sorts of instruments are huddled together at the very pinch to spare the man: so as in conclusion, that which the laws of the kingdom hold to be wilful murder, must pass for manslaughter. . . . Greatness is made a mask for guiltiness. . . . The least gratuity conveyed in a good hour into the close fist of an under sheriff strikes the bargain dead.'[67] In passages that evoke Henry VII's attack on livery and maintenance, Northampton urged freeholders to rely upon the justice of the kingdom, rather than the combinations of friends.

Finally, Northampton addressed the issue of combats which took place abroad. The king desired to supply the 'slackness' of the laws of England in punishing slaughters upon agreement to fight in foreign parts. He understood by conference with the judges that though there could be no procedure by common law, 'yet by appeal so often as it shall please us to appoint a Constable and Marshal of England, but for the present only, both to hear and adjudge the cause, the party thus offending may be condemned in that court to death (as by an act of parliament 1 Henry IV is evident').[68] This was a power that Northampton's grand-nephew the Earl of Arundel was to revive when he became Earl Marshal.

Northampton's efforts to end duelling are of interest for several reasons. His attempt to rationalise government administration was wedded to an attempt to rationalise behaviour both in the name of the king and of the state, so often mentioned in his tract. 'Reforming severity' was indeed an accurate description of Northampton's approach to government policy. How could such an approach be faulted when applied to duelling? And yet the tract had implications that link Northampton's view of the prerogative to the policy of 'Thorough' devised by Thomas Wentworth, Earl of Strafford, and William Laud, Archbishop of Canterbury, which in a similar way used the prerogative courts to reform bureaucracy and behaviour of which they did not approve. Words prompting a quarrel, according to Northampton's writings, were to be punished in the court of the Earl Marshal. But what would distinguish such words from the slanders and libels that Northampton had brought into Star Chamber in 1612 and 1613? Indeed, Sir William Holdsworth has argued that the use of the court of the Earl Marshal to try slanders became one of its major functions in the 1620s and led to its citation as a grievance in the Long Parliament.[69]

Northampton's tract did not end duelling in England. It did spell out a view of authority and political control which was bounded only by the structural inadequacies of the Stuart monarchy, the lack of means of enforcement and the dispensation of patronage in a way that undermined royal policy. While the tract emphasised moderation, Northampton always insisted on the control of language both oral and written. 'Subjects', he argued, were 'born to their prince and country more than to themselves, and have no right of interest so much as of their own lives, which is less than to call up their fellows to the sword without leave.'[70] At the same time, however, that he insisted on the king's inherent right to abolish duelling, or other practices of which he did not approve, Northampton would have radically bound the king's right to pardon. This intriguing mixture of divine right ideology and limitations on the monarch in the name of the state did not go unanswered.

VI

In November 1613 Northampton wrote to the king's secretary, Sir Thomas Lake, that he was awaiting the publication of the king's proclamation on duels before publishing his own extended treatise. In the same letter he discussed the naval commission which he had managed to revive despite the vested interests it threatened. It is not surprising that both should be mentioned together. Northampton's efforts to reform Jacobean bureaucracy and alter social behaviour were connected by more than chronology. In the first place the means he adopted were similar, that of royal commissions with wide-ranging powers. His ends, too, were much the same: to ensure the better functioning of the administration, and to put down social disorder. These ends were generally applauded, indeed demanded by officeholders and gentlemen alike. Why, then, did these efforts fail? For another commission to investigate the navy had to be mounted in 1618 and duelling continued in England until the nineteenth century. It is now possible to dismiss 'spleen' as the explanation. A close examination of Northampton's work on these commissions makes manifest his systematic approach to reform. Northampton's defeat may well be attributed to patronage practices which undermined investigations and new regulations. It is common among historians to blame James I for failing to hold his officials strictly to account. It may well be, however, that the structure of patronage at the Jacobean court precluded almost all efforts including the king's own to dislodge vested interests. Northampton wrote bitterly that had his earlier recommendations been implemented the king would have had an extra £100,000 on hand, which since had been pilfered. But 'so long as any man would complain of smart though for injustice, the commission was suspended instantly whereof the king's Exchequer yields too many weeping testimonies'. Yet a second hypothesis should be suggested as well. Northampton recognised that unless the Crown could pay its naval officers properly, it was useless to try to prevent corrupt practices. 'The vast sums that we owe them at this instant will put all courses of reformation quite out of frame . . . we have much ado with the little present money . . . to stop the wives and children from coming with outcries to the gate . . . it is but lost labour to pinch them of the proportions which they are at the present forced to steal.'[71]

Finally, opposition came from an unexpected source and provides another reason for the failure of reform in the Jacobean period. Northampton's methods were attacked as well as his goals. In two cases in 1613, James Whitelocke, a leading common lawyer and MP who had made a strong speech against impositions in 1610, argued on behalf of Sir Robert Mansell and Ralph Brooke that both the naval commission and the Earl Marshal's court were illegal. Asked by Sir Robert Mansell for an opinion on the authority of the 1613 commission, Whitelocke argued that its patent was too broadly drawn, granting it authority to punish offenders without providing the procedural safeguards guaranteed by Magna Carta. Whitelocke was accused of describing the commission as 'irregular, without precedent, strange, of a new mould and such as he hoped should never have place in this commonwealth and termed also the commissioners therein inquisitors'. Moreover, Whitelocke was retained in a case brought by Ralph Brooke, York Herald, against another herald. It will be recalled that Northampton's orders for the reformation of the office of arms included a provision that suits between officers were to be heard in the Earl Marshal's court. In 1612 and 1613 cases between officers were, none the less, brought in Chancery. Lord Ellesmere dismissed them. When Whitelocke argued on behalf of Brooke that the Earl Marshal, in the absence of a Constable, had no power by himself (or by commission) to keep a court, and therefore refused to submit to such jurisdiction, Ellesmere chastised him in strong language for touching the royal prerogative. Together, Ellesmere and Northampton, whose views of the prerogative usually coincided, along with Suffolk, another of the commissioners for the Earl Marshalship, went to complain to the king. Whitelocke was committed to the Fleet, where he joined Mansell, already in residence.[72]

Whitelocke's argument on behalf of Brooke was not new. Northampton had emphatically denied such a claim in his 1597 tract for Essex, citing his own research into the notes of fifteenth-century heralds whose distance from the fray made them 'less to be suspected of corruption or prevarication'. To seek a difference in jurisdiction between the Marshal and the Constable was idle.[73] The antiquaries who wrote memoranda for Northampton made much the same argument. It was probably in connection with his appointment to the subcommittee investigating the office of arms that Northampton asked Cotton in 1602 for information about the Marshal's prerogatives.

What had begun in the latter days of Elizabeth's reign as the claim of self-interested heralds in the absence of an Earl Marshal to an independent jurisdiction, was now transformed through the arguments of a leading common lawyer into an attack on the royal prerogative and its courts. Or at least that is the way the privy councillors and the king saw it. Whitelocke claimed he was not questioning the king's ability to establish commissions or name a constable who would have the requisite jurisdiction, but just that the Earl Marshal had none by himself. In both cases he questioned the way in which the commission had been drawn, not the royal prerogative. But each side heard the matter differently. Northampton complained of the 'private crosses and vexations which it threw upon the best endeavouring and deserving instruments to the great encouragement of fraud and abuse'. The Crown's legal officers, including Sir Francis Bacon, argued that Whitelocke and Mansell were wrong to question the right of the king to punish his own servants. Moreover, they suggested that the royal prerogative was as much a part of 'the law of the land' as the common law courts. To deny this would 'overthrow the king's martial power, and the authority of the Council table and the force of his Majesty's proclamations'.[74] Mansell and Whitelocke were released the following day and made apologies acknowledging the errors of their ways. When Brooke's case was finally heard in the Earl Marshal's court, the commissioners took care to recite their authority to examine such matters concerning two officers of arms. Still the issue of the Earl Marshal's jurisdiction continued to be raised for the next hundred years.[75]

Northampton's strongly worded tract on duelling in which he upheld the Earl Marshal's right to punish both quarrels and slanderous words may well have been a direct response to these challenges to royal authority. 'For princes may be truly said to hold rather a shadow than a strength of power, that leave it in the subjects' liberty either to scan their directions or to scan their authority.' Whitelocke himself breathed a sigh of relief when Northampton died just a few months later.[76] Northampton emphasised the role, indeed the obligation, of the prince to reform abuses and control anti-social behaviour. If the bureaucracy ceased to function effectively, if Parliament was careless or impotent, what was left but royal decree? Duelling was indeed a plague in Jacobean England, and Northampton's a worthy aim. But the procedure by which reform was carried out, even the very language in which it was couched, might prove to be as significant to its success or failure, as the more obvious obstruction caused by those whose financial interests were threatened by an end to corrupt practices.

Chapter 9

The Jacobean Privy Councillor in Parliament

The history of the Parliaments of James I is a tangled web, warped by the golden memory of Gloriana and enmeshed with the outbreak of civil war in the 1640s. Judgement has long since been passed on the Earl of Northampton's work in Parliament. Adjudged recklessly antagonistic to the Commons, Northampton was declared the destroyer of the Addled Parliament of 1614 by some contemporaries and later historians.[1] Yet in the hardening of Northampton's reputation, little attention has been paid to the details of his position as government spokesman or to his activities as committeeman on the many private Bills which flooded the House of Lords each session. At a time when historians are taking a fresh look at the workings of Parliament in the early seventeenth century, a close analysis of Northampton's work there provides a different context within which to view the role of the Jacobean privy councillor.[2]

For the Crown the meeting of Lords and Commons in a session of Parliament served several functions: the passing of legislation, the dissemination of information and marshalling of support, the airing of local problems and, most important, the granting of supply. There were six sessions of Parliament while Northampton served as privy councillor from 1603–14. In each different issues arose, among them union with Scotland, merchant grievances and wardship. With these central issues were entwined the continuing themes of the royal prerogative, parliamentary privilege and government finance. The next chapter will examine Northampton's position on these issues and his part in the Addled Parliament of 1614 which met abortively for two months; its abrupt dissolution ended the meeting of Parliament for seven years. This chapter analyses the many-sided role of the Jacobean privy councillor in Parliament, the preparations for a session, election patronage, committee work, and the rhetoric of policy.

I.   Preparing for Parliament

At his accession James I wanted to establish a harmonious relationship with his people. When he received petitions in 1603 and 1604 calling for redress of grievances involving religion, his feudal rights such as wardship and purveyance, and monopolies, he responded by convening the Hampton Court Conference to deal with ecclesiastical questions, by issuing a

proclamation against private monopolies and by stating his desire to call a
Parliament as soon as possible. An outbreak of plague postponed the meeting until 1604. In the interval lists of suggested legislation circulated in the
countryside. Wallace Notestein has written that these embodied matters
first raised in Parliament late in Elizabeth's reign which would continue to
be issues in the early Stuart Parliaments and reflected the views of 'the vocal
part of the country'.[3] Yet several of the suggested Bills were clearly government proposals. Some even reflected interests of Northampton, specifically
those on duels, the reform of the Earl Marshal's office and of the navy.
Other Bills would be referred to committees on which he sat, on which he
reported favourably.[4] This is not to suggest that Northampton had a hand
in drafting these lists or petitions. J. D. Mackie's hypothesis that Northampton was the author of one widely circulated petition, 'Advertisements
of a Loyal Subject to his Gracious Sovereign drawn from the Observation of
the People's Speeches', is based on little evidence.[5] For the first time in a
position of power, Northampton did not need to advertise. But Northampton might have been sympathetic to some of the issues raised by the anony-
mous author, including Scottish favourites and the king's liberality and
laxity in making knights. The Bills circulating in the countryside were a
potpourri of measures which included recognition of the king's title, removing the taint of treason from Mary, Queen of Scots, union with Scotland, as
well as ecclesiastical reforms and the repair of decayed towns,[6] and they
reflected views held by privy councillors and MPs alike. In short, at the
beginning of James's reign a consensus appeared to exist among the political nation on what the issues were perhaps – though not necessarily on their
resolution.

But legislation was not the central concern of the government. It has frequently been noticed how little new legislation it sponsored. Why then did
the Crown summon Parliament into session? At the beginning of almost
every reign a Parliament was held to recognise the new monarch's title,
establish a point of contact between the king and his people, and vote the
king the customs duties of tonnage and poundage.[7] Later supply became all
important for a chronically underfinanced Crown which repeatedly fell
short of a balanced budget at a time when it could not stay afloat on a
national debt. If the government's purpose, then, usually was supply, the
means were the satisfaction of the subject. Northampton spelled out this
quid pro quo of Jacobean politics in a letter to Robert Carr, decrying a
project for the discovery of concealed lands. Northampton's reasons were
two: first the evil of allowing one subject to fleece another in the name of the
king, and secondly the timing – a Parliament was about to be called: 'For
before the undertaking of that task in a captious and tickle time . . . the
subject's mind ought rather to be prepared than distempered.'[8]

This was Northampton's strategy for the preparation of parliamentary
sessions. What did it entail? For Northampton as for other officials the basic
method was the traditional redress of grievances and an effort to secure a

well-disposed House of Commons by the use of patronage.[9] The redress of grievances that Northampton had in mind was not merely cosmetic. His own earnest efforts at reform of the administration – of the navy, the ordnance, the office of arms and the Privy Seal – were part of that redress, often invoked in his speeches to Parliament. While Robert Cecil dominated the Privy Council Northampton played the faithful second in planning for Parliament. This meant constructing a package of administrative reforms which were ultimately termed the Great Contract – the exchange of the king's feudal revenues from wardship and purveyance for a fixed yearly income.

Northampton made explicit the connection between administrative reform, traditional redress of grievances, and hopes for a successful parliamentary session in a letter of 1605 to Sir Thomas Edmondes, the English ambassador in Brussels.

> At this instant we set hard about the preparation of matters for the parliament. We are about to take away the scandals raised upon purveyors and such other proling officers which were the subject of exception the last time. . . . The fair sweet royal hand that was wont to spread itself . . . hath now shut up itself so close . . . if men will forget the franchise of a Christmas at the first coming of our Master, when he neither knew the strength nor the weakness of his own estate, (as you know that in England Christmases are seldom kept without misrule), I dare undertake that henceforth they shall have no more cause to complain of that kind of proclivity.[10]

Administrative reform served as an important means of political management. In an effort to meet the Commons' legitimate grievances the Privy Council was concerned to gain control of royal finances and put an end to extravagance. Finally, a reference by Northampton to sweetening a bitter pill probably refers to the Council's attempts to put together the ingredients of the Great Contract. But the search for reform became entangled in other issues and structural difficulties. Northampton's portrait of the king's early days as a 'Christmas' was to prove a potent one. In 1621 James was still saying to the Commons that the court had learned that every day was not to be a Christmas.[11] By that time, their suspension of disbelief had ceased.

With the failure of the Great Contract in 1610–11, the Privy Council canvassed other means to raise needed revenue. But concern to secure the support of Lords and Commons limited flights of fancy. To the suggested enclosing of wastes and common lands, Northampton replied that it was not 'fit for improvement before the next parliament'.[12] This passage suggests that the meeting of Parliament served to limit the improvement of royal revenue.[13] Northampton may well have concluded that Parliaments which voted inadequate subsidies were an inefficient means of raising revenue. For there is no question that some devices with which Northampton became associated, such as the creation of baronetage, were likely to offend some members of Parliament. Yet the impact of any action on Parliament was always taken into consideration in the formation of royal policy.

II. Parliamentary Patronage

The Council's preparations for Parliament did not end with their contemplating redress of grievances. The election of a House of Commons 'well disposed' was important, too, and privy councillors used their electoral patronage to that end.[14] In the sixteenth and seventeenth centuries elections to the House of Commons were often shaped by the influence of important councillors and courtiers in their roles both as court officials with local influence and as leading landowners. Not the least important of the prerogatives available to the Lord Warden of the Cinque Ports was an extensive parliamentary patronage. This enabled Northampton to gratify the aspirations of leading country gentlemen and, at the same time, to find seats for his own servants. It has been suggested recently that in 1604 the Crown did not prepare for the election, but that in 1614 it consciously sought seats for its followers.[15] This analysis does not apply to Northampton. He took a firm grip on parliamentary patronage in 1604, particularly in the Cinque Ports, and continued to exercise his influence up to 1614.

Under Elizabeth, the Lord Warden's claim to name one of the two burgesses from each of the Cinque Ports had met with some resistance.[16] In January 1604 Northampton became Lord Warden and made real that claim. When New Romney resisted in February 1604 the lieutenant of Dover Castle conveyed Howard's displeasure to the town's officials.

> Remember I pray you and consider whether you do not expect that his Lordship at your request shall promise unto you a matter of a higher nature and importance than the simple request which he now proffereth unto you, knowing himself to be your Lord Warden by the king's election and letters patent absolutely, and therefore not tied otherwise than by ancient courtesy and custom to yield more to your request than you do now unto his.[17]

To this threat, which referred particularly to the Lord Warden's ability to help free the towns from taxation, New Romney responded by accepting his direction. In satisfaction the lieutenant wrote that all that was necessary when filling out the returns was to leave one space blank which the Lord Warden would then fill in.[18] In 1604 Northampton was able to name at least one and probably two of Dover's nominees – Sir Thomas Waller and George Bing, the brother of Northampton's servant, William Bing – and one each in New Romney, Rye and Sandwich. Thomas Unton, one of Northampton's household servants, was also returned for Winchelsea. In 1608 John Griffith, Northampton's secretary, filled one of Sandwich's seats, and in 1610 William Bing replaced one of New Romney's representatives.[19] The way in which nominations were made can be documented in detail in one particular case. When one of Rye's representatives, Thomas Hamon, died in 1607, Sir William Twysden, an eminent Kentish gentleman with court connections, requested the town to name his brother-in-law, Heneage Finch, to the position. Finch needed Northampton's approval in order to gain the seat. Twysden asked the Rye officials to postpone their election until he had spoken with the Lord Warden, who then wrote to the Rye officials:

> I make bold to recommend to your acceptance my request for the choice of Mr Heneage Finch. . . . The gentleman for his discretion and towardness in the study of the law shall be very able to perform that service to the credit of the corporation. . . . He will be willing in respect of his abode in this place [London] to ease you of that daily and large allowance which was before allotted to the predecessor. . . . I have found both his father [Sir Moyle Finch] and Sir William Twysden, his brother-in-law, so kindly and constantly affected to the furtherance of any good that my invention or industry, doth intend, or can devise to draw to your corporation.[20]

In this case Northampton used his parliamentary patronage to gratify three influential Kentish gentlemen and to reinforce his right to name at least one MP from each Cinque Port town. Wielding both the carrot and the stick, Northampton was able to make Finch one of Rye's representatives, reflecting the continuing invasion of gentry into borough seats characteristic of the Elizabethan period.

By 1614, as Sir John Neale has pointed out, the claim asserted by the Elizabethan Lord Wardens had become, in Northampton's formulation, an immemorial right: 'the ancient usage and privilege that myself and my predecessors have ever had in the nomination of one of the barons to be elected in the several ports.'[21] And Northampton was able to realise this right in 1614, influencing the nomination of eight or even ten of the Cinque Ports' fourteen representatives. These eight included two royal officials and two of Howard's merchant associates, Lionel Cranfield, who sat for Hythe, and Arthur Ingram for Romney. Four of his own local officials were also elected, Sir Robert Brett and Sir George Fane for Dover, William Bing and Thomas Godfrey for Winchelsea.[22] Godfrey wrote in his diary, 'William Bing, Captain of Deal Castle, who was also formerly my bedfellow in my Lord Privy Seal's house, and myself were chosen Burgess by the town of Winchelsea, 5 April 1614 the which parliament was dissolved and nothing done and concluded to be no session.'[23]

While the Cinque Ports provided the bulk of Northampton's parliamentary patronage, he was attentive to other spheres of influence. One of these was Cambridge University of which he became Chancellor in 1612. In 1614 Northampton sought to nominate one of the university's parliamentary members. Through his secretary, John Griffith, he suggested the candidacy of the courtier, Sir Miles Sandys. The franchise was vested in the Senate, composed of all Cambridge MAs, but the heads of ten houses attempted to put through the election of one of their number who had sat for the university in 1604. Although they emphasised the residency requirement which Sandys, a Cambridge graduate, did not meet, popular support as well as Northampton's as Lord Chancellor was on the side of Sandys and his election was accepted by the House of Commons.[24]

Northampton also influenced a few other seats. He placed his secretary, John Griffith, who sat for Sandwich in 1610, at Portsmouth in 1614. Norfolk's five boroughs traditionally under Howard sway may have provided Northampton with a few more seats. In 1604, Sir Charles Cornwallis, Northampton's long-time associate, was returned as Knight of the Shire and Sir Thomas Monson, one of Northampton's followers, sat for Castle Rising; in 1614 Sir William Twysden sat for Thetford, while another of his Finch brothers-in-law, Theophilus, sat for Great Yarmouth.[25] The continuing connection of Northampton with the Finches evidently overcame other alliances. Robert Drury, with long-time connections to Northampton, for instance, angled for a seat through Sir Robert Cotton. Understanding that there was to be a Parliament in 1614, he wrote to Cotton:

I sent to the Mayor of Thetford, as being lately become their nearest neighbour, I know they will respect me. They answered me with great affection, but withal how their love did engage them to the commandments of my Lord of Northampton. And if that I be forced to seek a knightship of the shire, that he will do me the favour, to let his tenants know his favour to me, leaving it to their own disposition. As in general I think it honest and honourable for every man to proceed no otherwise.[26]

Honourable or not, Northampton was apparently not always willing to leave parliamentary nominations to the local gentry. Instead he imported his Kentish supporters to sit for Norfolk boroughs where the Howards had held land for centuries. Furthermore, as Lord of the Manor of Bishop's Castle, Shropshire, Northampton asked the officials to nominate Sir William Cavendish, son and heir of a nobleman and a courtier, to replace William Twyneho, a patentee who held the seat in 1604. Northampton's argument is significant; 'for although the election is theirs by right, the inheritance of the borough is his, and therefore it cannot be feared that he will not be more careful than any to provide for the public weal of the town'.[27] This was not an idle promise, for at the urging of the council there, Northampton did prevent the creation of a market in a nearby town. As with machine politics in the Gilded Age, the 'tradeoff' was of economic advantage for votes.

Northampton was not always successful in his search for seats. This was notably true in Devon, seat of the barony with which King James at his accession had invested Northampton. In 1614 the town officials of Totnes regretfully informed him that his request had arrived too late. They had already promised the selection to their recorder, Sir George Carey, who refused to yield it to Northampton. Northampton met a similar refusal at Dartmouth in 1614.[28] Without office or traditional loyalties to reinforce his requests, the earl's influence was limited.

Several points should be made about the purpose and procedure of Northampton's parliamentary patronage. First of all it was indirect and frequently given through intermediaries, as in the nomination of Thomas Hitchcock for the Bishop's Castle seat. He was recommended by Dr Lionel Sharpe to Sir Charles Cornwallis who described the process this way in 1614: 'I . . . bestowed upon two gentlemen recommended unto me by Dr Sharpe letters recommendatory from the Earl of Northampton for two burgesships. The gentlemen were both unknown to myself, who confided only in him, that they were men of ability and fitness for the service.'[29] If Cornwallis did not know them, Northampton probably did not either. There is no reason therefore to assume that he chose the nominees personally. Furthermore, the evidence suggests that the clamour for seats came at least as much from prospective candidates as from the patron. As with other aspects of Jacobean patronage the patron was innundated with requests for favour. Northampton's purpose, then, was to assert his patronage rights bestowed by office and inheritance, and to elect men thought to be well disposed to the court. Frequently these were people with court connections, lawyers, merchants with royal patents, and landed gentry. The *assumption* was that the 'better, graver and more peaceable sort'[30] would necessarily support the Crown. This assumption explains why there is little indication that Northampton tried to control his nominees once they sat in the House of Commons. In fact, most are recorded as saying little or nothing in parliamentary proceedings. Furthermore, though Sir William Twysden and Sir Moyle Finch challenged Northampton in 1612 on the privileges of the baronets, family members sat in Norfolk boroughs in 1614.[31] Thomas Godfrey, Northampton's household servant, sat in several Parliaments in the 1620s, as well as the Short Parliament, and took the side of Parliament in the Civil War. Yet in the early years of the century he was part of a patronage network designed to harmonise the interests of the king and his subjects.[32] Parliamentary patronage was meant to conciliate local elites and to elect a House that would be receptive to the Crown's needs. It was not designed to ensure ideological purity. That is why passage of private Bills settling the private affairs of the political elite were of such importance to a parliamentary session and why Northampton found himself spending so many hours on committee work. For the *quid pro quo* supply was not only redress of grievances, but an opportunity for the local governors to air and settle their private and local problems.

III.   Parliamentary Committees and Private Bills

Although the privy councillors had dominated parliamentary proceedings under the Tudors it has long been argued that their influence declined in the early seventeenth century.[33] But this view overlooks two central functions of parliamentary meetings: the passage of private Bills and the presentation of government policy. In these areas a hard-working and conscientious privy councillor such as Northampton was constantly involved.

Northampton's own work in the House of Lords must be set within the framework of parliamentary structure.[34] Called into session by the king, the House of Lords was made up of those summoned personally because they were peers of the realm or spiritual lords, that is, members of the ecclesiastical hierarchy. Those who could not attend gave their proxies to other lords. Although only the lower House could introduce money Bills, both houses initiated legislation. Bills were given three readings: after the second they were assigned to a committee of members of the House who met to discuss, amend and decide whether to recommend acceptance, revision or dismissal. Such committees met at 7 or 8 a.m. or at 2 p.m. Normally the Lords sat in the morning though afternoon meetings were sometimes held when necessary. After the king's speech from the throne at the opening of Parliament, James's leading councillors, Salisbury, Ellesmere or Northampton, brought messages from the Crown. At times deputations of the Lords would wait on the king on an errand imposed by the House. On important issues, such as the union with Scotland and the Great Contract, major conferences were held with the House of Commons at which speeches would be made, principally by Salisbury, but often by Northampton.

How important was Northampton in the functioning of the Lords? While attendance need not connote importance, nor assignments, power, these statistics do provide an indication of how the government went about organising the work of the House of Lords. In 1604 Northampton attended fifty-seven of the seventy-one sittings, Salisbury thirty-three. In the second session begun in 1605, Northampton attended seventy-three of eighty-one, Salisbury thirty-two. In the third session of 1606–7, 105 sittings were held; Northampton was present for ninety-eight, Salisbury eighty-two, and in 1610, 106 at which Northampton was present for 100, Cecil seventy-one.[35] Frequently, then, Northampton attended when Salisbury did not, and it was not usual for both to be absent at the same time unless an important matter requiring conference with the Commons arose. Northampton and Salisbury were often named to committees even when absent, counter to the Lords' official practice.[36] As to proxies, Northampton received four in 1604, primarily from his relations: George Lord Audley, Thomas Lord Darcy, Henry Lord Berkeley. The fourth came from Lord Lumley who had originally given his to Darcy. At this first Parliament Salisbury received only three, while the others were distributed among various lords. It may be that power seemed in flux and Northampton as likely as Salisbury to occupy a prominent position in the government. By the second session, Salisbury's control was clear: Lumley and Berkeley gave their proxies again to Northampton, but Cecil now held nine others. In the third session, Northampton received only those of the Catholics Lumley and Lord Paget and in 1610 four, from the Catholic Lords Rutland and Scrope and his relations Audley and Berkeley.[37]

A parliamentary session provided the landed aristocracy and local interest groups the opportunity to regularise land transactions, to sort out disputed titles, change bequests and protect trade, markets and goods, while it allowed the Crown to restore the descendants of those who had been convicted of treason, naturalise aliens and change parish boundaries.[38] Much of the session was taken up with such business. Bills introduced on behalf of individuals or special interest groups required the same time and attention as the union with Scotland and the Great Contract. An important councillor such as Northampton might have a large number of private Bills to see through committee. In each session of James's first Parliament, Northampton sat on at least thirty-three committees, most concerned with private legislation. And in 1610, while Salisbury tried heroically to negotiate the Great Contract, Northampton was named to forty-eight committees.[39]

Northampton's activities shed some interesting light on the organisation and procedures of the committees of the Lords. Were important privy councillors named to committees purely for form's sake? It is certainly possible. Yet Northampton's speeches and notes in his writing book indicate that he took the job seriously whether the Bills concerned public or private business. For instance, in 1605–6 Northampton called for the judges and the learned counsel to attend the committees on swearing and sea coal in order to redraft the original Bills.[40] Furthermore, those whose interests the Bills affected were frequently called to testify for or against the Bills. In the case of Newcastle coal, merchants interested in the Bill both from London and Newcastle were invited to testify. The committees on free trade to Spain, Portugal and France, and on wines – committees on which Northampton sat – warned the merchants engaged in those trades to attend the Lords of the committee.[41] On the Bill disuniting the Hampshire parsonages of Ash and Deane, another member of the committee, Lord Saye and Sele, wrote to Robert Bowyer, clerk of the Parliaments, that the local officials from both villages were to be called to attend the committee.[42] Consultation with those concerned was an intrinsic part of the work of parliamentary committees and an important element in the Jacobean political process.

Bills were not rubberstamped. Even the slightest might undergo revision and the presence of a privy councillor was important. During the session of 1610, when he sat on forty-eight committees, Northampton served on every committee appointed from 14 February to 19 April: thirteen in all.[43] The meetings of committees in 1610 were frequently adjourned and it might be thought that this is explained simply by the lack of a quorum because the Lords were busy with the Great Contract. A further possibility, however, is that adjournments were to enable privy councillors to attend. For instance the Bill to allow Henry Jernegan to sell lands was appointed on 22 March and scheduled to meet on 27 March at 2 p.m. On 16 April it was put off until the afternoon of 18 April, and ultimately scheduled for the afternoon of 24 April to be held in the Council Chamber at Whitehall. Of those committees on which Northampton sat that were adjourned, eleven were scheduled to have at least one meeting at the Council Chamber.[44] Close scrutiny of the scheduling reveals no overlap: in no instance was Northampton scheduled to consider one Bill at the Parliament house while another on which he sat met at the Council Chamber. The evidence indicates that the inclusion of this privy councillor on a committee was not *pro forma*. Northampton attended frequently and spoke out strongly on Bills both in committee and in the Lords.

Northampton's participation on private Bills was frequently shaped by the patron–client relationship, local connections and official position. For instance, Bills that concerned Norfolk, traditional Howard territory, were often given to him, and in fact other Howards such as the Earl of Suffolk, the Lord Chamberlain, and the Earl of Arundel joined him on these committees. Several of the committees on which he sat examined Bills that concerned his clients. Sir John Holdich, John Arundell, Sir Robert Drury have family names long connected with the Howards.[45]

The restitution in blood of Sir John Davies, an old Essex follower and a suspected Catholic, provides a case in point. This Bill passed in the Lords after 'much ado', the clerk noted, and much debate. Davies had taken the oath of allegiance and had attended the established church but not yet taken communion. Reflecting his own priorities, Northampton argued that Davies had already come a long way, that 'it were very hard that for his religion he should . . . be excluded from his place in the world as a gentleman'. But Davies did not lack other supporters. Lord Chancellor Ellesmere spoke on his behalf and, most importantly, so did Salisbury. With that the bishops were swayed and assented to the Bill. The Bill died, however, in the Commons.[46] The difficulty encountered suggests the limitation of the efficacy of patron–client relations, when other crucial issues such as religion intervened.

The possibility that Davies had importuned several of the lords is not unlikely, for often in this period the patron–client relationship was shaped by inordinate pressure from below. The example of William Essex, an impoverished gentleman and a friend of Sir Robert Cotton, is illustrative. As a favour to Cotton, Northampton had become one of Essex's trustees. A Bill was introduced in Parliament to enable him to sell some of his lands because he was greatly in debt. Cotton, Robert Bowyer, clerk of the Parliaments, and Henry Elsyng who succeeded him in the post, were Essex's trustees too and Cotton sat on the Commons' committee considering the

Bill.[47] When the Bill was to be introduced into the House of Lords, it was delivered to Northampton in his garden, a procedure sufficiently out of the ordinary for the clerk to make note of it.[48] Furthermore, Northampton went so far as to speak out of order on Essex's behalf. 'Although the bill had but the first reading, yet my Lord Privy Seal did deliver Mr Essex, his necessity, and how much it stood him upon that he were utterly undone, if this bill should not pass. Being at the first reading, it was against the order of the House.'[49] Privy councillor or not, Northampton was subject to the rules of the upper House which was as jealous of its privileges as the lower. But the committee was designated to meet at the Council Chamber presumably so that Northampton might keep an eye on its deliberations.[50] Essex's Bill became law and later Northampton was prevailed upon to make him one of the first baronets.[51]

If Northampton's committee assignments were shaped frequently by patronage and local connections, he was often burdened with Bills which concerned title and restitution in blood, no doubt because of his important role as commissioner for the Earl Marshalship. He had spent much time in 1604 on the question of who was entitled to the Barony of Bergavenny: the Fanes, heirs general in the female line, or the Nevilles, who would inherit if the title had to descend to a male. The decision had gone for the Nevilles and the king as consolation had awarded to the Fanes the title of Le Despencer. In 1610 Lord Bergavenny wished to sell some lands and the question emerged once more. Northampton was related to Sir Francis Fane, whom he described as 'not only my kinsman but my friend, which is very seldom in this age for kindred and friendship to concur in one man'.[52] Both parties referred the matter to Northampton. His role in amending the Bill is graphically recorded by the clerk who noted that the additional words alluding to Bergavenny's counsel's arguments were inserted 'by my Lord Privy Seal's certificate remaining sewed in the journal book'.[53] Kinship in this case gave way to patriarchy; Bergavenny's Bill passed.

Work on such committees was important and time-consuming. Northampton was not originally appointed to the committee to consider the Act for the better execution of justice and suppression of criminal offenders in the northern parts of the kingdom, but he was added apparently to soothe the worries of lords concerned that the Bill might infringe their legal privileges.[54] For instance, Lord Sheffield wished to amend the Bill's provisions touching remanding of prisoners to state explicitly that it would not apply to peers. Perhaps because of negotiations with the Commons over the Great Contract, Salisbury and Northampton decided that they did not want to make an issue over a tangential and possibly touchy matter. Yet the Lords had to be appeased too. After the first conference with the House of Commons, Northampton compared the Bill to a 'stomach that hath good meat' that had first to be made 'good concoction and be turned into nourishment'. After further negotiations with the Commons, the Lords and even the king, Northampton was able to report success. Lord Sheffield withdrew his amendment and the king agreed to grant under the Great Seal an exception to the Bill once it became a statute which would safeguard peers from being remanded before an ordinary jury. Northampton reported that 'his Majesty when he understood by myself and some others . . . of the council of your willingness to give him contentment in this, which he called his bill . . . commanded me to give the whole House thanks and . . . commended your wisdom that you were so careful to keep your privileges'.[55]

Work on private Bills elicited from Northampton as much attention as central issues of policy. Frequently the issues of patronage, local connection and rank intertwined, as his work on preaching ministries suggests. While sitting on committees concerned with the union with Scotland and merchant grievances in 1606–7, Northampton also addressed Sir John Ackland's Bill providing for the nomination of a minister to preach and read divine service every week in the chapel at Columb John, Devon. The minister, who had to be a university graduate, was to be paid £10 a year, 'with sufficient meat, drink and lodging in the house of the said Sir John Ackland'.[56] In addition, Sir John was to build a school in the parish with lodgings attached where the minister was to teach. His total salary was to be £34 a year. The Bill seems of minor significance. Still Northampton spoke against it in the committee and on the floor of the House of Lords. Although the Bill's intention might be good, he suggested it breached the Privy Council's policy of encouraging husbandry. The sedentary life of reading and writing was 'fit for occupations, not for husbandry, less for the sword'.[57] In addition, this conversion into a preaching ministry of a prebend – endowed for the maintenance of a canon in a cathedral church – was the means to ruin cathedral churches. Northampton raised the alarm that there was abroad in the land the same humour against cathedral churches that prevailed in Henry VIII's time against abbeys. Finally, he suggested the Bill exhibited ingratitude towards the Courtenay family who had originally endowed the prebend.

Northampton's stand here suggests the view usually held of him: the secret Catholic, anti-Puritan who, because of his regard for the ancient nobility, opposed preaching ministries and education for those of low degree. Seemingly Northampton made this last view explicit. 'For my own part, I think that so many schools as there is, is a great decay unto learning, for the number of raw scholars makes such a division and is a cause to broach so many new opinions . . . when the scum are sent out of the university. . . . When men come from the university, though of mean understanding, yet will they not go to any trade. Their former life being so easy and without either trouble or pain.'[58]

Yet Northampton spoke favourably on a Bill similar to Ackland's brought forward in 1610 which established a hospital, a grammar school and maintenance of a preaching ministry in the town of Thetford, Norfolk. Why was this different? On this Bill he emphasised his own ties with Thetford and the county of Norfolk of which he was Lord Lieutenant, pointed out that the town was as poor as any in England, and called 'this work most charitable, best for instruction and religious, preaching is the means both to plant and increase truth in us'.[59]

Can Northampton's difference in attitude be explained only by sentimental or patronage ties to Norfolk? Probably not. Rather, along with the bishops, Northampton felt that control of the churches should remain with the ecclesiastical hierarchy. The Thetford Bill posed no threat to the cathedral church as the Ackland Bill did. Furthermore, Northampton was himself one of the most important benefactors in this period, establishing three hospitals for the elderly, one in Norfolk itself.[60] The Thetford Bill included a hospital, the Ackland Bill did not. Given his religious views, Northampton was clearly in favour of good works. These included the establishment of schools, particularly when they were linked with housing for the elderly. Finally, Northampton's central concern was to better the conditions of the clergy. His strong statement on free schools must be seen in its proper context, the Bill against non-residency which the House of Lords examined as a Committee of the Whole House.[61] The bishops wanted the flexibility to combine church livings so that they might better the position of local clergy; members of the lower House, eager to end absenteeism, wanted to ensure a godly ministry. Their ends were not far different. Northampton, like Salisbury, felt that the laity who had impropriated many church livings should contribute a portion of their impropriations to improve ministers' income. 'This cause', he said, 'must be concluded, not by arguments, but by charity.'[62] While Northampton's rhetoric might at times sound Laudian, it was in fact similar both in view and in tone to that of the Jacobean episcopacy. His stress on husbandry and station reflected his own education in the Tudor ideal of order. Northampton's rhetoric must always be understood in context; his point was not to do away with education but to ensure that endowments would be used to improve clerical incomes rather than to establish secular schools.

Northampton examined carefully each issue before him as a committee member and often wrote laborious opinions on even the most minor. This extensive committee work must be related to his work on the Privy Council which was manifold. Ironically, the Council was at once omnicompetent and lacking the apparatus to effectively administer its decisions. It sat as a court in Star Chamber, dealt with international affairs and domestic policy, placated ambassadors and issued licences to travel. Moreover, its members, especially Salisbury, Northampton and Ellesmere, had the responsibility to shepherd major issues of policy through Parliament, particularly by conferences between the two Houses. In addition, privy councillors sat on parliamentary committees concerned with private matters, making for an extraordinary work load, which required some division of labour.[63] So Salisbury took on the tasks of developing policy and negotiating with the Commons; to Northampton fell large amounts of committee work, particularly on private Bills, and the public presentation of the Crown's position on important issues.

IV. The Rhetoric of 'Divine Right'

Northampton always served as one of James's principal spokesmen. Yet historians have only noted his 'insulting' words.[64] Because Salisbury was too clever a politician to allow his own policies to be continually undermined by ill-considered rhetoric, a closer look at Northampton's speeches is in order. Decorated with allusions to biblical and classical authors and mediaeval legal precedents, what function did his orations serve? Northampton's speeches as a negotiator of the treaty with Spain and as a judge in the Gunpowder Plot trial suggest the answer. By adorning the government's position with precedent, metaphor and allusion, his rhetoric cloaked policy in the language of authority. Three major issues faced Parliament in the years 1604–11: union with Scotland, merchant grievances and the feudal rights ultimately bound up in the Great Contract. Northampton was actively engaged on all three. On each his words provided a microcosm of assumptions about the distribution of power and authority in the state and in Parliament itself. In the next chapter these issues will be examined closely. Here we look at the political assumptions with which he began his parliamentary career and the impact they may have had on his listeners.

On 26 March 1604 Northampton made his debut in the House of Lords at the passing of the Bill recognising King James's title. His lack of experience in parliamentary debate and politics did not prevent the 63-year-old novice from making a lengthy oration celebrating the monarch.

> I know very well that in a Senate of so great gravity and authority as this court presents it might...become me by the rule of vestas virgines to observe and learn some years before I began...to discourse....The world is ready to conceive those vessels to be most empty that are most apt to sound, and prejudice doth ever wait upon the thresholds of the first attempts. But...the very sound of such a recognition as may witness with one breath both my own singular affection and my Master's absolute and only right hath so far transported all the faculties and motions of a devoted soul...as the heart would choke and the very cask would break with the spirit of this strong infusion without some vent.[65]

In praising the king, Northampton made overt his own political views. No doubt Elizabeth I's 'gifts were great, her proceedings were advised and her ends were moderate'. But accident had provided most of her triumphs. 'By the...flaws of foreign states which England had most cause to fear many matters fell out happily for the securing of this princess and her kingdom whereof she nor her council could claim any greater operation than the fly that sat upon the cartwheel could of the great dust which the revolution did make'.[66]

James was another matter. Invoking miracles, prophecies and ancient records to garland the king's claim to the throne, Northampton proved at great length that he was descended from all the dynasties who had ever ruled in any of his dominions – excepting only the Roman emperors, 'who living in another climate' had been unable to make matches with local princesses and leave legitimate heirs.

Continuing, he laid out his own personal vision of the relation of king, Lords and Commons as he described the good fortune of having James as king. To the bishops he pointed out that James had restored episcopacy in Scotland and used 'a learned pen' to defend his religion. Coming closer to home, Northampton emphasised that the king had special regard for his nobility. Reflecting Northampton's own long-term interest in the reform of the giving of arms, the earl began his litany with James's order for the reformation of all abuses in the heralds' office. Secondly, Northampton stressed that the king had special regard for the employment of the highest born in the highest offices, noting 'the many scions of true noble houses planted at the council board, upon our saviour's own presumption that thistles cannot bring forth figs'. Thirdly, he took account of the king's liberality, 'granting to you whatsoever without over great enfeebling of his state'. Whatever the financial difficulties later on, in 1604 liberality was put forward as evidence of James's greatness. In so doing, Northampton was not just invoking self-interest but traditional aristocratic values in which bounty and largesse marked the great lord. Furthermore, reflecting the personal nature of the Lords' relationship with the monarch, Northampton acknowledged his own debt.

> The very stones of this place where I stand and speak would [accuse] me of ingratitude if I should not acknowledge what hath been effected by his powerful hand both in the branches and the root of that house whereof I descend.... For though this threshold worn with the steps of my progenitors can witness that my house was not the meanest in Manassas yet all the world can witness ... that I was *minimus in domo patris*.[67]

In this triumphant moment for the king and himself the humiliations of the past were washed away.

As he had stressed liberality to the Lords, so Northampton stressed redress of grievances and lower taxes to the Commons. James gave access to every person who had reason to complain and 'the king vows to burden you no further than ... the state hath interest'. The king, he said, would rather provide than receive contribution. Clearly the Council had not yet grasped the state of the royal finances. Peace and prosperity were the keynotes of his appeal to the Commons.

Northampton's glorification of the Lords' special relation to the king would not have sounded amiss in mediaeval England or even at the Tudor court. But there was no corresponding glorification of the Commons in the speech.

> Was it your desire that ... the ... chief agents ... be settled and fortified in that profession wherein you have established your chief content? Then

bow before the presence of that king which came not with a purpose to dissolve your laws and limits but to settle them. Were you weary of suspension from traffic which makes kingdoms rich? Then praise the change that gives you scope and liberty . . . to vent your own commodities . . . everywhere. Were you afraid of warring against some of the greatest princes of the world? . . . Then wonder at this conclusion that makes these Esaus honour you which formerly supplanted you. . . . Did your spirits faint with the very apprehension of those calamities which happen to those kingdoms often times that . . . are afraid to nominate a successor? Behold the root of Jesse branching every way . . . as all the birds of heaven are like to build on them.[68]

There are several striking aspects to Northampton's speech regarding the Commons. The first is the assumption that had he the will, the king could unsettle as well as settle their laws. Such a view was not, however, unique: it reflects James's own theory of the divine right of kings expressed most fully in the *Trew Law of Free Monarchies*.[69] Secondly, Northampton addresses the Commons as if they were primarily employed in trade. Certainly at the beginning of James's reign the merchants of the City called for the opening of previously closed markets, much as Northampton described, and they greeted the Anglo-Spanish peace treaty happily because it promised and delivered a boom in trade. But the House of Commons was not made up mainly of merchants but of landed gentry. Though many gentlemen held substantial holdings in some trading companies, Northampton's identification of them as merchants might grate on a body as sensitive to its rank and privileges as the House of Commons.[70] Thirdly, the Commons are treated as passive. Their role, unlike the Lords, who are given the highest employments, is to 'bow', 'praise', 'wonder', 'faint' and 'thank God', in short to applaud the king and those ministers responsible for his new policies. The only action they are perceived as undertaking is the traditional redress of grievances. While this agrees with mediaeval precedent, it does not accord with recent parliamentary history, such as the divisive debate in the last Parliament of Elizabeth over monopolies. While many MPs might agree with Northampton's view of the prerogative, they would be unhappy with his vision of their role in the state.

Northampton made this vision quite explicit. On the one hand, the Lords were 'an oracle', that is, messengers of the gods, persons of great wisdom; on the other, he conceived, he said, 'an image or Idea of the lower house as a theatre'.[71] In this image of theatre, the Commons were clearly the audience who were to respond with applause to the spectacle performed by the privy councillors set on work by the king who was only responsible to the Great Dramatist. Northampton's assessment of the Commons did change as we shall see but this view of parliamentary politics as theatre informed his speeches. The creation in 1610 of Prince Henry as Prince of Wales in a splendid pageant with the Lords and Commons in attendance underlines that this conception was not Northampton's alone. The theatrical image was a commonplace of sixteenth-century statecraft while plays and masques were the standard fare of Stuart court culture. But Northampton's metaphor may have provoked dissatisfaction among some of England's governors seated in the House of Commons who wished to play a larger part in the nation's affairs.

Chapter 10

Northampton and Parliamentary Issues, 1604–1614

The early Parliaments of James I provided a key element in the formulation of Crown policies: preparing for Parliament, responding to grievances, and adapting to the financial problems stemming from the chronic underassessment of parliamentary subsidies. Government policy underwent a fundamental shift after 1610 with the failure of the Great Contract. Furthermore, the conflict in relations between the king and Parliament were symbolised in the 'Addled' Parliament of 1614, so called because the king dissolved it after two months of wrangling, during which it passed no legislation and voted no supply. After that failure privy councillors such as Lord Chancellor Ellesmere and Sir Francis Bacon wrote thoughtful assessments of the causes of these difficulties and how they might be overcome.[1] Such problems shaped the king's attitude toward Parliament for the remaining eleven years of his reign and prompted further changes in policies devised by the Privy Council.

These early Parliaments have been subject to some scrutiny by historians. Wallace Notestein argued that in this period the House of Commons wrested control of parliamentary debate and proceedings from the few inexperienced privy councillors who were left in the lower House when most of their fellows were promoted to the Lords soon after James's accession. This winning of the initiative by the creation of the Committee of the Whole House laid the basis, Notestein argued, for an effective parliamentary opposition.[2] Other historians have blamed personal as well as structural causes, in particular James's lack of tact and finesse in dealing with his Parliaments. They have compared him unfavourably to Queen Elizabeth with her superb grasp of politics.[3] If Whig historians have stressed the ambition of the Commons and the obtuseness of the king, one recent historian has suggested that the Lords stood in the way of a monarch eager to meet his subjects half way. Others have suggested that members of the Commons were, in fact, often manipulated by the Lords who were their patrons.[4] But whatever the varying interpretations of the early Jacobean Parliaments, historians have been quite sure that they understood the role Northampton played. D. H. Willson called Northampton's speech on merchant grievances in 1607 highly insulting.[5] Notestein suggested that Northampton sabotaged Salisbury's efforts to secure the Great Contract.[6] Finally, all Stuart historians, whatever their persuasion, have accepted the traditional story that Northampton was guilty of the most sinister act of a government official: cynically plotting the destruction of the Parliament of 1614.[7] Each of these verdicts is wrong or at best inadequate. But the purpose of this chapter goes beyond revising the traditional estimate of the man. The re-examination of each of these issues provides a prism whose several sides show different aspects of the privy councillor in parliamentary politics.

Quentin Skinner has suggested that the Renaissance state, conducting its legal, political and diplomatic business through formal speeches and debates, emphasised the role of the rhetorician.[8] First and foremost, Northampton saw himself as the public orator, Cicero to James's Caesar, a characterisation that apparently had the blessing of the king. In the mid-sixteenth century, when Northampton himself taught rhetoric at Cambridge, what was required of a man who 'bestoweth his wit to play the Oratour'? The answer: 'by large amplification and beautifying his cause, the rhetorician is always known.'[9] In addition, within traditional Ciceronian rhetoric, style received renewed emphasis and good style meant the systematic repudiation of the speech of everyday life.[10] While Northampton's speeches are difficult for modern readers, and probably sounded old-fashioned to his audience, they reflected sixteenth-century fashions in rhetoric as well as the traditional desire to cloak political negotiation in a loftier, more erudite language. Northampton conceived his part in the presentation of important public issues such as union with Scotland, merchant grievances and the Great Contract as similar to the one he had performed in diplomatic missions and as a trial judge. His role was to impress, to educate and to persuade. Such a conception fits nicely with Northampton's notion of the privy councillor as oracle and his picture of the House of Commons as theatre.

Beyond this formal stance, Northampton's activities in Parliament were closely connected as well to his work on the Privy Council, particularly on foreign policy, government finance and administrative reform. Over the years his strategies changed. While he always remained the ideologue of divine right, he also tried to learn to negotiate with the Commons. Analysis of his work in Parliament suggests a new view of Privy Council politics and a more complex notion of the interrelationship of Lords and Commons which may provide comfort neither to Whigs nor revisionists.

I. Union with Scotland

When James VI of Scotland came to the English throne, he fervently wished for the union of England and Scotland, and as monarch of both foresaw little difficulty in realising his dream. In this he was greatly mistaken. Anti-Scottish feeling, strong in his southern kingdom, found vocal reflection in the House of Commons in 1604. The king therefore named a commission made up of representatives from both his dominions to study the matter. After two years of negotiation, the commission's report confined the union to these areas: border administration, hostile laws, commerce and natural-isation – the status of those born in Scotland before and after James became King of England. Sir Francis Bacon, who had played a significant role in formulating the commission's findings, presented the report in Parliament in 1606. In the end, James had to settle for a less than perfect union. Parliament passed an Act repealing each of those countries' laws that were directed against one another. But the union of the two kingdoms was left to Cromwell and Queen Anne. The issue of the post-nati was ultimately decided not by Parliament but in Calvin's case in 1608, by the judges who declared that those Scots born after James's accession to the English throne were entitled to English citizenship.[11]

Northampton took part in the debate on the union and also participated in the commission. His labours were acknowledged and assessed by James himself in a playful letter he wrote the earl.

If...I had desired you to have been diligent and careful in my affairs there, it had been, but to bid a running man go faster.... Your orations in parliament in advancement of the union are but words, but your officers' severity in Dover, are actions; a strange thing, that your natural avarice, and innate hatred to me, and all Scotland for my cause, should make you to cause your officers at such a time, pyke shillings from poor Scotsmen. Well I protest to God I thought you at my parting from you as honest a servant as ever king had.

James lauded his 'right trusty and right well beloved cousin and councillor' for his invocations of the benefits union with Scotland would bestow.[12] It seemed so simple in 1604.

Northampton's first efforts in conference on the union were concerned with the adoption of the new name, Great Britain. Members of the House of Commons led by Sir Edwin Sandys resisted the union and argued that even the adoption of a new name for England and Scotland threatened to dissolve English common law and the king's oath to uphold English rights. Recent arguments for 'devolution' and the re-establishment of a Scottish Parliament indicate that such feelings, whether on the English or Scottish side, have not completely died out. But Northampton's annoyance with the Commons is understandable too. A peaceful succession, the subduing of an ancient enemy not through war but through peace – what more could James's subjects wish? On 25 April 1604, one month into the first session, Northampton exercised his powers of persuasion, his rhetoric by turns reasonable, emotional, ironic. He emphasised the peace the king had established at home and abroad and argued that failure to endorse the union would have important international consequences. Drawing on information from English diplomats he argued that foreign observers noted 'the long pause which is taken upon the king's offer.... They will find the root of union to be very weak when the style is alone sufficient to stagger us.'[13]

To those members of the House of Commons who had argued that the change in name would dissolve English law, Northampton admitted that he was not so knowledgeable in common law, but argued that the change of a kingdom's title did not disturb civil law. Furthermore, he noted the sudden shyness of the Commons on the question of their power to cement the union. Northampton made ironic reference to parliamentary claims to political power, asking sarcastically, 'whether parliaments that change the state of religion, that alter questions of right, and in England are reputed as it were omnipotent may not dispose the same laws to attend the title of the same prince in conjoined and united parts... which before were severed?' His references ranged from the Romans, Franks and Italians to the Holy Roman Empire, but focused on two precedents in which the English themselves had offered the name of Great Britain to the Scots as parts of marriage pacts with daughters of Scottish monarchs, the most recent within living memory. 'I marvel in what corner of the world this fear of dissolving laws slept in the late time of King Edward VI when the Privy Council... made offer to the Scots of this union of name for clearing of all scruples and suspicious conceits in case the contract might go forward between their young queen and our sovereign.' His final argument was the most pointed:

I would gladly be informed also whether it be requisite or fit for us to stick upon that nicety in settling both kingdoms when the providence of God hath wrought more than the sword was able to enforce... and with great applause of all estates and qualities, if for the saving of much blood and establishing of an eternal peace it might in those days have been purchased at a price so easy and united by a bond so durable.[14]

In arguing for the royal policy of peace and unity, Northampton failed to recognise, however, that what he called a 'nicety' was the heart of the matter for some MPs. Sir Edwin Sandys replied by saying that Northampton's examples of the policies adopted by the Privy Council were not germane 'because it was never a matter treated in parliament, therefore could be not precedent for these proceedings'.[15]

The common law judges also disagreed with Northampton's analysis and asserted that the new name would indeed dissolve English laws and by implication, the king's oath to uphold the liberties of his subjects.[16] After this sudden reverse, the efforts of the privy councillors were bent to achieve whatever elements of union might be acceptable to the Scots and to the Commons. Salisbury suggested the establishment of the commission to negotiate with the Scots and bring back proposals to the next session of Parliament. Northampton was named to that body.

If negotiation with the Commons was difficult, negotiation with the Scots posed its own problems. The bitter fruit of centuries of hostility and fear that the more prosperous southern kingdom would swallow or overwhelm the northern was reflected in the suspicions of the Scottish commissioners. During the meetings of the commission, periodic reports were sent to Salisbury. One suggested that the details of the treaty be worked out by the king and his councillors: 'if we should enter now to advise of such matters with the commissioners, I fear the same should breed . . . great difficulties and more contention nor other propositions of greater consequence be done.' [17] Northampton's task, therefore, was to allay such suspicion in order to foster the drawing up of a document that would secure passage in the commission and in Parliament. It was not an easy task. Northampton had, however, already learned a lesson in conciliation. The union remained his goal. But the high-handed and ironic tone that he had used in conference with the House of Commons in 1604 changed to one of fervent and ingratiating persuasion.

While the evidence is unfortunately scant, it is clear that Northampton worked on the union in two ways, as the public orator who defined the issues, exhorted and assuaged the negotiators, and by privately gathering information on the issues the treaty posed. He performed the first role by painting a picture of the king in paternal images, as father and judge, and in the image of the healer, as physician and arbiter, who loved both his kingdoms without bias. James embodied the traditional virtues ascribed to mediaeval monarchs, according to Northampton, because he was 'so royal, so religious, so sincere and just'. [18]

He greeted the Scots in the strongest terms: 'we love you as our brethren, we embrace you as our countrymen, we value you as our kindest neighbours, we welcome you as our dearest friends.' Concerning the name of Great Britain, the issue on which he had strained so hard in Parliament, Northampton made the best of the Crown's defeat. He explained that the king 'misliketh not the names of England and of Scotland . . . but as they . . . may hereafter be abused out of factious desires to feed the springs . . . to convey pipes under ground of ancient hostility', like the conflicts of the Guelphs and Ghibellines, the white and red roses of York and Lancaster. The names of England and Scotland were to continue for the distinction of parts rather than the separation of kingdoms. Noting that the early church allowed no difference between Jew and Gentile when both acknowledged Christ, 'no more shall our age of an Englishman or Scot that live together in obedience of one monarchy. But as the names of Jew and Gentile did not cease immediately upon their reconcilement to one head no more need these.' [19] Such an analogy had of course political implications; this was divine right rhetoric with a flourish.

Northampton linked the differences between the countries in an organic metaphor to the king; they were the right and left hands, the king the head; they were twins of the same father (although the Scots were the younger son); playing on the metaphor he noted each was merely in unequal degrees from the sun. At the end of his peroration, Northampton let out all the stops in his plea for consensus:

It behooves us all not only with a word to wish but with our whole industry to provide that England and Scotland . . . may kiss one another . . . and
ever more like bright and cheerful cherubins in the propitiatory behold
one another . . . even as in that union by matrimony so in this of policy let
us be careful to provide as well by counsel as by caution that *quod deus
coniunxit homo non separet*.[20]

The new plan for union was presented to Parliament in 1606. There is
only scattered evidence of Northampton's part in efforts to get it through.
On 25 November 1606 the first conference with the Commons was held at
which the Lords urged the Commons' conferees, who had but limited
instructions, to debate the issues freely. Noting that he had a hand in the
framing of the articles, Northampton again urged approval because of the
expectations of those abroad and at home. He worried that 'some have
written that distraction would appear in the handling. He wished that he
might be a false prophet.'[21] He continued to speak at these conferences,
usually with Salisbury.[22] On the one hand he reflected King James's desires
and on the other the Commons' sensitivities, stating 'a perfect universal
union we present and there unto such restrictions as shall be fit'. He emphasised the notion of compromise, urging that the union must not founder on
disagreement over details, 'as when the worthy workman represented a
perfect picture to the view of many, one found one fault and other another
and one in the shoe, so said his Lordship in this exact well penned bill
somewhat in the shoe latchet may be loose'.[23]

Northampton's rhetoric now incorporated images of unity and consensus, but public orations were only part of his activities on parliamentary
issues. In private, his views were shaped by advice, information and precedents supplied most notably by Cotton, but by others too.

Cotton himself had in fact suggested the name of Britain for James's new
kingdom shortly after the king's accession.[24] Arguing that England and
Scotland were one in blood, language and religion, he went on to show that
James was descended from England's Saxon kings. There is no direct evidence that Cotton drew up this significant proposal at Northampton's
request; it may well have been for Salisbury or the king himself. But it is of
interest that Northampton repeatedly detailed James's genealogy while
speaking on the union in Parliament.[25] There is also direct evidence of his
drawing on Cotton's expertise while Northampton sat on the commission
drawing up the proposal for union, and during parliamentary debate in
1606.

The first question concerned free trade with the Scots:

Worthy Sir Robert Cotton . . . this day the Scots have propounded the
point of universal traffic and commerce. . . . I beseech you help to increase
my stock as well in this point as you have done in others by setting down
not only your own reasons of the difficulty or facility but whatsoever else

you can borrow from your friends either learned in the law or skilled in trade and traffic. It is a point of great importance and subject to great straits. . . . I wish they may enjoy [it] so far as it may be good for the weal of our country and the safety of our sovereign.[26]

This important letter suggests a flexibility or even uncertainty in North-ampton's approach to policy which his public speeches often masked. The tendency to see the Crown or the privy councillors as authoritarian, not allow-ing the Commons to participate in the political process, ignores the fact that on an informal basis many outside the government, whether at committee meetings or in proffering written advice, contributed to government policy. Northampton's mind was clearly not made up on the terms of trade with the Scots. He was open to argument. His concern for policy was no doubt aug-mented by his desire to appear well-informed in the Privy Council.

In the Commons' debate on the repeal of hostile laws in December 1606 the question arose as to whether escuage, incident to knight's service, was a hostile law and should, therefore, be repealed as well. Knight's service, the chief form of feudal tenure, obliged those holding land from the king to serve him for forty days a year in battle at their own charge or pay a fine called escuage or scutage. Northampton asked Cotton to prepare a brief for him on the issue, requesting 'any record or report of the first institution of scutage and the true motives that drew it first on and the conditions and circumstances that belong to it. . . . For these prove to what ends they have been imposed and levied.'[27] Since the history of an institution was key, Northampton believed, to its purpose, he tried his own hand at writing a piece on the matter, reciting eleven scutages imposed under King John. But he broke off abruptly after the words, 'which proves that the . . .'.[28] Cotton had more success.

Cotton began by discussing the antiquity of feudal tenure, noting that the principle of giving land in exchange for protection had been used by conquerors since the Romans, but was only fully established in England by the Norman Conquest. Most instances of knight's service had general appli-cation but some were limited to a single place. Cotton concluded, however, that escuage could not be repealed as a hostile law even when the service was specifically against the Scots.

Escuage general is no hostile law but a politic and fundamental law of the kingdom. . . . Escuage special to serve against the Scots . . . is not extin-guished in the tenure but suspended in the execution. And though during this suspension no penalty of escuage can be imposed by parliament . . . yet remaineth the tenure . . . and will yield other services concomitant as wardships, marriages and reliefs.[29]

It may seem peculiar that escuage should excite so much attention during discussion on union with Scotland that the Commons spent three days debating it. The reason is that while the tenure itself was of merely anti-quarian interest, built upon it was the feudal incident of wardship. When an heir to land held of the king came into his property during his minority, he became the king's ward and his wardship, land revenues and marriage rights could be sold for the king's profit. Administered through the Court of Wards, wardship had come to provide a sizeable part of the royal revenue. But for reasons economic and familial, wardship proved a constant irritant to the gentry. The debate in Parliament, ostensibly on hostile laws against the Scots, reflected the desires of some Commons members to be rid of wardship.[30]

Thomas Wilson, an MP, wrote an account of the debate for the Earl of Salisbury. 'Mr Fuller the first broacher of this business today pulled off his mask and said plainly that it tended to taking away of wards.' Fuller then added that there was 'no equity or reason in wardship, but that custom hath settled it'. Wilson summed up the debate by saying that 'the most and best that spake was for the remaining of escuage. But the generalest applause was upon them that would have it taken away.'[31] Some MPs turned the issue of hostile laws into a debate on the king's feudal rights. The Commons were soon to get their wish that wardship might be taken away with the government's offer of the Great Contract in 1610.

Despite the work of the commission for the union and the persuasion of the privy councillors, many members of the Commons remained unconvinced. At the end of the session the Commons did pass a modified Act repealing hostile laws directed against Scotland. When the Commons disagreed with royal policy, they used delay, limited instructions to conferees and tangential issues to affect that policy. This may not have been the winning of the initiative, but rearguard ambush, not a sign of the growing strength of the institution, but of its weakness.[32] As for Northampton, he had been unstinting in his efforts to achieve the king's goal in what he himself ruefully called 'endless labour on this rock of union'.[33] His speeches on the union in Parliament and to the commission show a changing rhetorical strategy, a growing sense of the need for consensus, coupled as always with his continuing appeal to divine right. Alongside the majestic language was a concern for the best advice he could secure on matters of policy and precedent. The issue of the English merchants' grievances against Spain which galvanised the session of 1606–7 provides important illustration.

II. Merchant Grievances

Much ink has been spilt analysing whether the debates on merchant grievances in the first Parliament of James I reflect advocates of free trade, the different interest groups represented in joint stock versus chartered companies or conflict between the outports and London.[34] Furthermore, historians have been content to echo S. R. Gardiner's verdict that the king and his councillors were intransigent in not yielding to the Commons' petition on the issue and impolitic in refusing compromise. Gardiner described Northampton's speech to a conference between the two Houses of Parliament in 1607 as one 'which hardly any other man in England would have allowed himself to utter. . . . He treated the Commons as if they were the dust beneath his feet.'[35]

The background to Northampton's speech is this. In 1606 English merchants complained of abuses by the Spaniards including the arrest of a ship for piracy, the seizure from English ships of commodities from the Low Countries – with which Spain was at war – and interference with trade to the West Indies. The Privy Council considered the grievances and lodged protests with the Spanish in some of the causes. In correspondence with Sir Charles Cornwallis, English ambassador to Spain, Salisbury repeatedly demanded redress and Cornwallis described his energetic if fruitless efforts to gain it.[36] On 25 February 1607 Sir Thomas Lowe, as governor of the Merchant Adventurers, petitioned the House of Commons. Although the Commons appointed a committee to examine the merchants' grievances, there appears to have been little discussion of the issue until May when the House sent Sir Edwin Sandys to the Lords to ask them to join in petitioning the king.[37] The Lords replied that while the message was 'somewhat strange' they too were concerned about such mistreatment and were willing to consider the matter. Sandys pointed out that the petition contained both a description of grievances and a call for legislation including Letters of Marque, which would allow English merchants to make reprisals against Spaniards and their goods. He went on to make an important distinction: the Commons embraced the petition's description of grievances but left redress to the king.[38] On 15 June the Lords agreed to a conference and that afternoon Northampton gave the speech that Gardiner characterised so scathingly. Salisbury set the stage for Northampton; war and peace, he argued, were matters for the king alone to decide. The merchants, Salisbury claimed, were making their private profit the public concern of the kingdom and the Commons were intruding into matters of foreign policy. King James had done all he could to insist on his subjects' right to trade with the Indies in the Spanish peace treaty negotiations; in fact, Spain had made no new laws to harass Englishmen. Finally, the merchants' demand for Letters of Marque would cause, if granted, a major economic loss of English goods in Spain, while reciprocal action by the English would catch only a trifle of Spanish trade. Salisbury then turned to the Commons' role, noting the many precedents that proved that such petitions to previous monarchs touching on war and peace had little success: these were *arcana imperii*, to be decided only by the king, advised by his Council.[39]

Northampton, who followed, made no additional points but explained why these were *arcana imperii*. Bacon, reporting to the lower House, described this speech as 'full of excellent matter and ornament and without iteration . . . the other Earl, who usually doth bear a principal part upon all important occasions . . . did deliver that he was persuaded that both houses did differ rather in credulity and belief, than in intention and desire: for . . . their Lordships . . . desired the reformation as much'.[40]

Northampton's language was more conciliatory than Salisbury's although his emphasis was on the constitutional limits of the power of the Commons. He explained that the Lords could not join in the petition because of

> the composition of our house, which he took in the first foundation thereof to be merely democratical, consisting of knights of shires and burgesses of towns, and intended to be those that have their residence, vocation, and employment in the places for which they serve: and therefore to have a private and local wisdom according to that compass, and so not fit to examine or determine secrets of state. . . . And although his Lordship acknowledged that there be diverse gentlemen in the mixture of our house, that are of good capacity and insight in matters of estate, yet that was the accident of the person, and not the intention of the place: and things were to be taken in the institution, not in the practice.[41]

Northampton's history was good but his stand was somewhat ingenuous since, as we have seen, he himself placed non-residents in borough seats.

Northampton iterated Salisbury's point that war and peace were the principal flowers of the Crown. The petition cast aspersions upon his Majesty and his conduct of foreign policy by implying that 'the king slept through the sobs of his servants until he was awaked with the thunder bolt of a parliament'.[42] After delineating the power of the monarch, Northampton went on to deal directly with the current issue. Bacon reported that 'his Lordship's conclusion was very noble . . . that what civil threats, contestation, art and argument can do, hath been used already to procure remedy in this cause, and a promise that if reason of state did permit, as their Lordships were ready to spend their breath in persuading that we desire, so they would be ready to spend their blood in the execution thereof'.[43]

The invocation of *raison d'état* raises the spectre of absolutism. Yet Northampton's argument that it was beyond Parliament's power to advise on matters of foreign policy, specifically on war and peace, was similar to Salisbury's and not unlike Sandys's when he brought the petition on merchant grievances to the Lords. Indeed, Northampton stressed the same lack of power in the upper House. In debate as to whether to join the House of Commons in petitioning the king, Northampton described the Lords as 'the higher House that are born councillors of the great estate' but avowed that in this case, 'it belongs not our element'.[44] Even his rhetoric was the same, but to the Lords, unlike the Commons, Northampton explained royal policy. Peace with Spain had just been recently concluded, and it was not unusual that old enmities should persist; such enmity toward Scotland, as

Northampton had painfully learned, hindered the union. He too argued that retaliation against Spain would cause greater loss in trade to the English. Northampton stressed, 'I would be glad to hear as well of a proportion to maintain the charge as of a petition to renew the war ... for though passion be a quick guide yet is it a slow paymaster.' Charles I's privy councillors were to make much the same point in 1628.[45]

In sum, how could councillors petition the king for action they had already undertaken at his direction? Even if adopted, the petition would be referred by the king to the Privy Council, 'where we are already'.[46] The differences in the speeches reflect Northampton's view of the differing functions of the Lords and Commons: the Lords made up of the king's natural advisers, who served as the conduit of his word to the Commons, representatives of local wisdom. But on this issue it is clear Northampton felt that neither House had authority to adopt the petition. Since both Northampton and Sandys agreed that the matter could only be remedied by the Council it is well worth asking what was the purpose of the petition: simply to remedy grievances or additionally to stir up anti-Spanish sentiment in the Commons, and at whose instigation?

Salisbury and Northampton had acted together again, the one attacking the merchants, the other articulating the historical and political reasoning on which the denial of the petition was based. Committed to the peace with Spain, both were concerned that its adoption might have damaged that new-born agreement. Were this all it would be enough to question Gardiner's and Willson's characterisation of Northampton's speech. But there is more. For this position Northampton had the support of one of the most respected members of the House of Commons, Sir Robert Cotton. Although much has been made of the Commons' use of historical precedent to buttress their arguments against the Crown,[47] in fact the Crown relied heavily on historical analysis, too, and often had as good historians.

When the Lords turned down the Commons' suit, they turned to the question of their privileges, that is, whether they had the right to present the king with such a petition. Many of them were unsure of their ground, as Sandys's own speeches had indicated. The day after the conference with the Lords, the Commons appointed a committee to look into the historical precedents. One member of that committee was Sir Robert Cotton.[48] But almost three weeks before Cotton had composed a brief for Northampton entitled 'An Answer to the Message of the Common House and Complaints of the Merchants', pointing out the 'reasons why the Lords may justly forbear to confer with the Commons house about the Spanish grievances'.[49] It served as the basis of both privy councillors' presentations. Cotton argued that it was improper to be discussed in Parliament because of the limitation of its power of redress, the kinds of causes it could properly handle and the 'judgement of parliament not to intermeddle with things proper either to other courts or the king's prerogative'. Parliament, he wrote, 'is to meddle with those matters only for which it is summoned ... the entertainment of other matters make long sessions'.[50] Parliament itself, Cotton argued, had recognised that these kinds of grievances were to be redressed at the council table.

How should Cotton's work for Northampton be characterised? In a system without institutional co-ordination between the executive and the legislature, informal methods were necessary. Salisbury operated through two means. The first was direct, through large conferences between both Houses at which he and Northampton and Lord Chancellor Ellesmere could speak to fifty or a hundred MPs at once. The second was indirect, through the use of friendly but seemingly independent MPs who were willing to raise issues the government wanted discussed. Nicholas Tyacke has suggested that Sir Robert Wroth's speech enumerating the Commons' grievances on the first day of business in the Commons was not the first challenge to a foreign king in the new reign that it was once considered. Instead, it was probably inspired by Salisbury himself.[51] In this way, trial balloons could be floated from which the government could later dissociate itself if necessary and policies could be suggested that the Commons might accept at their own initiative but not the Crown's. This ploy became a common practice in the early Stuart period and in many ways recognised the independence of the Commons as much as trying to control it directly through privy councillors. Cotton's relations with Northampton were even closer than those of Salisbury and Wroth. He had been providing Northampton with advice and briefs for several years. Their work on the union with Scotland and on merchant grievances points to an important new nexus between the Privy Council and Commons taking place now informally since the number of privy councillors in the lower House had been reduced.[52]

Moreover, if Northampton's working partnership with Cotton inside Parliament suggests a different story from that told by Gardiner, evidence from a source outside Parliament suggests yet another twist to the story. In October 1605 Sir Charles Cornwallis, ambassador to Spain on Northampton's nomination and considered crypto-Catholic and pro-Spanish by his contemporaries, lamented the delays of the Spaniards in rectifying wrongs against English merchants. He wrote to Salisbury to suggest another strategy: 'a galliard motion in parliament grounded upon some reason for leaving this peace with large offer for support of the king's charges which made known to the [Spanish] Ambassador would so awake their dull spirits as very shortly I doubt not but I shall be able to write that which will be both pleasing and profitable to his Majesty.' Cornwallis repeated the same proposal to Northampton: 'somewhat said and done this parliament to incite the king against Spain . . . (and that made known here) will, I doubt not, much further me in the service I have parposed . . . I have lately written two general letters to my Lord of Salisbury much to this purpose.'[53] Cornwallis's suggestion of planting such a motion is startling but its open discussion in official dispatches suggests that such a ploy was common enough to need no explanation and that Parliament could be used by the Crown to influence foreign policy. Such a suggestion was a corollary to Northampton's repeated comment that foreign nations closely observed parliamentary sessions.

Neither councillor responded directly to this suggestion; the 1605 session was overtaken by the Gunpowder Plot. Merchant grievances went unattended and it might be thought that there was no connection between Cornwallis's suggestion and the discussion of the issue two years later. The oppressions of English merchants continued, however, to figure large in his correspondence. In June 1606 Salisbury wrote that the principal business before the Council was 'complaints which are daily multiplied on all sides about the courses held in Spain against his Majesty's service'. Against these wrongs, the king's subjects were soliciting Letters of Marque 'to right themselves as well as they can, in such places where they have been wronged'. Salisbury noted that the clamour was directed at the Council because the merchants felt they were getting nowhere with Cornwallis in Spain. In July 1606 the entire Council wrote to Cornwallis that it could 'hardly find a sufficient and just answer to refuse or deny their suit...though we have a disposition...to stop the...clamour...by all other means'.[54] In November 1606, as matters continued to drag on, Cornwallis again suggested 'this next session of parliament will come very fitly to give them a feeling that the king my sovereign shall not want means to undertake and maintain the wars if he be enforced. Neither can I doubt that so many gross injuries as there be published to be daily offered to his subjects here by this arrogant nation will be let pass by either of the Houses without an earnest motion of revenge, and a liberal offer of means to effect it.'[55]

Did the Crown plant the motion? There is no direct evidence but the chronology is suggestive. In January 1607 Salisbury described a meeting with the Spanish ambassador which had produced little but protestations of better usage in the future. In February, when the Spanish ambassador and the archduke's ambassador presented their own grievances and suggested further meetings, Salisbury suggested that 'the parliament now approaching, and many other businesses being at hand, it might be deferred until the ambassador should receive a further answer to our complaints formerly delivered'.[56] It was also in February that Sir Thomas Lowe, who had close connections with the court, raised the motion in Parliament.

If Salisbury did wish the issue raised in Parliament his intent was to bring pressure on Spain by an attack on the treaty and a proposal to vote large subsidies as if to endorse renewal of war. Indeed the *Commons Journal* described the councillors' response in conference in just that way: 'it was conceived and uttered by the Lords, that if the Commons were at anytime made acquainted with such causes, it were with one of these two purposes; that either they should make some declaration of their affections or else minister aid of money, the sinews of war.'[57] The call for Letters of Marque, however, would not support royal policy but alter it.

Instead of the traditional picture of Crown and opposition locked in struggle, the issue of merchant grievances points up just how complex the workings of Parliament were. The Spanish merchants were eager to gain redress in whatever manner they could; MPs were sympathetic to their losses but uncertain as to the appropriate remedy; the English ambassador, at a loss to gain restitution from the Spanish, eagerly tried to use parliamentary pressure; privy councillors, who had worked hard for the same end as the Commons, could not endorse their remedy which would bring more evils than it would cure. At the end of the session Salisbury explained to Cornwallis the Council's negative response to the petition in almost the same words he had used in conference, but summed up the session in positive terms, 'his Majesty having received good contentment in their proceedings'.[58]

III.   The Great Contract

The parliamentary session of 1610 reveals Northampton much changed from the 'vestal virgin' of 1604. He was now strongly aware of the realities of Stuart government, of the overspending of the early years and of the need to reach the Commons not only by grandiloquence but also by negotiation. Throughout this extraordinary session he stressed in conference the administrative reforms that the court had undertaken, and painted a harsh but realistic picture of the alternatives the Crown would be driven to were the Great Contract not concluded.

The Great Contract, proposed by Lord Treasurer Salisbury to Parliament in 1610, was the most innovative proposal of the early Stuart period.[59] Trading the king's feudal rights and tenures, particularly wardship, for a settled and steady income would have ended the old notion that the king should 'live of his own', and established in its place the public funding of the state. The initiative looked forward to the settlement of 1660. But that took a civil war. There is evidence that Salisbury had conceived the idea as early as 1604 and throughout the earlier sessions of the Parliament in 1604, 1605–6, 1606–7 the issues of purveyance, feudal tenures and wardship had been repeatedly raised in the Commons, sometimes at Salisbury's suggestion. The nobility and gentry, who dominated both Houses of Parliament, were those primarily affected by the feudal incidents of relief and wardship; purveyance proved a continuing irritant to the general populace. Northampton himself had worked on the problem of purveyance after it was raised in the first session.[60]

From February to July 1610 both Houses debated and conferred on the Great Contract. By the time of adjournment in 1610 a tentative agreement had been reached on the rights the king would give up and the amount the subjects would contribute, but there had been no consideration of how that support would be levied. At its reconvening in October, it was clear the

Contract was lost; members of the Commons who had to answer to constituents came back wanting to bind the king more securely and gain larger concessions; the king, his debts increased and furious that earlier negotiations had been fruitless, raised his demands and the Contract fell to the ground. The consequences were the mulcting of those very revenues that the king and Salisbury had offered in exchange for a sound and regular income.

Some historians have suggested that Northampton helped to undermine the Great Contract in order to injure Salisbury in the king's regard. But Northampton's role in the negotiations and in the session as a whole have not been examined. In fact, he actively backed Salisbury's initiative in speeches in the Lords and at conferences with the Commons. In addition, he shouldered the heavy work of the private Bills brought before the House of Lords that Salisbury could not attend to.

In his first speech in conference with the Commons, Northampton took up the cudgels for the Great Contract. Accused of persistently patronising the Commons, Northampton's words in 1610 belie it. Never did he try harder to gain the support of the Commons. He began by recognising the worth of the members and the common background they shared with the Lords. He referred to their

> learned and grave judgements not sorted by succession but selected by free choice out of all the seminaries of experience and wisdom . . . [casting] his eyes upon many his kinsmen, many his friends, and many whom society of life made familiar to him . . . though our status were divided, our degrees were different, yea our speeches sometimes dissonant, yet our minds and ends were uniform.[61]

This language is important. For the haughty Northampton, who had written on the leprosy of the low-born in 1597 and lauded the high status of those on the Privy Council in 1604, to praise those chosen by election not birth was conciliatory indeed. Repeatedly, Northampton distinguished between the abilities of members of the Commons and their constitutional role. Moreover, Northampton's words stressed consensus of the Council and the Commons. Clearly, he was trying to exercise all the suasion of which he was capable.

Northampton echoed Salisbury's speech calling for supply and support. Supply was the traditional monies Parliament voted the king on specific occasions; support was Salisbury's innovative suggestion for a fixed yearly income for the monarch. The king, Northampton argued, had every cause to ask for support both because of need and the virtues of his person. Painting a picture of what James had done for the realm, Northampton recapitulated past efforts at reform, particularly those with which he himself had been involved. He returned to the issue of foreign policy, raising the spectre of the Pope's excommunication of James and what it might have wrought.

Instead, the king had brought peace, had repaired the church fabric and weeded out schism. The king's generosity was a function of majesty but 'howsoever out of nature, ignorance of our state or importunity of suitors, his Majesty had seemed overliberal, yet now at length he meant to make a stay'.[62] To those who said the proposal of the Great Contract was unusual, Northampton replied with mediaeval precedents from Richard II, Henry III and Henry IV. Like his contemporaries both on the Council and in the Commons, Northampton shared a set of assumptions which viewed Stuart monarchy as the direct heir of the mixed monarchy of the fourteenth and fifteenth centuries. Such precedents might then be immediately relevant and as we have seen were invoked by councillors as well as MPs. But Northampton was always practical. He went beyond traditional notions of necessity defined by war or extraordinary circumstances to argue that the king had the right to call on his subjects for support in peacetime. His overriding principle was the maintenance of the monarchy. The king had done his part by extending his ordinary revenues, reforming his administration and limiting his bounty. Now it was up to the Commons to reciprocate.[63]

In these early days of the session Northampton served as an envoy from one House to another and from the king to both. Northampton did not try to sow discord by his reports; Salisbury congratulated him and said he had never heard any man deliver a better one.[64] On 12 March Northampton brought James's message to both Houses giving the Commons leave to treat of tenures. Northampton said the king agreed because of 'your humility, not to deal without leave until it were granted; dutifulness, referring it unto his judgement; understanding, desiring the Lords to join with you in your petition; discretion, in not propounding your desires *gratis* but with recompense'. While these qualities which Northampton ascribed to the Commons may not have accorded with some members' view of their role, it did with the king's. Northampton's tone was hopeful. Calling wards 'the fair Helen', he reported that the king allowed them to treat of tenures despite the fact that by so doing, 'he blasteth the flower of his regality'. Then Northampton added his own views. He urged them to proceed 'without rubs or lets'. 'You know the king's estate, the verifying whereof you have been offered to have been showed records. I can bring no record but the record of affection; but speaking unto you I take myself to be at home.' Then he added the words, obvious in themselves, yet a theme which was to grow as the session went on: 'as long as there is a monarchy, you must maintain the monarch.' Another version spells it out more explicitly and perhaps more ominously: 'We had better help him now whilst he is able to concur with us than at the last when you must bear him more heavy and that he must crush you, for whilst we hold monarchy we must maintain the monarch.'[65] Northampton's stock warning was not a jeremiad of the Civil War to come, but a realistic picture of the options the king and his ministers would face. Furthermore, it is important to make the distinction that the king would crush his subjects not through arbitrary political power, but with the weight of debt. Lord Chancellor Ellesmere, often thought to have had little love for Northampton, praised his report, saying 'that Lord, who delivered his Majesty's pleasure unto us, conveyed it as well and clearly as ever he saw the purest water brought by the best conduit'.[66]

The Commons' opening offer of £100,000 was clearly a disappointment to the Crown. Northampton's immediate reaction was, for once, succinct: 'The Commons have made an offer. The question is whether it be a sufficient offer for the king.' By the end of April, he voiced some doubt: 'this business hath many links, I think this circle is very round and the chiefest points in question.'[67] As the matter dragged into June, Northampton said in conference that there was no reason for the Crown to offer more until they had seen what the Commons would give. But in conference with the House that afternoon he urged: 'is it nothing to have a man's son freed from wardships which I hold a great burden unto the subject? Therefore as the casting of a bell everyone throws in somewhat to make the sound better, so if we like the sounding of this bell, let us every one cast in somewhat.' By July agreement looked near and Salisbury argued the distance was so little and the bargain so advantageous, 'if you should not accept it you would hereafter repent yourselves'.[68] As the session wore on Northampton no longer spoke on the Great Contract. But the reason for his silence seems apparent: Northampton sat on forty-eight committees during the 1610 session, an overwhelming load. While Salisbury tried heroically to negotiate with the Commons, Northampton was shouldering much of the private business of the Lords.

At a conference between the two Houses in October when Parliament reassembled after recess, during which MPs had consulted with their constituents, one of the king's ministers made a last effort on behalf of the Contract:

I am no physician to anatomise the king's wants; but except you redeem the things which before I spake of, they must be more pressed than they have been. I speak not by way of menace; for when it comes to that I shall be miserable. I do not say the king shall send you an Empson and a Dudley, but this I say, the king must not want.[69]

But the speaker was not the authoritarian Northampton threatening future retribution by government officials turned extortionists. It was Salisbury, in extremity as the Contract failed. In this Salisbury and Northampton were as one. The commons understood the message too. ''Twas to be feared,' one MP said, 'if he could not take with the right hand, he would take it with the left'.[70] And there was fear too that 'the leak in the cistern' would continue unabated.

Why did the Great Contract fail? A contemporary wrote that the sum was too large for a subject to pay and too little for the king to receive.[71] This analysis recognised both the king's needs and the importance of placing the monarchy on a wider financial base. But the MPs had undergone close questioning during the summer recess on how the Contract would be financed. They came back determined to strike a harder bargain. Obviously frustrated, the king increased his demands, the Commons refused to pay and the Contract was lost.

With the Contract a failure, Northampton made a last-ditch effort to get the traditional subsidies from the Commons. Once again he began by extolling the Commons, 'the rare and worthy parts with which so many members of that body are endued, as well by nature as by erudition', and promised not to cloy their 'stomachs that have surfeited upon so many dainties and delightful fruits with a sallet of coleworts twice sodden'.[72] He did not have to report that the king was in want, he said, and urged them to think of how neglect of the king would be thought of abroad. Invoking the unity of the kingdom at the time of the Armada, Northampton raised the spectre of war and how it would be impossible to call Parliament together to raise funds, in case of such an emergency.

Northampton predicted what would follow the failure to vote the king money. On the crucial matter of patronage, he posed the dilemma that would face the aristocracy 'that prefer our sons, our nephews, our allies and friends, to the king's service in hope of bountiful reward'. Were the king to turn his patronage to his own profit, the consequences would be drastic:

> The fry that is repelled from the ocean must of necessity return to the tainting of the rivers in which they were first bred. The gentry and nobility enforced to improvement of their fortunes to the uttermost for the maintenance and support of the cadets of their own families will cut the subject to the bone.[73]

Northampton's was a sophisticated analysis of how patronage functioned in the larger political system. In providing the fundamental link between the Crown and the political elite, patronage had important economic consequences. He suggested that it provided the elasticity that allowed a paternalist order to exist. Were that favour to cease or to cost more, all subjects would suffer because the elite would be forced thoroughly to mulct its tenants and those who had economic relationships with them.

Northampton emphasised that the common good was involved in the satisfaction of the king and went on to address several objections. To those who argued that the ordinary charges should be paid for by the king, he challenged traditional notions that the king should 'live of his own' and denied any formal record of it. He pointed out that princes were forced by variation of fortune to change their course. Therefore the service of the state could not be tied to any certain rules either of art or economy. The king had tried to extend ordinary means as far as he could; he had mortgaged and even sold his own land and improved the customs. He was 'willing to improve as much as the subject will bear . . . but where the state is slothful to supply, it is above the skill of kings to make themselves alchemists'. To those who argued impertinently that much had been given he replied naming the king's expenses. Demands on the subject were greater under Elizabeth and yet supplies were yielded with greater alacrity. If it were answered that England was then at war, he pointed out the benefits the king had brought by making peace. Furthermore, stressing Elizabeth's stinginess, he said that 'it is not long since we found cause to complain of bounty in a king'.[74]

To their final excuse, that they must return to their counties and account for their vote of subsidies, this was Northampton's advice. Tell them, he said, the king and his family are in good health, the kingdom at peace, the subjects in union, the laws in strength and swords turned into coulters. James had given ear to propositions preferred by the Commons for the common good such as no king since the Conquest had listened to.

You may let them know that the world is enamoured of the king's justice, foreign parts affected to his amity...we stand more obliged to his Majesty than to those that went before, the surety of succession, the maintenance of public justice, the fruits of bounty, the instances of clemency with as many other moral virtues and regal merits as occasion could urge or zeal offer.

This is a view of James not often heard, either from contemporaries or later historians, yet it reflects the achievements of the reign which were not insubstantial compared to the Tudors'. But Northampton expressed his view most explicitly in this passage:

Proportion should rather be the rule of our imitation than precedent... for so long as empire and subjection are relatives, supplies and satisfaction must be concomitant according to...necessity. Wherefore whether we leave precedents or follow precedents, whether princes'...hand[s] be open or close, yet this rule must ever hold, that so long as subjects live under monarchy they are bound to maintain the monarch.[75]

Northampton's view of the prerogative accorded with that of Ellesmere and other privy councillors who believed that by the Great Contract the king had offered to bind both his hands which no earthly power could effect.[76] But in urging the voting of subsidies, Northampton made the traditional conjunction of supply and the satisfaction of the subject.

The public record shows Northampton supporting Salisbury and the Great Contract at every turn. There is some evidence, however, that he had private doubts. In his own papers are jottings which, though not a coherent statement, raise doubts about the wisdom of abolishing wardship. Reviewing the justification for that ancient custom, he argued that with the father dead, the king, the father of his country, provides care, protection and defence. With the abolition of wardship 'the ward shall lose many helps which the law gives'. As he so often did, Northampton took note of the foreign implications. He suggested that the alteration showed distrust of the king and worried about its effect on foreign ambassadors. 'Some will think he sells his prerogative, others that his people mistrust [him].' Northampton then went on to make two points of particular significance. To begin with, he questioned the efficacy of the bargain: 'Make the fine what you will it may be cut off or spent, then is the return upon the subject who pays for it.... Ill for the subject himself for when these pensions are worn out, the subject's purse must pay for it.' In line with his view that so long as there was a monarchy the monarch had to be maintained, Northampton pointed out the inadequacy of the Contract to prevent further financial demands on the subject – an argument made by MPs, too.

Northampton went on to make a crucial distinction between administrative reform and bartering away the prerogative. Where Elizabeth had compounded for purveyance with her subjects' gratitude, James was urged to give it up altogether. 'The state which joyed under a woman in the ease of pursuivants by monopolies now are taught to reject the monopolies.' He ended with the suggestion of the offer of marriage of wards. One paragraph which Northampton crossed out defines his concern most clearly: 'Discouragement of the king's affection in doing good when all his grace is returned to his own prejudice; what he reforms they abolish, monopolies with limitations, pursuivants with composition. Desire to take away abuses of the wards with taking the wards away.'[77] Northampton's assessment of the difficulties in giving up wardship was quite practical. Undated, his comments may have been written in 1604, 1607 or 1610. Similar doubts on the wisdom of the Great Contract were expressed in 1610 by Sir Julius Caesar and with hindsight in 1615 by Sir Francis Bacon. The loyal second to Salisbury may have been merely Northampton's pose but to assume that he was secretly undermining the Great Contract requires evidence that has not been found. Looking for a villain, Notestein draws on Northampton's reputation, his personality and his relationship with Sir Robert Carr, the king's favourite, to suggest that the earl helped the failure. There is evidence that Carr and Sir Thomas Lake, the king's principal secretary, may have added heat to the king's frustration at the reconvening of Parliament by claiming that the Commons were drawing up a petition to send home the Scots. But Northampton cannot be connected to these or any other clandestine efforts.[78] For whatever Northampton's private doubts he engaged along with Salisbury to bring the Contract to fruition with every ounce of persuasion, reasoning and even threat that he could muster.

The failure of the Great Contract in 1610 had a profound effect on the court. As Northampton predicted it embittered James toward his Parliament and toward Salisbury, his parliamentary manager. The Council now turned to the very devices that Salisbury and Northampton had warned would result from the failure of the Great Contract. Northampton was energetic in trying to raise funds through projects such as the baronetage and by administrative reforms such as the short-lived revival of the naval commission. While such reform might be looked on favourably by many, the use of prerogative commissions would encounter resistance from Members of Parliament such as James Whitelocke, who questioned the method if not the end. In the wake of the demise of the Great Contract, Parliament was not called into session for three years while the court sought to put its own house in order.

IV. The Addled Parliament

Northampton's role in the abrupt dissolution of the Addled Parliament has been often retold: he opposed it from the outset because he favoured alliance with Spain which paid his pension. Without a Parliament, the king would be dependent on a Spanish dowry. When nevertheless the king called a Parliament in 1614, Northampton actively worked to bring about its abrupt dissolution, planting an inflammatory speech in the House of Commons and then encouraging the king to dissolve Parliament. The plot succeeded and Northampton paraded in triumph through London with his co-conspirator Sir Charles Cornwallis and scores of followers. Cornwallis later admitted his part in planting the speech. He was clapped in the Tower for sowing the seeds of discord between the king and his subjects. And what of Northampton? He had died a week after the dissolution and therefore was beyond earthly judgement.[79]

In 1612 and 1613, as the expedients and projects of the past two years failed to match hopes or the king's increasing debts, suggestions were made in the Privy Council that the king call another Parliament.[80] Northampton's view was decidedly negative and his analysis of the difficulties acute, based on his knowledge that recently devised means of raising money would be attacked and his despair at controlling the flow of favour. While Northampton's desire for the Spanish alliance must have played some role in his calculations, so did his belief that sessions of Parliament had to be carefully prepared; to ensure a well-affected Parliament, redress of grievances and administrative reforms had to be undertaken. With the failure of the Great Contract, the government had indeed been driven as Salisbury and Northampton had warned to improve the king's revenues to the greatest extent possible, 'extracting as it were the very strokings of the udder from the cow'.[81] Northampton argued that there were several impediments to a successful session. First of all, foreign difficulties, such as the death of Henry IV in France and the insecurity of the Duchy of Cleves, invoked in 1610 to gain supply, were no longer of moment. The king's daughter had just been married so that could not be raised as a just motive for supply. Since the Crown had been unable to increase its income markedly from wardship, licences of alienation or post fines, the Commons would not value them as highly as in the previous session. Moreover, 'the king's retribution better trusted then than now', he had not punished those guilty of 'extraordinary insolvencies'. Finally, Northampton noted among the impediments 'infinite grudge upon the baronets' and 'hand closed promised by my Lord of Northampton (worse)'.[82]

To this analysis, Northampton added his own experience with Parliaments and parliamentarians in 1610 and 1613. The Irish Parliament of 1613 had provided a dress rehearsal for later Stuart politics. After the king created forty new boroughs to secure a Protestant majority, members of both Houses had held 'secret conventicles' to organise opposition. On the opening day of the session the Catholic rump chose its own speaker but withdrew after a scuffle around the speaker's chair and refused to participate, so that the Crown was not able to organise Parliament. As we have seen, Northampton had coped with the problem successfully. Another session of the Irish Parliament was scheduled for 1614; it is hardly surprising that he thought it impossible for the Crown to prepare for and organise two Parliaments at once. Closer to home he skirmished with Sir Thomas Beaumont, who befriended the Earl of Essex during his annulment proceedings with Frances Howard. It is significant that Northampton attacked him on political grounds. In the session of 1610 Beaumont had first questioned purveyance and the legality of impositions and then gone on to challenge Northampton's basic argument for supply, that above all the monarch must be maintained. 'Policy is the bond of society, but the laws are the spirit of the kingdom . . . if [the king] or his ministers shall leap over them or break them down, what have we to secure us?' What Beaumont saw as a constitutional question, however, Northampton regarded as mere obstruction, calling him 'that notorious knave that opposed the king so powerfully in parliament and the Lords of the Council since at the board in maintaining the refusal of Leicestershire to answer and supply the purveyance'.[83] Given his views, it was no wonder that Northampton was pessimistic about another meeting of Parliament.

But the financial problems remained unsolved. Supporters of a Parliament, such as Sir Henry Neville, argued if the king granted the promises of 1610 the subjects would gladly vote him sufficient revenues. What Neville proposed amounted to the revival of the Great Contract. Consultation with leading MPs had suggested to Neville that only such concessions would elicit contribution and he offered to manage Parliament in return for office: the Secretaryship of State.[84] Sir Francis Bacon, another proponent of calling Parliament, advocated that the Crown do everything possible to elect a Commons which would be well disposed to aid the king.

Although recent scholarship has clearly marked the differences between the plans of Neville and Bacon, both contemporaries and later historians confused these schemes and labelled them 'undertaking'. Analysts of the Addled Parliament assert that the Howard faction led by Northampton played the role of dissemblers, supporting the 'undertakers', to prove to the king that Parliament would never heed his necessities – their end, to turn him decisively in the direction of Spain, the Spanish marriage and the Spanish dowry.[85]

Northampton's position must be distinguished, however, from that of his nephew, Thomas Howard, Earl of Suffolk, and the favourite, Somerset. Although Northampton disagreed with them he was losing influence to this new alliance. In a series of letters written in February 1614 Northampton, already ill, reported to Somerset and the king the deliberations of the Privy Council on the question of calling Parliament. Repeatedly he emphasised the need for preparation: endorsing the traditional redress of grievances and attention to elections. But Northampton emphatically repudiated Neville and the 'undertakers', and their 'pragmatic invention or hasty prosecution':

> We have taken order that all the requests and aggrievances which were given in at the breaking up of the last parliament may be brought in the same day to be scanned by the Lords to the reasonable end that upon the breaking of the bunch we may make election as well of the things which his majesty may grant without hurt, as of the burdens wherein they may be also eased without either scandal to the justice of the state or prejudice to his Majesty.[86]

On Saturday, 16 February, Northampton reported to Carr the Council's final decision, a consensus that Parliament should be called, 'and though some were more confident than others . . . yet all resolved upon the necessity of a parliament'.

By 1614 Northampton no longer dominated the Council. His nephew Suffolk and William Herbert, Earl of Pembroke, had been appointed to bring in the demands that would be asked of the king at this meeting of Parliament. To Somerset, his son-in-law, Suffolk wrote that Pembroke, a supporter of Neville's programme, had said that diverse lords who spoke with many wise Parliament men 'found they declined from the undertakers and only myself and he were believers' in its success.[87] Then Suffolk told this story about Northampton to the favourite:

> I must make you laugh to tell you that my Lord Privy Seal soberly says to me, 'my lord you incline before the council too much to these undertakers.' This troubles me nothing for if we may do our master the service we ought by our dissembling, I am well contented to play the knave a little with them which you must give me dispensation for following your direction.[88]

But Northampton did not dissemble. To Somerset he reasserted his views that preparation, not undertaking, was what was wanted.

> To be plain with your Lordship so many difficulties are upon the contemplation of this subject as if there were any possibility in repairing or

supplying the king's estate by any other means, the greater part of us would hold this time worst fitted and the means less prepared than we would wish, but necessity will perhaps draw us to adventure rather than to suffer. For it is true that there may be good parliaments but we find not as true that we can meet with any demonstrations of certainty.[89]

It is clear, however, that there was a new axis of influence at court. Northampton began to slide from power in the last months of his life as he declined as well in health. In April he was ill (although one observer thought he was more sick in mind than body).[90] His last attendance at the Privy Council was on 22 February when the meeting was held at Northampton's house. His signature was last affixed to a Privy Council order on 30 March.[91] He who had been the stalwart in serving as government spokesman in the Lords missed the opening of Parliament and attended none of its sessions.[92] He sat on no committees, received no proxies. In short, Northampton was no longer in political control when the Addled Parliament met.

Let us now turn our attention to the Commons in 1614. If we suspend our knowledge of Hoskyns's inflammatory speech on 3 June, do we see a harmonious session undermined by conspiracy? In examining the session it is important to look at its chronology and tempo. The Commons began the session by arguing about the rumours of undertaking and suggesting that efforts to gain seats for the Crown were unusually great. Then impositions came to the fore. Members argued that they were illegal although the judges had ruled otherwise in Bate's case. The Lords refused to join in a petition to the king on the matter and Bishop Neile made a speech attacking the Commons for raising the issue. The Commons responded by focusing on Neile's speech as a breach of the Commons' privileges. In all of this there seemed little concern for supply. The session, bogged down in recrimination, seemed to be going nowhere.[93]

In fact, the House of Commons had proved so unruly from the beginning of the session that leaders such as William Hakewill argued against so many Committees of the Whole House.

On 12 May, a month into the session, Sir Warwick Hele moved that the next day be appointed to give Bills the second reading to find the Lords something to do. Furthermore, on 21 May, in the debate on impositions, citing biblical prophecies, Thomas Wentworth, son of Peter, referred to Henry IV, saying, 'in the midst of his glory he died like a calf that had his throat cut by a butcher, but far be it from my Lord the king that aught so should befall him.'[94] Four days later, the Commons resolved to forbear from all business until they had answer from the Lords as to how they would provide satisfaction in punishing Neile. Sir Samuel Sandys verbally wrung his hands, speaking of the 'inevitable misery that we that came to reform disorders have nothing but disorders among us'. Finding them unresponsive to his message asking them 'to fall to matters that concerned the state', James sent again telling them to prepare a Bill for the continuation of statutes and to attend his Majesty in the House of Lords for dissolving Parliament unless they provided a speedy and effectual course for his supply.[95]

This chronology is significant because Hoskyns had not yet invoked the Sicilian Vespers and Northampton had not attended Parliament in two months. And if there was a conspiracy it was more likely to be caused by those at the scene, not by Northampton lying ill at Greenwich.

Then John Hoskyns made his speech urging the king to send the Scots home, and raised the spectre of the Sicilian Vespers. The king contacted the Spanish ambassador who held out the hope of the Spanish dowry to make up the king's debts. The king told Northampton of his resolve and, within an hour of the royal visit, Northampton sent news of it to the Spanish ambassador.[96] Immediately after, the king dissolved Parliament.

Hoskyns was imprisoned in the Tower for his speech along with Wentworth and two other MPs. He claimed that Dr Lionel Sharpe had given him the speech and promised him the protection of Cornwallis, even perhaps of Northampton. Cornwallis admitted writing a speech which he wished to deliver in the Commons himself. When he found he had applied too late for a seat, he sought to have someone else give it. He had in mind Thomas Hitchcock who had secured his seat at Bishop's Castle through Northampton's influence transmitted by Cornwallis and Sharpe. Cornwallis wanted to make two points. The first point was to support the king's right to levy impositions. And Hitchcock did make a speech upholding impositions. But the second part of the speech he either refused to make or omitted and so Sharpe, Cornwallis's emissary, moved on to Hoskyns. Cornwallis wanted the king to increase the number of Englishmen who served him as gentlemen of the privy chamber and asked the king to tell Scots not to come to England. He swore that he did not mean to attack those already there. As presumptuous as that might sound to James's ears; the speech Hoskyns gave was much more inflammatory and Cornwallis denied its authorship.[97]

What are we to make of this episode? Certainly Northampton might have agreed with Cornwallis's speech as planned; he had long complained of those around the king who wasted the mite his administrators were able to save. Further, it was not unusual to plant speeches in the Commons. As we have seen, such dabbling happened in 1604 and continued into the 1620s. Cornwallis himself repeatedly suggested it.[98] Moreover, it would be a mistake to see Hoskyns as Gardiner did, as the innocent who did not know the meaning of what he said, for 'he had not studied history very deeply'. This is unlikely. Hoskyns was well educated. He received his BA and MA at New College and became a member of the Middle Temple, where he supervised students. He was a stalwart of the 'Mitre' circle of wits which included various lawyers, merchants and poets. In addition, he was acquainted with several members of the Society of Antiquaries. Furthermore, Hoskyns had made a violent speech against the Scots in 1610; it did not take Cornwallis and Sharpe to suggest the theme. Finally, Hoskyns realised how inflammatory his speech was: he began by saying it might be the last . . . [99] So it seems more reasonable to see Hoskyns not as the innocent tool or victim of the pro-Spanish interests, but as a member of the Commons who agreed with the idea of sending home the Scots, a cry that might unite a variety of factions. In addition, Thomas Hitchcock, who seems but a footnote in the story, has something important to tell us. It was perfectly possible for him to refuse to make the speech about the Scots while agreeing to endorse impositions.[100] A new paradigm of the relations of the Lords and Commons must go beyond simple manipulation to one where MPs freely accepted and rejected suggestions from the Lords who were their patrons.

What of Northampton's role in the breakdown of the 1614 Parliament? That he was neither surprised nor displeased may well be true. Bacon later accused him of providing a haven for those who opposed the undertakers.[101] That he took an active role in destroying the session remains unproven. Contemporary observers were less certain of Northampton's part than recent historians have been. While suggesting that there was a general rumour in court that Northampton was 'somewhat implicated in that business', Henry Wotton noted that Cornwallis had cleared 'my Lord of Northampton from any manner of understanding with him therein upon his salvation; which yet is not enough (as I perceive among the people) to sweep the dust from his grave'. What Wotton reported, then, was rumour, not necessarily his own opinion, let alone fact. He noted that Hoskyns claimed he had been promised the protection of others at court besides Northampton. Like Wotton, John Chamberlain suggested that others might have been involved. One candidate was Sir Edward Phelips, father of Sir Robert Phelips and Master of the Rolls, whom he noted had lost the royal favour in the wake of the dissolution, 'for there be many presumptions that his hand was in it, his son being so busy and factious in the House, and Hoskyns one of his chief consorts and minions so far engaged, besides divers untoward speeches of his own'.[102]

Such contemporary suggestions that others were involved in the plot have been neglected by historians. Certainly there were widespread rumours that the seeds of discord were being sown perhaps by some outside the House of Commons. But Northampton is not the only or even the most likely suspect. Lake had told the king in 1610 that there were inflammatory speeches in the Commons to send the Scots home.[103] Suffolk had pretended to support the undertakers. While in the Tower, Hoskyns claimed he had been promised Somerset's support. In short, others had had as good a motive and better opportunity to set the conspiracy on foot. In the end, there was no need; the king was on the verge of dissolving Parliament even before Hoskyns made his speech. Hindsight and scapegoating has obscured the fact that the session was out of control from the beginning. Northampton's parade through London 'as yt were in triumph' was the last great spectacle for a dying man upon his return from Greenwich.[104]

What conclusions can be drawn from this study of Northampton's role in Parliament? First of all, it is no longer possible to accept the traditional portrait of Northampton; he was hardworking, often conciliatory and always concerned to prepare parliamentary sessions so that both the representatives and the king were able to secure their ends: the redress of grievances and supply. His work as a privy councillor was multifaceted and parliamentary sessions frequently dealt with issues that first came before the Council. In addition, work on private business took up much of the session. Racing between committee meetings on private Bills and conferences between Lords and Commons on important public issues such as the Great Contract taxed individual councillors and the resources of the Privy Council itself.

Secondly, analysis of Privy Council factions and the playing out of their conflicts in Parliament must be carefully done: factions were fluid at the Jacobean court both in their adherents and their stand on issues. Up until 1611 Northampton acted as an ally of Salisbury, who dominated the Council and the court's parliamentary activities. Furthermore, it is an error to assume that the Howard faction was united in 1614: in fact Northampton disagreed with and was losing power to Suffolk and Somerset. Thirdly, Northampton's exalted view of the prerogative was similar to that held by others in the Commons and the Lords. Wallace Notestein suggested that if James had listened more to Salisbury and Bacon and not to Northampton and his ilk, opposition in the Commons might have melted away. Yet Northampton was the ally of Salisbury and his views of preparation for Parliament accorded with Bacon's — they both opposed the 'undertakers' in 1614.[105] On the relation of the prerogative to parliamentary petitions concerning foreign policy Northampton's stand was shared by as influential a member of the House of Commons as Sir Robert Cotton. Indeed Lord Chancellor Ellesmere, the highest ranking official on the Privy Council, believed with Northampton that the royal prerogative could not be bridled. It is interesting to ask why Northampton and Ellesmere have been perceived differently both by contemporaries and later historians. It is, I suggest, the linkage of their view to other issues: Ellesmere, Protestant and anti-Spanish, was never called authoritarian as was Northampton, Catholic and pro-Spanish, despite the fact that Ellesmere's view of the early Jacobean Parliaments was as jaundiced as Northampton's.[106]

Certainly Northampton understood the need for consultation within the early Stuart political system. In his committee work and in his development of policy, Northampton frequently called on those affected by legislation and those learned in law and trade. Such informal consultation was useful in making policy and managing Parliament as well as assuaging grievances.

Nevertheless, while Northampton's view of the prerogative may not have been unusual, there is a critical problem with his rhetoric. Northampton's major role in Parliament was that of the orator. He frequently invoked the image of ancient Rome. He used precedent, allusion, metaphor to articulate

Jacobean policy. This he did well, even if at length, and in an old-fashioned or artificial style. Northampton's failure lay not in what he *did* say about divine right, for these ritualistic statements were accepted by his listeners. His failure lay in what he did *not* say. In all his words there was a fatal lacuna: what was missing was both a recognition and invocation of the rights and liberties of the Commons. In the Apology of 1604, a committee of the Commons explicitly rehearsed the ancient rights and properties of Englishmen as embodied in the House of Commons. It is even possible that the Apology included a specific rejoinder to Northampton's rhetoric in the following words:

> It has been told to our faces by some of no small place, and the same spoken also in the presence of your Majesty, that, on the 24th of March was twelvemonth, we stood in so great fear that we would have given half we were worth for the security wherein we now stand. . . . We contrariwise most truly protest the contrary, that we stood not at that time . . . in any doubt or fear at all.

This protestation captures the spirit and even the words of Northampton's first speech to Parliament in which he had suggested that the Commons were weary, afraid and faint with apprehension at Elizabeth's death.

It is true that from 1604 to 1611 Northampton learned to modulate his language and to negotiate with the Commons. But he rarely acknowledged a mutual understanding of the delicate connections between divine right and those rights and liberties represented in the Commons. This may not have been critical in the first Parliament of James I. By 1628, however, J. G. A. Pocock has suggested that the Commons and the king no longer shared a common constitutional language.[107] Furthermore, the seizure in 1629 of Sir Robert Cotton's library by the Crown, which in 1607 had been at Northampton's disposal, reflected and symbolised a breakdown in the earlier interdependence of Council and Commons characteristic of the early years of James's reign. Despite his efforts both formal and informal to make the political system work, Northampton's failure to give public voice to the implicit political contract between the king and his people may have contributed in some part to that breakdown. None the less, Northampton's work in Parliament was diligent, prepared and at once eloquent and practical. In particular, his description of the financial expedients to which the Crown would be driven without adequate means of supply was prescient. It described not merely policies adopted immediately after the failure of the Great Contract but applied with particular force to the 1630s and the development of 'Thorough'. By his orations in praise of Caesar, emphasising the good he had done the kingdom in fostering its peace and prosperity, Northampton bent all his efforts to avoid this outcome. If he was unable to convince his countrymen, it was not for want of trying.

Chapter 11
Perspectives

The early years of the seventeenth century were both peaceful and prosperous. In 1608 Northampton described Jacobean England this way:

> at home, our Lord be praised, all things are so quiet and so likely to continue in that temper, as suspicions may cease, the dogs that began to bark at persons strange at their first entrance, do now grow familiar and the justice of the state is now so well approved and so generally tested by all sorts, as howsoever some may mutiny in particular, as no time, no state, no policy shall ever want mutineers, yet the main is carried upon the poles of justice and with the direction of intelligence.[1]

Although not the conventional view of the period, Northampton's is reasonably accurate; it should now be clear that the Jacobean court needs re-evaluation. Similarly, Northampton's own reputation is open to revision. Shortly after Northampton's death, Sarmiento, a sophisticated if not disinterested observer, described him to Philip III: 'in consideration of the Earl's courage, virtue, prudence and refinement he was for all this accounted the first gentleman of the kingdom and with reason.' Noting that he was a connoisseur whose London residence was one of the finest in Europe, the ambassador concluded by saying, 'I considered it of use to provide such a detailed report to your Majesty about this gentleman because he was unique in his qualities and virtues and in his devotion to your Majesty's service.' Sarmiento's was not of course the only view. Sidney suggested he was more mourned on the continent than in London; Chamberlain thought him vindictive in death as in life.[2] With a clever mind attuned to the cause of court favour, Northampton was a master manipulator both of people and circumstance, yet he was not without principles. These remained steady, if not popular, throughout his life: advocacy of peace with Spain, maintenance of royal power, support for authority and tradition.

Was Northampton a monster who dissembled with God or the most noble among the learned? Such epithets are only single shafts of light through a prism illuminating his character. Intelligent, cultivated, articulate, Northampton brought a keen sense of analysis to the Crown's problems, if not the imagination to invent workable solutions. (His colleagues were no more successful.) Yet in one way Northampton may have differed from his fellow councillors. Because of the traumatic childhood loss of his father, his family's fall from favour and the years as a conspirator, he was often consumed by envy and bitterness. As a result he acknowledged few if any ethical constraints. His quest for power was tempered, however, if not by scruples, then by *Realpolitik*: Northampton did not follow Mary, Queen of Scots, to the scaffold and counselled Essex to moderation. At the end of his life, did his personal anxieties coincide with the stresses of the Jacobean court so that, finally, there were no limits to the actions he would undertake to remain in favour? Or did he perceive himself in the Overbury case once again the reluctant conspirator? No final answer can be given in the case of so complex a personality as Northampton operating in so uncertain a *milieu*. In a court culture which emphasised the theatrical in both its public and its private gestures, Northampton was the unsurpassed wearer of masks. But, if doubt remains in assessing his character, it lingers as well in analysing the *mentalité* of other Jacobeans. King James declared with rough sexual humour that for some trivial offence he would have not only Northampton's head as 'King Henry, my noble predecessor, got his father's' but his whole body.[3] Robert Cecil, the foremost royal servant of the period, who had suffered none of Northampton's deprivations, helped to destroy his own brother-in-law Cobham in order to hold on to power. Perhaps Northampton was, after all, 'a fit man for the conditions of these times'.

If Northampton's personality remains veiled in the same obscurity as his prose, his career provides much new information about the workings of the Jacobean court. As a privy councillor Northampton was diligent and pragmatic; while seeking to preserve the Tudor state and Elizabethan practices in patronage and policy, he saw the need for administrative reform. In the creation of his own clientage he cultivated traditional ties, whether with the Howard family connections or in the Cinque Ports, with the town oligarchs or with the gentry of Kent and Sussex. At the same time recognising that one of the most important functions of court patronage was to reward local magistrates, he secured good servants and services for the king. In this nexus of patron and client Northampton fused favour and policy.

The relationship of patronage and policy went one step farther at the Jacobean court. In his investigations Northampton pinpointed certain types of patronage practices as the underlying cause of corruption. His remedies of salaries, promotion on merit and an end to the buying and selling of offices were important systematic reforms, but the Jacobean government was without the means to implement them. Northampton had to rely instead on interim measures such as sales of Crown lands and titles, and the playing off of disaffected merchants and officials to raise funds and control the bureaucracy. Using the old system, he tried to provide answers to economic and administrative problems that were often intractable.

Northampton was neither as innovative as Salisbury, who constructed the Great Contract, nor as systematic as Cranfield, who established several reform commissions in the later Jacobean period. Like them his own personal profits stemmed from the very system he was trying to reform. But compared to either Northampton's income was moderate and he had fewer debts. For him prestige mattered more than profit.

While some of Northampton's efforts failed due to lack of skill and implementation, in the main the causes were structural. Northampton wrestled with government machinery that worked with difficulty at best. Through his circle of scholars, merchants and officeholders who advised him on policy, Northampton sought to overcome the shortcomings of the Privy Council and of early modern administration. His description of Council meetings provided poignant evidence that the Crown continued to labour under great difficulties until its financial and bureaucratic apparatus had undergone some structural change in the wake of seventeenth-century revolutions, economic change and warfare.

Northampton's career suggests several historical perspectives, stretching backward to the 1530s and forward to the Restoration and beyond. It has been argued by G. R. Elton that an administrative revolution occurred under Henry VIII that replaced household with bureaucratic government.[4] Henry's reign did produce important changes in the Tudor constitution but some eighty years later Jacobean government remained intensely personal. Salisbury controlled administration and policy almost until his death. While sharing some power and profits with other councillors, he often bypassed the Privy Council so that in 1612 Northampton was hard pressed to organise its proceedings. The office of Secretary of State through which Salisbury had managed most government business declined in importance after his death. Middle- and lower-ranking officials of the administration such as the Privy Seal clerks often operated independently of ministers in their own interest and frequently used their personal acquaintances or servants as deputies. Northampton's reliance on private advisers, which I have described as a brains trust, was not new. Similar groups of advisers had been used by Thomas Cromwell in the 1530s and Lord Burghley and Robert Cecil under Elizabeth. Moreover, reform depended on bringing such private agents into the government itself. Northampton used Cotton and Cranfield to oversee the naval and treasury commissions. Indeed, when Cranfield mounted his investigations of the navy, household and ordinance as Lord Treasurer, one of his solutions was to bring in his own servants to oversee business.[5]

But if government was still personal, there was a strong sense of the need for change. Later Stuart ministers admired the France of Louis XIV and sought to borrow the innovations of Colbert. The use of experts and statistics did not begin, however, with William Petty. Such efforts can be traced back at least to the reform commissions of the early Stuarts. While historians have often focused on warfare as the stimulus to rationalisation of bureaucracy, these initiatives began during the Jacobean peace.[6]

The widely held notion of a breakdown in Elizabethan patronage networks under James must be re-examined. In the 1590s Howard was a member of Essex's following but remained on good terms with Cecil; indeed his alliance with Cecil laid the foundation for the structure of Jacobean patronage. Factional rivalries in that decade and later may well have been more complex and less polarised than previously thought. New to office in 1603, Northampton, the courtier nonpareil, established close contacts with local elites. Although he rewarded fellow Catholics, his patronage was notable for its lack of ideological rigour and for the variety of clients to whom he provided favour. In addition, aristocrat and bourgeois were closely connected at the Jacobean court. Merchants like Cranfield, Ingram and Swinnerton gained power and profit not in spite of the ancient nobility, of whom Northampton was a chief representative, but through him. Court and country, Catholic and Protestant, nobleman and merchant were connected in Northampton's patronage. If this was true of Northampton, what does the patronage of other important Jacobean and Caroline figures look like? Did they maintain such broad-based connections? Has emphasis on royal favourites prevented historians from seeing the continuation of such networks into the 1620s and beyond? Indeed, given the structural problems of early Stuart reward, is it possible to consider even the use of royal favourites as a functional adaptation to the problem of too many suitors? Such questions about Stuart patronage need to be explored further.

Finally, one further parallel suggested by Northampton's work is the policy of 'Thorough' in the 1630s. Administrative reform, rationalisation of bureaucracy and behaviour were the hallmarks of Northampton's policy and of other officials who were his contemporaries, such as Salisbury, Cranfield, Ellesmere, Bacon and Sir John Coke. In the 1630s Charles I employed Thomas Wentworth, Earl of Strafford and Archbishop Laud to undertake similar reforms. Like Salisbury and Northampton, they were driven to financial expedients such as the revival of fiscal feudalism and projects when parliamentary and royal revenues declined and they too fell back on the prerogative courts to enforce their policies. This is not to suggest a well thought out and consistent policy from 1603 to the 1630s but rather that similar problems engendered similar responses both within the court and without. While an MP, Wentworth had been a champion of parliamentary privilege. Once in office his policies resembled Northampton's. Both sought to cut down expenses, to maintain patronage in the hands of privy councillors, to regain control over the lower levels of the bureaucracy and to use Star Chamber and the Court of Earl Marshal to impose royal authority. In the same way such methods of reform generated opposition from those whose vested interests were under attack. One Scottish courtier, disgruntled with efforts to oversee the plantation of Ulster and force undertakers to meet their commitments, called the earl 'as proud as the devil ... and the most vindictive man that breathes'.[7] While the rhetoric is familiar the target was not Northampton but Strafford, whose policies provoked descriptions of his character similar to earlier ones of Salisbury, Northampton and Buckingham. Northampton's career thus challenges us to think again about the court of the early Stuarts: to analyse the content and context of social relationships, to chart the emergence of a rationalised bureaucracy and of the modern state; and to understand the development of an ideological challenge to royal power constructed at least in part in reaction to centralising government and authority in seventeenth-century England.

Notes

Introduction

1 Hugh Trevor-Roper, 'The general crisis of the seventeenth century', in *Crisis in Europe, 1560–1660*, ed. T. H. Aston, London, 1965, pp. 82–3.

2 For the fullest exposition of this view see Perez Zagorin, *The Court and the Country*, New York, 1970.

3 Some of the important studies of local communities include: T. G. Barnes, *Somerset 1625–1640: A County's Government During the 'Personal Rule'*, Cambridge, 1961; Peter Clark, *English Provincial Society from the Reformation to the Revolution; Religion, Politics and Society in Kent, 1500–1640*, Hassocks, 1977; Alan Everitt, *The Community of Kent and the Great Rebellion*, Leicester, 1966; Anthony Fletcher, *A County Community in Peace and War: Sussex 1600–1660*, London, 1975; A. H. Smith, *County and Court, Government and Politics in Norfolk, 1558–1603*, Oxford, 1974; J. S. Morrill, *Cheshire 1630–1660, County Government and Society during the English Revolution*, Oxford, 1974. For a discussion of the localist focus of some of these studies, see Clive Holmes, *The Eastern Association in the English Civil War*, Cambridge, 1974, ch. 1, as well as his article, 'The county community in Stuart historiography', *Journal of British Studies*, 19 (1980), 54–73, and David Underdown, 'Community and class: Theories of local politics in the English revolution', in *After the Reformation, Essays in Honor of J. H. Hexter*, ed. Barbara C. Malament, Philadelphia, 1980.

4 Among the important studies of parliamentary sessions, see Robert Ruigh, *The Parliament of 1624*, Cambridge, 1971; Conrad Russell, *Parliaments and English Politics 1621–1629*, Oxford, 1979; Robert Zaller, *The Parliament of 1621: A Study in Constitutional Conflict*, Berkeley, 1971. Editions of the debates in Parliament have appeared for 1610 and 1628 and the Short Parliament: E. R. Foster (ed.), *Proceedings in Parliament, 1610*, 2 vols, New Haven, 1966; *Commons Debates, 1628*, ed. Robert C. Johnson, Mary Frear Keeler, Maija Jansson Cole and William B. Bidwell, New Haven, 1977; *Proceedings of the Short Parliament of 1640*, ed. W. C. Coates and Esther S. Cope, Camden Society, 4th series, 19, London, 1977. On an allied topic, see Derek Hirst, *The Representative of the People? Voters and Voting in England under the Early Stuarts*, Cambridge, 1975.

5 See Russell, *Parliaments and English Politics, 1621–1629*, pp. 1–35; D. Hirst, 'Court, country and politics before 1629', in *Faction and Parliament; Essays on Early Stuart History*, ed. Kevin Sharpe, Oxford, 1978, pp. 105–37.

6 J. E. Neale, 'The Elizabethan political scene', in *Essays in Elizabethan History*, London, 1958, p. 84.

7 M. Prestwich, *Cranfield, Politics and Profits under the Early Stuarts*, Oxford, 1966, pp. 223–6.

8 See G. E. Aylmer, *The King's Servants*, London, 1961; Joel Hurstfield, *Freedom, Corruption and Government in Elizabethan England*, Cambridge, Mass., 1973, pp. 137–62, 183–96, 294–325.

9 E.R. Turner, *The Privy Council of England in the Seventeenth and Eighteenth Centuries, 1603–1784*, 2 vols., Baltimore, 1927, I pp. 137–8; D. Hirst, 'The Privy Council and problems of enforcement in the 1620s', *Journal of British Studies*, 18 (1978), 46–66.

10 Joel Hurstfield, *The Queen's Wards*, London, 1958; 'Church and State, 1558–1612: The task of the Cecils', in *Freedom, Corruption and Government*, pp. 79–103. Prestwich, *Cranfield*; R. H. Tawney, *Business and Politics under James I*, Cambridge, 1958.

11 W. Notestein, *The House of Commons, 1604–1610*, New Haven, Conn., 1971, p. 547, n. 6.

12 'Truth Brought to Light', *Somers Tracts*, 2nd edn, London, 1809, II, 267.

13 Anthony Weldon, 'The court and character of King James', in *Historical and*

Biographical Tracts, ed. George Smeeton, 2 vols, Westminster, 1820, I, 8. Weldon's tract was first published in 1650. Cf. also Arthur Wilson, *The History of Great Britain Being the Life and Reign of King James I*, London, 1653; Francis Osborne, *Traditional Memoirs of the Reign of King James I*, London, 1658.

14 [William Sanderson], *Aulicus Coquinariae*, London, 1650, p. 65. Cf. Godfrey Goodman, *The Court of King James I*, ed. J. S. Brewer, 2 vols, London, 1839. In 1811 Sir Walter Scott reprinted several of these tracts in his *Secret History of the Court of James the First*, 2 vols, Edinburgh, 1811, as did Smeeton in his *Historical and Biographical Tracts*. John H. Jesse repeated the now traditional gossip in his *Memoirs of the Court of England*, 4 vols, London, 1840. In compositions.

15 S. R. Gardiner, *The History of England from the Accession of James I to the Outbreak of the Civil War*, 10 vols, London, 1883–4, I, pp. 93–4.

16 Prestwich, *Cranfield*, pp. 105–6.

17 Hurstfield, 'The morality of early Stuart statesmen', *History*, 56 (June 1971), 235–43, and 'Political corruption in modern England: the historian's problem', *History*, 52 (1967), 16–34.

Chapter 1. 'A Man Obscured'

1 Quoted in G. F. Nott, *The Works of Henry Howard, Earl of Surrey, and of Sir Thomas Wyatt, the Elder*, 2 vols, London, 1816, I, p. 446 n. Nott provides a lengthy and useful, if not complete, discussion of Howard's life during the reign of Elizabeth.

2 This description of the Howard family is based on Gerald Brennan and Edward P. Stratham, *The House of Howard*, 2 vols, New York, 1908, as well as the *DNB* and G. E. C[okayne], *Complete Peerage*, 13 vols, London, 1910–59. See also Lacey Baldwin Smith, *The Mask of Royalty*, London, 1971, for a discussion of the fall of the Howards at the end of Henry VIII's reign.

3 B.L. Add. Mss. 6298, f. 285.

4 Oxford, Bodl. Lib. Mss. 616, f. 3. The first English translation of *The Courtier* was that of Sir Thomas Hoby in 1561. In 'Note No. 67: The poet Earl of Surrey's library', *Book Collector*, V (1956), 172, Bent Juel-Jenson described a 1541 Italian edition of *The Courtier* which bears Henry Howard's name and numerous manuscript annotations both in Italian and Latin with citations to an edition of Cicero. Howard described his own reading in his *Defensative against the Poyson of Supposed Prophecies*, A.3.

5 Nott, *Surrey*, I, pp. 429, 477: the University of Cambridge to James I; p. 478: King James to the University of Cambridge, June 1612; p. 481: The Warden and Fellows of New College to the Earl of Northampton, May 1609.

6 See Brian Levack, *The Civil Lawyers in England, 1603–1641*, Oxford, 1973.

7 B. L. Lansdowne Mss. 109, ff. 113, 114, 116; A. G. R. Smith, *Servant of the Cecils: The Life of Sir Michael Hickes, 1543–1612*, London, 1977.

8 H. E. Malden, *Trinity Hall*, London, 1922, p. 113; Nott, *Surrey*, I, p. 430.

9 Nott, *Surrey*, I, 428–9, xv n.b. In a letter to his son in 1620, the Earl of Arundel noted that 'my grandfather of Norfolk and his brother, my good uncle of Northampton, were both bred as pages under Bishops'.

10 J. A. Bossy, 'The character of Elizabethan Catholicism', in *Crisis in Europe, 1560–1660*, ed. T. H. Aston, New York, 1965, p. 242.

11 ibid., pp. 223–46; P.R.O. S.P. 31, 12, 34, Sarmiento to Philip III, 30 June 1614. I am grateful to Caroline Hibbard, Derek Hirst and Alan Smith for their suggestions about Northampton's religious outlook.

12 B.L. Cotton Mss. Titus C VI, f. 13v, 23 October (1571?); Neville Williams, *Thomas Howard, Fourth Duke of Norfolk*, New York, 1964, pp. 126–9.

13 Williams, *Thomas Howard*, pp. 126–254.

14 B.L. Cotton Mss. Titus C VI, f. 13v, Henry Howard to Lord Burghley, 23 October (1571?).

15   John Smyth, *The Berkeley Manuscripts*, 3 vols, Gloucester, 1883, II, 265–449.
16   J. A. Bossy, 'English Catholics and the French marriage, 1577–1581', *Recusant History*, 5, (1960), 2–16. See also Wallace MacCaffrey, 'The Anjou match and Elizabethan foreign policy', in *The English Commonwealth*, ed. P. Clark, A. G. R. Smith, N. Tyacke, Leicester, 1979. See also Howard's letters of this period: B.L. Cotton Mss. Titus C VI, ff. 5–6, 30.
17   *Cal. S.P. Span. 1580–1586*, p. 315, 6 March 1582. Mendoza noted that Howard wrote him twice a week details of all that passed concerning Flanders, France and Scotland. He claimed too to have persuaded him not to go on a mission abroad.
18   *Cal. S.P. Span. 1580–1586*, pp. 448–9, 28 February 1583.
19   B.L. Cotton Mss. Titus C VI, ff. 166–166v, 5 July 1608.
20   Nott, *Surrey*, I, 437, 439 n; HMC *Salisbury*, 13, 193, 20 July (1581?); HMC *Appendix to the Second Report*, p. 41; *Cal. S.P. Scot.* II, 938, Henry Fagot to ?, April 1583; B.L. Cotton Mss. Caligula C VII, 260, 11 Dec. 1583; HMC *Laing*, I, 34–5. In 1586 Thomas Morgan informed Mary that he had written to Henry Howard who had been ordered to live in Sir Nathanial Bacon's house, HMC *Salisbury*, 3 and 4, 136.
21   B.L. Cotton Mss. Titus C VI, ff. 5–5v; Bossy, 'English Catholics and the French marriage', pp. 2–16.
22   B.L. Cotton Mss. Titus C VI, f. 17, October 1572, from Audley End. See also f. 24, Henry Howard to Lord Burghley, 5 October 1573; f. 29, 4 September 1577; f. 32v, 1584.
23   ibid., f. 6.
24   *A Defense of the Ecclesiastical Regiment in Englande defaced by T.C. in his replie against D. Whitgifte*, London, 1574, STC 10393; Lord Henry Howard's 'Answer to the Gaping Gulf' in *John Stubb's Gaping Gulf*, ed. Lloyd E. Berry, Charlottesville, 1968; 'Regina Fortunata', B.L. Egerton Mss. 944, *c.*1576; 'A Dutiful Defense of the Lawful Regiment of Women', Oxford, Bodl. Lib. Mss. 903.
25   Howard wrote that 'prophecies of wicked men are a kind of science which was never grafted by our heavenly Father, and therefore can be good for no man that is well affected', and cited a Spanish proverb, 'God created man as a scholar in this life to learn, man hath not made himself a Master to command or countermand what is above his horizon', p. 8.
26   B.L. Cotton Mss. Titus C VI, ff. 39–39v, Howard to Lord Burghley presenting a book of prayers which he composed and wrote out in Latin himself; Lambeth Palace, Bacon Papers 653, ff. 48–48v, Howard to the Lord Treasurer, sending book of prayers; B.L. Cotton Mss. Titus C VI, ff. 52, 55–55v, Howard to Robert Cecil in which are mentioned works sent in 1593 and 1595; Howard translated 'The Emperor Charles V's political instructions to his son Philip II' from Spanish. In it he referred to the twelve years that he had been banished from the queen's presence and to the work he had presented to her the previous year, B.L. Lansdowne Mss. 792, ff. 1–1v.
27   Lambeth Palace, Bacon Papers 653, ff. 48–48v.
28   This was not a unique combination; see Bossy, 'The character of Elizabethan Catholicism', *supra*.
29   B.L. Cotton Mss. Titus C VI, f. 5v; 'stories' refers to histories.
30   'Answer to the Gaping Gulf', in Berry, p. 179; *A Defense of the Ecclesiastical Regiment in Englande*, pp. 11, 4; B.L. Cotton Mss. Titus C VI, f. 579.
31   'Answer to the Gaping Gulf' in Berry, pp. 194, 165.
32   Robert Lacey, *Robert, Earl of Essex*, London, 1971, pp. 209–10, 283.
33   Oxford, Bodl. Lib. Mss. 903, 'A Dutiful Defense of the Lawful Regiment of Women', f. 4.
34   This portrait of Howard is at the Mercers' Company in London. Roy Strong in *The English Icon*, London, 1969, p. 59, identifies it as painted by a follower of Custodis patronised mainly by the provincial gentry; see also Roy Strong, *The Elizabethan Image*, London, 1969, p. 49 and T. Birch, *Memoirs of the Reign of Queen Elizabeth*, 2 vols, London, 1754, I, p. 227.
35   J. E. Neale, 'The Elizabethan political scene', *Essays in Elizabethan History*, London, 1958, pp. 59–84.

36 B.L. Add. Mss. 4112, f. 90, Anthony Bacon Mss., Birch transcripts, 26 January 1595.
37 Birch, *Queen Elizabeth*, II, pp. 358–9, 363, 68–70; HMC *Salisbury*, 8, 371, Howard to Essex (? September 1598), 169, Essex to Howard, 17 May 1598; B.L. Add. Mss. 4121, f. 88v, 3 October 1596, Earl of Shrewsbury to Henry Howard; ff. 111–111v, Howard to A. Bacon, 9 October 1596.
38 Birch, *Queen Elizabeth*, II, pp. 365–7, 30 December 1597.
39 Folger Shakespeare Library V b.7, p. 41; this ms. is the only known copy of the tract. Although catalogued *c*.1600, it is more likely to have been written in late 1597 or 1598. Essex went off to Ireland in March 1599.
40 Birch, *Queen Elizabeth*, II, p. 246.
41 Lambeth Palace Mss., Bacon papers, vol. 659, f. 224.
42 B.L. Add. Mss. 4120, ff. 114–114v, Lady Catherine Howard to Mr Anthony Bacon, 23 August 1596; Add. Mss. 4120, 120v–121, Essex to Henry Howard, 28 August 1596, Birch, *Queen Elizabeth*, II, 359.
43 Lambeth Palace Mss., Bacon papers, vol. 655, f. 11, 9 January 1597. See also Arthur Collins, *Letters and Memorials of State*, London, 2 vols, 1746, II, 49–50, 4 May 1597. Hereafter cited as *Sidney Letters*. I am grateful to Fritz Levy for this reference to Howard as go-between for Essex and Sidney.
44 B.L. Cotton Mss. Titus C VI, ff. 479v–480.
45 B.L. Add. Mss. 4123, f. 95v, 27 April 1597.
46 Birch, *Queen Elizabeth*, II, pp. 359, 326; B.L. Add. Mss. 4120, ff. 120v–121, 28 August 1596; Lambeth Palace Mss., Bacon papers, vol. 659, f. 391, 3 October 1596.
47 Lambeth Palace Mss., Bacon papers, vol. 658, f. 208, 7 January 1597.
48 HMC *Salisbury*, 9, 125–6.
49 B.L. Add. Mss. 22563, Weymouth Papers, ff. 39–40, Howard to Bacon (? December 1599). This is a copy; Birch, *Queen Elizabeth*, II, pp. 459–60 prints both Bacon's and Howard's letters with some variations.
50 HMC *Salisbury*, 10, 328–9; *Cal. S.P. Dom. 1598–1601*, p. 475, ? September 1600.
51 HMC *Salisbury*, 11, 33, February 1601. Sir William Temple wrote to Cecil after the uprising's failure protesting that 'being of that faction in Essex House which wholly allowed the course held by the right noble Lord Harry, I was never admitted to any conference, so as I had no hand in the contriving of any plots, was never made acquainted with them'. I am grateful to Fritz Levy for this citation.
52 HMC *Salisbury*, 9, 101, Sir John Davies to Cecil, 1601 (*c*. 2 March); 151, Davies to Sir John Popham, March 1601; 423, Davies to Cecil, 12 October 1601; 323, Sir William Constable to Cecil, 5 August 1601. B.L. Cotton Mss. Vitellius C XVII, ff. 341–66, contain some of the confessions of Essex's associates written in Henry Howard's hand. Whether they were notes made by Howard for Cecil or for his own benefit is not clear. Henry Cuffe admitted the plot against Cecil to convince the queen that the latter meant to secure the succession for the Spanish Infanta. Cuffe also stated that Essex's intent 'was to have been an humble suitor to the queen after his access to her for assembly of a parliament . . . and never to have dealt otherwise than by submission', f. 342v. See also Joel Hurstfield, 'The succession struggle in late Elizabethan England', in *Freedom, Corruption and Government in Elizabethan England*, Cambridge, Mass., 1973.
53 Birch, *Queen Elizabeth*, II, pp. 68–70; HMC *Salisbury*, 6, 271, Howard to Cecil, 20 July 1596. In 1593 and 1595 Howard sent him philosophical and religious tracts reminding Cecil that his long disgrace had come 'rather by destiny than deserving'. B.L. Cotton Mss. Titus C VI, ff. 52, 55–55v; Lambeth Palace Mss., Bacon papers, vol. 655, f. 116, February 1597.
54 B.L. Lansdowne Mss. 109, f. 111, Henry Howard to Mr Hickes; HMC *Salisbury*, 8, 187, Gilbert, Earl of Shrewsbury to Cecil, 1 June 1598. *Cal. S.P. Dom. 1598–1601*, p. 312, William Tresham to Howard, 28 August 1599; Nott, *Surrey*, I, p. 443.
55 HMC *De L'Isle and Dudley*, II, 397, 30 September 1599; Nott, *Surrey*, I, p. 443.
56 HMC *De L'Isle and Dudley*, II, 481, 30 August 1600.

57   J. MacLean (ed.), *Letters from Sir Robert Cecil to Sir George Carew*, Camden Society, o.s. 88, London, 1864, 23.

58   Helen Stafford, *James VI of Scotland and the Throne of England*, New York, 1940, p. 203. Hereafter cited as Stafford, *James VI*.

59   John Bruce (ed.), *Correspondence of King James VI of Scotland with Sir Robert Cecil and Others in England*, Camden Society, o.s. 68, London, 1861, 1–2. Hereafter cited as Bruce, *Correspondence*. Another part of the secret correspondence is published in David Dalrymple, Lord Hailes (ed.), *The Secret Correspondence of Sir Robert Cecil with James VI of Scotland*, Edinburgh, 1766, hereafter cited as Hailes, *Secret Correspondence*. The fullest discussion of the succession problem is in Stafford, *James VI*. Cf. also Joel Hurstfield, 'The succession struggle in late Elizabethan England', and P. M. Handover, *The Second Cecil: The Rise to Power 1563–1604*, London, 1959. Unfortunately Howard's contacts with King James prior to 1601 have not come to light. I am grateful to Fritz Levy for an illuminating discussion of this letter.

60   B.L. Cotton Mss. Titus C VI, f. 176v.

61   Stafford, *James VI*, pp. 257, 281–3; Stafford quotes a brief prepared by Howard evidently for Cecil which argues the legitimate basis for government ministers to have secret and unauthorised contacts with officials of other states, and perhaps provides his rationale for his own dealings with the Spanish during James's reign. 'Again suppose that you should take that liberty that many worthy councillors have done in holding better correspondency with neighbour states than princes in their passions admit and, respecting more your oath to serve with fidelity than the custom of the court or of the time, should keep a vent open whereby malice might evaporate by clearing doubts and jealousies that might cause wars, dissensions and practices. ... Suppose that you should compass such a kind of credit with the Queen of England's neighbour and ally against her express wish ... tending to the queen's security ... what quarrel could a just or worthy prince pretend against a minister thus diligent in preventing dangers?'

62   Quoted in Edward Edwards, *The Life of Sir Walter Raleigh*, 2 vols, London, 1868, I, p. 442. The original draft, 'Contra Rawlegh and Cobham', is in B.L. Cotton Mss. Titus C VI, ff. 382–92.

63   Bruce, *Correspondence*, p. 8; Hailes, *Secret Correspondence*, pp. 30, 35; Stafford, *James VI*, p. 275. When Howard warned Bruce against Sir Anthony Shirley, a one-time ambassador to Persia, Bruce answered with some asperity that James had been introduced to Shirley by Anthony Bacon with Howard's privity. Bruce, *Correspondence*, p. 40.

64   B.L. Cotton Mss. Titus C VI, f. 171, Howard to Lady Raleigh, 4 July 1603.

65   Edwards, *Raleigh*, I, pp. 436–44. In this draft Howard compared Cobham and Raleigh to the notorious Empson and Dudley. He wrote that the queen must see the peril of protecting persons odious to the multitudes. Although Empson and Dudley had been of service to Henry VII, 'yet at the coming in of Henry VIII no sacrifice besides their lives could be found proximate for the people's discontent'.

66   Stafford, *James VI*, pp. 259, 267–8. Bruce, *Correspondence*, pp. 50–1, Bruce to Howard, 25 March (1603). On another occasion Bruce wrote Howard that '30 is settled upon the centre of 10 and 3, where you will find him rest constant and immoveable'; Bruce, *Correspondence*, p. 41.

67   Bruce, *Correspondence*, pp. 50–1, Bruce to Howard, 25 March 1603.

68   *Cal. S.P. Dom. 1603–10*, p. 2; Edward Bruce, Lord Kinloss, to Henry Howard, 9 April 1603; HMC *Salisbury*, 15, 44, 58, Ralph Grey to Cecil, 12 April 1603, Thomas Lake to Cecil, 25 April 1603; N. E. McClure (ed.), *The Letters of John Chamberlain*, 2 vols, Philadelphia, 1939, I, pp. 191–2.

69   B.L. Cotton Mss. Titus C VI, ff. 169–71v, 4 July 1603. For a discussion of the Main and Bye plots of 1603 see S. R. Gardiner, *The History of England from the Accession of James I to the Outbreak of the Civil War*, 10 vols, London, 1883–4, I, 108–39. For a very harsh assessment of Howard's role in the secret correspondence see Edwards, *Raleigh*, I, pp. 175ff, and P. M. Handover, *The Second Cecil*, London, 1959, p. 240. Howard's actual suggestions to Cecil of how to handle Raleigh and Cobham amounted to cutting off the

springs of bounty and bore no relationship to the crimes with which they were charged in 1603. See Edwards, *Raleigh*, I, pp. 436–44.

70 One historian who has discussed these patronage connections is Peter Clark, *English Provincial Society from the Reformation to the Revolution; Religion, Politics and Society in Kent, 1500–1640*, Hassocks, 1977.

71 See, for example, W. Notestein, *The House of Commons, 1604–1610*, New Haven, 1971, p. 547; D. H. Willson, *King James VI and I*, London, 1956, pp. 178, 269, 335.

72 B.L. Cotton Mss. Titus C VI, f. 480.

73 Oxford, Ashmolean Mss. 1729, ff. 90–90v, James to Privy Council, 16 May 1603.

Chapter 2. The Organisation of Influence

1 HMC *10th Report*, II, Gawdy Mss. 88, John Holland to Sir Bassingbourn Gawdy, May or June 1603.

2 For a discussion of these lands and their division, see Chapter 4.

3 See Joel Hurstfield, 'The succession struggle in late Elizabethan England', in *Elizabethan Government and Society, Essays presented to Sir John Neale*, ed. S. T. Bindoff, Joel Hurstfield and C. H. Williams, London, 1961; Neville Williams, *Thomas Howard, Fourth Duke of Norfolk*, London, 1964.

4 Much of the discussion of the Tudor–Stuart patronage system is based on Wallace MacCaffrey, 'Place and patronage in Elizabethan politics', in *Elizabethan Government and Society, Essays Presented to Sir John Neale*, pp. 95–126, hereafter cited as MacCaffrey, 'Place and patronage'; J. E. Neale, 'The Elizabethan political scene', in *Essays in Elizabethan History*, London, 1958, pp. 59–84, hereafter cited as Neale, 'The Elizabethan political scene'. G. E. Aylmer, *The King's Servants*, London, 1961, treats extensively the conditions of office, appointment, promotion, tenure, fees, social identity and political leanings of Charles's officials.

5 E. R. Foster, *Proceedings in Parliament, 1610*, 2 vols, New Haven, 1966, I, p. 6.

6 Lawrence Stone, *The Crisis of the Aristocracy*, Princeton, 1966, pp. 71–4, 99–100.

7 For an analysis of the connections between wardship and patronage see J. Hurstfield, *The Queen's Wards*, London, 1958.

8 MacCaffrey, 'Place and patronage in Elizabethan politics', p. 108.

9 Aylmer, *The King's Servants*, p. 248.

10 Neale, 'The Elizabethan political scene', p. 61.

11 B.L. Stowe Mss. 168, ff. 169–70, 10 October 1605. See also Northampton's letter to Charles Cornwallis, Oxford, Bodl. Tanner Mss. 75, f. 263v, 1607.

12 See for instance Brian Levack, *The Civil Lawyers in England, 1603–1641*, Oxford, 1973.

13 See A. H. Smith, *County and Court; Government and Politics in Norfolk, 1558–1603*, Oxford, 1974, pp. 57–61; Stone, *The Crisis of the Aristocracy*, p. 38.

14 Aylmer, *The King's Servants*, pp. 110, 105, 97.

15 *Cal. S.P. Dom. 1611–1618*, p. 475.

16 See T. M. Coakley, 'Robert Cecil in power: Elizabethan politics in two reigns', in *Early Stuart Studies*, ed. Howard Reinmuth, Minneapolis, 1970, pp. 64–94; Joel Hurstfield, 'Church and State, 1558–1612: The task of the Cecils', in *Freedom, Corruption and Government in Elizabethan England*, Cambridge, Mass., 1973, pp. 79–103.

17 B.L. Cotton Mss. Titus C VI, f. 188v. Salisbury to Northampton (n.d., probably 1608–12), Vespasian C X, ff. 91v–92, Northampton to Charles Cornwallis. W. Notestein, *The House of Commons, 1604–1610*, New Haven, 1971, p. 547, described Northampton's personality as unnatural and warped. 'Northampton hated Salisbury. ...He was jealous of Salisbury's influence over the king; that power he craved for himself.' One *may* accept the latter as true without accepting the former.

18 See for instance: D. H. Willson, *The Privy Councillors in the House of Commons, 1604–1629*, Minneapolis, 1940, pp. 17–18, who describes the Spanish or Howard faction as 'a worthless and treacherous lot', lumping Nottingham together with Northampton and Suffolk.

19 Sir John Harrington, *The Letters and Epigrams of Sir John Harrington*, ed. N. E. McClure, Philadelphia, 1930, p. 112. HMC *Salisbury*, 18, 136, 12 May 1606. HMC *Salisbury*, 16, 258, (1604 before 20 August); HMC *Salisbury*, 19, 162, 25 June 1607; HMC *Salisbury*, 15, 166, 2 July 1603; *Cal. S.P. Dom. 1603–10*, p. 54; HMC *Salisbury*, 19, 160, 24 June 1607; HMC *Salisbury*, 15, 84 (before 13 May 1603). *Cal. S.P. Dom. 1603–1610*, 275, 1605; HMC *Salisbury*, 17, 314, 10 July 1605, 322–3, 16 July 1605.

20 HMC *Salisbury*, 15, 323, 11 December 1603; HMC *Salisbury*, 15, 317–19, 10 December 1603; *Cal. S.P. Dom. 1603–1610*, 130, 8 July 1604.

21 *Letters of Sir Francis Hastings, 1574–1609*, ed. Claire Cross, Somerset Record Society, 68, (1969), 108, 30 December 1606. Notestein, *The House of Commons*, pp. 161–2.

22 HMC *Salisbury*, 17, 31, 22 January 1605.

23 HMC *Salisbury*, 19, 435 (1607, after June).

24 *The Acts of the Parliaments of Scotland*, ed. T. Thomson, Edinburgh, 1966, III, 563, c. 41. I am grateful to Jennifer Wormald for the reference.

25 Stone, *The Crisis of the Aristocracy*, pp. 72–6.

26 P.R.O. S.P. 14, 13.

27 P.R.O. S.P. 14, 37, 168.

28 P.R.O. S.P. 14, 37, 176.

29 P.R.O. S.P. 14, 37, 177.

30 Oxford, Bodl. Lib. Tanner Mss. 75, f. 265, 1607.

31 HMC *Salisbury*, 18, 251–2, 26 August 1606. Cf. Sir John Holles to Sir John Digby, HMC *Portland*, 9, 32 (after 20 June 1613): glad to have Digby's assurance of free speech, Holles remained anxious even though 'the greatest pirate of this kind of merchandise' was gone. Salisbury's interception or investigation of private letters was evidently well known.

32 T. Birch, *The Court and Times of James I*, 2 vols, London, 1849, I, 390–7, Lord Thomas Howard to Sir John Harrington, 1611. Cf. P.R.O. S.P. 14, 62, 44, Sir John Bennett to Dudley Carleton, 27 March 1611: 'Sir Robert Carr was created Baron of Winwich . . . he hath broken the ice; who and what will follow God knows.' P. R. Seddon, 'Robert Carr, Earl of Somerset', *Renaissance and Modern Studies*, IV (1970), 46–68.

33 *Cal. S.P. Dom. 1603–1610*, p. 265, 4 December 1610; HMC *Buccleuch*, I, 102, John Moore to Winwood, 29 October 1611.

34 P.R.O. S.P. 14, 64, 23, 9 June 1611.

35 Birch, *Court and Times of James I*, I, p. 191, George Calvert to Sir Thomas Edmondes, 1 August 1612.

36 N. E. McClure (ed.), *The Letters of John Chamberlain*, 2 vols, Philadelphia, 1939, I, p. 352, 27 May 1612; HMC *Mar and Kellie*, II, 40–1, 22 June 1612.

37 HMC *Mar and Kellie*, II, 42.

38 P.R.O. S.P. 14, 71, 36, 10 August 1612; for a description of the factions battling over the Secretaryship see T. Moir, *The Addled Parliament of 1614*, Oxford, 1958, pp. 10–30; Clayton Roberts and Owen Duncan, 'The parliamentary undertaking of 1614', *English Historical Review*, 93 (July 1978), 481–98; Seddon, 'Robert Carr, Earl of Somerset'.

39 Cam. Univ. Lib. Mss. Dd. 3.63, f. 50v (1613).

40 Moir, *The Addled Parliament*, p. 74; because the king insisted on controlling his own patronage, Northampton left 'assignations to places and preferments absolutely to [the king's] own election as the flower which he says doth most content him of all those that grow within the pale of prerogative. Sir Thomas Lake expects and many wish him well but the time is yet to come wherein any councillor hath opened his mouth to the king for that honour.' B.L. Cotton Mss. Titus C VI, f. 500v.

41 HMC *Mar and Kellie*, II, 52, Fenton to Mar (c.June 1613); 51–2, 20 May 1613; 55–6, 27 October 1613; B.L. Cotton Mss. Titus C VI, f. 91v, 1611–13.

42 HMC *Salisbury*, 16, 319, 28 September 1604.

43 *Chamberlain*, I, p. 463, 8 July 1613.

44 M. Prestwich, *Cranfield: Politics and Profits under the Early Stuarts*, Oxford, 1966, pp. 120–1, 125; B.L. Cotton Mss. Titus C VI, f. 118, 24 February 1614.

45 Prestwich, *Cranfield*, pp. 67–9, 127–9, Nat'l Lib. of Wales, Carreg-lwyd Mss. 621, BMab 652/1. For a discussion of Ingram's relations with the Howards, particularly as merchant banker to Nottingham and Suffolk, cf. A. F. Upton, *Sir Arthur Ingram*, Oxford, 1961.
46 B.L. Cotton Mss. Titus C VI, f. 135 (after 4 July 1613).
47 A. G. R. Smith, 'The secretariat of the Cecils, circa 1580–1612', *English Historical Review*, 83, (July 1968), 481–504.
48 B.L. Cotton Mss. Titus C VI, f. 113, 1613.
49 Levack, *The Civil Lawyers in England, 1603–1641*, p. 51.
50 *Chamberlain*, I, pp. 602–3.
51 P.R.O. S.P. 14, 70, 55, Northampton to Rochester, 20 August 1612.
52 P.R.O. S.P. 14, 71, 6, Rochester to Northampton, 8 October 1612; Birch, *Court and Times of James I*, I, pp. 335–6, Rev. Thomas Larkin to Sir Thomas Puckering, 21 July 1614.
53 B.L. Cotton Mss. Titus C VI, f. 106v, Northampton to Rochester, April–May 1613.
54 ibid. One provision of Salisbury's 1608 memorandum had required officials not to seal certain types of grants, and Northampton as Lord Privy Seal was its most notable enforcer. See below, Chapter 8.
55 B.L. Cotton Mss. Galba E I, ff. 276–7v, 19 January 1604; HMC *Buccleuch*, I, 106, John Moore to Sir John Winwood, 10 May 1612.
56 P.R.O. S.P. 14, 75, 29, Northampton to Lake, ? November 1613.
57 Cam. Univ. Lib. Mss. Dd. 3.63, f. 50v, Northampton to Rochester, 1613.
58 B.L. Cotton Mss. Titus C VI, f. 115v, November 1613.
59 L. P. Smith, *The Life and Letters of Sir Henry Wotton*, 2 vols (Oxford: 1907), II, 41.
60 B.L. Cotton Mss. Titus C VI, f. 93v, February 1614.
61 ibid., f. 107 (after 21 February 1614). Northampton's remarks, which may indicate a loss of favour, find some support in a letter written by the Dowager Countess of Arundel to her son Thomas, Earl of Arundel, Northampton's grand-nephew and heir in February 1614. Noting that Northampton had been ill and kept to his chamber, she added 'many flying reports...that his Lordship take some grief upon some unkindness but I leave all to God to believe no more reports than I know to be true'. She had noted previously a report before Christmas that Suffolk was to be made Lord Treasurer. HMC *Cowper*, I, 81. For a discussion of the changing political constellations at court in 1614 see Chapter 10.
62 B.L. Cotton Mss. Titus C VI, ff. 88–88v, 1612–13.
63 P.R.O. S.P. 14, 35, 78.
64 B.L. Cotton Mss. Titus C VI, f. 117.
65 B.L. Cotton Mss. Titus C VI, f. 107.
66 For recent works see Beatrice White, *A Cast of Ravens*, New York, 1965 and G. V. Akrigg, *Jacobean Pageant*, New York, 1962, pp. 190–205. I plan to reconsider some of the evidence in a volume on *Patronage and Corruption in Early Stuart England*.
67 D. H. Willson, *King James VI and I*, London, 1956, p. 340; Cam. Univ. Lib. Mss. Dd. 3.63, f. 17.
68 Cam. Univ. Lib. Mss. Dd. 3.63, f. 52.
69 Cam. Univ. Lib. Mss. Dd. 3.63, ff. 54, 35, 36v–37v.
70 White, *A Cast of Ravens*. Descriptions of the trial were published by A. Amos, *The Great Oyer of Poisoning*, London, 1846; W. Cobbett, *Complete Collection of State Trials*, II, London, 1809.
71 Birch, *Court and Times of James I*, I, p. 375.
72 See for example *Chamberlain*, I, p. 466, 8 July 1613; Chester City Record Office, CR 63, 2, 19, Davenport's Commonplace Book, ff. 2v–14v. I am grateful to Richard Cust for this reference; Akrigg, *Jacobean Pageant*, pp. 200–7.
73 Those letters cited by the prosecution are Cam. Univ. Lib. Mss. Dd. 3.63; the portions used are marked. See also Henry E. Huntingdon Lib., Ellesmere, Mss. 5979, 'Breviate of evidence against the Earl of Somerset in the poisoning of Sir Thomas Overbury', which cites portions of Northampton's letters.

Chapter 3.   A Jacobean Patronage Network

1   See G. E. Aylmer *The King's Servants*, London, 1961; W. MacCaffrey, 'Place and patronage in Elizabethan politics', in *Elizabethan Government and Society*, ed. S. T. Bindoff, J. Hurstfield and C. H. Williams, London, 1961; J. E. Neale, 'The Elizabethan political scene', in *Essays in Elizabethan History*, London, 1958; *Patronage in the Age of the Renaissance*, ed. G. Lytle and S. Orgel, Princeton, 1982.

2   See, for instance, Eleanor Rosenberg, *Leicester, Patron of Letters*, New York, 1955, and Lewis Namier, *The Structure of Politics at the Accession of George III*, London, 1929.

3   See H. R. Trevor-Roper, 'The general crisis of the seventeenth-century', in *Crisis in Europe, 1560–1660*, ed. T. H. Aston, London, 1965, pp. 82–3. For the most extensive development of this view see P. Zagorin, *The Court and the Country*, New York, 1970.

4   J. P. Cooper, *The Wentworth Papers, 1597–1628*, Camden Fourth Series, 12, London, 1973, pp. 1–8; Derek Hirst, 'Court, country and politics before 1629', in *Faction and Parliament: Essays on Early Stuart History*, ed. Kevin Sharpe, Oxford, 1978, pp. 105–27.

5   This description of the administrative structure of the Cinque Ports is based on K. M. E. Murray, *The Constitutional History of the Cinque Ports*, Manchester, 1935. For the characterisation of Northampton as an absentee Lord Warden, see Peter Clark's impressive study, *English Provincial Society from the Reformation to the Revolution: Religion, Politics and Society in Kent, 1500–1640*, Hassocks, Sussex, 1977, pp. 309–12. *Cal. S.P. Dom. 1595–1597*, 505, 30 September 1597, Cobham's patent, endorsed 'A copy of the patent of Henry, Lord Cobham, For Henry, Lord Howard', and dated 5 January 1604, the day Howard succeeded.

6   B.L. Stowe Mss. 743, f. 26, 26 February 1612; P.R.O. S.P. 14, 48, 243, an earlier memorandum setting forth orders for the discipline of the garrison at Sandgate Castle, provided that 'no soldier put away his place but with the privity and consent of the captain, that he may give knowledge thereof to the Lord Warden or his lieutenant'.

7   *Calendar of the White and Black Books of the Cinque Ports, 1432–1955*, ed. Felix Hull, London, 1966, pp. 358–414, *passim*; Thomas Moir, *The Addled Parliament of 1614*, Oxford, 1958, p. 47; *Cal. White and Black Books*, pp. 397, 413, 431; P.R.O. S.P. 14, 66, 32, 1611; *Cal. White and Black Books*, pp. 325, 360, 366; P.R.O. S.P. 14, 66, 31, 1611. Two Thomas Kennets were Cinque Ports officials in the early seventeenth century, one a jurat of Folkestone, the other clerk of Faversham; one of them was in addition also under-porter of Sandgate Castle. *Cal. White and Black Books*, pp. 410, 414; 376–456, *passim*; P.R.O. S.P. 14, 66, 31.

8   *Cal. White and Black Books*, pp. 346, 348; P.R.O. S.P. 14, 66, 32, 1611; *Cal. White and Black Books*, p. 360; P.R.O. S.P. 14, 66, 31; *Cal. White and Black Books*, p. 400; Nat'l Lib. of Wales, Carreg-lwyd Mss. 240, BMab 651/1; P.R.O. S.P. 14, 66, 31; *Cal. White and Black Books*, pp. 365–88, *passim*; HMC *13th Report*, 4, Rye Mss. 183, 132; Nat'l Lib. of Wales, Carreg-lwyd Mss. 240, BMab 651/1.

9   MacCaffrey, 'Place and patronage in Elizabethan politics', pp. 122–3.

10   P.R.O. S.P. 14, 74, 85.

11   E. P. Shirley, 'An inventory of the effects of Henry Howard, K.G., Earl of Northampton, taken on his death in 1614 together with a transcript of his will', *Archaeologia*, 42 (1869), 377, hereafter cited as 'Will'; P.R.O. S.P. 14, 66, 32; 'Will', *Archaeologia*, 42 (1869), 377; *Cal. S.P. Dom. 1611–18*, 311. Anthony Sanders of Eton, identified as one of Northampton's retainers, was also a gunner of Dover Castle with a fee of eight pence a day. John Harris, a gunner and soldier at Sandgate Castle who was paid six pence a day, was probably the brother-in-law of Christopher Harris, one of Northampton's servants to whom he left £50; Nat'l Lib. of Wales, Carreg-lwyd Mss. 240, BMab 651/1; P.R.O. S.P. 14, 66, 32; 'Will', *Archaeologia*, 42 (1869), 377; P.R.O. S.P. 14, 66, 31. Peter Webster, a servant to whom Northampton left £40 in his will, petitioned Zouche for the arrears of his fee as a gunner at Sandgate Castle, 'Will', *Archaeologia*, 42 (1869), 377; *Cal. S.P. Dom. 1611–18*, 340, 1615(?).

12   'Will', *Archaeologia*, 42 (1869), 378; P.R.O. S.P. 14, 81, 77; 'Truth Brought to Light',

Somers Tracts, 2nd edn, London, 1809, II, 397; J. E. Neale, *The Elizabethan House of Commons*, pp. 53–4; *Cal. S.P. Dom. 1611–18*, 462; Aylmer, *The King's Servants*, pp. 289–91.

13   John Jaggard was dismissed for non-residency after Zouche took office. These offices were often treated as freehold property. William Dowland, a servant of Northampton who had accepted a gunner's place instead of the £30 left him in the earl's will, petitioned Zouche to be allowed to sell it since he planned to retire to the country. John Goodwin, a jurat of Dover who had purchased a gunner's place from one of Northampton's servants, found that though such purchases were allowed by Northampton they were now unlawful. Having paid the price, Goodwin pleaded with Zouche that the transaction be allowed to stand. *Cal. S.P. Dom. 1611–18*, 311, ? October 1615; 298, ? July 1615; *Cal. White and Black Books*, p. 136. The position of Richard Austen, who held a gunner's position during Northampton's tenure, was challenged for non-residency, *Cal. S.P. Dom. 1611–18*, 311.

14   HMC *13th Report*, 4, Rye Mss., 183, 28 March 1627; see John K. Gruenfelder, 'The Lord Wardens and elections, 1604–1628', *Journal of British Studies*, 16, (Fall 1976), 1–23; Derek Hirst, *The Representative of the People?*, Cambridge, 1975, pp. 210–13, 207–9.

15   HMC *Sackville*, I, 155; *Cal. S.P. Dom. 1611–18*, 46; 'Truth Brought to Light', *Somers Tracts*, II, 366; *Cal. White and Black Books*, p. 398.

16   *Cal. S.P. Dom. 1603–10*, 626; *Cal. S.P. Dom. 1611–18*, 376; Clark, *English Provincial Society*, pp. 275–6.

17   *Cal. S.P. Dom. 1623–1625 and Addenda*, 547, ? 1613; that Ward was accused of embezzlement did not hinder his officeholding. P.R.O. S.P. 14, 66, 32; P.R.O. S.P. 14, 76, 17, 2 February 1614; *Cal. S.P. Dom. 1603–10*, 620, 25 June 1610; B.L. Stowe Mss. 743, f. 20, Northampton to Sir Thomas Waller, 2 December 1608; *Cal. White and Black Books*, pp. 400, 418, 155, 421.

18   *Cal. White and Black Books*, p. 124; Nat'l Lib. of Wales, Carreg-lwyd Mss. 1812, 2 December 1607, BMab 656/1.

19   Cam. Univ. Lib. Mss. Dd. 3.63, f. 16, Northampton to Rochester, June 1614; London County Council, *Survey of London*, 18, London, 1937, p. 51; *Chamberlain*, I, 542, 30 June 1614. Brett had already profited from his position as a gentleman usher at court with a £200 annuity and a lease of the moiety of the king's coppicewoods in the forest of Whittlewood, and a grant of all coat and conduct money since the tenth year of Elizabeth due and not paid into the Exchequer and of all fines for the non-payment of the same; *Cal. S.P. Dom. 1603–10*, 370, 525, 581. Coat and conduct money was a tax assessed to provide a coat and travelling expenses for each man furnished for military service.

20   MacCaffrey, 'Place and patronage in Elizabethan politics', p. 97.

21   See L. L. Peck, 'Patronage, policy and reform at the court of James I: The career of Henry Howard, Earl of Northampton', Ph.D. thesis, Yale University, 1973, ff. 82–8.

22   P.R.O. S.P. 14, 76, 20, II.

23   Inner Temple, Petyt Mss. 538, 17, ff. 274–274v. In a letter to Salisbury, Northampton thanked him for supporting the Lord Warden's authority in the Cinque Ports, an authority Northampton claimed 'appears by all precedents hath been ever absolute'. B.L. Cotton Mss. Faustiana C II, ff. 23 ff., contains 'A calendar of such records as are contained in the book delivered by Mr. Kniveton to my Lord Privy Seal concerning Dover and the Sink Ports'; /A° 1610, 4 January. Marked with Robert Bowyer's characteristic notation, this calendar may have served in part as the basis of Bowyer's advice. Furthermore, it indicates Northampton's continuing personal search for historical precedents on which to base his authority in the Cinque Ports. For Bowyer's notations, see Elizabeth Read Foster, *Proceedings in Parliament, 1610*, 2 vols, New Haven, 1966, I, xxii.

24   G. R. Elton, *The Tudor Revolution in Government*, Cambridge, 1962, pp. 134–5. Bishop Foxe, Lord Privy Seal from 1487 to 1516, and the Earl of Manchester in the 1630s, did preside over the court; G. Elton, *The Tudor Constitution*, Cambridge, 1962, pp. 184–90; Aylmer, *The King's Servants*, p. 47.

25 I. S. Leadam, *Select Cases in the Court of Requests, 1497–1569*, Selden Society, 12, (1898), cxxiii.

26 B.L. Cotton Mss. Titus C VI, f. 113, Northampton to Somerset, 1613; Cam. Univ. Lib. Mss. Dd. 3.63, f. 17v, Northampton to Somerset, 1613; A. G. R. Smith, 'The secretariat of the Cecils, circa 1612', *English Historical Review*, 83 (July 1968), 500–3.

27 Elton, *The Tudor Revolution*, pp. 270–4.

28 *Cal. S.P. Dom. 1595–97*, 560, Reynolds to the queen (1597?). Another time, referring to ecclesiastical appointments, he observed that benefices were commonly taken up in the post and few remained unfilled till the incumbents were dead if they were once on the way to heaven. *Cal. S.P. Dom. 1601–3*, 231, E. Reynolds to O. Reynolds, 2 August 1602.

29 *Cal. S.P. Dom. 1598–1601*, 66, 26 June 1598; 158, January 1599.

30 P.R.O. S.P. 14, 1, 38, 20 April 1603.

31 *Cal. S.P. Dom. 1603–10*, 223, 9 June 1605, E. Reynolds to O. Reynolds; 307, 31 March 1606, E. Reynolds to O. Reynolds; P.R.O. S.P. 14, 19, 250; Aylmer, *The King's Servants*, pp. 69–96. He was willing to lend his brother £50 to secure a place, and Owen Reynolds became assistant to the clerk of the parliaments, Robert Bowyer. *Cal. S.P. Dom. 1601–03*, 120, E. Reynolds to O. Reynolds, 5 November 1601. On Owen Reynolds's death Edward Reynolds sent Salisbury a variety of official documents found in his brother's papers; *Cal. S.P. Dom. 1603–10*, 602, 25 April 1610. E. R. Foster, 'The painful labour of Mr Elsyng', *Transactions of the American Philosophical Society*, n.s., vol. 62, pt 8, 1962, p. 11.

32 *Cal. S.P. Dom. 1598–1601*, 536, 6 January 1601. *Cal. S.P. Dom. 1603–10*, 270, 10? December 1605, E. Reynolds to O. Reynolds.

33 P.R.O. S.P. 14, 26, 12, Edward Reynolds to O. Reynolds, 13 January 1607.

34 *Cal. S.P. Dom. 1611–18*, 167, 8 January 1613. Petition of clerks of Signet and Privy Seal to the king.

35 P.R.O. S.P. 14, 34, 82; S.P. 14, 34, 90; S.P. 14, 35, 230B, 6 July 1610; S.P. 14, 35, 53.

36 P.R.O. S.P. 14, 77, 59, E. Reynolds to Francis Mills, 9 July 1614. *Cal. S.P. Dom. 1611–18*, 338, 12? December, 20 December 1615; 399, 23 December 1615, 346, [January] 1616.

37 *Cal. S.P. Dom. 1611–18*, 350, 19 February 1616; 391, 17 August 1616; 472, 10 June 1617. Saddler, Worcester's secretary, whom Reynolds termed 'dangerous', also angled for a gratuity, 391, 17 August 1616.

38 *Cal. S.P. Dom. 1611–18*, 351, 23 February 1616; 369, 30 May 1616.

39 *Cal. S.P. Dom. 1611–18*, 401, (October) 1616; 391, 17 August 1616; 422, 2 January 1617; *Cal. S.P. Dom. 1619–23*, 177, 8 September 1620.

40 *Cal. S.P. Dom. 1611–18*, 81, 16 October 1611; P.R.O. S.P. 14, 66, 101, Reynolds to Northampton, 30 October 1611.

41 *Cal. S.P. Dom. 1611–18*, 84, 90, 102; Salisbury apparently authorised this disbursement, 103, 28 December 1611; 117, Thomas Packer to Salisbury, January 1612.

42 P.R.O. S.P. 14, 34, 57, 29 June 1608; *Cal. S.P. Dom. 1611–18*, 272, 345, 346, 452, 401; *Cal. S.P. Dom. 1619–23*, 328, ? 1621. John Packer married Francis Mills's daughter and received his reversion in 1604. Reynolds may also have been connected to Mills through his wife's first husband.

43 On the creation of the baronetage see L. Stone, *The Crisis of the Aristocracy*, Princeton, 1966, pp. 82–97; Katherine S. Van Erde, 'The Jacobean baronets: An issue between king and Parliament', *Journal of Modern History*, 33 (June 1961), 137–47; J. G. Nichols, 'The institution and early history of the dignity of baronet', *Herald and Genealogist*, 3 (1866), 193–212. The money was earmarked for the army in Ulster.

44 Stone, *The Crisis of the Aristocracy*, p. 85.

45 Quoted in Nichols, 'The institution and early history of the dignity of baronet', 206–9, Strode to Tolemache, 10 May 1611. Strode wrote his friend several letters detailing the course of the negotiations.

46 The following paragraphs are based on G. E. C[okayne], *Complete Baronetage*, 6 vols, Exeter, 1900–9; *DNB*, Harleian Society *Visitations* and county histories.

47 For Finch's connections to Essex see Clark, *English Provincial Society*, pp 262, 309.

48 I am grateful to Conrad Russell for this point which needs to be developed more fully for the entire period up to 1640. For Northampton's parliamentary patronage see Chapter 9.

49 For the most recent discussion of Cotton's role, see Kevin Sharpe, *Sir Robert Cotton, 1586–1631*, Oxford, 1979, pp. 123–30.

50 B.L. Cotton Mss. Julius C III, f. 358, 144; f. 13 December 1608; f. 367 (after 1608).

51 B.L. Cotton Mss. Julius C III, f. 265, 1611; f. 107, 1611; f. 42, 14 August 1611.

52 VCH *Berkshire*, IV, 254; *Cal. S.P. Dom. 1603–10*, 562, 25 November 1609.

53 Van Erde, 'The Jacobean baronets', 139. Van Erde does not name the fifteen Catholics she finds in the baronetage. Neither does she connect the large number of Catholics with the influence of Northampton.

54 Hope Mirrlees, *A Fly in Amber, Being an Extravagant Biography of the Romantic Antiquary Sir Robert Cotton*, London, 1962, pp. 293–4; Le Strange Mordaunt, Richard Mollineux, Richard Fleetwood, Walter Aston and Thomas Bendishe were other baronets suspected of Catholic leanings; Van Erde, 'The Jacobean baronets', 139; Aylmer, *The King's Servants*, p. 357.

55 Van Erde, 'The Jacobean baronets', 139–41; Northampton cited this hostility, in a memorandum, B.L. Cotton Mss. Cleo F VI, f. 331.

56 *Cal. S.P. Venetian 1603–7*, 42, 28 May 1603.

57 HMC *Salisbury*, 19, 52–3, King James to Salisbury, 22 February 1606.

58 HMC *Salisbury*, 18, 238–9, Lake to Salisbury, 17 August 1606; HMC *Various Collections*, 3, Tresham Papers, 139–47; P.R.O. S.P. 14, 70, 25, Northampton to Rochester, 3 August 1612; P.R.O. S.P. 14, 70, 46, Northampton to Rochester, 12 August 1612.

59 *The Visitation of Kent, 1619–21*, Harleian Society, 42 (1898), 11–12; M. F. Pritchard, 'The significant background of the Stuart Culpeppers', *Notes and Queries*, 205 (November 1960), 408–16; 'Will', *Archaeologia*, 42 (1869), 377.

60 T. Birch, *The Court and Times of James I*, 2 vols, London, 1849, I, 54, Northampton to Sir Thomas Edmondes, 2 May 1606.

61 P.R.O. S.P. 14, 65, 95, 31 August 1611.

62 HMC *Salisbury*, 19, 63, 7/17 March 1607.

63 A. G. Lee, *The Son of Leicester*, London, 1964, p. 142; *Cal. S.P. Dom. 1603–10*, 614; quoted in Lee, *The Son of Leicester*, p. 155. Stone, *The Crisis of the Aristocracy*, p. 399, notes the long-standing enmity of the Dudleys and the Howards and says that 'in 1603 the Howards came into their own again and the last of the Dudleys fled into embittered exile in Italy'. In fact, Henry Howard was Dudley's patron. For the Star Chamber case in which Dudley was fined for calling himself the Earl of Leicester and Warwick, see J. Hawarde, *Les Reportes del Cases in Camera Stellata, 1593–1609*, London, 1894, pp. 169 ff., 198 ff. He was one of the few judges who decided that the witnesses to Lady Sheffield's marriage to the Earl of Leicester – by which Dudley claimed legitimacy – should not be suppressed (p. 220).

64 B.L. Cotton Mss. Titus B VII, f. 414, Thomas Morgan to James I, 14 June 1608.

65 B.L. Cotton Mss. Titus C VI, ff. 166–167v, 5 July (1608); the *DNB* incorrectly states that Morgan probably died in 1606.

66 *Cal. S.P. Venetian 1607–10*, 517, 23 June 1610.

67 Arthur P. Kautz, 'The selection of Jacobean bishops', in *Early Stuart Studies*, ed. Howard Reinmuth, Minneapolis, 1970, pp. 152–79.

68 Thomas Atkinson was named to Winfarthing by John Holland, trustee of the Howard family. In 1610 John Cole, Northampton's assignee, granted the benefice of Stratton to Peter Raye who held it with Starston; another assignee gave the living of Aldeborough to Richard Moore which he held united with Redenhall. In 1614 John Griffith, Northampton's secretary, named Edmund Hammond to Alburgh; Francis Blomefield, *History of Norfolk*, London, 1805–10, I, pp. 181–90; V, pp. 187, 351; VIII, p. 72. In 1610 Northampton granted to John Foyle, gentleman, the advowson of the rectory of Cattistock, Dorset, on the death of the incumbent, John Mayo; Nat'l Lib. of Wales, Carreg-lwyd Mss. 56, 30 April 1610.

69 William Younger, MA from Cambridge, held the living of St Mary's church in South Walsham to which he had been named in 1601 by the Bishop of Norwich. In 1612

Northampton named him to St Laurence's in the same town. In 1610 Howard presented John Rose, an Oxford alumnus, to All Saints, Gillingham, where Rose also held St Mary's on the Bacon family's nomination. Abacuc Cadywold was presented by Northampton to Wacton Magna in 1613 while he held the advowson of Wacton Parva. Blomefield, *Norfolk*, XI, p. 138; VIII, p. 9; V, pp. 295–303. Of all his appointees one of the few with court connections was John Blague, an MA from Cambridge, who was the son of Thomas Blague, chaplain to Queen Elizabeth and Dean of Rochester from 1592 until his death in 1611. The next year Northampton presented Blague to the parishes of Denton with 136 communicants and Earsham with 260 communicants, the largest of the benefices in Northampton's gift. Blomefield, *Norfolk*, V, p. 315; Thomas Blague, *DNB*.

70 B.L. Cotton Mss. Julius C III, f. 156, Thomas Dove to Cotton, 13 April 1608; f. 121, 1 December 1608. Patronage was a two-way street. Although Northampton could do nothing for William Cotton, Bishop of Exeter, Cotton could do something for him. Northampton asked for and got a prebend and the place of canon residentiary for John Bridgeman, later Bishop of Chester. Northampton's reward was Bridgeman's panegyric. Invoking God's blessing on the earl and his family, Bridgeman prayed 'that this land may long enjoy you and his Majesty or his issue never want a Howard to serve him in the honorablest affairs and place of the commonweal'. B.L. Harleian Mss. 7002, f. 295, Bridgeman to Northampton, 11 September 1613.

71 HMC *Salisbury*, 16, 327–8, Tooker to Cecil, 9 October (1604); Birch, I, 108, Rev. John Sanford to Sir Thomas Edmondes, 6 May 1610. 'Upon the remove of the Bishop of Gloucester Dr Tooker . . . had thought to have succeeded and had a grant of it from the king but Dr Tomson, Dean of Windsor, hath carried it from him.'

72 B.L. Cotton Mss. Julius C III, f. 371, 23 December 1609.

73 F. C. Dietz, *English Public Finance, 1558–1641*, New York, 1964, p. 388 and note.

74 *Cal. S.P. Irish 1611–14*, 282, Northampton to Lake, 29 August 1612.

75 See Peck, 'Patronage, policy and reform at the court of James I', pp. 82–8.

76 Aylmer, *The King's Servants*, pp. 258, 259, 265, 267, 273.

77 Lawrence Stone, 'The educational revolution in England, 1560–1640', *Past and Present*, 28 (July 1964), 41–80.

78 Aylmer, *The King's Servants*, p. 268.

79 Northampton's household servants have been culled from the lists in Nat'l Lib. of Wales, Carreg-lwyd Mss. 240, BMab 651/1; 'Will' and 'Inventory', *Archaeologia*, 42, (1869), 347–78. Peck, 'Patronage, policy and reform at the court of James I', pp. 82–8.

80 Neale, 'The Elizabethan political scene', p. 67.

81 *Cal. S.P. Dom. 1611–18*, 128; Foster, *Alumni Oxon.* 'Will', *Archaeologia*, 42 (1869), 377; G. E. C [okayne], *Complete Baronetage*.

82 *Visitation of Gloucester, 1623*, Harleian Society, 21; Foster, *Alumni Oxon.*

83 *DNB*; Aylmer, *The King's Servants*, pp. 384–5; *Cal. S.P. Dom. 1611–18*, 510.

84 'Will', *Archaeologia*, 42 (1869), 377.

85 Neale, *The Elizabethan House of Commons*, pp. 53–4; Aylmer, *The King's Servants*, pp. 289–91; 'Will', *Archaeologia*, 42 (1869), 377; Foster, *Alumni Oxon.*; Nat'l Lib. of Wales, Carreg-lwyd Mss. 308; 'Will', *Archaeologia*, 42 (1869), 377; Aylmer, *The King's Servants*, p. 362; 'Will', *Archaeologia*, 42 (1869), 377.

86 *Cal. S.P. Dom. 1603–10*, 497; 'Will', *Archaeologia*, 42 (1869), 377; *Cal. S.P. Dom. 1611–18*, 110, 230; Nat'l Lib. of Wales, Carreg-lwyd Mss. 771, 2236, 597, 1538.

87 Blomefield, *History of Norfolk*, V, p. 456.

88 *Visitation of Kent, 1619–21*, Harleian Society, 42, 27–8. Venn, *Alumni Cant.*, I. *Cal. S.P. Dom. 1603–10*, 457; 'Will', *Archaeologia*, 42 (1869), 377.

89 B.L. Lansdowne Mss. 235, ff. 1–15v, Thomas Godfrey's diary.

90 B.L. Lansdowne Mss. 235, f. 2. During Northampton's tenure as Lord Warden the franchise for the election of local officials in Sandwich was restricted to twenty-four free men in addition to the mayor and jurats. Traditionally, the franchise had been open to the 'commons, free men and better sort of inhabitants' of Sandwich, or so it was claimed in the 1620s; B.L. Add. Mss. 33512, f. 18. Under Northampton's predecessor, Lord

Cobham, it had first been limited to forty-eight and then thrown open. The Privy Council at Northampton's request ordered the franchise to be limited to twenty-four, 'and those to be of the better, graver, and more peaceable sort', HMC *Buccleuch*, I, 48. In 1626 this limited franchise was attacked by inhabitants of Sandwich on the grounds that a faction had got control of the town government, that the town had decayed under its rule, and that the town was unable to take its part in defending the realm. The petition linked open franchise to defence of the realm; B.L. Add. Mss. 33512, f. 18. For a discussion of the disorders in Sandwich from the 1590s on, cf. D. Hirst, *The Representative of the People?*, Cambridge, 1975, p. 207.

91 B.L. Lansdowne Mss. 235, f. 3v.
92 P.R.O. S.P. 14, 70, 34, Northampton to King James, 10 August 1612; f. 35, Northampton to Sir Charles Cornwallis, 10 August 1612.
93 P.R.O. S.P. 14, 70, 35. Northampton's words were strong: 'Kings have placed provosts not de jure but de facto and so have they granted many pardons for wilful murder.' He emphasised the origin of the institution rather than more recent practice.
94 N. E. McClure (ed.), *The Letters of John Chamberlain*, 2 vols, Philadelphia, 1939, I, p. 542.
95 Cam. Univ. Lib. Mss. Dd. 3.63, f. 16, my italics.
96 L. P. Smith (ed.), *The Life and Letters of Sir Henry Wotton*, 2 vols, Oxford, 1907, II, p. 41, Wotton to Bacon, 25 June 1614.

Chaper 4. Profit from Office

1 N. E. McClure (ed.), *The Letters of John Chamberlain*, 2 vols, Philadelphia, 1939, I, p. 539; T. Birch, *The Court and Times of James the First*, 2 vols, London, 1849, I, pp. 324–5.
2 E. P. Shirley, 'An inventory of the effects of Henry Howard, K.G., Earl of Northampton, taken on his death in 1614, together with a transcript of his will', *Archaeologia*, 42 (1869), 347–78; hereafter cited as 'Inventory', and 'Will'. The letter writers varied in their estimates of Northampton's legacies. See H. S. Scott (ed.), *The Journal of Sir Roger Wilbraham*, London, 1902, pp. 113–14; L. P. Smith, *The Life and Letters of Sir Henry Wotton*, 2 vols, Oxford, 1907, II, pp. 38–40. *Chamberlain*, I, 541–2; Birch, I, 324–5.
3 H. S. Scott (ed.), *Journal of Sir Roger Wilbraham*, pp. 113–14. Wilbraham estimated the earl's worth at £120,000 but this seems exaggerated. The figure of £80,000 assumes that Northampton's landed estates were worth fifteen to twenty times their yearly yield.
4 Smith, *Wotton*, II, p. 38. See Lawrence Stone, *The Crisis of the Aristocracy*, Oxford, 1966, pp. 760–1.
5 *Cal. S.P. Dom. 1595–1597*, 505. B.L. Add. Mss. 12514, ff. 46–47v. 'For my Lord of Northampton. Touching the Lord Warden's authority.'
6 *Cal. S.P. Dom. 1603–10*, 152, 626; K. M. E. Murray, *The Constitutional History of the Cinque Ports*, Manchester, 1935, pp. 120–38.
7 KAO, New Romney Borough Records, CP, W110, Northampton to the mayor and jurats of New Romney, 2 February 1604.
8 *Cal. S.P. Dom. 1603–10*, 468; P.R.O. S.P. 14, 76, 17, 2 February 1614; Lawrence Stone, *Family and Fortune*, Oxford, 1973, p. 286 n.
9 *Calendar of the White and Black Books of the Cinque Ports, 1432–1955*, ed. Felix Hull, London, 1966, pp. 125–30.
10 *Cal. White and Black Books*, p. 137, General Brotherhood at New Romney, 21 July 1612.
11 P.R.O. S.P. 14, 61, 43, 1 February 1611, *Cal. S.P. Dom. 1603–10*, 428, 5 May 1608.
12 G. E. Aylmer, *The King's Servants*, London, 1961, p. 211; *Cal. S.P. Dom. 1603–10*, 445, 4 July 1608.
13 P.R.O. C. 54, 1766, 30 May 1604, Indenture between Northampton and Suffolk.
14 The manor of Cattistock was part of the Howard of Bindon holdings which came to Northampton; John Hutchins, *The History and Antiquities of the County of Dorset*,

Westminster, 1861, p. 355. Margaret Viscountess Bindon and her husband, Sir Edmund Ludlow, sued the earl over Marnhull manor, also in Dorset. P.R.O. Chancery Proceedings, Series II, Bundle 283, No. 2.

15   John Holland and others were trustees for Northampton and Suffolk for the manors in the county of Norfolk; W. A. Copinger, *The Manors of Suffolk*, Manchester, 1908, IV, 200; Edward Stafford and Peter Gay were Northampton's trustees for various lands in East Greenwich, P.R.O. Wards 5, 29. The attorneys, Francis Plowden and Andrew Blunden, were his trustees for the manor of Clun in Shropshire; P.R.O. C. 54, 1786, 30 June 1604; HMC, *10th Report*, IV, Corporation of Bishop's Castle, p. 406.

16   B.L. Add. Mss. 27401, ff. 24–5, 'An acquittance to Owen Shepherd, my Lordship's Receiver General of part of his collection and charge for the whole year ended at Michelmas this year 1604'. The difficulty in assessing Northampton's landed income arises because there are few accounts and they do not include all of the lands that Northampton amassed as listed in the feodary surveys made in the 1620s. Other accounts include Arundel Castle Mss. MD 500, a survey of Northampton's lands in Suffolk, Cambridgeshire and Lincolnshire, and Arundel Castle Mss. A 1255, Northampton's steward's accounts for 1613 for Norfolk, Suffolk and Lincolnshire, which appear incomplete. The yearly rentals given in 1604 are close to those in B.L. Lansdowne Mss. 58, ff. 58–60v: 'manors and lands as did come to the Queen's Majesty's hands by the attainder of the late Duke of Norfolk' (1588?). When the Earl of Arundel sued out his lands in the 1620s, the Court of Wards assigned values to Northampton's lands that were very low; P.R.O. Wards 5, 29. Eleven Norfolk manors were valued at £60 by the feodary survey, which both the Elizabethan note and Shepherd's 1604 account put at above £350.

17   Nat'l Lib. of Wales, Carreg-lwyd Mss. 630, 'An abstract taken of the estate as well as of the means of discharge', 27 September 1616.

18   Arundel Castle Mss. MD 500, ff. 6–6v. See also Arundel Castle Mss. A 1255.

19   P.R.O. C. 54, 1830, 20 January 1606; C. 54, 2157, 6 May 1613; Frebridge had previously been rented to Francis Gawdy for £20 a year.

20   P.R.O. C. 54, 2168, 10 November 1613; C. 54, 2162, 20 November 1613; Oxford, Bodl. Lib., Jones Mss. 20, f. 88, 27 June 1622, 'A note of all the lands and possessions of the hospital founded by the right honorable Henry Howard, Earl of Northampton, in East Greenwich and likewise of the present yearly revenue thereof.' For an earlier transaction with Brett for some land on which Northampton House was built see P.R.O. C. 54, 2044, 6 July 1610. For purchases of land in East Greenwich see C. 54, 2046, 25 October 1610; C. 54, 2105, 6 February 1611. For Sedgeley see Nat'l Lib. of Wales, Carreg-lwyd Mss. 630.

21   Stone, *The Crisis of the Aristocracy*, pp. 142, 760–1.

22   Stone, *Family and Fortune*, pp. 59, 272–5.

23   Smith, *Wotton*, II, p. 40; HMC *Cowper*, I, 84.

24   HMC *Sackville*, I, 154–5. Temple Newsam Mss. TN P06 XI (1), Cranfield to Ingram, 18 August 1607. See R. H. Tawney, *Business and Politics under James I*, Cambridge, 1958, pp. 103–4; M. Prestwich, *Cranfield: Politics and Profits under the Early Stuarts*, Oxford, 1966, pp. 69–70; A. F. Upton, *Sir Arthur Ingram*, London, 1961.

25   *Cal. S.P. Dom. 1603–1610*, 413.

26   HMC *Sackville*, I, 155. Sir William Waad, Arthur Ingram, Robert Hawey, William Angell, Lionel Cranfield, William Massam; Joan Thirsk, *Economic Policy and Projects*, Oxford, 1978, pp. 83–93.

27   Hatfield House Mss. M 485/28, Cecil Papers, CXXV. Although this is marked (1610?), it is more likely to date from before 14 March 1608 when Northampton was granted the farm with a rent to the king of one-quarter of the revenue.

28   Nat'l Lib. of Wales, Carreg-lwyd Mss. 621, BMab 652/1, 28 November 1624: Northampton asked that port officers refrain from collecting the impost on starch since it was granted to him by the king and he had let it to Ingram, Dalby and others. *Cal. S.P. Dom. 1603–10*, 430.

29   Prestwich, *Cranfield*, p. 107. There is evidence that he was trying to revive the starch

duties in 1613; B.L. Cotton Mss. Cleo F VI, ff. 99–99v (1612–1613?): 'the importation of starch is likely to prove his Majesty a good benefit having once received a judgement at the common law as a public nuisance to the whole state by destruction of grain so as no more of that kind might be made within the realm.'

30 *Cal. S.P. Dom. 1611–18*, 145–6. Temple Newsam Mss. TN P07 III (33): 'The accounts between my Lord and Sir Arthur Ingram as well upon the contract as for the annuity of £3,000 per annum payable to his Lordship out of the customs of Ireland.' Victor Treadwell, 'The establishment of the farm of the Irish customs, 1603–1613', *English Historical Review* (1978), 580–602.

31 Joel Hurstfield, *The Queen's Wards*, London, 1958.

32 P.R.O. Wards 9, 162, 7 James; *Cal. S.P. Dom. 1611–1618*, 145–6.

33 John Smyth, *The Berkeley Manuscripts*, 3 vols, Gloucester, 1883, II, pp. 265–449.

34 Smyth, *The Berkeley Manuscripts*, II, pp. 431–2; 14 February 1612. John Griffith valued the wardship at £1200 in his calculations of the estate; Nat'l Lib. of Wales, Carreglwyd Mss. 630, 27 September 1616. The agreement reached in an out-of-court settlement called for £300 in ready money, the rest to be paid in three instalments. While Griffith agreed to this, the other executors did not and they wound up in their own legal tangle.

35 *Cal. S.P. Spanish 1580–86*, 315–16, 364, 403.

36 *Cal. S.P. Ven. 1603–07*, 175, 239, Nicolo Molin-Doge, 25 August 1604, 4 May 1605.

37 Henri Lonchay and Joseph Cuvalier, *Correspondance de la cour d'Espagne sur les affaires des Pays-Bas au XVIIe Siècle*, 6 vols, Brussels, 1923–37, I, p. 156. For a discussion of efforts to gain toleration see A. J. Loomie, 'Toleration and diplomacy: The religious issue in Anglo-Spanish relations, 1603–1605', *Transactions of the American Philosophical Society*, n.s. vol. 53, pt 6 (1963).

38 P.R.O. S.P. 31, 12, 35, Sarmiento to Philip III, 17 October 1614. For a discussion of the Spanish pensioners see Charles Carter, *The Secret Diplomacy of the Hapsburgs 1598–1625*, New York, 1964, as well as Garrett Mattingly, *Renaissance Diplomacy*, Baltimore, 1964.

39 *Cal. S.P. Ven. 1610–13*, 135. In 1605 Zuniga, then Spanish ambassador, had listed the pensions he had paid to English courtiers; B.L. Add. Mss. 31, 111.

40 P.R.O. S.P. 31, 12, 34, Sarmiento to Philip III, 5 October 1613; B.L. Add. Mss. 31, 111, 'Extracts from Sarmiento's accounts Feb. 2/12/1614'; P.R.O. S.P. 31, 12, 35, 15 February 1614: 'List of the feigned names mentioned in Sarmiento's letter to the Duke of Lerma.'

41 P.R.O. S.P. 31, 12, 36, 10 February 1615; a gold ducat was worth 9s 4d. It is also possible that Northampton wanted the money used to pay a debt. I am grateful to Professor Joel Hurstfield for this point.

42 Cam. Univ. Lib. Mss. Dd. 3.63, ff. 35v–36, 45, Northampton to Rochester (1613); Prestwich, *Cranfield*, p. 129. A mark was two-thirds of a pound.

43 B. E. Supple, *Commercial Crisis and Change in England, 1600–42*, Cambridge, 1964, pp. 37–58.

44 Prestwich, *Cranfield*, p. 168; Astrid Friis, the author of the major work on the project, *Alderman Cockayne's Project and the Cloth Trade*, London, 1927, p. 252 and F. H. Durham, 'Relations of the Crown to trade under James I', *Transactions of the Royal Historical Society*, n.s. 13 (1899), 214, all rely on the statement cited in the text from 'Truth Brought to Light', *Somers Tracts*, 2nd edn, London, 1809, II, p. 280. It should be noted that there was no Lord Treasurer from 1612–14; Suffolk became Lord Treasurer after Northampton's death.

45 B.L. Cotton Mss. Titus C VI, ff. 108–9, Northampton to Rochester.

46 HMC *Rutland*, 4, 463, 465–6, 473, 492–4, 500; all but one of these gifts can be traced in the inventory of Northampton's goods made after his death. Northampton's executors got less for them than the retail price Rutland had paid; 'Inventory', *Archaeologia*, 42 (1869), 347–78.

47 *Cal. S.P. Irish 1608–10*, 521–2, 31 October 1610.

48 P. Zagorin, *The Court and the Country*, New York, 1970, p. 138. Cf. M. Perceval-Maxwell, *The Scottish Migration to Ulster in the Reign of James I*, London, 1973.

49 Theodore Rabb, *Enterprise and Empire: Merchant and Gentry Investment in the Expansion of England, 1575–1630*, Cambridge, 1967, pp. 31, 82, and 'List of Names'. Northampton was also an honorary member of the French and Spanish companies, both shortlived attempts to create regulated monopolies in trades which had long been established.

50 *Cal. S.P. Colonial*, I, 21, 2 May 1610.

51 Gillian T. Cell, 'The New Foundland Company: A study of subscribers to a colonizing venture', *William and Mary Quarterly*, 3rd ser., 22 (1965), 611–25.

52 Stone, *The Crisis of the Aristocracy*, p. 547.

53 E. B. Chancellor, *The Private Palaces of London*, London, 1908, p. 51.

54 London County Council, *Survey of London*, London, 1900–, vol. 18, 5–6, 10–11, 23; vol. 20, 89. P.R.O. C. 54, 2044, 2168, 2162; A. J. Loomie, *Spain and the Jacobean Catholics, 1613–1624*, Catholic Record Society, 68 (1978), 39.

55 HMC *Sackville*, I, 265, May 1612.

56 P.R.O. S.P. 14, 66, 44, 2 October 1611.

57 B.L. Cotton Mss. Titus C VI, ff. 95–7, 1613, Northampton to Rochester; *Cal. S.P. Dom. 1603–10*, 197, 19 February 1605.

58 P.R.O. S.P. 14, 75, 45, Northampton to Sir Thomas Lake, 11 December 1613; f. 46 provides specifics of the fees attached to the keepership of the park.

59 *Cal. S.P. Dom. 1611–18*, 216.

60 P.R.O. S.P. 14, 75, 45. Of the same matter Northampton wrote that 'the disgrace beside is somewhat greater than I would willingly undergo without the least desert in my declining years'. P.R.O. S.P. 14, 75, 40, Northampton to Lake, 9 December 1613.

61 'Inventory', *Archaeologia*, 42 (1869), 347–78.

62 Northampton apparently possessed a portrait of Prince Henry, described in the inventory as 'a large Prince Henry on horseback in arms', which has been called the 'earliest large-scale equestrian portrait of a royal personage in English painting'. Roy Strong, *The Elizabethan Image*, London, 1970, p. 81. Strong cites Northampton's inventory but mistakenly assumes him to have lived at Audley End, built by his nephew, Thomas Howard, Earl of Suffolk; Roy Strong, *The English Icon*, London, 1969, p. 43; 'Inventory', *Archaeologia*, 42 (1869), 347–78.

63 'Inventory', *Archaeologia*, 42 (1869), 347–78. Arundel bought his library and some other household goods for £529. Nat'l Lib. of Wales, Carreg-lwyd Mss. 372, BMab 651/1, 27 September 1616.

64 Stone, *The Crisis of the Aristocracy*, p. 546.

65 *Cal. S.P. Dom. 1603–10*, 356; W. K. Jordan, *The Charities of Rural England*, London, 1961, p. 125.

66 F. Blomefield, *History of Norfolk*, 11 vols, London, 1805–10, IX, 55–6.

67 W. K. Jordan, *Social Institutions in Kent, 1480–1660*, London, 1961, p. 48; W. K. Jordan, *The Charities of London*, London, 1960, p. 147; Oxford, Bodl. Lib. Jones Mss. 20, f. 88.

68 'Will', *Archaeologia*, 42 (1869), 377.

69 Leeds, Temple Newsam Mss. TN P0 7 III (33).

70 *Chamberlain*, I, 497.

71 'Inventory', *Archaeologia*, 42 (1869), 350.

72 HMC *Downshire*, IV, 433–4.

73 'Will', *Archaeologia*, 42 (1869), 375–6.

74 W. L. Spiers, 'The notebook and account of Nicholas Stone', *Walpole Society*, 7 (1919), 4.

75 Stone, *Family and Fortune*, p. 282 and Introduction.

Chapter 5. The Jacobean Privy Councillor

1 For a discussion of the development and structure of the Privy Council in the sixteenth and seventeenth centuries, see D. E. Hoak, *The King's Council in the Reign of Edward VI*,

Cambridge, 1976; E. R. Turner, *The Privy Council, 1603–1784*, Baltimore, 1927, Vol. I;
Michael Pulman, *The Elizabethan Privy Council in the Fifteen-Seventies*, Berkeley, 1971.

2   Derek Hirst, 'The Privy Council and problems of enforcement in the 1620s', *Journal of British Studies*, 18 (Fall 1978), 46–66; Conrad Russell, *Parliaments and English Politics, 1621–1629*, Oxford, 1979, pp. 64, 70 ff.

3   See for instance P.R.O. S.P. 14, 15, 87, Northampton to Lake, urging the latter to tell the king to burn Northampton's letters, 'for my eye tells me when the king is here that letters are a prey which many hunt after'.

4   B.L. Add. Mss. 39853, f. 83, 10 April 1607.

5   P.R.O. S.P. 14, 15, 97, Northampton to Lake, 22 October 1605.

6   B.L. Stowe Mss. 170, ff. 81–2, 5 July (1608?).

7   Turner, *The Privy Council*, I, 35–66; Hoak, *The King's Council*, pp. 227–8; Pulman, *The Elizabethan Privy Council*, pp. 81–2.

8   J. Hawarde, *Les Reportes del Cases in Camera Stellata, 1593–1609*, London, 1894, p. 175; see also the case of the Earl of Northumberland, p. 299.

9   27 May 1603, 7 November 1606, 14 October 1607, 18 November 1607, 16 June 1608, October 1608 (no date); Hawarde, *Camera Stellata*.

10 Hawarde, *Camera Stellata*, pp. 228, 236, 292; for the most recent view that Ellesmere was a member of a faction in the Council opposed to Northampton see L. B. Knafla, *Law and Politics in Jacobean England, The Tracts of Lord Chancellor Ellesmere*, Cambridge, 1977, pp. 90–4.

11 A. J. Loomie, 'Toleration and diplomacy; the religious issue in Anglo-Spanish relations, 1603–1605', *Transactions of the American Philosophical Society*, vol. 53, pt 6, Philadelphia, 1963.

12 Hawarde, *Camera Stellata*, pp. 189–91, 268–9.

13 P.R.O. S.P. 14, 70, 61, ? August 1612.

14 The Henry E. Huntington Library, Ellesmere Manuscripts, 2605. The manuscript is headed 'A Brief of the Examinations lately taken before the Lords at Whitehall November 1612', and contains the examinations of those later convicted as well as Anthony Duisburgh, a student at Cambridge, and Abraham Speckett, who provided information. The manuscript is endorsed 'A Brief of the Examinations for the L. Privy Seal'. For the case itself, see T. B. Howell, *A Complete Collection of State Trials . . .*, London, 1816, II, 862–4.

15 N. E. McClure (ed.), *The Letters of John Chamberlain*, 2 vols, Philadelphia, 1939, I, p. 396. Star Chamber also heard 'the case of Sir Peter Buck . . . an officer . . . of the navy, who hath lain some good while in prison, for having written to a friend of his at Dover a letter containing this news, "that some of the Lords had kneeled down to the king for a toleration in religion"; besides some particular aspersion in the said letter of my Lord Privy Seal, whom likewise of late a preacher or two have disquieted: whereby he hath been moved, besides his own nature and (as some think also) besides his wisdom, to call these things into public discourse, *quae spreta exolescunt.*' L. P. Smith (ed.), *The Life and Letters of Sir Henry Wotton*, 2 vols, Oxford, 1907, II, pp. 22–3, 17 May [1613]. Northampton was a vigorous and persistent investigator of corruption in the navy; the identity of his accuser suggests a counter-attack.

16 Hawarde, *Camera Stellata*, pp. 176–7; 227–8.

17 H. E. H. Lib., El 2606, 20 December 1612, warrant under the signet for discharge of Sir Richard Cox, knight, Henry Mynours, sergeant of carriages, Henry Vernon, Thomas Goodrich and Thomas Lake, gent., for scandalous words, judgement given in Star Chamber against 'our trusty and right wellbeloved cousin and councillor the Earl of Northampton. . . . For that our said cousin the Earl of Northampton hath out of his honourable and compassionate disposition made humble and earnest suit unto us to remit unto all the persons above named, not only their imprisonment but also their fines which we are for his sake pleased to do.' *A. P. C. 1613–1614*, p. 42, 20 May 1613; Ingraham was released again upon the suit of the Lord Privy Seal.

18 Hawarde, *Camera Stellata*, p. 313.

19 ibid., p. 220.
20 ibid., pp. 276, 241.
21 ibid., p. 311.
22 See Ellesmere's injunctions to the justices of the peace, Hawarde, *Camera Stellata*, pp. 186–7; for the views of such a justice of the peace, see Richard Cust and Peter Lake, 'Sir Richard Grosvenor and the rhetoric of magistracy', *Bulletin of the Institute of Historical Research*, 54, May 1981, 40–53.
23 Hoak, *The King's Council*, pp. 136, 141; Pulman, *The Elizabethan Privy Council*, p. 164.
24 Quoted in Hoak, *The King's Council*, p. 107.
25 For attendance see *A. P. C. 1613–1614*; Hoak, *The King's Council*, pp. 34–90 and Pulman, *The Elizabethan Privy Council*, pp. 164–8.
26 *Cal. S.P. Ven. 1610–1613*, 438, 26 October 1612.
27 P.R.O. S.P. 14, 70, 49, 59.
28 P.R.O. S.P. 14, 70, 46, 49; P.R.O. S.P. 14, 71, 1, 7 October 1612.
29 P.R.O. S.P. 14, 70, 54.
30 See for instance A. G. R. Smith, 'The secretariat of the Cecils,' *English Historical Review*, 83 (July 1968), 481–504.
31 P.R.O. S.P. 14, 70, 46, 36.
32 P.R.O. S.P. 14, 70, 46, 54.
33 Cam. Univ. Lib. Mss. Dd. 3.63, ff. 12–14, January 1614.
34 B.L. Cotton Mss. Titus C VI, ff. 98–9. 'That benefit which may be made by the devising of some proportion of equality between the gold and the silver dependeth upon an exact conference between the Lord Knyvet ... and the officers of the mint whereof the Lords shall have an account very shortly when the officers are ready.'
35 P.R.O. S.P. 14, 70, 79, 29 September 1612.
36 B.L. Cotton Mss. Titus C VI, 104v.
37 P.R.O. S.P. 14, 75, 38.
38 P.R.O. S.P. 14, 70, 79, 29 September 1612. B.L. Cotton Mss. Vespasian C IX–CXI; Stowe Mss. 172–4 contain Cornwallis's and Edmondes's correspondence. It is to be hoped that Simon Adams will clarify the foreign policy of the period in his forthcoming work on the subject.
39 P.R.O. S.P. 14, 70, 79, 29 September 1612, S.P. 14, 71, 1, 7 October 1612; S. R. Gardiner, *The History of England from the Accession of James I to the Outbreak of the Civil War*, 10 vols, London, 1883–4, II, p. 247.
40 V. S. Treadwell, 'The establishment of the farm of the Irish customs, 1603–1613', *English Historical Review*, 93 (July 1978), 599.
41 *Cal. S.P. Ireland 1603–1606*, 'Introduction', xliv. In 1608 Northampton asked for and got a special briefing about a particular pirate, *Cal. S.P. Ireland 1606–1608*, 395, 15 January 1608.
42 B.L. Cotton Mss. Titus B X, ff. 188–90v, Chichester to Northampton, 7 February 1608; ff. 196–8, 5 February 1609; *Cal. S.P. Ireland 1611–1614*, 421, 17 September 1613.
43 'Letter-Book of Sir Arthur Chichester, 1612–1614', *Analecta Hibernica*, no. 8, pp. 5–177; hereafter cited as 'Chichester Letter-Book'; Chichester to Archbishop of Canterbury, p. 56, 23 October 1612. Chichester enjoyed considerable patronage in ecclesiastical appointments.
44 'Chichester Letter-Book', pp. 23–4, 23 May 1612; p. 76, 6 February 1613.
45 ibid., p. 63, 21 December 1612; p. 40, 6 August 1612; p. 45, 24 September 1612.
46 For analysis of Ireland and the impact of English policy in the early seventeenth century see Aidan Clarke's 'The Irish economy', and 'Pacification, plantation and the Catholic question, 1603–1623', in *A New History of Ireland*, ed. T. W. Moody, F. X. Martin, F. J. Byrne, Oxford, 1976, pp. 168–231; for the difficulties of administering the plantation see M. Perceval-Maxwell, *The Scottish Migration to Ulster in The Reign of James I*, London, 1973; for the problems posed by the plantation of Virginia see Edmund Morgan, 'The Labor Problem at Jamestown, 1607–1618', *American Historical Review*, 76 (1971), 595–611.

47   B.L. Cotton Mss. Titus C VI, ff. 307–8.
48   B.L. Cotton Mss. Titus B X, ff. 402–7, 285, 263–4.
49   *Cal. S.P. Ireland 1606–1608*, 404–5. *Cal. S.P. Ireland 1608–1610*, 521–2, 31 October 1610. For Gardiner's sympathetic treatment of Chichester's rule and analysis of the plantation, see *History*, I, pp. 358–441.
50   ibid.; Sir Hugh Wirrall, one of Northampton's English 'undertakers', wrote to Northampton also commenting on the poorer sort of Briton coming to Ireland; B.L. Cotton Mss. Titus B X, f. 287, (*c.*1614).
51   See Morgan, 'The Labor Problem at Jamestown, 1607–1618'; 'Chichester Letter-Book', pp. 30–3, 50ff., 74–5.
52   Perceval-Maxwell, *The Scottish Migration to Ulster in the Reign of James I*.
53   'Chichester Letter-Book', pp. 95, 70ff., 97–9, 102. T. W. Moody, 'The Irish parliament under Elizabeth and James I', *Proceedings of the Royal Irish Academy*, vol. 45, sect. C, pp. 41–81.
54   'Chichester Letter-Book', p. 106; B.L. Cotton Mss. Titus C VI, ff. 135–6v, 1613; Cam. Univ. Mss. Dd. 3.63, f. 1ff. (*c.*17 July 1613); f. 231, August 1613; *Cal. S.P. Ireland 1611–1614*. Cornwallis, no longer ambassador to Spain, repeated to Northampton some 'homely' words he had heard: 'these Irish are a scurvy nation, and are as scurvily used'.
55   Cam. Univ. Mss. Dd. 3.63, f. 6v, Northampton to Rochester.
56   'Chichester Letter-Book', pp. 126, 151, 150.
57   Clarke, in *A New History of Ireland*, p. 216; Clarke (p. 215) argues that the king 'dealt roughly' with the Irish delegation at an audience in April but three months later his decision was 'incongruously conciliatory'. But this is the precise mix which characterised Jacobean government: the combination of the rhetoric of divine right and pragmatic policy.
58   'Chichester Letter-Book', pp. 149–50. *Cal. S.P. Ireland 1611–1614*, 432.
59   B.L. Cotton Mss. Titus C VI, ff. 102–4v.
60   For an important discussion of seventeenth-century notions of government finance see G. L. Harriss, 'Medieval doctrines in the debates on supply, 1610–1629', in *Faction and Parliament*, ed. K. Sharpe, Oxford, 1978, pp. 73–103.
61   See Russell, *Parliaments and English Politics 1621–1629*, pp. 49–50.
62   B.L. Cotton Mss. Titus C VI, ff. 101–101v, Northampton to Rochester. For land sales during Northampton's tenure as treasury commissioner see *Cal. S.P. Dom. 1611–1618*, 171, 181, 24 February and 23 April 1613.
63   *Chamberlain*, I, 358, 17 June 1612.
64   See for instance P.R.O. S.P. 14, 75, 23, 23 November 1613; S.P. 14, 75, 31, 2 December 1613, Northampton to Lake; Cam. Univ. Lib. Mss. Dd. 3.63, f. 42, Northampton to Rochester; 'Chichester Letter-Book', p. 132.
65   For a discussion of Jacobean projects see Joan Thirsk, *Economic Policy and Projects*, Oxford, 1978; F. C. Dietz, *English Public Finance, 1558–1641*, New York, 1932, pp. 144–81; Lynn Muchmore, 'The project literature: an Elizabethan example', *Business History*, 45 (1971), 474–87; see also B.L. Lansdowne Mss. 156, ff. 43, 54, 318, 436; P.R.O. S.P. 14, 61, 25, S.P. 14, 63, 22–4.
66   Maurice Beresford, 'The common informer, the penal statutes and economic regulation', *Economic History Review*, 10 (1957), 221–37.
67   B.L. Cotton Mss. Titus B V, ff. 194, 196, 203, 246, 253, 307, 309, 388, 399. Others concerned the king's claim to certain lands left by the sea in Lincolnshire and Cambridgeshire, the pre-emption of tin, patent for salt and a proposition for granting privileges in trade to aliens.
68   P.R.O. S.P. 14, 56, 47, 48.
69   B.L. Cotton Mss. Titus C VI, ff. 108–9.
70   ibid. Astrid Friis, *Alderman Cockayne's Project and the Cloth Trade*, London, 1927, provides the fullest description of this project. See also B. E. Supple, *Commercial Crisis and Change in England, 1600–1642*, Cambridge, 1959, pp. 33–51; P.R.O. S.P. 14, 72, 70, 160.

71   P.R.O. S.P. 14, 71, 89, 1612.
72   Supple, *Crisis*, pp. 197–224; Joyce Appleby, *Economic Thought and Ideology in Seventeenth-Century England*, Princeton, 1978, pp. 24–51. P.R.O. S.P. 14, 70, 29, 7 August 1612, Northampton to Rochester. For position papers on farthing tokens see S.P. 14, 70, 40–4; S.P. 14, 72, 135–42.
73   B.L. Cotton Mss. Titus C VI, ff. 135–6v, Northampton to Rochester; for another example of the Council's effort at supervision see B.L. Lansdowne Mss. 152, f. 99, 23 July 1612: 'It is agreed that some merchants be appointed to go down to view the works and to report to the Lords in what state they are.' See also Anthony Upton, *Sir Arthur Ingram*, Oxford, 1961.
74   B.L. Cotton Mss. Titus B IV, ff. 100–4.
75   B.L. Egerton Mss. 2877, f. 167v; Hutton recommended Sir John Bennet to Northampton; Bennet, judge of the Prerogative Court of Canterbury, was impeached in 1621 for taking bribes.
76   B.L. Add. Mss. 58833; I am grateful to Conrad Russell for bringing this document to my attention. It is dated 1617, but appears to have been drawn up earlier. For instance, Nicholas Charles is listed as Lancaster Herald, but he had died in November 1613. Similarly, John Raven, who is listed as Richmond Herald, died in February 1615. In short, the present document apparently was based on an earlier one drawn up during Northampton's tenure as treasury commissioner; see Russell, *Parliaments and English Politics, 1621–1629*, p. 51; See also B.L. Cotton Mss. Titus B IV, f. 178, where Northampton notes under the entry 'pensions': 'That the list be reviewed every quarter to see how many die and what is spared.'
77   B.L. Cotton Mss. Cleo F VI, f. 96 ff. Northampton also noted that the number of judges might be reduced to their ancient number, but that would take time. The contemporary notion that office was vested in its holder made administrative reform difficult.
78   B.L. Cotton Mss. Cleo F VI, ff. 97, 105–105v. For a discussion of Hay's career see Roy Schreiber's forthcoming study.
79   B.L. Cotton Mss. Cleo F VI, ff. 99–100v.
80   ibid., ff. 102, 100–100v.

Chapter 6.   Advisers on Policy: Scholars and Officeholders

1   See L. Peck, 'Patronage, policy and reform at the Court of James I: The career of Henry Howard, Earl of Northampton', ch. III, 'The Scholars' (PhD thesis, Yale University, 1973).
2   For the development of English historical studies in the sixteenth century see F. J. Levy, *Tudor Historical Thought*, San Marino, 1967; F. Smith Fussner, *The Historical Revolution*, New York, 1962; May McKisack, *Medieval History in the Tudor Age*, Oxford, 1971; *English Historical Scholarship*, ed. Levi Fox, London, 1956; Robin Flower, 'Laurence Nowell and the discovery of England in Tudor times', *Proceedings of the British Academy*, 21 (1935); C. E. Wright, 'The dispersal of the monastic libraries and the beginning of Anglo-Saxon studies, Matthew Parker and his circle: A preliminary study', *Transactions of the Cambridge Bibliographical Society*, I (1949–53), 203–37. For the continental scholarship which influenced English antiquaries see Donald R. Kelley, *Foundations of Modern Scholarship, Language, Law and History in the French Renaissance*, New York, 1970; Quentin Skinner, *The Foundations of Modern Political Thought*, 2 vols, Cambridge, 1978.
3   Linda Van Nordern, 'The Elizabethan Society of Antiquaries', (PhD dissertation, UCLA, 1946); Kevin Sharpe, *Sir Robert Cotton, 1586–1631, History and Politics in Early Modern England*, Oxford, 1979, pp. 17–48.
4   Ernst Flugel, 'Die älteste englische Akademie', *Anglia: Zeitschrift für die englische Philologie*, 32 (1909), 265–8; Van Nordern, 'The Elizabethan Society of Antiquaries',

pp. 420–8. See also Thomas Kuhn, *The Structure of Scientific Revolutions*, Chicago, 1962.
5   B.L. Cotton Mss. Julius C III contains several hundred letters addressed to Cotton. Sharpe, *Sir Robert Cotton*, provides a detailed study of Cotton's career.
6   B.L. Cotton Mss. Julius C III, ff. 56–7, George Calvert to Cotton, 30 March 1621.
7   R. B. Wernham, 'The public records in the sixteenth and seventeenth centuries', in *English Historical Scholarship*, ed. Levi Fox, p. 50.
8   B.L. Cotton Mss. Julius C III, f. 102.
9   *Cal. S.P. Dom. 1611–1618*, 305.
10 B.L. Harleian Mss. 6018, ff. 154v, 172. See also Colin Tite, 'The early catalogues of the Cottonian Library', *British Library Journal*, vol. 6 (1980), pp. 144–57.
11 B.L. Harleian Mss. 6018, ff. 155v, 160, 185–6v.
12 B.L. Cotton Mss. Titus C I, f. 140.
13 B.L. Cotton Mss. Titus C VI, f. 140 (undated).
14 For a discussion of the painting see Roy Strong, *Tudor and Jacobean Portraiture*, 2 vols, London, 1969, I, pp. 351–3.
15 K. R. Andrews, 'Caribbean rivalry and the Anglo-Spanish Peace of 1604', *History* (February 1974), 1–17.
16 ibid., 8, 17.
17 A. J. Loomie, 'Toleration and diplomacy: The religious issue in Anglo-Spanish relations', *American Philosophical Society*, n.s., vol. 53, pt 6, 1963, 52.
18 Quoted in Maurice Lee, *James I and Henri IV: An Essay in English Foreign Policy 1603–1610*, Urbana, 1970, p. 42.
19 B.L. Cotton Mss. Vespasian C XIII, ff. 158–9, 'Discourse upon the king's necessity to make peace or keep wars with Spain'.
20 B.L. Cotton Mss. Vespasian C XIII, ff. 160–2. 'A discourse whether it be fit for England to make peace with Spain'. Even after the peace treaty was signed, Northampton received advice which he described as 'way to expulse the Spaniard'; Cotton Mss. Galba E 1, f. 276.
21 R. D. Hussey, 'America in European diplomacy, 1597–1604', *Revista de Historia de America*, 41 (June 1956), 1–30.
22 B.L. Cotton Mss. Vespasian C XIII, ff. 47–52.
23 B.L. Cotton Mss. Vespasian C XIII, ff. 401–2.
24 B.L. Cotton Mss. Vespasian C XIII, f. 47.
25 A report of the negotiations by Sir Thomas Edmondes, now catalogued as B.L. Add. Mss. 14033, was published as an appendix to Philip Watson's *A History of the Reign of Philip III*, 2nd edn, 2 vols, London, 1786. The account of the negotiations given here is based on Edmondes's report. Another account exists in HMC *Appendix to the 8th Report*, the Earl of Jersey Manuscripts. For Cotton's brief see B.L. Cotton Mss. Vespasian C XIII, ff. 47–52, of which a copy is Earl of Leicester, Holkham Hall Mss. no. 677, ff. 253–7.
26 Cotton, 'Reasons for the trade into the East and West Indies', B.L. Cotton Mss. Vespasian C XIII, f. 48. Watson, *History of the Reign of Philip III*, II, pp. 252, 264, 265. See S. E. Morrison's *Admiral of the Ocean Sea, A Life of Christopher Columbus*, 2 vols, Boston, 1942, I, p. 118.
27 Watson, *History of the Reign of Philip III*, II, p. 252; B.L. Cotton Mss. Vespasian C XIII, p. 50.
28 B.L. Cotton Mss. Vespasian C XIII, f. 50.
29 B.L. Cotton Mss. Vespasian C XIII, ff. 47–52. 'Now it may be objected that such restraints, as they now expect, have been obtained, but it is plain, that no otherwise, than under special suit, favour and grace.' Cotton cited the example of Elizabeth agreeing to the Portuguese request not to allow English merchants or mariners to sail to Ethiopian parts.
30 HMC *Appendix to 8th Report*, Earl of Jersey Mss., f. 97v.
31 B.L. Cotton Mss. Vespasian C XIII, ff. 47–52.

32 Watson, *History of the Reign of Philip III*, II, p. 265.
33 P.R.O. S.P. 94, 10, ff. 215–16v.
34 P.R.O. S.P. 14, 19, 10.
35 P.R.O. S.P. 14, 19, 12.
36 For a full account of the Gunpowder Plot see David Jardine, *A Narrative of the Gunpowder Plot*, London, 1857.
37 *A True and Perfect Relation of the whole proceedings against the late most barbarous Traitors, Garnet, a Jesuite and his confederats: Contayning sundry speeches delivered by the Lords Commissioners at their Arraignments, for the better satisfaction of that that were hearers, as occasion was offered; the Earl of Northampton's speech having bene enlarged upon those grounds which are set downe and lastly all that passed at Garnet's Execution*, London, 1606, sig. 4; STC 11619a. Hereafter cited as *A True and Perfect Relation*.
38 *A True and Perfect Relation*, sig. Cc 3v.
39 B.L. Cotton Mss. Titus C VI, ff. 142, 150.
40 B.L. Cotton Mss. Titus C VI, f. 153.
41 B.L. Cotton Mss. Titus C VI, f. 160.
42 *Cal. S.P. Ven. 1603–1607*, 438–9, 7 December 1606.
43 B.L. Cotton Mss. Titus C VI, f. 142. 'Worthy knight if among all your monuments you have any collection of as many ancient laws before the conquest as you can get, let this bearer wait your leisure to bring them hither.'
44 *A True and Perfect Relation*, sig. Ii 4v; Hh1v–Hh2, Ee 3v.
45 *Cases Collected and Reported by Sir Francis Moore* (2nd edn, London, 1675), p. 821, 'Gooderick's Case'. Hereafter cited as *Moore's Reports*. Bellarmine, who engaged in an extensive pamphlet war with King James on the question of papal power, never mentioned such a letter from Northampton; Jardine, *A Narrative of the Gunpowder Plot*, p. 223. Northampton pressed several such cases, and in one the defendant was fined £3,000; N. E. McClure (ed.), *The Letters of John Chamberlain*, 2 vols, Philadelphia, 1939, I, pp. 304, 509.
46 See Sharpe, *Sir Robert Cotton*, for further details of some other briefs Cotton prepared for Northampton.
47 B.L. Cotton Mss. Cleo F VI, f. 51 ff.
48 B.L. Cotton Mss. Cleo F VI, f. 73.
49 B.L. Cotton Mss. Cleo F VI, f. 144, f. 381.
50 B.L. Cotton Mss. Titus C VI, f. 145.
51 E. Goldsmid, *Cotton Posthumi*, Edinburgh, 1884, p. 30. This is the printed version of Cotton's 'Means to Repair the King's Estate . . .'.
52 *Cotton Posthumi*, p. 32.
53 B.L. Cotton Mss. Cleo F VI, f. 53v.
54 *Cotton Posthumi*, p. 43.
55 B.L. Cotton Mss. Cleo F VI, ff. 102, 99–99v.
56 B.L. Cotton Mss. Titus B IV, f. 100v. 'Black money' was copper or debased silver coinage.
57 William Noy, *A Treatise of the Rights of the Crown*, London, 1715, appears to have been copied with several errors from a manuscript of Cotton's treatise.
58 *Cotton Posthumi*, pp. 54–5.
59 P.R.O. S.P. 14, 53, 65, April? 1611; F. C. Dietz, *English Public Finance, 1558–1641*, New York, 1964, p. 148.
60 P.R.O. S.P. 14, 54, 61, April? 1611.
61 *Chamberlain*, I, pp. 325, 329.
62 B.L. Cotton Mss. Julius C III, f. 7, 26 March 1612.
63 *Chamberlain*, I, p. 345, 29 April 1612.
64 B.L. Cotton Mss. Cleo F VI, f. 90v.
65 B.L. Cotton Mss. Titus C VI, f. 144v.
66 Cam. Univ. Lib. Mss. Dd. 3.86, no. 8, f. 1. Dodderidge's tract is printed in part in Thomas Hearne, *A Collection of Curious Discourses*, 2 vols, London, 1771, I, pp. 163–7.

67 Cam. Univ. Lib. Mss. Dd. 3.86, no. 8, ff. 1–2v. In doing so Norfolk seems to have drawn on the precedent of the Duke of Clarence, the Lord High Constable under Henry V.

68 Cam. Univ. Lib. Mss. Dd. 3.86, no. 8, f. 4.

69 Francis Thynne, 'A Discourse of the Duty and Office of an Herald of Arms', in Hearne, *Curious Discourses*, I, 147, 148, 156. Hereafter cited as Thynne, 'Heralds'; Thynne's writings on the Cinque Ports are in B.L. Add. Mss. 12514, ff. 46–7. Like Northampton Thynne had provided information on the Earl Marshalship to Essex in 1597, B.L. Cotton Mss. Vespasian C XIV, ff. 395, 400.

70 Thynne, 'Herald', *Curious Discourses*, I, pp. 147–8. Thynne referred to a table he had prepared for Northampton listing the faults of the office. It is probably P.R.O. S.P. 14, 44, 76, 77, mistakenly calendared as April? 1609, *Cal. S.P. Dom. 1603–1610*, 505.

71 Thynne, 'Herald', *Curious Discourses*, I, pp. 156–7.

72 Edmund Bolton, *Elements of Armories*, London 1610; B.L. Cotton Mss. Julius C III, f. 28; Bolton referred to the 'great effects' expected because of Northampton's 'special care for reformation'.

73 B.L. Cotton Mss. Julius C III, f. 28, Bolton to Cotton, 19 July 1610.

74 B.L. Cotton Mss. Titus B V, f. 211, Bolton to Northampton, 11 March 1611. See also F. E. Baldwin, *Sumptuary Legislation and Personal Regulation in England*, Baltimore, 1926, pp. 161, 189.

75 B.L. Cotton Mss. Titus B V, ff. 211–211v; Maurice Beresford, 'Habitation versus improvement: The debate on enclosure by agreement', in *Essays in the Economic and Social History of Tudor and Stuart England in Honour of R. H. Tawney*, ed. F. J. Fisher, Cambridge, 1961, pp. 40–69, points out that Bolton's was becoming a minority view in the early seventeenth century. I am grateful to Peter Clark for comments on Bolton's project.

76 B.L. Cotton Mss. Titus B V, f. 211v.

77 Philip Styles, 'Politics and historical research in the sixteenth and seventeenth centuries', in *English Historical Scholarship*, ed. L. Fox, London, 1956, p. 52; Van Nordern, 'The Elizabethan College of Antiquaries', p. 469. Unlike the Society of Antiquaries in existence from 1586 to 1614 the Academy Royal would be run by the Crown, would not establish a national library and would not stress original research.

78 B.L. Cotton Mss. Julius C III, ff. 28, 19 July 1610; 30, 16 October 1612; 32. Bolton was unable to make use of Northampton's good offices in 1612 because he could not go to Ireland at the time.

Chapter 7. Advisers on Policy: The Merchants

1 *Journals of the House of Lords*, 22 vols, London, 1846, III, 343b.

2 B. E. Supple, *Commercial Crisis and Change in England, 1600–1642*, Cambridge, 1959. The literature on mercantilism is extensive: for a guide see D. C. Coleman (ed.), *Revisions in Mercantilism*, London, 1969.

3 Supple, *Commercial Crisis*, pp. 225–53.

4 B.L. Cotton Mss. Galba E I, ff. 145–7. The full title reflects Northampton's characteristic concerns: 'A discourse of the first beginning of clothing in England, the success thereof, the benefit this realm receiveth thereby in traffic with foreign nations, the necessity of redressing diverse abuses of corrupt merchants in their several trades and the means to reform them.' Galba E I contains a number of tracts on economic questions prepared for Northampton.

5 ibid., f. 164v; *Cal. S.P. Dom. 1603–1610*, 135, 21 July 1604.

6 Menna Prestwich, *Cranfield, Politics and Profits Under the Early Stuarts*, Oxford, 1966, pp. 49–51, 83, 62. Hereafter cited as Prestwich, *Cranfield*.

7 Quoted in Prestwich, *Cranfield*, p. 116.

8 N. E. McClure (ed.), *The Letters of John Chamberlain*, 2 vols, Philadelphia, 1939, I, p. 463, 8 July 1613.

9   Prestwich, *Cranfield*, pp. 122–3, 127, 125. The right to purvey Gascon wines to the Household was gained for Cranfield through the favour of the Earl of Somerset, Northampton's friend and ally. R. H. Tawney, *Business and Politics under James I*, Cambridge, 1958, focuses on Cranfield's early business career and his years as government minister, but pays little attention to his relations with Northampton. See also Victor Treadwell, 'The establishment of the farm of the Irish customs, 1603–1613', *English Historical Review*, 93 (1978), 580–602.

10 Prestwich, *Cranfield*, p. 467. For a different view of Cranfield see Michael Young, 'Illusions of grandeur and reform at the Jacobean court', *Historical Journal*, 22 (1979), 53–73.

11 HMC *Sackville*, I, 273–82.

12 P.R.O. S.P. 14, 70, 25, Northampton to Rochester, 3 August 1612.

13 P.R.O. S.P. 14, 70, 29, 7 August 1612.

14 P.R.O. S.P. 14, 70, 47, Northampton to Lake, 12 August 1612.

15 P.R.O. S.P. 14, 70, 25.

16 P.R.O. S.P. 14, 70, 46, Northampton to Rochester, 12 August 1612.

17 P.R.O. S.P. 14, 70, 46, 47.

18 HMC *Sackville*, I, 276–7. Cranfield's memorandum is entitled 'A Plain and true Relation concerning the banishing of English cloth by the Archduke out of his dominions'. Like Needham, Cranfield noted that originally cloth had been made from English wool in Flanders and reimported into England. 'This appeareth plainly by old records, for the first custom paid for cloths was inward.'

19 HMC *Sackville*, I, 277–8. Northampton paraphrased Cranfield's argument in the letter he sent to Rochester announcing that he had sent the merchant to the king. P.R.O. S.P. 14, 70, 30, 8 August 1612.

20 HMC *Sackville*, I, 279–80.

21 HMC *Downshire*, III, 236, William Trumbull to Salisbury, 13 January 1613. According to article six of the 1506 treaty between England and the House of Burgundy, it was unlawful for the Prince of the Netherlands to banish cloth or impose duties other than those then in use. While the archduke's Privy Council considered banishing English cloth, Trumbull, the English ambassador, submitted article six to them for consideration.

22 HMC *Downshire*, IV, 12.

23 HMC *Downshire*, III, 137, Northampton to Trumbull, 25 December 1612; IV, 5, John Kendrick to William Trumbull, 4 January 1613.

24 HMC *Downshire*, IV, 95, William Trumbull to King James I, 26 April 1613.

25 Many of these proposals are contained in B.L. Cotton Mss. Titus B V.

26 Prestwich, *Cranfield*, p. 184. F. C. Dietz, *English Public Finance, 1558–1641*, New York, 1964, p. 373. Hereafter cited as Dietz, *Finance*.

27 P.R.O. S.P. 14, 70, 83, Northampton to Rochester, September 1612. Northampton pointed out that 'the reasons of the party opposite did only tend to the destruction of the impositions themselves but of the 3*d* . . . no man brought so much as likelihood to meet with our instances'.

28 N. S. B. Gras, *The Early English Customs System*, Cambridge, 1918, p. 66. Northampton on another occasion articulated this argument by referring to 'that maxim that above the 12*d* in the pound which the subject pays, the foreigner must pay 3*d* in any kind'. Cam. Univ. Lib. Mss. Dd. 3.63, f. 11.

29 B.L. Cotton Mss. Titus C VI, ff. 89–90, Northampton to (Rochester) (before 6 May 1613). The Privy Council met to consider Caron's further objections in 1614; Cam. Univ. Lib. Mss. Dd. 3.63, ff. 11–15, Northampton to Rochester (*c*.10 January 1614).

30 A. P. Newton, 'The establishment of the great farm of the English customs', *Transactions of the Royal Historical Society*, 4th ser., I (1918), 129–55. Hereafter cited as Newton, 'Great Farm'. On customs on French wines farmed by John Swinnerton in the 1590s, for instance, the Crown made £2,408 less by its own direct administration than by the farm.

31 HMC *Salisbury*, 16, 319, Earl of Dorset, Lord Treasurer, to Cecil, 28 September 1604.
32 There had been a great fluctuation in receipts from 1594 to 1603 with a high in 1595 of £120,000 and a low in 1599 of £81,000. Dietz, *Finance*, p. 328 n.
33 Dietz, *Finance*, p. 331. Newton, 'Great Farm', 150.
34 Newton, 'Great Farm', 155; Robert Ashton, 'Revenue farming under the early Stuarts', *Economic History Review*, 2nd ser., VII–VIII (1954–6), 311; see also Ashton, 'Deficit finance in the reign of James I', *Economic History Review*, 2nd ser., 10 (1957–8), 15–29.
35 *Chamberlain*, I, 243, Chamberlain's information was correct; cf. Dietz, *Finance*, p. 332.
36 P.R.O. S.P. 14, 71, 3, Northampton to the king, 8 October 1612; Dietz, *Finance*, p. 154, is incorrect in citing Dorset as the 'late Lord Treasurer' who berated Swinnerton. In the context of the letter it is apparent that Northampton is referring to the end of the second patent in December 1611, when the rent was raised from £120,000 to £136,000 and his reference within the same paragraph to the 'little Lord' makes it certainly Salisbury. Northampton went on to note that Salisbury mitigated the increase by newly including within the Great Farm the Scottish custom and licence of beer.
37 B.L. Cotton Mss. Titus C VI, ff. 84–84v, Northampton to the king (June 1612–August 1612?). Arthur Ingram received £200 as did John Wolstonholme, and Richard Carmarthan and Sir William Ryder received £140; the rest was divided among the waiters and searchers in London and the outports.
38 B.L. Cotton Mss. Titus C VI, ff. 84–84v.
39 Newton, 'Great Farm', 153.
40 Quoted in HMC *Sackville*, I, 284. On 20 August, when he had not yet had an answer, Northampton asked Rochester 'to move the king for me that it may please him to make a stay of his hand to any specific warrant for the putting of it to the seal till I may wait on him'. P.R.O. S.P. 14, 70, 55, Northampton to Rochester, 20 August 1612.
41 HMC *Sackville*, I, 283, 288–9.
42 HMC *Sackville*, I, 291–3, 294. Cranfield claimed they also wished to prevent the king from securing the loan from the City, because the customs would be used as collateral and the farmers' practices might be discovered.
43 HMC *Sackville*, I, 295–6; Prestwich, *Cranfield*, p. 117; Cranfield calculated Swinnerton's offer of a £100,000 fine as good as £105,000 because it was to be paid beforehand.
44 P.R.O. S.P. 14, 71, 3, 8 October 1612.
45 Dietz, *Finance*, p. 333.
46 B.L. Cotton Mss. Titus C VI, ff. 84–84v.
47 P.R.O. S.P. 14, 71, 3, 5, Northampton to the king, 8 October 1612; and to Rochester.
48 P.R.O. S.P. 14, 71, 18, Lord Chancellor Ellesmere and Northampton to the king, 11 October 1612; James Spedding (ed.), *The Letters and the Life of Francis Bacon*, 7 vols, 1861–74, IV, 337, noted that this letter was composed by Bacon, the solicitor-general, who had been appointed to inquire into the legal aspects of the customs farms. This opinion was upheld in Chancery in June 1613, and the profits of the wine farm then sequestered. HMC *Sackville*, I, 306.
49 Dietz, *Finance*, p. 346.
50 In several different papers, Cranfield gave the profit variously as £15,194 and £15,224; the farmers claimed their yearly profit was £9,473, but the addition of several omitted items brought that up to £12,310. HMC *Sackville*, I, 301.
51 HMC *Sackville*, I, 303. Cranfield gathered information from an employee of the wine farmers as to the management charges of the farm when Swinnerton had held it, amounting to £471.
52 B.L. Cotton Mss. Titus C VI, ff. 134–134v, Northampton to Rochester (undated; before April 1613).
53 HMC *Sackville*, I, 306.
54 P.R.O. S.P. 14, 72, 1, and 1.1, Swinnerton to Rochester, 1 January 1613; P.R.O. S.P. 14, 74, 36, Northampton to Rochester, 24 July 1613.
55 HMC *Sackville*, I, 308. Swinnerton did receive the sweet wine farm as consolation and he sold the sweet wine farm in the outports to Cranfield; Dietz, *Finance*, p. 347.

56 HMC *Sackville*, I, 309. In 1621 Cranfield estimated that even this lease gave the farmers a profit of £9,288; Prestwich, *Cranfield*, p. 118.

57 Prestwich, *Cranfield*, p. 120.

58 P.R.O. S.P. 14, 74, 36, Northampton to Rochester, 24 July 1613.

59 Prestwich, *Cranfield*, p. 124.

60 P.R.O. S.P. 14, 70, 46.

61 B.L. Cotton Mss. Julius C III, f. 259, Thomas Milles to Cotton, 15 July 1604. This was not the first position paper of Milles that had been circulated to royal officials. He had prepared a statement of his views on reviving the staple system which was read by Sir Thomas Fanshawe, Remembrancer of the Exchequer, who showed it to Lord Burghley. Milles, *The Customer's Apology*, London, 1601, was circulated among members of the Privy Council; Milles also dedicated a tract to Lord Ellesmere, 'An out-port customer's accompt of all his receipts' (1612?). The presentation copy is at the Henry E. Huntington Library.

62 *DNB* 'Thomas Milles'; Phoebe Sheavyn, *The Literary Profession in the Elizabethan Age*, New York, 1964, pp. 41–4; Eleanor Rosenberg, *Leicester, Patron of Letters*, New York, 1955, pp. 6–7.

63 *The Catalogue of Honour*, London 1610, STC 17926; *The Customer's Alphabet and Primer*, London, 1608, STC 17927; *The Customer's Replie or Second Apology*, London, 1604, STC 17932.

64 B. M. Cotton Mss. Julius C III, f. 260, Thomas Milles to Cotton, 27 March 1609.

65 B. E. Supple, *Crisis and Change in England, 1600–1642*, Cambridge, 1964, pp. 29–30, 231; for varying views of the free trade movement see T. K. Rabb, 'Sir Edwin Sandys and the Parliament of 1604', *American Historical Review*, 69 (1964), 661–9; Robert Ashton, 'The parliamentary agitation for free trade in the opening years of the reign of James I', *Past and Present*, 38 (1967), 40–55; T. K. Rabb, 'Free trade and the gentry in the Parliament of 1604', *Past and Present*, 40 (1968), 165–73; 'Jacobean free trade again', *Past and Present*, 43 (1969), 151–7; Pauline Croft, 'Free trade and the House of Commons 1605–1606', *Econ. Hist. Rev.*, 2nd ser., 28 (1975), 17–27.

66 Thomas Milles, *The Customer's Alphabet and Primer*, London, 1608, STC 17927, sig. G 2a, I. Hereafter cited as Milles, *Alphabet*.

67 Milles, *Alphabet*, sig. K.

68 Newton, 'Great Farm', 143; Milles, *Alphabet*, sig. E 2a.

69 Supple, *Crisis*, pp. 73–99, 163–97.

70 Supple, *Crisis*, p. 182; T. S. Willan, 'The foreign trade of the provincial ports', in *Studies in Elizabethan Foreign Trade*, Manchester, 1959, p. 76.

71 B.L. Cotton Mss. Julius C III, f. 259.

72 T. S. Willan, *A Book of Tudor Rates*, Manchester, 1962, xlvii.

73 Tobias Gentleman, *England's Way to Win Wealth and to Employ Mariners*, London, 1614, STC 11745, p. 42; hereafter cited as Gentleman, *England's Way*.

74 J. F. Larkin and P. L. Hughes, *Stuart Royal Proclamations*, I, Oxford, 1973, pp. 217–19; *Cal. S.P. Dom 1603–1610*, 509, ? May 1609, Petition of the fishermen of the Cinque Ports to the king showing that Netherlanders drive them from their fishing and sell fresh fish in England against the law; Gentleman emphasised Northampton's position as Lord Warden by including in the dedication several of the earl's titles: Constable of the Castle of Dover, Lord Warden, Chancellor and Admiral of the Cinque Ports.' Gentleman, *England's Way*, sig. A2–A3.

75 P.R.O. S.P. 14, 37, 79, 17 November 1608. S.P. 14, 48, 92–4.

76 P.R.O. S.P. 14, 48, 92–4. Larkin and Hughes, *Stuart Royal Proclamations*, I, p. 219. Although this tax was a new imposition in England, it formed part of the king's revenue in Scotland. J. R. Elder, *The Royal Fishery Companies of the Seventeenth Century*, Aberdeen, 1912, p. 7; T. W. Fulton, *Sovereignty of the Seas*, London, 1911, p. 124. Rainsford reviewed his project in 1611, P.R.O. S.P. 14, 47, 164.

77 *Sir William Monson's Naval Tracts*, ed. M. Oppenheim, Navy Records Society, vol. 47, pp. 236–7. Monson wrote memoranda on English fishing in 1609: P.R.O. S.P. 14, 47, 112–14. For Northampton's support of Newfoundland fishing, see Chapter 4 above.

78   Gentleman, *England's Way*, sig. A2v–A3. Gentleman compared the project to the offer of Sebastian Cabot to King Henry VII for the discovery of the West Indies.

79   Fulton, *Sovereignty of the Seas*, pp. 88–9; Elder, *The Royal Fishery Companies of the Seventeenth Century*, p. 2; James T. Jenkins, *The Herring and the Herring Fisheries*, London, 1927, pp. 68–71; hereafter cited as Jenkins, *The Herring*.

80   Robert Hitchcock in his *A Politique Platt for the Honor of the Prince*, London, 1581, advocated that £80,000 be raised to support herring fisheries and 400 boats built for the trade. He estimated his scheme would bring in £400,000; Fulton, *Sovereignty of the Seas*, pp. 97–8. John Keymer described the Dutch fishing trade in a ms. written in 1601 and presented to James in 1605 or 1606. To emulate the Dutch, the English fishermen needed not only proper boats – the ones they had were too light – but re-education as well. They fished only seven weeks while the Dutch fished twenty-six. 'This is the life of these people where great riches is to be gotten.' Keymer, *Observations made upon the Dutch Fishing About the Year 1601*, London, 1664; on Keymer see also M. F. Pritchard (ed.), *Original Papers Regarding Trade in England and Abroad Drawn up by John Keymer for the Information of James I*, New York, 1967.

81   Gentleman, *England's Way*, pp. 3–4.

82   Gentleman, *England's Way*, pp. 10–11, 13. The merchant ships carried the herring to Russia, Prussia, Poland, Denmark and Sweden. In return they received hemp, flax, cordage, cables, iron, wax, pitch, tar, barrel-boards – the staples of shipbuilding – in addition to gold and silver.

83   Gentleman, *England's Way*, pp. 6–8.

84   Gentleman, *England's Way*, pp. 46, 42.

85   Gentleman, *England's Way*, pp. 23, 25, 27–9, 35. At times the fishing towns were their own enemies. Colchester men, for example, in order to catch sprats, put out their nets in the King's Channel in the Thames and caught instead young herring which they sold at Billingsgate for twopence a peck. They thereby destroyed an entire crop of summer herrings worth 20–30 shillings a barrel, pp. 19–20.

86   Gentleman, *England's Way*, pp. 36, 39, 8.

87   Gerard de Malynes, *Lex Mercatoria*, London, 1622, pp. 242–4; Thomas Mun, *England's Treasure by Forraign Trade*, London, 1664, Ch. xix.

Chapter 8.   Administrative Reform and the Problems of Corruption

1   B.L. Cotton Mss. Titus C VI, ff. 77–77v. The 'old treasurer' referred to was the Earl of Dorset.

2   See G. E. Aylmer, *The King's Servants*, London, 1961; J. Hurstfield, *The Queen's Wards*, London, 1958.

3   See for example H. R. Trevor-Roper, 'The general crisis of the seventeenth century', in *Crisis in Europe, 1560–1660*, ed. T. H. Aston, London, 1965, pp. 82–3.

4   J. Hurstfield, 'Political corruption in modern England: The historian's problem', *History*, 52 (1967), 16–34; L. Peck, 'Court patronage and government policy: The Jacobean dilemma', in *Patronage in Renaissance Europe*, ed. Stephen Orgel and Guy Lytle, Princeton, 1982; 'Corruption at the court of James I: The undermining of legitimacy', in *After the Reformation, Reappraisals in Honour of J. H. Hexter*, ed. Barbara C. Malament, Philadelphia, 1980, pp. 75–90.

5   J. S. Nye, 'Corruption and political development: A cost-benefit analysis', in *Political Corruption*, ed. Arnold J. Heidenheimer, New York, 1970, pp. 566–7. Nye defines corruption as 'behaviour which deviates from the formal duties of a public role because of private-regarding, pecuniary or status gains'.

6   B.L. Cotton Mss. Titus B V, f. 283ff. is Northampton's analysis of the abuses in ecclesiastical courts.

7   Cam. Univ. Lib. Mss. Dd. 3.63, f. 44v, n.d.; B.L. Stowe Mss. 170, ff. 81–2, 5 July 1608.

8   Allegra Woodworth, 'Purveyance for the Royal Household in the reign of Queen Eliza-beth', *Transactions of the American Philosophical Society*, n.s., 35, pt 1 (1945), 18; G. E. Aylmer, 'The last years of purveyance, 1610–1660', *Econ. Hist. Rev.* 10 (1957–8), 82; J. J. N. McGurk, 'Royal purveyance in the shire of Kent, 1590–1614', *Bulletin of the Institute of Historical Research* (1977), 58–68.

9   HMC *Salisbury*, 16, 326, 7 October (1604).

10 Nat'l Lib. of Wales, Carreg-lwyd Mss. 634, 'A brief and true discourse of the king's Majesty's cart-takers . . . By Robert Fletcher yeoman purveyor of carriages for the removes only of his Majesty's most honourable Household, wherein he hath served 30 years and more with great trouble, losses and scandal. October the 15th 1605.' Hereafter cited as Fletcher, 'Brief and true discourse'.

11 Fletcher, 'Brief and true discourse', ff. 7, 6, 14.

12 P.R.O. L.S. 13, 168, f. 187v, 'Articles to be observed by Edward Cosins, Clerk of the Carriage 10 June 1605'.

13 D. H. Willson (ed.), *The Parliamentary Diary of Robert Bowyer, 1606–1607*, Minneapolis, 1931, pp. 10–11, 16–17, 32 n. For the value of purveyance see Aylmer, 'The last years of purveyance', 86; F. C. Dietz, *English Public Finance, 1558–1641*, New York, 1964, p. 424.

14 Willson, *Bowyer*, pp. 55, 62, 67.

15 Willson, *Bowyer*, p. 37 n, Salisbury to the Earl of Mar, 9 March 1606.

16 Woodworth, 'Purveyance for the Royal Household in the reign of Queen Elizabeth', pp. 19, 76.

17 P.R.O. L.S. 13, 168, ff. 368–71.

18 H.E.H. Lib., Hastings Mss. 15058, 15059.

19 B.L. Cotton Mss. Titus F IV, f. 329.

20 H.E.H. Lib., Hastings Mss. 15058, f. 1, 29 October 1612.

21 H.E.H. Lib., Hastings Mss. 15059, ff. 1–2v.

22 ibid., ff. 2v–3.

23 *Cal. S.P. Ireland 1611–1614*, 100, Sir Humphrey Winche to Salisbury, 3 September 1611.

24 H.E.H. Lib., Hastings Mss. 15059, f. 2v.

25 G. R. Elton, *The Tudor Revolution in Government*, Cambridge, 1962, p. 261.

26 P.R.O. S.P. 14, 51, 42, 1 February 1611; S.P. 14, 32, 38, 5 May 1608.

27 W. J. Jones, 'Ellesmere and politics, 1603–1617', *Early Stuart Studies*, ed. Howard S. Reinmuth, Minneapolis, 1970, pp. 57–9.

28 P.R.O. P.S.O. 3, Ind. 6744, November 1607; Ind. 6745, May 1615.

29 P.R.O. P.S.O. 3, Ind. 6745, January 1614, April 1614, April 1612, May 1612.

30 P.R.O. P.S.O. 3, Ind. 6745, September 1611, March 1610, April 1611.

31 For a discussion of these commissions, see Michael Oppenheim, *A History of the Admin-istration of the Royal Navy and of Merchant Shipping in Relation to the Navy*, London, 1896, pp. 184–95; Prestwich, *Cranfield: Politics and Profits under the Stuarts*, Oxford, 1966, pp. 211–18; Michael Young, 'Illusions of grandeur and reform at the Jacobean court', *Historical Journal*, 22 (1979), 53–73; L. Peck, 'Problems in Jacobean administration: Was Henry Howard, Earl of Northampton, a reformer?', *Historical Journal*, 19 (1976), 835–40.

32 Inner Temple, Petyt 538, vol. 6, f. 117; Oppenheim, *Royal Navy*, pp. 189–95.

33 B.L. Cotton Mss. Julius F III, ff. 1–2v, Julius F III contains the testimony given before the 1608 naval commission. These depositions have been published by A. P. McGowan, *The Jacobean Commissions of Inquiry, 1608 and 1618*, Navy Record Society, 116, London, 1971.

34 B.L. Cotton Mss. Titus C VI, f. 148.

35 B.L. Cotton Mss. Julius F III, ff. 98, 5, 9, 84, 219–219v.

36 B.L. Cotton Mss. Julius F III, ff. 15, 26.

37 B.L. Cotton Mss. Titus C VI ff. 154–155v. Northampton's introduction to the commis-sion's report, B.L. Royal Mss, 18A, 34, contains his marginal corrections and signature. Trinity College, Cambridge R.7.22 is another copy with Northampton's corrections. B.L. Add. Mss. 9334 contains a draft of Cotton's report corrected by Northampton; P.R.O.

S.P. 14, 41, 1, the formal report of the commission, is bound together with an analytical draft of the report in Cotton's hand; S.P. 14, 41, 2. Trinity College, Cambridge R.5.1. is another copy of the commission's report; R.5.4, 'Orders to be Established for the future government of the navy to prevent the former abuses'.

38 Oppenheim, *Royal Navy*, pp. 190, 203–4; *Cal. S.P. Ven. 1607–1610*, 290, 25 June 1609. B.L. Royal Mss. 18A, 34, ff. 5v–7v.

39 B.L. Add. Mss. 9334, f. 33 (also Trinity College, Cambridge Mss. R.5.4); Cotton Mss. Titus B V, f. 283.

40 B.L. Cotton Mss. Titus B IV, f. 100v; B.L. Add. Mss. 9334, f. 20. For a discussion of sale of offices in the period see K. W. Swart, *Sale of Offices in the Seventeenth Century*, The Hague, 1949, pp. 45–67; Aylmer, *The King's Servants*, pp. 225–39. Beinecke Library, Yale, Osborne Mss. 631 is a copy of Northampton's translation, 'The sum of diverse directions of governments which Charles V left to his son Philip II', which describes sale of office as preferable to impositions.

41 B.L. Cotton Mss. Titus C VI, ff. 495–495v.

42 Sir Anthony Wagner, *The Heralds of England*, London, 1967, pp. 199–262.

43 Folger Shakespeare Library Mss. Vb. 7, ff. 37–8.

44 John Guillim, *A Display of Heraldry*, London, 1724, Appendix, p. 47. Folger Shakespeare Library Mss. Vb. 7.

45 B.L. Cotton Mss. Faustiana E I, ff. 176–176v. The abuses complained of included embezzlement and giving arms to 'Most base, abject and mechanical persons'.

46 ibid., ff. 178, 176–176v, f. 175. The heralds claimed that they had prompted the House of Commons to petition the queen for the commission.

47 ibid., f. 175.

48 ibid., f. 127.

49 Folger Shakespeare Library Mss. Va. 157, no foliation.

50 B.L. Cotton Mss. Faustiana E I, ff. 182–4v.

51 B.L. Cotton Mss. Titus C I, f. 97v.

52 B.L. Cotton Mss. Titus C I, f. 428 ff. Northampton's tracts on the Earl Marshalship are contained in this volume.

53 B.L. Add. Mss. 9334, f. 20.

54 B.L. Cotton Mss. Titus C I, f. 432v.

55 ibid., f. 528v.

56 J. F. Larkin and P. L. Hughes, *Stuart Royal Proclamations*, Oxford, 1973, No. 126, against pocket daggers, 16 January 1613; No. 132, against the publication of reports of duels, 15 October 1613, and No. 136.

57 See Oxford, Ashmolean Mss. 856 and B.L. Cotton Mss. Titus C I. The former attributes 'Duello Foil'd' to Northampton but Titus C I, f. 358 ff. is 'Duello Foil'd' with underlinings and annotations by Northampton which suggests it was written by someone else; ff. 206 ff. is a piece against duelling in his own hand.

58 H.E.H. Lib., El 406; for a discussion of duelling see F. R. Bryson, *The Sixteenth-Century Italian Duel*, Chicago, 1938; Robert Baldick, *The Duel*, New York, 1965; C. A. Thimm, *A Complete Bibliography of Fencing and Duelling*, London, 1896.

59 'A Publication of his Majesty's Edict and severe Censure against Private Combats and Combatants', STC 8498 accompanied 'A proclamation against private challenges and combats: With articles annexed for the better directions to be used therein, and for the more judicial proceeding against offenders', 4 February 1614; Larkin and Hughes, *Stuart Royal Proclamations*, No. 136, p. 305.

60 'A Publication of his Majesty's edict', pp. 24–5, 36–9, 34, 95, 41–2.

61 ibid., pp. 44, 27, 49.

62 ibid., pp. 21, 47–9, 59.

63 ibid., pp. 14–15, 22–5, 49–50.

64 ibid., pp. 104, 107–8; Larkin and Hughes, *Stuart Royal Proclamations*, pp. 302–8.

65 'A Publication of his Majesty's edict', pp. 53, 54, 66–7, 118.

66 ibid., pp. 71–3, 82–3.

67 ibid., pp. 74–8, 83–4.
68 ibid., pp. 100–1.
69 William Holdsworth, *A History of English Law*, I, Boston 1922, 578–80; see also P. H. Hardacre, 'The Earl Marshal, the Heralds and the House of Commons, 1604–1641', *International Review of Social History*, II (1957), 118–19.
70 'A Publication of his Majesty's edict', p. 59.
71 P.R.O. S.P. 14, 75, 32.
72 Bulstrode Whitelocke, *Liber Famelicus of Sir James Whitelocke*, Camden Soc., O.S. vol. 70, London, 1858, pp. 38–40; Gardiner, *The History of England from the Accession of James I to the Outbreak of the Civil War*, 10 vols, London, 1883–4, II, 187–91; G. D. Squibb, *The High Court of Chivalry*, Oxford, 1959, pp. 42–5; N. E. McClure (ed.), *The Letters of John Chamberlain*, 2 vols, Philadelphia, 1939, I, pp. 186–7. P.R.O. S.P. 14, 74, 2, 13 June 1613.
73 Folger Shakespeare Lib. Vb. 7, f. 13; B.L. Cotton Mss. Titus C I, ff. 140–140v.
74 P.R.O. S.P. 14, 74, 2, 13 June 1613; P.R.O. S.P. 14, 75, 32, 18 November 1613.
75 Squibb, *High Court of Chivalry*, pp. 42 ff., 144–7.
76 'A Publication of his Majesty's edict', p. 18; B. Whitelocke, *Liber Familecus of Sir James Whitelocke*, p. 39.

Chapter 9. The Jacobean Privy Councillor in Parliament

1 S. R. Gardiner, *The History of England from the Accession of James I to the Outbreak of the Civil War*, 10 vols, London, 1883–4, I, 353. W. Notestein, *The House of Commons, 1604–1610*, New Haven, 1971, and D. H. Willson, *The Privy Councillors in Parliament, 1604–1629*, Minneapolis, 1940, accept and expand Gardiner's portrait of Northampton; Thomas Moir, *The Addled Parliament*, Oxford, 1958, echoes this view. For contemporary views see L. P. Smith, *The Life and Letters of Sir Henry Wotton*, 2 vols, Oxford, 1907, II, pp. 38–40, Wotton to Sir Edmund Bacon, 16 June 1614; T. Birch, *The Court and Times of James the First*, 2 vols, London, 1849, I, pp. 323–4, Rev. Thomas Larkin to Sir Thomas Puckering, 18 June 1614.
2 The revisionist view of early Stuart Parliaments was sparked by Geoffrey Elton, 'A high road to civil war?' and 'Studying the history of Parliament', in *Studies in Tudor and Stuart Politics and Government*, Cambridge, 1974, II, pp. 3–12 and 162–82 and Conrad Russell, 'Parliamentary history in perspective, 1604–1629', *History*, 61 (February 1976). The December 1977 issue of the *Journal of Modern History* was devoted to revisionist views of early Stuart politics; see Mark Kishlansky, 'The emergence of adversary politics in the long Parliament', *JMH*, 49 (December 1977), 617–40; Paul Christianson, 'The peers, the people and parliamentary management in the first six months of the long Parliament', 575–99; James E. Farnell, 'The social and intellectual basis of London's role in the English civil wars', 641–60. For replies to these views see J. H. Hexter, 'Power struggle, Parliament and liberty in early Stuart England', and Derek Hirst, 'Unanimity in the Commons, aristocratic intrigues and the origins of the English Civil War', *JMH*, 50 (March 1978), 1–50; 51–71. K. M. Sharpe (ed.), *Faction and Parliament*, Oxford, 1978, contains several articles addressing different aspects of the revisionist view of parliamentary politics. See also Elton, 'Parliament in the sixteenth century: functions and fortunes', *Historical Journal*, 22 (1979), 255–78; the fullest exposition of the challenge to the Whig interpretation of the period from 1604–1640 as marking the campaign for the subject's liberties in opposition to the authoritarian action of the monarchy can be found in Conrad Russell, *Parliaments and English Politics, 1621–1629*, Oxford, 1979.
3 Notestein, *The House of Commons*, pp. 47–54, discusses the two versions of proposed bills, P.R.O. S.P. 14, 6, 99, and Northumberland Mss. Letters and Papers VII, Alnwick Castle Mss. R. Munden, in 'The politics of accession', M.Phil., University of East Anglia, 1974, analyses these proposals at length and suggests that they amounted to a

moderate programme reflecting the concern of the politically active gentry, pp. 152–4, 387–92.

4 Northampton sat on committees considering the union, the ecclesiastical courts and recusants, against swearing, for confirmation of the king's letters patent and forests. His own interests are reflected in the Act for the more severe repressing of duels, and especially, the Act for the better direction of the Earl Marshal's court and the repressing of abuses and errors in heraldry and arms. This proposal is found only in the Alnwick Castle Mss.

5 J. D. Mackie in his article 'A loyal subject's advertisement as to the unpopularity of James I's government in England 1603–1604', *Scottish Historical Review*, 23, no. 89 (October 1925), 1–17, 155–7, dates the tract between May 1603 and August 1604 and claims Northampton as its author based on his deductions that the author is English and politically important. Noting that few Englishmen were close to James with the exceptions of Howard and Cecil, Mackie limits his canvas to these two possibilities, dismissing Cecil as 'not the man to commit to paper a frank statement of his views' (p. 7). He backs up his attribution by noting that the tract is found in a secretary's copy in the Fortescue papers, which had belonged to John Packer, clerk of the Privy Seal and secretary to the Earls of Somerset and Buckingham, and that Howard was both Lord Privy Seal and Somerset's closest political ally. Several points may be made against this attribution. It is not clear why the author must have been of political importance or why Howard and Cecil are the only two possibilities. In style the tract is unlike Howard's mannered prose, the expression of support for the Low Countries against Spain runs counter to his inclinations, and the tract was evidently a popular one and can be found in ms. copy in many collections, including the Cotton copy presented in the *Somers Tracts* and one at Trinity College, Cambridge. If Cecil would not write such a paper, it is even more unlikely that Howard would. One reason educed by Mackie to prove Howard the author of the 'Advertisement' was Howard's use of the Latin phrase *Principiis obsta, sero medicina paratur …* in a private letter, when it also occurs in the 'Advertisement'. It might equally be argued that Matthew Hutton was the author of the tract since he too uses the same phrase (from Ovid's *Rèmedia Amoris*) and in a letter to Northampton in 1605. My thanks to Conrad Russell for this attribution. See B.L. Add. Mss. 29829 for yet another use of the phrase in a letter to Northampton dated July 1603.

6 See Munden, 'The politics of accession', pp. 387–92.

7 See for example, Conrad Russell, *Parliaments and English Politics*, pp. 45–6. Parliament had been held at the beginning of every reign at least since 1379.

8 B.L. Cotton Mss. Titus C VI, ff. 122–122v, 1613–14.

9 D. H. Willson, *The Privy Councillors in Parliament*, pp. 133–4; J. Spedding (ed.), *The Letters and the Life of Francis Bacon*, 7 vols, London, 1861–74, V, pp. 176–91.

10 B.L. Stowe Mss. 168, f. 169v, 10 October 1605; Hawarde, *Les Reportes del Cases in Camera Stellata, 1593–1609*, London, 1894, pp. 193–5, for the punishment of a deputy purveyor in April 1605.

11 Quoted in Robert Zaller, *The Parliament of 1621*, Berkeley, 1971, pp. 22, 35.

12 B.L. Cotton Mss. Cleo F VI, ff. 99–99v.

13 See Russell, 'Parliamentary history in perspective'.

14 See for instance John K. Gruenfelder, 'The electoral patronage of Sir Thomas Wentworth, Earl of Strafford, 1614–1640', *Journal of Modern History*, 49 (December 1977), 557–74; Robert W. Kenny, 'The parliamentary influence of Charles Howard, Earl of Nottingham, 1586–1624', *Journal of Modern History*, 39 (September 1967), 215–32.

15 The classic work on parliamentary patronage is J. E. Neale, *The Elizabethan House of Commons*, London, 1963; see also Thomas Moir, *The Addled Parliament of 1614*, pp. 52–3. Further evidence of the Crown's concern about elections is found in Northampton's letter to the JPs of Buckinghamshire to inquire into the background of the Goodwin–Fortescue contest, Oxford, Bodl. Lib., Rawlinson Mss. D918, f. 35.

16 Neale, *The Elizabethan House of Commons*, pp. 204–12.

17 Quoted in K. M. E. Murray, *The Constitutional History of the Cinque Ports*, Manchester,

1935, pp. 98–9, 28 February 1604. Murray mistakenly dates this as 1603 when it should be 1604 since reference is made to King James.

18 Murray, *Cinque Ports*, p. 99. Cf. the gratuity of £10 granted by the ports to Thomas Rogers, a servant of Northampton, for his pains on behalf of the ports in the last Parliament, 'when the Ports were drawn in question concerning the not paying of subsidies'. *Cal. White and Black Books*, p. 383. The practice of leaving one space blank on the election returns appears to contravene James's proclamation concerning the elections.

19 *Official Returns of Members of Parliament*, I, 1213–1702, 2 vols, London, 1878, 442–8; see John K. Gruenfelder, 'The Lord Wardens and elections, 1604–1628', *Journal of British Studies*, 16 (Fall 1976), 1–23.

20 HMC *13th Report*, IV, Rye Mss. 134–5, Sir William Twysden to Mayor and 'his brethren' of Rye, 26 September 1607; Same to Same, 12 October 1607; the Lord Warden to the Mayor and Jurats of Rye, September 1607. Rye tried to make use of its London friends in 1610. It addressed an appeal to Griffith, Twysden, Finch and its other member, John Young, reciting the Lord Warden's promise of his aid in obtaining a grant of tonnage to the town, which at threepence a ton would be used for the improvement of the decayed harbour. They begged their assistance in passing the Bill. HMC *13th Report*, IV, Rye Mss., 146, 20 November 1610.

21 Quoted in Neale, *The Elizabethan House of Commons*, p. 12.

22 *Official Returns of Members of Parliament*, I, 1213–1702; Appendix, XLI; Moir, *The Addled Parliament of 1614*, p. 51. Thomas Watson, teller of the Exchequer, who sat for Rye and Sir Thomas Smyth, a fiscal officer of the Crown who sat for Sandwich, were Northampton's nominees, according to Moir, and Edward Hendon who sat for Rye may have been, too; p. 47. Gruenfelder, 'The Lord Wardens and elections', suggests that in 1604 Northampton named a representative at Hastings, Sir George Carew, and in 1605, Sir Edward Hales, and at Hythe, C. Tolderrey; in 1614 Hales again sat for Hastings; p. 23. He does not cite George Bing who sat for Dover in 1604.

23 B.L. Lansdowne Mss. 235, f. 3.

24 Moir, *The Addled Parliament of 1614*, pp. 39–41.

25 Moir, *The Addled Parliament of 1614*, p. 47. Cf. Neale, *The Elizabethan House of Commons*, pp. 186–8, for the Duke of Norfolk's traditional influence in his county and Neville Williams, *Thomas Howard, Fourth Duke of Norfolk*, London, 1964, pp. 75–6.

26 R. C. Bald, *Donne and the Drurys*, Cambridge, 1959, pp. 128–9. Drury did not get the Thetford seat and eventually sat for the borough of Rye, perhaps as Northampton's nominee.

27 HMC *10th Report*, IV, Bishop's Castle Mss. 406, Northampton to Bailiff and Burgesses of Bishop's Castle, 21 October 1610. Notestein, *The House of Commons*, p. 168, suggests that Twyneho had been Northampton's nominee. Twyneho's smalt patent was condemned as a grievance by the Commons in 1606.

28 HMC *3rd Report*, Corporation of Totnes Mss., pp. 346–7, Northampton to Totnes, 20 February 1614; Carey had requested the nomination in 1604 but his letter arrived too late. I am grateful to Norah Fuidge for this point. Moir, *The Addled Parliament of 1614*, pp. 47–51.

29 P.R.O. S.P. 14, 77, 44.

30 HMC *Buccleuch* I, 48. At Northampton's request, the Privy Council ordered the franchise of Sandwich limited to 24.

31 See above, Chapter 3.

32 B.L. Lansdowne Mss. 235, ff. 1–13v, Thomas Godfrey's diary.

33 Willson, *The Privy Councillors in the House of Commons*, pp. 3–23.

34 See Elizabeth Read Foster, 'Procedure in the House of Lords during the early Stuart period', *Journal of British Studies*, V (1966), 56–73 and Sheila Lambert, 'Procedure in the House of Commons in the early Stuart period', *English Historical Review* 95 (1980), 753–81.

35 *L.J.* II.

36 H.L.R.O. Main Papers, H.L. 27 January 1597 to 1 June 1607, f. 150, an order of 1607,

stated that no absent lord was to be named a member of a committee unless particularly interested in the Bill by virtue of holding some office concerned with the subject matter of the committee. Were he at a committee meeting in rooms or chambers near the Parliament he was to be deemed present.

37   *L.J.* II, 263, 355, 499, 548.

38   I am grateful to Conrad Russell for the last two points.

39   *L.J.* II.

40   *L.J.* II, 369, 6 February and 392, 10 March 1606. I am grateful to Prof. Foster for advice on committees in the Lords which she will discuss at length in her forthcoming study of the House of Lords under the early Stuarts.

41   *L.J.* II, 370, 8 February 1606, 405, 1 April 1606.

42   H.L.R.O. Main Papers, H.L. ff. 22–3, 20 May 1610.

43   H.L.R.O. Braye Mss. 62 contains the committee appointment books beginning in 1610. Northampton was named to five committees in one day, *L.J.*, II, 24 February 1606; 380–1. Notestein, *The House of Commons*, p. 440, suggests that privy councillors in the House of Commons could not possibly have attended all the committees they were appointed to.

44   H.L.R.O. Braye Mss. 62. Those adjourned to the Council chamber concerned the private land transactions of Sir Henry Crispe, William Essex, Henry Jernegan, Charles Walgrave and Lady Despencer, the parsonages of Frome Whitfield, Dorset, and Ash and Dean, Southampton, the hospital of Thetford, the subcommittee on non-residency and pluralities, and the reform of the abuses of sailors and the companies of Salters and Brewers.

45   H.L.R.O. Braye Mss. 62, ff. 157, 158; *L.J.* II. For Holdich's Bill see *L.J.* II, 373, 14 February; 429, 10 May; 431, 13 May 1606. Holdich's Bill ran into difficulties in the lower House, *C.J.* I, 312, 24 May 1606; D. H. Willson (ed.), *The Parliamentary Diary of Robert Bowyer, 1606–1607*, Minneapolis, 1931, p. 179. The Bill was put off until the 1610 sessions when it passed; E. R. Foster, (ed.), *Proceedings in Parliament, 1610*, 2 vols, New Haven, 1966, I, pp. 135–7. *C.J.* I, 447. Others in whose legislation Northampton may have interested himself include Lord Windsor, Charles Paget, Charles Walgrave. On 2 July 1610 Northampton was 'first committee' to examine an Act concerning marsh lands in Norfolk and Suffolk. Suffolk and Arundel joined him on the committee, Braye Mss. 62, f. 161. Listed first in the appointment books, the 'first committee' often received the bill and reported back to the House.

46   H.L.R.O. Petyt 538, vol. 8, f. 199, Foster, *Proceedings in Parliament*, I, pp. 60–3, 205–7; II, p. 368.

47   B.L. Cotton Mss. Julius C III, f. 42, *VCH* Berkshire, IV, 254; *Cal. S.P. Domestic 1603–1610*, p. 562, *C.J.* I, 394, 16 February 1610; P.R.O. C. 54, 2049, 20 June 1610; P.R.O. C. 66, 1787, 1791, 1806, 8 February 1610, 14 June 1610, 4 December 1610; other trustees included Thomas Harrison and Edward Lord Wotton.

48   H.L.R.O. Braye Mss. 62, f. 166, 24 April 1610.

49   Foster, *Proceedings in Parliament*, I, pp. 38, 67, 215. The Bill had its second reading on 26 April and passed the Lords on 28 April.

50   The Archbishop of York was 'first committee', but after its first meeting the committee was adjourned to the Council Chamber. Also named to it was the Earl of Arundel. H.L.R.O. Braye Mss. 62, f. 148.

51   See above, pp. 53–4, Foster; *Proceedings in Parliament*, I, pp. 194–5.

52   H.L.R.O. Abergavenny Peerage Mss. 16 June 1610, Northampton's draft of report on precedence of baronies; Foster, *Proceedings in Parliament*, I, pp. 86–7, 147.

53   H.L.R.O. Braye Mss. 62, f. 152v, 19 May 1610; H.L.R.O. Main Papers, H.L. f. 37, 18 June 1610.

54   H.L.R.O. Braye Mss. 62, f. 157v; the Lord Privy Seal is inserted as 'first committee' and a note reads that by order dated 30 June he and Lord Knollys were added to the committee and that the Lord Chief Justices and the Lord Chief Baron were to be added to the legal officers attendant on the committee.

55   Foster, *Proceedings in Parliament*, I, pp. 137, 140, 247.
56   H.L.R.O. Main Papers, H.L., March 1607, ff. 143 ff. These papers show the close work the committees did even on minor Bills.
57   B.L. Cotton Mss. Titus C VI, ff. 454–5.
58   Foster, *Proceedings in Parliament*, I, p. 79.
59   ibid., I, pp. 37, 40–1. The Lord Privy Seal was 'first committee', and joined by Suffolk, Arundel and Nottingham no doubt because of the Norfolk/Howard connection. H.L.R.O. Braye Mss. 62, f. 147, 17 March 1610.
60   This Bill was introduced in the previous session; *Bowyer*, p. 6.
61   The debate is recorded in Foster, *Proceedings in Parliament*, I, pp. 75–9, 229–36. Northampton spoke for committing the Bill while the bishops wanted it thrown out altogether; ibid., pp. 72–3. The Archbishop of Canterbury made the salient point that 'the taking away of a benefice is a wrong unto him from whom it is taken because it may be he hath paid dearly for it', p. 76.
62   Foster, *Proceedings in Parliament*, I, p. 235. Northampton sat on another committee examining a Bill uniting the parishes of Frome Whitfield to provide a preacher and free school. The committee conferred with townspeople before drawing up a new Bill which was ultimately passed despite the Archbishop of Canterbury's initial objections; ibid., pp. 235, 33, 193.
63   D. Hirst, 'The Privy Council and the problems of enforcement', *Journal of British Studies*, 18 (Fall 1978), 46–66; Foster, 'Procedure in the House of Lords during the early Stuart period', 66.
64   *Bowyer*, p. 339v; such was Willson's description. Northampton was described by Sir Henry Montagu, an MP, as 'the learned earl', p. 48.
65   B.L. Cotton Mss. Titus C VI, f. 408.
66   ibid., f. 408v. Northampton's assessment is the same as Conrad Russell's in *The Crisis of Parliaments*, Oxford, 1971, pp. 244–5.
67   ibid., f. 413. This image of his house as the meanest in Manassas dates back at least to the 1580s. See Oxford Bodl. Lib. Mss. 903. 'A Dutiful Defense of the Lawful Regiment of Women', ff. 4 ff.
68   ibid., ff. 413–13v. With his reference to difficulties created by failure to nominate a successor, Northampton celebrated his own role in the secret correspondence which laid the foundation for a peaceful succession.
69   'The Trew Law of Free Monarchies' (1598), in *The Political Works of James I*, ed. C. H. McIlwain, New York, 1965, pp. 53–70.
70   R. H. Tawney, *Business and Politics under James I*, Cambridge, 1958, pp. 14–18; T. K. Rabb, *Enterprise and Empire; Merchant and Gentry Investment in The Expansion of England, 1575–1630*, Cambridge, Mass., 1967. My thanks to Conrad Russell and Peter Clark for these points.
71   B.L. Cotton Mss. Titus C VI, f. 408v. On another occasion, Northampton referred to the judges as oracles; Foster, *Proceedings in Parliament*, I, p. 65.

Chapter 10.   Northampton and Parliamentary Issues, 1604–14

1   'Things to be Considered of before a Parliament to be Called (1615)', in Louis Knafla, *Law and Politics in Jacobean England, The Tracts of Lord Chancellor Ellesmere*, Cambridge, 1977, pp. 263–73; James Spedding (ed.), *The Letters and the life of Francis Bacon*, London, 7 vols, 1861–74, V, pp. 176–91.
2   Wallace Notestein, 'The winning of the initiative by the House of Commons', *Proceedings of the British Academy*, 11 (1924–5), 125–75.
3   See for instance, D. H. Willson, *The Privy Councillors in The House of Commons, 1604–1629*, Minneapolis, 1940, pp. 13–16.
4   See Roger Munden, 'The politics of accession: James I and the Parliament of 1604', M.Phil., University of East Anglia, 1974; see previous Chapter, Note 3.

5 D. Willson, *The Parliamentary Diary of Robert Bowyer, 1606–1607*; hereafter cited as *Bowyer*. See also S. R. Gardiner, *The History of England from the Accession of James I to the Outbreak of the Civil War*, 10 vols, London, 1883–4, I, p. 353.

6 W. Notestein, *The House of Commons, 1604–1610*, New Haven, 1971, pp. 502, 569n. 27.

7 See for instance Willson, *The Privy Councillors*, pp. 140–2. Clayton Roberts and Owen Duncan, 'The Parliamentary undertaking of 1614', *English Historical Review*, 93 (July 1978), pp. 481–98.

8 Quentin Skinner, *The Foundations of Modern Political Thought*, Cambridge, 1978, I, p. 31.

9 Quoted in W. S. Howell, *Logic and Rhetoric in England, 1500–1700*, New York, 1961, pp. 101.

10 ibid., pp. 117–18.

11 For a discussion of the union see Brian Levack, 'The proposed union of English law and Scots law in the seventeenth century', *Juridical Review* (1975), pt ii, 97–115; on Bacon's role see Joel J. Epstein, 'Francis Bacon and the issue of union, 1603–1608', *Huntington Library Quarterly* (1970), 121–32. For the parliamentary proceedings, see Notestein, *House of Commons*, pp. 211–54; D. H. Willson, 'James I and Anglo-Scottish unity', in *Conflict in Stuart England*, ed. W. Aiken and B. Henning, London, 1960, pp. 43–55.

12 B.L. Cotton Mss. Titus C VI, f. 178.

13 ibid., f. 431. See Cotton Mss. Vespasian C X, f. 143, where Cornwallis cites the Spaniards' great interest in what occurred in Parliament.

14 B.L. Cotton Mss. Titus C VI, ff. 431–2.

15 P.R.O. S.P. 14, 7, 74, ff. 232v–233.

16 Spedding, *Bacon*, III, p. 200, quoting a letter from Cecil to the Earl of Mar, 28 April 1604.

17 P.R.O. S.P. 14, 10 A, 39.

18 B.L. Cotton Mss. Titus C VI, ff. 429–429v. Northampton made explicit his role as public orator in his speech before the commission, referring to 'my last hallowe and applause'; f. 433.

19 B.L. Cotton Mss. Titus C VI, f. 429–429v.

20 ibid., f. 433.

21 *C.J.*, I, 1004.

22 See for instance *Bowyer*, pp. 326–7, recording Bacon's report: 'Then 2 speeches were used by 2 great persons who commonly set at the upper end of the table (the Earls of Salis[bury] and Northampton.)' See also *Bowyer*, p. 224.

23 *Bowyer*, pp. 224, 326–7.

24 P.R.O. S.P. 14, 1, 3.

25 See Northampton's first speech in Parliament, B.L. Cotton Mss. Titus C VI, ff. 408–14, and *Bowyer*, p. 224, 7 March 1606.

26 B.L. Cotton Mss. Titus C VI, f. 163v. Cotton's answer can be found in 'A consideration whether the subjects of Scotland shall be admitted into an equality of trade with the subjects of England'. B.L. Cotton Mss. Titus F IV, ff. 63–8v. See K. S. Sharpe, *Sir Robert Cotton, 1586–1631*, Oxford, 1979, pp. 116–17, 152–4, for other aspects of Cotton's work on the union.

27 B.L. Cotton Mss. Titus C VI, f. 149.

28 B.L. Cotton Mss. Titus F IV, f. 61v.

29 ibid., f. 62.

30 Joel Hurstfield, *The Queen's Wards*, London, 1958.

31 *Bowyer*, pp. 201n–202; *C. J.*, I, 1007, 4 December 1606.

32 See Conrad Russell, 'Parliamentary history in perspective, 1604–1629', *History*, 61 (February 1976), 11–27, for the view of Parliament as a declining institution.

33 B.L. Add. Mss. 39, 853, f. 83. Northampton to Charles Cornwallis, 10 April 1607.

34 Robert Ashton, 'The parliamentary agitation for free trade in the opening years of the reign of James I', *Past and Present*, 38 (1967), 40–55; T. K. Rabb, 'Free trade and the gentry in the Parliament of 1604', *Past and Present*, 40 (July 1968), 165–73; Ashton,

'Jacobean free trade again', *Past and Present*, 43 (May 1969), 151–7; Pauline Croft, 'Free trade and the House of Commons, 1605–1606', *Economic History Review*, 28 (1975), 17–27.

35   Gardiner, *History*, I, p. 353; *Bowyer*, p. 339n.

36   Cf. B.L. Cotton Mss. Vespasian C IX, *passim*.

37   *Bowyer*, p. 293. See Gardiner, *History*, I, pp. 340–53. For the merchant's petition see P.R.O. S.P. 14, 26, ff. 127 ff. For a response to the petition see P.R.O. S.P. 14, 27, 52–54v which argued that the king and Privy Council had tried to deal with legitimate grievances, that Parliament was not accustomed or fit to deal with matters of war and peace – these were the province of king and Council – and suggested that the merchants' presentation of the petition to Parliament was intended 'to stir up discontents among the subjects against the present government'; f. 53. Willson in *Bowyer*, p. 333, states that this is an outline of Salisbury's speech. Because it contains points such as the above that Salisbury did not include in his speech, it may be a brief prepared for him.

38   *Bowyer*, pp. 320–2.

39   Spedding, *Bacon*, III, p. 349. The entire speech can be found on pp. 347–59. Salisbury's speech is also recorded in *Bowyer*, pp. 333–9.

40   Spedding, *Bacon*, III, p. 360.

41   Spedding, *Bacon*, III, p. 360; *Bowyer*, p. 339.

42   Spedding, *Bacon*, III, pp. 360–1, *Bowyer*, p. 339. See P.R.O. S.P. 14, 27, f. 53: 'The merchants ought to have satisfied themselves, without troubling the House of Parliament, as though his Majesty, and his council had carried themselves too remiss in it, and therefore needed a spur from Parliament.'

43   Spedding, *Bacon*, III, p. 361. *Bowyer*, p. 339 n. Northampton's speech in his own hand is found in B.L. Cotton Mss. Titus C VI, ff. 435–435v.

44   B.L. Cotton Mss. Titus C VI, f. 442.

45   ibid., ff. 442v–443. See Conrad Russell, '1628: War and the Petition of Right', prepared for a conference on the Petition of Right, held at Washington University, 20–1 October 1978; *Parliaments and English Politics, 1621–1629*, Oxford, 1979, pp. 323 ff.

46   B.L. Cotton Mss. Titus C VI, ff. 442–3.

47   See for example Christopher Hill, 'The Norman yoke', *Puritanism and Revolution*, London, 1969, pp. 58–125; F. S. Fussner, *The Historical Revolution*, New York, 1962; F. J. Levy, *Tudor Historical Thought*, San Marino, 1967.

48   *Bowyer*, pp. 332–3.

49   B.L. Cotton Mss. Titus F IV, ff. 295v–298. The piece is dated 28 May 1607.

50   B.L. Cotton Mss. Titus F IV, f. 297. Cf. Titus C VI, ff. 446–446v. While Cotton provides a list of historical precedents, P.R.O. S.P. 14, 27, ff. 52–4v, focuses on the concrete difficulties of the merchants and their causes and how the Privy Council has responded in terms of its policy toward Spain.

51   Nicholas Tyacke, 'Wroth, Cecil and the parliamentary session of 1604', *Bulletin of the Institute of Historical Research*, 50 (1977), 120–5. See T. Rabb, 'Sir Edwin Sandys and the Parliament of 1604', *American Historical Review*, 69 (1964), 647–8.

52   During the same session Northampton thanked Cotton 'for your notes . . . for the matter hath been bravely handled in the lower House and in our House it is like enough to find some hammering'. B.L. Cotton Mss. Titus C VI, f. 149.

53   B.L. Cotton Mss. Vespasian C IX, ff. 177v–178, 187v.

54   ibid., ff. 461v, 466 ff.

55   ibid., ff. 591v–592.

56   ibid., ff. 668v; Vespasian C X, f. 40.

57   *C.J.*, I, 340–2, 348.

58   B.L. Cotton Mss. Vespasian C X, ff. 148v–149v.

59   For a discussion of wardship, see Joel Hurstfield, *The Queen's Wards*; for the negotiations in the Parliament of 1610 on the Great Contract, see Notestein, *House of Commons*, pp. 255–434. The most recent discussion is that of A. G. R. Smith, 'Crown, Parliament and finance: The Great Contract of 1610', in *The English Commonwealth*, ed. P. Clark, A. G. R. Smith and N. Tyacke, Leicester, 1979.

60 See Tyacke, 'Wroth, Cecil and the parliamentary session of 1604', and above, Chapter 8. In 1610 Northampton presented the king's view: 'Purveyance, etc., he is willing should be taken away, if you can devise him any course how to maintain his honour and the necessaries for his house,' E. R. Foster (ed.), *Proceedings in Parliament, 1610*, 2 vols, New Haven, 1966, I, pp. 35–6. Purveyance fell more heavily on the southern countries; those representing the north of England might feel they were striking a poor bargain by agreeing to the Great Contract. I am grateful to Conrad Russell for this point.

61 Foster, *Proceedings in Parliament*, II, p. 40. Foster notes that the report of Northampton's speech in B.L. Harleian Mss. 777 is apparently from a copy of the speech itself, 40n.

62 ibid., II, p. 45.

63 For a discussion of the parliamentary debates on supply during the early Stuart period, see the important article by G. L. Harriss, 'Medieval doctrines in the debates on supply, 1610–1629', in *Faction and Parliament*, ed. K. Sharpe, Oxford, 1978, pp. 73–103.

64 Foster, *Proceedings in Parliament*, I, pp. 33–4.

65 ibid., I, pp. 35–6, II, p. 55.

66 ibid., I, p. 43 n. Ellesmere apparently referred to Northampton's 12 March speech.

67 ibid., I, pp. 198, 68.

68 ibid., I, pp. 118, 146. Salisbury added that 'This must not be taken as a menace'.

69 ibid., II, p. 301.

70 ibid., II, p. 317.

71 HMC *Downshire*, II, 388, John More to William Trumbull.

72 Foster, *Proceedings in Parliament*, I, pp. 259–60.

73 ibid., I, p. 265.

74 ibid., I, pp. 268, 272. See also Harriss, 'Medieval doctrines in debates on supply', p. 85.

75 Foster, *Proceedings in Parliament*, I, pp. 274–5, 270. For the changing definition of necessity see Harriss, 'Medieval doctrines in the debates on supply', pp. 73–103.

76 ibid., I, p. 265. On 20 March Ellesmere said, 'this matter is the greatest that ever was spoken of . . . which would not have been suffered to come into dispute in the days of your Majesty's predecessors'; I, p. 42. His view of the prerogative is expressed in the following passage: 'The king's prerogative was a matter of so high a nature and so tender and jealous to be treated of, that he durst not meddle therein'; II, p. 156.

77 B.L. Cotton Mss. Titus C VI, ff. 499–499v.

78 Notestein, *House of Commons*, pp. 429, 569–70 n: 'Carr and Northampton were on good terms. It is easy to suspect that Northampton was involved in these shady transactions.' For Lake's role see Foster, *Proceedings in Parliament*, II, p. 346 n.

79 L. P. Smith, *The Life and Letters of Sir Henry Wotton*, 2 vols, Oxford, 1907, II, p. 39, 16 June 1614; N. E. McClure (ed.), *The Letters of John Chamberlain*, 2 vols, Philadelphia, 1939, I, p. 539, 9 June 1614. The traditional story can be found in full in Willson, *The Privy Councillors in the House of Commons*, pp. 140–2. 'Northampton and the other Howards, with whom Somerset was now allied, regarded this parliament with the deepest aversion. . . . Northampton then set himself to wreck its work and bring about its dissolution. . . . These efforts culminated in his succesful intrigue at the end of the parliament to increase its turbulence and thus anger the king and bring about a dissolution. . . . Northampton's intrigue was only too successful.' Gardiner put forward the same story although somewhat more cautiously, *History*, II, pp. 247–8. T. Moir, *The Addled Parliament of 1614*, Oxford, 1958, fleshes out the story but accepts Gardiner and Willson's view. Clayton Roberts and Owen Duncan, 'The parliamentary undertaking of 1614', tend cautiously to accept the traditional version of Northampton's role.

80 See Roberts and Duncan, 'The parliamentary undertaking of 1614', for an analysis of the events leading up to the calling of Parliament in 1614 which agrees with the argument presented here that Northampton did not support 'undertaking'.

81 Quoted in Foster, *Proceedings in Parliament*, I, p. 264.

82 B.L. Cotton Mss. Titus F IV, f. 331.

83 Foster, *Proceedings in Parliament*, II, p. 318; Cam. Univ. Lib. Mss. Dd. 3.63, f. 37v;

'Chichester Letter-Book', *Analecta Hibernica*, no. 8, pp. 70–102; Victor Treadwell, 'The House of Lords in the Irish Parliament of 1613–1615', *English Historical Review*, 80 (1965), 92–107; Aidan Clarke, 'Pacification, plantation and the Catholic question, 1603–1623', in *A New History of Ireland*, ed. T. W. Moody, F. X. Martin, F. J. Byrne, Oxford, 1976, pp. 168–231.

84 Roberts and Duncan, 'The parliamentary undertaking of 1614', 481–98.

85 Moir, *The Addled Parliament*, pp. 25, 68, 140–5.

86 B.L. Cotton Mss. Titus F IV, ff. 329ff.; HMC *Cowper*, I, 81.

87 B.L. Cotton Mss. Titus F IV, ff. 332–40.

88 B.L. Cotton Mss. Titus F IV, ff. 340–1. Moir, *The Addled Parliament*, p. 68, omits the phrase 'which you must give me dispensation for following your direction', which provides the crucial information that Suffolk was following Somerset's instructions.

89 B.L. Cotton Mss. Titus F IV, ff. 329 ff. Peter Seddon, 'Robert Carr, Earl of Somerset', *Renaissance and Modern Studies*, IV (1970), 46–68, argues that Somerset was not involved in the breakup of the session once it began.

90 HMC *Downshire*, IV, p. 362, Sir John Throckmorton to William Trumbull; *Chamberlain*, I, 526, 14 April 1614.

91 *A.P.C. 1613–1614*, pp. 364, 397, 40.

92 The printed *Lords Journal* lists Northampton as present on both 7 April and 7 June 1614. An examination of H.L.R.O. Original Journals, No. 8 [1614], ff. 281, 337, shows that he was not present on either occasion. Petyt 538, vol. 8, f. 278 shows 'Comes South-ton Custos privati Sigilli' as present on 15 April, obviously mistaking Southampton for Northampton.

93 On 5 May, for instance, there were complaints of disorder in the House. Kenneth Spencer Research Library Mss. 237, transcript of Maija J. Cole, pp. 19–20. I am grateful to Maija Cole for permission to quote from her transcript of this important parliamentary diary for 1614 which she is editing for publication.

94 Kenneth Spencer Research Library Mss. E 237, 3 May, Cole transcript, pp. 14–15, 40, 80. See also *Wotton*, II, p. 36, 8 June 1614.

95 ibid., pp. 107, 99, 103–4, 115. The latter message was sent on 3 June 1614.

96 C. H. Carter, *The Secret Diplomacy of the Hapsburgs*, Columbia, 1964, p. 130.

97 P.R.O. S.P. 14, 77, 43, 44. Cornwallis denied that Hoskyns had been paid £20 for the speech, which Sharpe apparently alleged. He never implicated Northampton during his many months in the Tower. Cf. *Wotton*, II, p. 39.

98 Tyacke, 'Wroth, Cecil and the parliamentary session of 1604'; Conrad Russell, 'The foreign policy debate in the House of Commons, 1621', *Historical Journal*, 20 (1977), 289–309; 'The examination of Mr Mallory after the Parliament of 1621', *Bulletin of the Institute of Historical Research*, 50 (1977), 125–32. Furthermore, Notestein, *House of Commons*, p. 576, points out that it was a common practice for MPs who spoke for Bills to be paid for their efforts; *Chamberlain*, I, p. 540; L. B. Osborn, *The Life, Letters and Writings of John Hoskyns*, New Haven, 1937, p. 75.

99 Osborn, *John Hoskyns*, pp. 1–15; Kenneth Spencer Research Library Mss. E 237, Cole transcript, p. 120.

100 P.R.O. S.P. 14, 77, 44, 22 June 1614.

101 Spedding, *Bacon*, V, p. 182.

102 *Wotton*, Letters, II, p. 39; *Chamberlain*, I, pp. 540–1. Willson, *The Privy Councillors in Parliament*, p. 140 n; *Chamberlain*, I, p. 540, explained the reason for the plot: 'there was much ado and great dispute, before a parliament could be procured, and the contrary part to make good their opinion sought by all means to embroil and bring it to nothing.'

103 Foster, *Proceedings in Parliament*, II, p. 346 n.

104 *Chamberlain*, I, p. 540.

105 Notestein, *House of Commons*, p. 502. See Roberts and Duncan, 'The parliamentary undertaking of 1614'.

106 For Ellesmere's views on the prerogative, see Knafla, *Law and Politics in Jacobean*

England, pp. 197–201, 254–73. See also W. J. Jones, *The Elizabethan Court of Chancery*, Cambridge, 1967. It is interesting to note Northampton's statements on John Cowell's *The Interpreter*, condemned in the Parliament of 1610 for suggesting that the king was not bound by the common law. The Privy Council sought to mollify an infuriated House of Commons. Both Salisbury and Northampton stated the king's view that he was 'as absolute a monarch as ever was here' but would certainly uphold the common law. Salisbury suggested one reason, 'knowing that he is upon the stage and hath a great enemy, the Pope', and that such issues might raise questions of the relation between the king and his people. Northampton reported that James thought the matter too high for the author to deal with and the king's 'own affection to observe, execute, maintain the law. For remedy, it pleaseth the king that the book shall be suppressed'. Foster, *Proceedings in Parliament*, I, pp. 185–9. But of course the king's affection to uphold the common law suggested that he had a choice, and the prerogative could not be limited. Northampton shared James's view on the issue.

107 Pocock, 'Propriety, liberty and valour; ideology, rhetoric and speech in the 1628 debates', unpublished paper prepared for a conference on the Petition of Right, Washington University, 20–1 October 1978.

Chapter 11. Perspectives

1 B.L. Cotton Mss. Vespasian C X f. 339v.
2 Quoted in A. J. Loomie, *Spain and the Jacobean Catholics, 1613–1624*, Catholic Record Society, 68 (1978), pp. 38–40. N. E. McClure (ed.) *The Letters of John Chamberlain*, 2 vols, Philadelphia, 1939, I, 542; HMC *Downshire*, IV, 433–4.
3 Cecil Papers 134: 71 (1605?). I am grateful to Prof. G. P. V. Akrigg for this reference.
4 G. Elton, *The Tudor Revolution in Government*, Cambridge, 1953.
5 G. Elton, *Reform and Renewal; Thomas Cromwell and the Commonwealth*, Cambridge, 1973; A. G. R. Smith, 'The Secretariat of the Cecils', *English Historical Review*, 83 (July 1968), 481–504; M. Prestwich, *Cranfield: Politics and Profits under the Early Stuarts*, Oxford, 1966, pp. 228–30.
6 J. H. Plumb, *The Origins of Political Stability, England, 1675–1725*, Boston, 1967, pp. 24–5. For a study of the expansion of bureaucracy under pressure of war in the late seventeenth century, see H. C. Tomlinson, *Guns and Government*, London, 1979. On the impact of war generally in Europe, see G. Parker and L. Smith, *The General Crisis of the Seventeenth Century*, London, 1978.
7 National Museum of Scotland, Gordon-Cumming Papers, Dep. 175, Box 65, No. 275, 3 August 1636.

Selected Bibliography

Manuscript Sources

ARUNDEL CASTLE

MD 500	Survey of Northampton's lands
A 1255	Northampton's steward's accounts, 1613

BRITISH LIBRARY

Additional Manuscripts

4112, 4120, 4123	Anthony Bacon manuscripts; Birch's Transcripts
6298	Biographical sketch of Northampton, *c*.1607
9334	Draft of Sir Robert Cotton's report of 1608–9 naval commission, corrected by Northampton
12514	Francis Thynne's brief on the Cinque Ports
14033	Report of Spanish peace treaty negotiations
22563	Henry Howard–Francis Bacon letters
27401	Account of Northampton's receiver-general, 1604.
33512	Correspondence and papers of corporation of Sandwich, Kent
39853	Sir Charles Cornwallis's correspondence
31111	Gondomar's accounts, 1614
58883	List of royal officeholders *c*.1613–17

Cotton Manuscripts

Cleopatra F VI	Treasury commission papers, 1612–14
Galba E I	Treasury commission papers, 1612–14, Jacobean tracts
Faustiana C II	Calendar of records concerning the Cinque Ports
Faustiana E I	Papers on the heralds' office
Julius C III	Sir Robert Cotton's correspondence
Julius F III	Naval commission of 1608–9, proceedings
Titus B IV	Treasury commission papers, 1612–14
Titus B V	Jacobean project literature
Titus B VII	Letter from Thomas Morgan to James I
Titus B X	State papers Irish, *temp*. James I
Titus C I	Papers of the office of Earl Marshal
Titus C VI	Northampton's letters and papers
Titus F IV	Parliamentary papers, *temp*. James I
Vespasian C IX, X, XI	Sir Charles Cornwallis's correspondence
Vespasian C XIII	Tracts on peace with Spain
Vespasian C XIV	Francis Thynne's analysis of the Earl Marshalship, 1597
Vitellius, C XVII	Confessions of Essex conspirators
Caligula C VII	Howard's contacts with Mary, Queen of Scots

Egerton Manuscripts

944	Henry Howard's 'Regina Fortunata'
2877	Letter from Matthew Hutton to Northampton

Harleian Manuscripts

6018	Catalogue of Sir Robert Cotton's manuscripts with loan lists
7002	Miscellaneous letters 1584–1619

Lansdowne Manuscripts
58   Duke of Norfolk's lands in possession of Crown, *c*.1588
109   Henry Howard's correspondence with Michael Hickes
235   Thomas Godfrey's diary
152, 156   Sir Julius Caesar's papers
792   Henry Howard's translation of Charles V's political instructions to
                          his son Philip II

Royal Manuscripts
18A   Northampton's introduction to the 1608–9 naval commission
                          report

Stowe Manuscripts
168, 170   Papers and correspondence of Sir Thomas Edmondes
743   Northampton's letters to Sir Thomas Waller, lieutenant of Dover
                          Castle

CAMBRIDGE UNIVERSITY

Trinity College Manuscripts
R.5.1   Naval commission report of 1608–9
R.5.4   'Orders to the established for the future government of the navy',
                          1609
R.7.22   Northampton's introduction to naval commission report

University Library Manuscripts
Dd. 3.63   Northampton's letters to Somerset
Dd. 3.86, no. 8   Sir John Dodderidge's treatise on heralds

FOLGER SHAKESPEARE LIBRARY

V. b. 7   Henry Howard's 'brief discourse on the right use of giving arms'
V. a. 157   William Smith's discourse on the officers of arms

HOUSE OF LORDS RECORD OFFICE

Abergavenny Peerage Manuscripts
Braye Manuscripts 62   Committee appointment books 1610
Main Papers   Parliamentary papers 1604–1614
Original Journals   1614

HOLKHAM HALL

677   Sir Robert Cotton's brief on trade to the Indies

HENRY E. HUNTINGTON LIBRARY

Ellesmere Manuscripts
406   Ellesmere correspondence
2605   Examinations taken in libel case brought by Northampton in Star
                          Chamber, 1612
2606   Warrant for release of defendants in libel case
5979   Evidence against Somerset in the poisoning of Sir Thomas Overbury

Hastings Manuscripts
15058, 15059   Sir Robert Jacob's letters to Northampton

INNER TEMPLE

Petyt 538/6   Thomas Norris to Sir John Coke about the navy, 1603
Petyt 538/8   Parliamentary papers
Petyt 538/17   Letter from Northampton to Salisbury

KENT ARCHIVES OFFICE

CP/W110   New Romney Borough Records

LAMBETH PALACE MANUSCRIPTS

653, 655, 658, 659   Anthony Bacon papers

LEEDS PUBLIC LIBRARY

Temple Newsam Manuscripts
                               Sir Arthur Ingram's papers
TN PO 7 III (33)   Irish customs farm
TN PO 6 XI (1)   Starch patent

NATIONAL LIBRARY OF WALES

Carreg-lwyd Manuscripts
                               John Griffith's papers
56   Northampton's grant of rectory of Cattistock, Dorset
240   Lists of Northampton's household servants
372   Northampton's household goods
621   Correspondence about Northampton's starch patent
630   Abstract of Northampton's estate, 1616
634   Robert Fletcher's brief on the abuses of cart-takers

OXFORD UNIVERSITY

Ashmolean Manuscripts
856   'Duello Foil'd'
1729   Letter of James I to Privy Council

Bodleian Manuscripts
616   Henry Howard's 'Treatise on natural philosophy'
903   Henry Howard's 'Dutiful Defense of the Lawful Regiment of Women'

Jones Manuscripts
20   Note of lands and possessions of Trinity Hospital, Greenwich

Rawlinson Manuscripts
D 918, f. 35   Northampton's letter to JPs of Buckinghamshire re Goodwin v. Fortescue

Tanner Manuscripts
75   Sir Charles Cornwallis's correspondence

PUBLIC RECORD OFFICE

Chancery 54, 66   Northampton's land transactions
Lord Steward's Office
13, 168   Papers of the Lord Steward's Office, James I

Privy Seal Office
Index 6744, 6745   Indices to privy seal grants

State Papers
14   State Papers, James I
31/12   Gondomar's correspondence
94/10   Northampton's letter to Sir Thomas Edmondes

Court of Wards
Wards 5/29, 9/162   Northampton's wardships, feodary surveys

NATIONAL MUSEUM OF SCOTLAND

Gordon-Cumming Papers
Dep. 175, Box 65   Seventeenth-century correspondence

Printed Works: Primary Sources

Acts of the Privy Council of England, 1603–1604; 1613–1614 (London: 1907–21).

'Advertisements of a loyal subject to his gracious Sovereign drawn from the observation of the people's speeches', *Somers Tracts*, 2nd edn (London: 1809).

A True and Perfect Relation of the Whole Proceedings against the late most barbarous traitors, Garnet, a Jesuite and his confederats ... (London: 1606).

Birch, Thomas, *Memoirs of the Reign of Queen Elizabeth*, 2 vols (London: 1754).

Birch, Thomas, *The Court and Times of James the First*, 2 vols (London: 1849).

Bolton, Edmund, *The Elements of Armories* (London: 1610).

Bruce, John (ed.), *Correspondence of King James VI of Scotland with Sir Robert Cecil and Others in England*, Camden Society, o.s. vol. 78 (London: 1861).

Calendar of State Papers, Colonial Series, Vol. 1 (London: 1860).

Calendar of State Papers, Domestic Series, 1547–1625, 12 vols (London: 1856–9).

Calendar of State Papers Relating to English Affairs, Preserved Principally in the Archives of Simancas, Vol. 3, 1580–6 (London: 1896).

Calendar of State Papers Relating to English Affairs ... *in the Archives and Collections of Venice*, Vol. 10, 1603–7; Vol. 11, 1607–10; Vol. 12, 1610–13 (London: 1900–5).

Calendar of the State Papers Relating to Ireland of the Reign of James I, Vol. 1, 1603–6; Vol. 2, 1606–8; Vol. 3, 1608–10; Vol. 4, 1611–14 (London: 1874–7).

Calendar of the State Papers Relating to Scotland, Vol. 2 (London: 1858).

Calendar of the White and Black Books of the Cinque Ports, 1432–1955, ed. F. Hull (London: 1966).

Cases Collected and Reported by Sir Francis Moore, 2nd edn (London: 1675).

Cobbett, W. (ed.), *Complete Collection of State Trials*, Vol. 2 (London: 1809).

Collins, Arthur, *Letters and Memorials of State*, 2 vols (London: 1746).

Cooper, J. P., *The Wentworth Papers, 1597–1628*, Camden Society, 4th ser., Vol. 12 (London: 1973).

Cross, Claire (ed.), *Letters of Sir Francis Hastings, 1574–1609*, Somerset Record Society, Vol. 68 (Frome: 1969).

Foster, Elizabeth Read (ed.), *Proceedings in Parliament, 1610*, 2 vols (New Haven: 1966).

Gentleman, Tobias, *England's Way to Win Wealth and to Employ Mariners* (London: 1614), STC 11745.

Goldsmid, Edmund (ed.), *Cotton Posthumi* (Edinburgh, 1884).

Hailes, David Dalrymple, Lord (ed.), *The Secret Correspondence of Sir Robert Cecil and James VI of Scotland* (Edinburgh: 1766).

Hawarde, John, *Les Reportes del Cases in Camera Stellata, 1593–1609* (London: 1894).

Historical Manuscript Commission Reports:
First and Second Reports with Appendices (London: 1874).
Third Report with Appendix (London: 1872).
Eighth Report with Appendices (London: 1881).
Tenth Report, Appendix II, Gawdy Mss. (London: 1885).
Twelfth Report, Appendix I, Earl of Cowper Mss.; *IV*, Bishop's Castle Mss. (London: 1888
Thirteenth Report, Appendix IV (London: 1892).
Duke of Buccleuch Mss., I (London: 1899).
De L'Isle and Dudley Mss., II (London: 1934).
Marquis of Downshire Mss., II, III, IV (London: 1938–40).
Laing Mss., I (London: 1914).
Earl of Mar and Kellie, Mss., 2 vols (London: 1904–30).
Duke of Portland Mss., IX (London: 1905).
Duke of Rutland Mss., IV (London: 1905).
Sackville Mss., I (London: 1940).
Marquis of Salisbury's Mss., 24 vols, (London: 1883–1976).
Various Collections, III (London: 1904).

Howard, Lord Henry, 'Answer to the gaping gulf', in *John Stubb's Gaping Gulf*, ed. L. E. Berry (Charlottesville: 1968).

Howard, Lord Henry, *A Defense of the Ecclesiastical Regiment in Englande defaced by T. C. in his replie against D. Whitgifte* (London: 1574), STC 10393.

Howard, Lord Henry, *A Defensative against the Poyson of Supposed Prophecies* (London: 1583).

Howard, Lord Henry, *A Publication of his Majesty's Edict and Severe Censure against Private Combats and Combatants* (London: 1614), STC 8498.

Howell, T. B., *A Complete Collection of State Trials . . .* (London: 1816).

Journals of the House of Commons, I (London: 1803).

Journals of the House of Lords, II (London: 1846).

Keymer, John, *Observations made upon the Dutch Fishing about the Year 1601* (London: 1664).

Knafla, L. B., *Law and Politics in Jacobean England, The Tracts of Lord Chancellor Ellesmere* (Cambridge: 1977).

Larkin, J. F. and Hughes, P. L., *Stuart Royal Proclamations*, I (Oxford: 1973).

Leadam, I. S. (ed.), *Select Cases in the Court of Requests, 1497–1569*, Selden Society, Vol. 12 (London: 1846).

'Letter-Book of Sir Arthur Chichester, 1612–1614', *Analecta Hibernica*, no. 8, 5–177.

Lonchay, Henri and Cuvalier, Joseph (eds), *Correspondance de la Cour d'Espagne sur les Affaires des Pays-Bas au XVIIe Siecle*, Vol. 1 (Brussels: 1923).

McClure, N. E. (ed.), *The Letters of John Chamberlain*, 2 vols (Philadelphia: 1939).

McGowan, A. P., *The Jacobean Commissions of Inquiry, 1608 and 1618*, Navy Record Society, Vol. 116 (London: 1971).

MacLean, J. (ed.), *Letters from Sir Robert Cecil to Sir George Carew*, Camden Society, o.s. Vol. 88 (London: 1864).

Malynes, Gerard de, *Lex Mercatoria* (London: 1622).

Milles, Thomas, *The Customer's Apology* (London: 1601).

Milles, Thomas, *The Customer's Replie, or Second Apology* (London: 1604).

Milles, Thomas, *The Customer's Alphabet and Primer* (London: 1608).

Milles, Thomas, *The Catalogue of Honour* (London: 1610).

Milles, Thomas, *The Mystery of Iniquity* (London: 1611).

Mun, Thomas, *England's Treasure by Forraign Trade* (London: 1664).

Noy, William, *A Treatise of the Rights of the Crown* (London: 1715).

Oppenheim, Michael (ed.), *Sir William Monson's Naval Tracts*, Navy Records Society, Vol. 47 (London: 1914).

Pritchard, M. F. (ed.), *Original Papers Regarding Trade in England and Abroad Drawn up by John Keymer for the Information of James I* (New York: 1967).

Return of the Names of Every Member to Serve in each Parliament, Vol. I, 1213–1702 (London: 1878).

Scott, H. S. (ed.), *The Journal of Sir Robert Wilbraham* (London: 1902).

Shirley, E. P. (ed.), 'An inventory of the effects of Henry Howard, K.G., Earl of Northampton, taken on his death in 1614, together with a transcript of his will', *Archaeologia*, vol. 42 (1869), 347–78.

Smith, L. P. (ed.), *The Life and Letters of Sir Henry Wotton*, 2 vols (Oxford: 1907).

Spedding, James (ed.), *The Letters and the Life of Francis Bacon*, 7 vols (1861–1874).

Spiers, W. L., 'The notebook and account of Nicholas Stone', *Walpole Society*, 7 (1919).

Thynne, Francis, 'Discourse of the duty and office of an herald of arms', in *A Collection of Curious Discourses*, ed. Thomas Hearne (London: 1771).

'Truth Brought to Light', *Somers Tracts*, 2nd edn, Vol. II (London: 1809).

Whitelocke, Bulstrode, *Liber Famelicus of Sir James Whitelocke*, Camden Society, old series, Vol. 70 (London: 1858).

Willson, D. H. (ed.), *The Parliamentary Diary of Robert Bowyer, 1606–1607* (Minneapolis: 1931).

Printed Works: Secondary Sources

Akrigg, G. P. V., *A Jacobean Pageant*, (New York: 1962).

Amons, A., *The Great Oyer of Poisoning* (London: 1846)

Andrews, K. R., 'Caribbean rivalry and the Anglo-Spanish peace of 1604', *History*, vol. 59 (1974), 1–17.

Appleby, Joyce, *Economic Thought and Ideology in Seventeenth-Century England* (Princeton: 1978).

Ashton, Robert, 'Revenue farming under the early Stuarts', *Economic History Review*, 2nd ser., vol. 7–8 (1954–6), 310–22.

Ashton, Robert, 'Deficit finance in the reign of James I', *Economic History Review*, 2nd ser., vol. 10 (1957–8), 15–29.

Ashton, Robert, 'The parliamentary agitation for free trade in the opening years of the reign of James I', *Past and Present*, vol. 38 (1967), 40–55.

Ashton, Robert, 'Jacobean free trade again', *Past and Present*, vol. 43 (1969), 151–7.

Aylmer, G. E., 'The last years of purveyance, 1610–1660', *Economic History Review*, vol. 10 (1957–8), 81–93.

Aylmer, G. E., *The King's Servants* (London: 1961).

Bald, R. C., *Donne and the Drurys* (Cambridge: 1959).

Baldwin, F. E., *Sumptuary Legislation and Personal Regulation in England* (Baltimore: 1926).

Beresford, Maurice, 'The common informer, the penal statutes and economic regulation', *Economic History Review*, vol. 10 (1957), 221–37.

Beresford, Maurice, 'Habitation versus improvement: the debate on enclosure by agreement', in *Essays in Economic and Social History of Tudor and Stuart England in Honour of R. H. Tawney*, ed. F. J. Fisher (Cambridge: 1961).

Blomefield, Francis, *History of Norfolk*, 11 vols (London: 1805–10).

Bossy, J. A., 'English Catholics and the French marriage, 1577–1581', *Recusant History*, vol. 5 (1960), pp. 2–16.

Bossy, J. A., 'The character of Elizabethan Catholicism', in *Crisis in Europe, 1560–1660*, ed. T. H. Aston (New York: 1965).

Brennan, Gerald and Stratham, Edward P., *The House of Howard* (New York: 1908).

Carter, Charles, *The Secret Diplomacy of the Hapsburgs, 1598–1625* (New York: 1964).

Cell, Gillian, 'The New Foundland company, a study of subscribers to a colonizing venture', *William and Mary Quarterly*, 3rd ser., vol. 22 (1965), 611–25.

Chancellor, E. B., *The Private Palaces of London* (London: 1908).

Clark, Peter, *English Provincial Society from the Reformation to the Revolution: Religion, Politics and Society in Kent, 1500–1640* (Hassocks: 1977).

Clarke, Aidan, 'Pacification, plantation and the Catholic question, 1603–1623', in *A New History of Ireland*, ed. T. W. Moody, F. X. Martin, F. J. Byrne (Oxford: 1976).

Coakley, T. M., 'Robert Cecil in power: Elizabethan politics in two reigns', in *Early Stuart Studies*, ed. H. Reinmuth (Minneapolis: 1970).

Coleman, D. C., *Revisions in Mercantilism* (London: 1969).

Croft, Pauline, 'Free trade and the House of Commons, 1605–1606', *Economic History Review*, 2nd ser., vol. 28 (1975), 17–27.

Cust, Richard and Lake, Peter, 'Sir Richard Grosvenor and the rhetoric of magistracy', *Bulletin of the Institute of Historical Research*, vol. 54 (1981), 40–53.

Dietz, Frederic C., *English Public Finance, 1558–1641* (New York: 1964).

Durham, F. H., 'Relations of the Crown to trade under James I', *Transactions of the Royal Historical Society*, n.s. vol. 13 (1899), 199–247.

Edwards, Edward, *The Life of Sir Walter Raleigh* (London: 1868).

Elder, J., *The Royal Fishery Companies of the Seventeenth Century* (Aberdeen: 1912).

Elton, Geoffrey, *The Tudor Constitution* (Cambridge: 1962).

Elton, Geoffrey, *The Tudor Revolution in Government* (Cambridge: 1962).

Elton, Geoffrey, 'A high road to civil war?', in *Studies in Tudor and Stuart Politics and Government*, vol. 2 (Cambridge: 1974), pp. 3–12.

Elton, Geoffrey, 'Studying the history of parliament', in *Studies in Tudor and Stuart Politics and Government*, Vol. 2 (Cambridge: 1974), pp. 162–82.

Elton, Geoffrey, 'Parliament in the sixteenth century: functions and fortunes', *Historical Journal*, vol. 22 (1979), 255–78.

Epstein, Joel, 'Francis Bacon and the issue of union, 1603–1608', *Huntington Library Quarterly*, vol. 33 (1969), 121–32.

Flower, Robin, 'Laurence Nowell and the discovery of England in Tudor times', *Proceedings of the British Academy*, vol. 21 (1935), 47–73.

Flugel, Ernst, 'Die älteste englische Akademie', *Anglia*, vol. 32 (1909), 265–8.

Foster, Elizabeth Read, 'The painful labour of Mr Elsyng', *Transactions of the American Philosophical Society*, n.s., vol. 62, pt 8 (1962).

Foster, Elizabeth Read, 'Procedure in the House of Lords during the early Stuart period', *Journal of British Studies*, vol. 5 (1966), 56–73.

Friis, Astrid, *Alderman Cockayne's Project and the Cloth Trade* (London: 1927).

Fulton, T. W., *Sovereignty of the Seas* (London: 1911).

Fussner, F. Smith, *The Historical Revolution* (New York: 1962).

Gardiner, S. R., *The History of England from the Accession of James I to the Outbreak of the Civil War*, 10 vols (London: 1883–4).

Gardiner, S. R., *What Gunpowder Plot Was* (London: 1897).

Godfrey, Walter, *The College of Arms*, London Survey Committee Monograph no. 16 (London: 1963).

Goodman, Godfrey, *The Court of James I*, ed. J. S. Brewer, 2 vols (London: 1839).

Gras, N. S. B., *The Early English Customs System* (Cambridge: 1918).

Gruenfelder, John K., 'The electoral patronage of Sir Thomas Wentworth, Earl of Strafford, 1614–1640', *Journal of Modern History*, vol. 49 (December 1977), pp. 557–74.

Gruenfelder, John K., 'The Lord Wardens and elections, 1604–1628', *Journal of British Studies*, vol. 16 (1976), 1–23.

Handover, P. M., *The Second Cecil: The Rise to Power, 1563–1604* (London: 1959).

Hardacre, P. H., 'The Earl Marshal, the heralds and the House of Commons, 1604–1641', *International Review of Social History*, vol. 2 (1957), 106–25.

Harriss, G. L., 'Medieval doctrines in the debates on supply, 1610–1629', in *Faction and Parliament*, ed. K. Sharpe (Oxford: 1978), pp. 73–103.

Hasted, Edward, *History of Kent* (London: 1886).

Hexter, J. H., *Reappraisals in History* (New York: 1963).

Hexter, J. H., 'Power struggle, Parliament and liberty in early Stuart England', *Journal of Modern History*, vol. 50 (1978), 1–50.

Hill, Christopher, *Puritanism and Society* (London: 1958).

Hirst, Derek, *The Representative of the People? Voters and Voting under the Early Stuarts* (Cambridge: 1975).

Hirst, Derek, 'Court, country and politics before 1629', in *Faction and Parliament*, ed. K. Sharpe (Oxford: 1978), pp. 105–37.

Hirst, Derek, 'The Privy Council and problems of enforcement', *Journal of British Studies*, vol. 18 (1978), 46–66.

Hoak, D. E., *The King's Council in the Reign of Edward VI* (Cambridge: 1976).

Holdsworth, William, *A History of English Law*, Vol. I (Boston: 1922).

Holmes, Clive, 'The county community in Stuart historiography', *Journal of British Studies*, vol. 19 (1980), 54–73.

Howell, W. S., *Logic and Rhetoric in England, 1500–1700* (New York: 1961).

Hurstfield, Joel, *The Queen's Wards* (London: 1958).

Hurstfield, Joel, 'Political corruption in modern England: the historian's problem', *History*, vol. 52 (1967), 16–34.

Hurstfield, Joel, 'The morality of early Stuart statesmen', *History*, vol. 56 (1971), 235–43.

Hurstfield, Joel, 'The succession struggle in late Elizabethan England', in *Freedom, Corruption and Government in Elizabethan England* (Cambridge, Mass.: 1973).

Jardine, David, *A Narrative of the Gunpowder Plot* (London: 1857).

Jenkins, James T., *The Herring and the Herring Fisheries* (London: 1927).

Jesse, John H., *Memoirs of the Court of England*, 4 vols (London: 1840).

Jones, W. J., 'Ellesmere and politics, 1603–1617', in *Early Stuart Studies*, ed. H. Reinmuth (Minneapolis: 1970).

Jones, W. J., *The Elizabethan Court of Chancery* (Cambridge: 1967).

Jordan, W. K., *The Charities of London* (London: 1960).

Jordan, W. K., *Social Institutions in Kent, 1480–1660*, Kent Archaeological Society, Vol. 75 (Ashford, England: 1961).

Jordan, W. K., *The Charities of Rural England, 1480–1660* (New York: 1962).

Juel-Jenson, Bent, 'The poet Earl of Surrey's library', *The Book Collector*, vol. 5 (1956), 172.

Kautz, A. P., 'The selection of Jacobean bishops', in *Early Stuart Studies*, ed. H. Reinmuth (Minneapolis: 1970).

Kelley, Donald, *Foundations of Modern Scholarship, Language, Law and History in the French Renaissance* (New York: 1970).

Kenny, R. W., *Elizabeth's Admiral: The Political Career of Charles Howard, Earl of Nottingham, 1536–1624* (Baltimore: 1970).

Khan, Shafaat Ahmed, *The East India Trade in the Seventeenth Century* (Oxford: 1923).

Lacey, Robert, *Robert, Earl of Essex* (London: 1971).

Lee, A. G., *The Son of Leicester* (London: 1964).

Lee, Maurice, *James I and Henri IV: An Essay in English Foreign Policy, 1603–1610* (Urbana: 1970).

Levack, Brian, *The Civil Lawyers in England, 1603–1641* (Oxford: 1973).

Levack, Brian, 'The proposed union of English law and Scots law in the seventeenth century', *Juridical Review*, vol. 20 (1975), 97–115.

London County Council, *Survey of London* (London: 1900–), vols 18, 20.

Loomie, A. J., 'Toleration and diplomacy: the religious issue in Anglo-Spanish relations, 1603–1605', *Transactions of the American Philosophical Society*, n.s. vol. 53, pt 6 (1963).

Loomie, A. J., *Spain and the Jacobean Catholics, 1613–1624*, Catholic Record Society, vol. 68 (1978).

MacCaffrey, Wallace, 'Place and patronage in Elizabethan politics', in *Elizabethan Government and Society*, ed. S. T. Bindoff, J. Hurstfield and C. H. Williams (London: 1961).

MacCaffrey, Wallace, *The Shaping of the Elizabethan Regime* (Princeton: 1968).

MacCaffrey, Wallace, 'The Anjou match and Elizabethan foreign policy', in *The English Commonwealth*, ed. P. Clark, A. G. R. Smith and N. Tyacke (Leicester: 1979).

McGurk, J. J. N., 'Royal purveyance in the shire of Kent, 1590–1614', *Bulletin of the Institute of Historical Research*, vol. 50 (1977), 55–68.

Mackie, J. D., 'A loyal subject's advertisement as to the unpopularity of James I's government in England, 1603–1604', *Scottish Historical Review*, vol. 23 (1925), 1–17, 155–7.

McKisack, May, *Medieval History in the Tudor Age* (Oxford: 1971).

Malden, H. E., *Trinity Hall* (London: 1922).

Mayes, Charles R., 'The sale of peerages in Stuart England', *Journal of Modern History*, vol. 29 (1957), 21–37.

Mirrlees, Hope, *A Fly in Amber* (London: 1962).

Moir, Thomas, *The Addled Parliament of 1614* (Oxford: 1958).

Moody, T. W., 'The Irish parliament under Elizabeth and James I: a general survey', *Proceedings of the Royal Irish Academy*, vol. 45, sect. C, pp. 41–81.

Muchmore, Lynn, 'The project literature: An Elizabethan example', *Business History*, vol. 45 (1971), 474–87.

Munden, Roger, 'James I and "the growth of mutual distrust": king, commons, and reform', in *Faction and Parliament*, ed. K. Sharpe (Oxford: 1978), pp. 43–72.

Murray, K. M. E., *The Constitutional History of the Cinque Ports* (Manchester: 1935).

Neale, J. E., 'The Elizabethan political scene', in *Essays in Elizabethan History* (London: 1958).

Neale, J. E., *The Elizabethan House of Commons* (London: 1963).

Newton, A. P., 'The establishment of the great farm of the English customs', *Transactions of the Royal Historical Society*, 4th ser., vol. 1 (1918), 129–55.

Nichols, J. G., 'The institution and early history of the dignity of baronet', *Herald and Genealogist*, III (1866), 193–212.

Notestein, Wallace, *The House of Commons, 1604–1610* (New Haven: 1971).

Notestein, Wallace, 'The winning of the initiative by the House of Commons', *Proceedings of the British Academy*, vol. 11 (1924–5), 125–75.

Nott, G. F., *The Works of Henry Howard, Earl of Surrey, and of Sir Thomas Wyatt, the Elder*, 2 vols (London: 1816).

Nye, J. S., 'Corruption and political development: a cost-benefit analysis', in *Political Corruption*, ed. Arnold J. Heidenheimer (New York: 1970).

Oppenheim, Michael, *A History of the Administration of the Royal Navy and of Merchant Shipping in Relation to the Navy, from MDIX to MDCLX* (London: 1896).

Osborn, L. B., *The Life, Letters and Writings of John Hoskyns, 1566–1638* (New Haven: 1937).

Osborne, Francis, *Traditional Memoirs of the Reign of King James I* (London: 1658).

Peck, Linda Levy, 'Court patronage and government policy: the Jacobean dilemma', in *Patronage in Renaissance Europe*, ed. S. Orgel and G. Lytle (Princeton: 1982).

Peck, Linda Levy, 'Corruption at the court of James I; the undermining of legitimacy', in *After the Reformation*, ed. B. Malament (Philadelphia: 1980).

Peck, Linda Levy, 'Problems in Jacobean administration: Was Henry Howard, Earl of Northampton, a reformer?', *Historical Journal*, vol. 19 (1976), pp. 831–58.

Peck, Linda Levy, 'Patronage, policy and reform at the court of James I: the career of Henry Howard, Earl of Northampton', Ph.D. thesis, Yale University, 1973.

Perceval-Maxwell, M., *The Scottish Migration to Ulster in the Reign of James I* (London: 1973).

Pocock, J. G. A., *The Ancient Constitution and the Feudal Law* (Cambridge: 1957).

Pocock, J. G. A., 'Propriety, liberty and valour; ideology, rhetoric and speech in the 1628 debates', unpublished paper prepared for a conference on the Petition of Right, Washington University, 20–1 October 1978.

Prestwich, Menna, *Cranfield: Politics and Profits under the Early Stuarts* (Oxford: 1966).

Pritchard, M. F., 'The significant background of the Stuart Culpeppers', *Notes and Queries*, no. 205 (1960), 408–16.

Pulman, Michael, *The Elizabethan Privy Council in the Fifteen-Seventies* (Berkeley: 1971).

Rabb, Theodore K., 'Sir Edwin Sandys and the Parliament of 1604', *American Historical Review*, vol. 69 (1964), pp. 646–70.

Rabb, Theodore K., *Enterprise and Empire: Merchant and Gentry Investment in the Expansion of England, 1575–1630* (Cambridge, Mass.: 1967).

Rabb, Theodore K., 'Free trade and the gentry in the parliament of 1604', *Past and Present*, vol. 40 (1968), 165–73.

Roberts, Clayton, *The Growth of Responsible Government in Stuart England* (Cambridge: 1966).

Roberts, Clayton and Duncan, Owen, 'The parliamentary undertaking of 1614', *English Historical Review*, vol. 93 (1978), 481–98.

Rosenberg, Eleanor, *Leicester, Patron of Letters* (New York: 1955).

Ruigh, Robert, *The Parliament of 1624* (Cambridge: 1971).

Russell, Conrad, *Parliaments and English Politics, 1621–1629* (Oxford: 1979).

Russell, Conrad, 'Parliamentary history in perspective, 1604–1629', *History*, vol. 61 (1976), pp. 1–27.

Russell, Conrad, 'The examination of Mr. Mallory after the parliament of 1621', *Bulletin of the Institute of Historical Research*, vol. 50 (1977), 125–32.

Russell, Conrad, 'The foreign policy debate in the House of Commons in 1621', *Historical Journal*, vol. 20 (1977), 289–309.

(Sanderson, William), *Aulicus Coquinariae* (London: 1650).

Scott, Sir Walter, *Secret History of the Court of James I*, 2 vols (Edinburgh: 1811).

Seddon, P. R., 'Robert Carr, Earl of Somerset', *Renaissance and Modern Studies*, vol. IV (1970), pp. 46–68.

Sharpe, Kevin (ed.), *Faction and Parliament, Essays on Early Stuart History* (Oxford: 1978).

Sharpe, Kevin, *Sir Robert Cotton, 1586–1631* (Oxford: 1979).

Sheavyn, Phoebe, *The Literary Profession in the Elizabethan Age* (New York: 1964).

Skinner, Quentin, *The Foundations of Modern Political Thought*, 2 vols (Cambridge: 1978).

Smith, A. G. R., 'The secretariats of the Cecils, circa 1580–1612', *English Historical Review*, vol. 83 (1968), 481–504.

Smith, A. G. R., *Servant of the Cecils: The Life of Sir Michael Hickes, 1543–1612* (London: 1977).

Smith, A. G. R., 'Crown, parliament and finance: the Great Contract of 1610', in *The English Commonwealth*, ed. P. Clark, A. G. R. Smith and N. Tyacke (Leicester: 1979).

Smith, Lacey Baldwin, *The Mask of Royalty* (London: 1971).

Smyth, John, *The Berkeley Manuscripts*, 3 vols (Gloucester: 1883).

Stafford, Helen, *James VI of Scotland and the Throne of England* (New York: 1940).

Stone, Lawrence, 'The educational revolution in England, 1560–1640', *Past and Present*, vol. 28 (1964), 41–80.

Stone, Lawrence, *The Crisis of the Aristocracy* (Princeton: 1966).

Stone, Lawrence, *Family and Fortune* (Oxford: 1973).

Strong, Roy, *The English Icon* (London: 1969).

Strong, Roy, *The Elizabethan Image* (London: 1969).

Styles, Philip, 'Politics and historical research in the sixteenth and seventeenth centuries', in *English Historical Scholarship*, ed. L. Fox (London: 1956).

Supple, B. E., *Commercial Crisis and Change in England, 1600–1642* (Cambridge: 1959).

Swart, K. W., *The Sale of Offices in the Seventeenth Century* (The Hague: 1949).

Tawney, R. H., *Business and Politics under James I* (Cambridge: 1958).

Tite, Colin, 'The early catalogues of the Cottonian Library', *British Library Journal*, vol. 6 (1980), pp. 144–57.

Treadwell, V. S., 'The House of Lords in the Irish parliament of 1613–1615', *English Historical Review*, 80 (1965), 92–107.

Treadwell, V. S., 'The establishment of the farm of the Irish customs, 1603–1613', *English Historical Review*, vol. 93 (1978), 580–602.

Trevor-Roper, Hugh, 'The general crisis of the seventeenth century', in *Crisis in Europe, 1560–1660*, ed. T. H. Aston (London: 1965).

Turner, E. R., *The Privy Council of England in the Seventeenth and Eighteenth Centuries, 1603–1784*, 2 vols (Baltimore: 1927).

Tyacke, Nicholas, 'Wroth, Cecil and the parliamentary session of 1604', *Bulletin of the Institute of Historical Research*, vol. 50 (1977), 120–5.

Upton, A. F., *Sir Arthur Ingram* (Oxford: 1961).

Van Erde, Katherine S., 'The Jacobean baronets: An issue between king and parliament', *Journal of Modern History*, vol. 33 (1961), 137–47.

Wagner, Sir Anthony, *The Heralds of England* (London: 1967).

Watson, Philip, *The History of the Reign of Philip III*, 2nd edn, 2 vols (London: 1786).

Weldon, Anthony, 'The court and character of King James', in *Historical and Biographical Tracts*, ed. G. Smeeton, 2 vols (London: 1820).

White, Beatrice, *A Cast of Ravens* (New York: 1965).

Willan, T. S., 'The foreign trade of the provincial ports', *Studies in Elizabethan Foreign Trade* (Manchester: 1959).

Willan, T. S., *A Book of Tudor Rates* (Manchester: 1962).

Williams, Neville, *Thomas Howard, Fourth Duke of Norfolk* (London: 1964).

Willson, D. H., *The Privy Councillors in the House of Commons, 1604–1629* (Minneapolis: 1940).

Willson, D. H., *King James VI and I* (London: 1956).

Willson, D. H., 'James I and Anglo-Scottish unity', in *Conflict in Stuart England*, ed. W. Aiken and B. Henning (London: 1960).

Wilson, Arthur, *The History of Great Britain, Being the Life and Reign of King James* (London: 1653).

Woodworth, Allegra, 'Purveyance for the royal household in the reign of Queen Elizabeth', *Transactions of the American Philosophical Society*, n.s. vol. 35, pt 1 (1945).

Wright, C. E., 'The dispersal of the monastic libraries and the beginning of Anglo-Saxon studies, Matthew Parker and his circle: a preliminary study', *Transactions of the Cambridge Bibliographical Society*, vol. 1 (1949–53), 202–37.

Young, Michael, 'Illusions of grandeur and reform at the Jacobean court', *Historical Journal*, vol. 22 (1979), 53–73.

Zagorin, Perez, *The Court and the Country* (New York: 1970).

Zaller, Robert, *The Parliament of 1621* (Berkeley: 1971).

Index